Marion Klaskow

The Social Forces in Later Life:

An Introduction to Social Gerontology

The Social Forces in Later Life:

An Introduction to Social Gerontology

Robert C. Atchley
Miami University
Oxford, Ohio

Designer: Gary A. Head

Editor: Irene Elmer/Kevin Gleason

ISBN-0-534-00186-6

L. C. Cat. Card No.: 72-84067

Printed in the United States of America

3 4 5 6 7 8 9 10   76 75 74

Preface

This book is a basic introductory text for advanced undergraduates or beginning graduate students in social gerontology. After the basic perspectives on social gerontology as a discipline have been laid down, and following a brief summary of the biological and psychological "facts of life" concerning physical aging, the bulk of the book deals with the interplay between various social and social-psychological forces and the aging individual.

Writing a basic text in as broad a field as social gerontology is quite a task, one that could never have begun without a great deal of help. From the first, many of my ideas came out of interchanges with Clark Tibbitts; despite a harried schedule, he was always willing to offer his incisive criticisms. Also, I gained a great deal of basic knowledge and a chance to organize the subject by writing two correspondence courses in gerontology for the George Washington University program in Long-Term Health Care Administration under Leon Gintzig.

I would like to thank Bernice L. Neugarten, Ethel Shanas, Hiram J. Friedsam, Paul B. Maves, James H. Schulz, Nathan W. Shock, Mildred M. Seltzer, among many others for their encouragement and suggestions for improving initial drafts of the book; and particularly strong thanks are due to Lillian Troll who provided hundreds of fine suggestions for improvements throughout. And for reviewing later stages of the manuscript I thank Walter J. Cartwright, Stephen J. Cutler, Gary D. Hampe, and D. G. McTavish. Finally, I owe a special debt to David T. Lewis, whose inspiring classes and keen interest in students attracted me to the profession of sociology in the first place, and gratitude to Fred Cottrell who has taught me more than I used to think there was to know.

Because this is the first edition of a text in a field where there has never been an established introductory text, there are bound to be inadequacies. The data in this book and the instructor's manual to accompany it are as current as I could make them, but in a rapidly developing field knowledge gets out of date quickly. But the prime test of any text is whether it serves well the students and teachers who use it. In this regard I must depend on those who use the book to suggest improvements and help me make it better.

Contents

Part One **Introduction**

1   The Scope of Social Gerontology   3

2   Approaches to the Study of Social Gerontology   21

Part Two **The Aging Individual**

3   Biological Aging   43

4   The Psychology of Aging   51

5   The Psychological Foundations of Behavior   73

Part Three **Age Changes in Situational Context**

6   Role Changes in Later Life   99

7   Health   113

8   Finances   139

9   Retirement   153

10   Recreation and Leisure   177

11   Independence and Dependency   189

12   Personal Adjustment to Aging   199

Part Four **Societal Response to the Aging**

13   Societal Disengagement   219

14   The Economy   227

15   Politics and Government   239

16   Community   257

17   Moorings in the Community: Religion and Voluntary Associations   281

18   Primary Relationships: Family, Friends, and Neighbors   291

19   Epilogue: What Does It All Mean?   327

General Bibliography   336

Glossary   339

Index   343

Contents

Part One   **Introduction**

1   The Scope of Social Gerontology   **3**

Gerontology Defined 4; Social Gerontology 5; The Stages of Later Life 6; What Makes Aging an Important Area for Study? 8; The Rise of Aging as a Social Problem 8; Some Important Gaps in Knowledge 16; Summary 18; Bibliography 19

2   Approaches to the Study of Social Gerontology   **21**

Characteristics of Social Gerontology as a Discipline 21; Scientific Knowledge 23; Impressionistic Knowledge 24; Social Criticism 24; The Role of Methodology 26; Methodological Problems in Social Gerontology 26; The Role of Theory 30; Prominent Theories in Social Gerontology 31; Other Theories 37; Summary 38; Bibliography 39

Part Two   **The Aging Individual**

3   Biological Aging   **43**

Results of Senescence 47; Conclusion 48; Bibliography 49

4   The Psychology of Aging   **51**

Sensory Processes 51; Perceptual Process 57; Psychomotor Performance 58; Complex Per-

*formance 60; Mental Functioning 61;
Conclusion 70; Bibliography 71*

5   The Psychological Foundations of Behavior   **73**

*Drives 73; Research Illustration 1: Motivation
of Aged Persons 77; Research Illustration 2:
Aging and the Decline of Emotional Response 79;
Attitudes 81; Personality 82; The Self
86; Social Roles 87; Age Changes in Self-
Concept 87; Age Changes in Self-Esteem 89;
Summary 91; Bibliography 92*

Part Three   **Age Changes in Situational Context**

6   Role Changes in Later Life   **99**

*Positions 99; Social Roles 99; Retirement
102; Research Illustration 3: The Role Count
104; Widowhood 106; Dependency 107;
Disability and Sickness 108; The Role of the
Institutional Resident 110; Other Important
Changes 110; Summary 111; Bibliography 112*

7   Health   **113**

*General 114; Chronic Conditions 115;
Duration 115; Mental Illness 116; Research Illustration 4: Social Isolation and Mental
Illness in Old Age 118; Treatment 120;
Impairment and Disability 121; Institutionalization 123; Death 128; Variations 130;
Helping the Chronically Ill or Disabled Older Person 131; Summary 132; Bibliography
133*

8   Finances   **139**

*The Financial Need 139; Assets 144;
Level of Living 146; The Future 147;
Conclusion 148; Bibliography 149*

9   Retirement   **153**

*The Link Between Man and His Work 154;
The Evolution and Institutionalization of Retirement
155; The Retirement Concept 156; Retirement as Process 157; Retirement Prepara-*

tion   *159;*   *The Retirement Decision   161;*
Research Illustration 5: Health as an Early Retire-
ment Factor   164;   Retirement as Event   166;
Retirement as a Role   167;   The Consequences
of Retirement   168;   Research Illustration 6:
The Effect of Retirement on Personal Adjustment
169;   The Future of Retirement   172;   Sum-
mary   173;   Bibliography   173

10   Recreation and Leisure   177

Summary   186;   Bibliography   187

11   Independence and Dependency   189

Summary   197;   Bibliography   198

12   Personal Adjustment to Aging   199

Some General Reactions to Aging   200;   Suc-
cessful Aging   204;   A Case of Successful Aging
209;   Summary   213;   Bibliography   214

Part Four   **Societal Response to the Aging**

13   Societal Disengagement   219

Summary   225;   Bibliography   226

14   The Economy   227

Older People as Workers   228;   Older People as
Consumers   230;   Summary   236;   Bib-
liography   237

15   Politics and Government   239

Political Participation   239;   Political Power
244;   Government and Older People   249;
Summary   254;   Bibliography   255

16   Community   257

Health   259;   Social Services   260;   Trans-
portation   268;   Housing   270;   Education
273;   Summary   274;   Bibliography   275

17   Moorings in the Community: Religion and
                 Voluntary Associations   281

Religion   281;   Voluntary Associations   287;
Conclusion   288;   Bibliography   289

18   Primary Relationships: Family, Friends, and
Neighbors   **291**

*The Older Couple   293;   Widows and Widowers
297;   Older Bachelors and Spinsters   298;
Sexuality in Older People   299;   Trends in
Marital Status   300;   The Older Parent Role
301;   The Grandparent Role   303;   Research
Illustration 7: The Changing American Grandparent
304;   The Great-Grandparent Role   307;
The Sibling Role   307;   Summary of Kinship
Roles   308;   Family Structure   308;   Family
Values   310;   Family Functions   311;
Family Dynamics   313;   Friends and Neighbors
316;   Research Illustration 8: Social Integration
of the Aged   317;   Summary   320;   Bib-
liography   322*

19   Epilogue: What Does It All Mean?   **327**

*Research   327;   Training   329;   Policy and
Planning   329;   The Future of Social Gerontology   333;   Bibliography   333*

General Bibliography   **336**

Glossary   **339**

Index   **343**

The Social Forces in Later Life:

An Introduction to Social Gerontology

Part One   Introduction

The two introductory chapters that comprise Part I deal with the *discipline* of social gerontology. Chapter 1 defines social gerontology and provides the background essential for understanding the emergence of human aging as an important field within social science. Chapter 2 gives the characteristics of the discipline—its various types of knowledge, the methodology for learning about aging, and some of the prominent theories which form the nucleus for research on the social aspects of aging.

1

The Scope of Social Gerontology

The following case histories were adapted from the Kansas City Study of Adult Life:

Case 1

This retired semiskilled government employee was seventy at the beginning of the study. He lived with his wife and had grown children and several grandchildren. He mentioned his wife as a most admired person, wonderful, congenial, and pleasing; the only thing wrong, he indicated with a chuckle, was that she kept him working around the house.

He thoroughly enjoyed being retired and did not miss his work. He had worked hard and worried a lot, and liked being free of all that. He thought of himself as "more mellow, more settled and less tempted." He loved his children and grandchildren and enjoyed *short* visits from them. One neighbor said she felt toward him as a daughter toward a father. He had lived in the same house for more than twenty years, knew several neighbors, considered a few of them as friends, but did very little visiting. His nights were almost always dreamless in the last half of his life. He had absolutely no telephone calls.

The clinical psychologist found no evidence of anxiety or depression. His family and close friends spoke of him with real affection, and expressed concern for his health, about which he himself never complained. He was in no way alienated, anomic, or isolated, and he coped extremely well. The exchange of energy between himself and his wife appeared in good balance, and certainly he gave as much or more into his social system than he took out of it.[1]

---

[1] Adapted by permission from Richard H. Williams and Claudine G. Wirths, *Lives Through the Years* (New York: Atherton Press, 1965), pp. 37–39.

Case 2

Dependency is not always a voluntary state—it can be forced upon an aging person most cruelly. This eighty-year-old widow is a good example of what can happen when an older person becomes physically incapable of doing for herself and is left emotionally **to** her own devices because everyone else is too busy or too bored to care.

At the beginning of the study, she was far from being in this position. She lived with her widowed daughter, mothered the daughter's seventeen-year-old son, and pulled her share of the load of keeping house. At the time of the first interview she was bright and hard working and looked rather young for her age. She found it hard to think of herself as eighty, and yet, except for one physically disabled sister on the West Coast, she was the only one of her generation left.

The last interview, four years after the initial one, showed that the respondent had failed drastically. She had sprained her back and was confined to a chair or bed. A niece and a granddaughter were also living in the apartment, as well as a great-granddaughter, making a total of five in the rather small quarters. Noise and confusion abounded, and the respondent was left sitting helplessly in the midst of this bedlam. Her own role was clearly that of a nonparticipant. Occasionally she was able to hold the baby and feed it or wash a few dishes, but there her services ended, of necessity. Everyone else was too busy or too bored with her to give her more than nominal attention, and she was dying of loneliness in this mass of people.

She described her daily round as one of deadly monotony—nothing to do, nothing she could do, just sit from meal to meal and then to bed for a poor night's sleep. They were all too occupied to take her visiting or to church, and although she did not want to resent this, she did. She did not want to be a "crank" and tried to guard her tongue, but this was hard, as she still seemed mentally alert to what was going on. For this reason, she really welcomed the interviewers. They were someone to talk to who was interested in her, and at least they relieved the boredom.[2]

Gerontology Defined

These two short vignettes illustrate the substance of gerontology. It is a complex subject, wandering far and wide across the traditional lines of academic study. Yet it never strays from a basic concern with *older people*.

---

[2] *Ibid.,* pp. 48–49.

Doctors study the illnesses of older people, biologists study the physical changes aging brings to the cells of the body, psychiatrists study mental illness among older people, psychologists study age changes in sensory perception, economists study the income requirements of older people, architects design special housing for older people, and the sociologist studies the relationship between older people and their society and culture. Almost every area of study dealing with man or his needs has a branch which deals with older man. All of these tiny branches of these many fields come together under the name of gerontology—literally the logic of aging.

There are four related but separate aspects to the study of aging. The biological aspect deals with physical aging—the body's gradual loss of the ability to renew itself. The psychological aspect deals with the sensory processes, perception, motor skills, intelligence, problem-solving, understanding, learning, drives, and emotions of the aging individual. The biological and psychological changes which occur with advancing age coupled with the social environment of the individual produce a third aspect—the behavioral. This aspect of aging deals with attitudes, expectancies, motives, the self-image, social roles, personality, and psychological adjustment to the situation. Finally, the sociological aspect of aging deals with the society in which aging occurs, the influence this society has on the aging individual, and the influence he has on it. The older person's health, income, work, and leisure, as these relate to his family, friends, voluntary associations, and religious groups, as well as to society in general, the economy, the government, and the community are all part of the sociology of aging.

These four aspects of aging—biological, psychological, behavioral, and sociological—are all interrelated in the life of any older person.

Social Gerontology

Social gerontology is a subfield of gerontology which deals primarily with the nonphysical aspects of aging. Clark Tibbitts, one of the founding fathers of social gerontology, describes it as "concerned with the developmental and group behavior of adults following maturation and with the social phenomena which give rise to and arise out of the presence of older people in the population."[3]

Biological and psychological aspects of aging are of interest to the social gerontologist only insofar as they influence the way the individual and society adapt to each other. Yet because biology and psychology are

---

[3] Clark Tibbitts, "The Future of Research in Social Gerontology," in *Age with a Future,* ed. P. From Hansen (Copenhagen: Munksgaard, 1964), p. 139.

at the root of the social aspects of aging, the social gerontologist must understand as much as he can about these areas.

The Stages of Later Life

Defining "older person" is no easy task, for a number of reasons. In the first place, aging begins very early in life. Biologists agree that almost as soon as the organism stops growing it begins the process of growing old. In the second place, it is possible to measure age in two quite different ways. Chronological age is calendar age. The life cycle is a sequence of events in the life of an individual which begins with birth and ends with death. In between there are many stages, events, and phases. The terms childhood, adolescence, adulthood, middle age, later maturity, and old age refer to some of these phases. The chronological age of an individual is important in understanding aging only because it provides clues as to the current phase of the individual's life cycle.

In the search for a definition of "old person," childhood and adolescence can be ruled out early. Both obviously refer to periods in the life cycle when the organism is still growing. Young adulthood can also be ruled out because although the aging process has technically started, none of the manifestations of aging have yet appeared. It is more difficult to rule out middle age, later maturity, and old age.

Aging is a gradual process with relatively few abrupt changes and it varies, sometimes greatly, from individual to individual. "It has been customary to assume that old age sets in somewhere during the seventh decade of life, and, until recently, much of the research and the majority of action programs have focused on the period beginning at or near age 65. It is now recognized, however, that the real turning point comes much earlier. On the basis of present knowledge, it seems possible to identify three stages of advanced adulthood: middle age, later maturity and old age."[4]

Middle age   is the period when the individual first becomes aware of the fact that he is growing old. Although the correlation is not perfect, this phase of the life cycle usually occurs during the forties and fifties. At this time the individual becomes aware that he has less energy than he used to, and he begins to see a need for intellectual activities to replace more physical pursuits as sources of satisfaction.

Chronic illness becomes more prevalent. In the fifties, vision and

---

[4] Clark Tibbitts, *Handbook of Social Gerontology* (Chicago: University of Chicago Press, 1960), p. 9.

hearing begin to fail. Women pass through menopause, usually a difficult transition. The work career often reaches a plateau, and the children have left home by the time most couples reach their early fifties. Some women go back to work; others sit around the house wondering what to do with themselves. This can be a frustrating period for both men and women because it marks the close of childrearing and sometimes work careers and an end to the satisfactions they brought. Yet it can also mark a new beginning for a marriage or a new occupational career, and so provide new sources of satisfaction.

Finally, middle age is the time when most people come to grips with the fact that death is real, and not just something that happens to someone else.

Later maturity   is marked by an even greater awareness of aging and by a difficulty in remaining future-oriented. Chronologically it often corresponds to the sixties and seventies. There is a drastic reduction in available energy during this period, and the individual becomes very aware of his failing eyes and ears.

Long-term chronic health problems begin to limit activity during this period. Retirement and the accompanying reduction of income combine with poor health to reduce the individual's personal contacts. Deaths of relatives and friends and movement of children also reduce his social environment. Most women are widows by the time they reach their mid-sixties.

Notwithstanding all this, later maturity can be a pleasant period. Most people retain a fair measure of physical vigor, and this, coupled with freedom from responsibilities, makes later maturity one of the most open and free periods in the life cycle for those prepared to take advantage of it.

Old age   is the beginning of the end. It is characterized by extreme frailty, disability, or invalidism. Mental processes slow down. The individual thinks a lot about himself and his past and tries to find some meaning in life. At this point the individual knows the end is very near. Activity is greatly restricted. Loneliness and boredom are thought to be common. This is not apt to be a very pleasant period.

The effects of aging are present in all three phases. Nevertheless, when we talk about older people we will be talking about the last two phases in combination. Chronologically, this means roughly those in their very late fifties and older.

Caution: It is important to emphasize that these categories are based on sets of characteristics which seem to go together in a majority of cases. Seldom will a particular individual show each and every symptom typical of a given phase, but most older people should approximate the symptoms of one of these phases. A second important point is that these categories are based on characteristics *other than* chronological age. While chronological age is related to phases of the life cycle in most cases, this relation is not a necessary one. The important point is whether one has the characteristics of old age, not whether one has reached a certain age. One person could be in old age at fifty-five and another could be in later maturity at eighty-five.

What Makes Aging an Important Area for Study?

In American society interest in the problems of older people is currently high. The Federal Government has created a special department called the Administration on Aging, and most states now have an administrative body devoted to the problems of aging. The reason behind this concern with older people is that their situation has come to be defined as a social problem—that is, a situation affecting a large group of people that is believed by them or others to be a source of difficulty or unhappiness. We generally believe that the more we know about a problem, the easier it is to solve. The sheer press of practical problems can thus force the development of science, and in the area of social gerontology there is a conspicuous overabundance of problems in search of solutions.

Yet, there is another significant motive for the study of social gerontology. The quest for knowledge for its own sake has always played a part in science, and many scientists will attest to the fact that no matter how noble the cause, it is very difficult to stay with a task which does not possess some degree of intrinsic fascination. For some people, observing the intricacy of social relationships is like watching a campfire—it never becomes tiresome or boring. For these people the study of gerontology can become an end in itself.

The Rise of Aging as a Social Problem

But why is aging a social problem? Surely the fact that large numbers of people now live to reach old age is one of modern society's greatest achievements. Yet most people look forward to old age with fear and apprehension.

The roots of the problem are complex. Modern science and technology have created a world in which the average individual will live his allotted threescore and ten. Yet society has not been prepared to receive this large new group of older members.

There are three major trends which have brought about the current situation. The first is related to the way the population has grown, the second is related to increased urbanization and industrialization, and the last is related to the increased pace of social change.

Population Growth

If we use the widely accepted criterion of age sixty-five or over to operationally define *older people,* then what changes have taken place in this category since the beginning of the century?

The most obvious change has been the dramatic increase in the *numbers* of older people. In 1900 there were slightly more than three million older people in the United States and in 1970 there were over 20 million—a six-fold increase and nearly double the increase for the general population.

This increase resulted from several factors. First, births have increased steadily over the past 100 years. Second, a larger proportion of those born are now surviving to age sixty-five than was formerly the case. Third, the large numbers of people who migrated to the United States in the late nineteenth and early twentieth centuries are becoming older. Of these factors, the increasing size of the baby crop is by far the most important.[5]

Table 1. Percent of Total Population Age 65
and Over, U. S., for Selected Years

	1900	1930	1940	1950	1960	1970	2000 (projected)
Percent Age 65 and Over	4.0	5.4	6.8	8.1	9.2	9.6	11.1

Source: U. S. Bureau of the Census

In addition to increasing numbers, there has also been a steady rise in the *proportion* of older people in the U. S. population since 1900 (See Table 1).

Obviously, the same factors which influence the numbers of older people also influence their percentage of the total. In this case, however, the

[5] Henry D. Sheldon, "The Changing Demographic Profile," in *Handbook of Social Gerontology,* ed. Clark Tibbitts (Chicago: University of Chicago Press, 1960), p. 41.

percentage of older people rose slowly because all of the factors which increased the older population did so only slightly faster than births increased the younger population. This kept the percentage of older people relatively stable in spite of large increases in numbers.

The number of older people will probably continue to increase rapidly over the next few decades. And the proportion of the population sixty-five and over may actually increase more than projected in Table 1 if the birth rate decline which began in 1958 continues.

Life expectancy is the average number of years persons born in a given year can be expected to live under the conditions prevailing in that year. For example, life expectancy in the United States was just over forty-nine years at the beginning of the century. This means that people born in 1900 could be expected to live an average of forty-nine years under the conditions of 1900. By 1965 life expectancy in the United States had risen to seventy years. This is certainly a significant increase in the average length of life, and it helps explain why so many people are surviving to become older people.

One important aspect of the increase in life expectancy is that women have enjoyed a greater increase as compared to men. In 1900 the life expectancy for women in the U. S. was just under fifty-one years, and for men it was not quite forty-eight years, a difference of about three years in favor of the women. In 1965, however, women had a life expectancy of almost seventy-four years as compared with nearly sixty-seven for men, a difference of seven years. Thus, women have increased their advantage with regard to life expectancy. Some population experts have estimated that if this trend continues, older women will outnumber older men by two to one by the year 2000.

Urbanization

In 1900 only about 40 percent of the U. S. population lived in cities. By 1960 this figure had risen to 70 percent, and by the year 2000 we can expect somewhere in the neighborhood of 90 percent of our population to be living in metropolitan areas. What about older people? Are they as "urbanized" as the general population? In 1960, 70 percent of the population sixty-five years of age and older was urban, the exact same figure that applied for the general population. From this we can infer that as the rest of the nation moved into urban areas, its older people moved too.

Among urban areas of different size, however, older people do appear to differ slightly from the general population. Table 2 shows that older people tend to be slightly overrepresented in central cities and in cities of less than 10,000 population, while they tend to be underrepresented in the urban fringe, the area where most of the "bedroom" suburbs are. By and large, however, older people do not seem to settle in disproportionate numbers in any particular size community.

Nevertheless, there are geographic areas of the country where older people do live in disproportionate numbers. Everyone knows that older people congregate in Florida and California. However, there are several other states in which older people are even more heavily represented. Nationwide, older people constitute 9 to 10 percent of the total population, yet sizable areas of Kansas, Nebraska, Iowa, Missouri, Oklahoma, and Texas have more than 17 percent older people. Florida and California

Table 2. Percentage of Urban Population by Size of Place, U. S. Population and Age Group 65 and Over, 1960

| | *Percent Urban Population* | | | |
U. S. Total	Central Cities	Urban Fringe	Cities of 10,000– 49,999	Cities of 2,500– 9,999
125,268,750	46.3	30.2	12.9	10.6
Age Group 65 and Over				
11,526,190	49.8	23.7	13.8	12.6

Source: U. S. Bureau of the Census

gained older people through migration, but in the Middle and Southwestern states the movement of young people *out* left older people overrepresented in many areas. Thus, most of the overrepresentation of older people has resulted indirectly from urbanization of the young rather than from movement by the old.

Another important result of our rapid urbanization has been change within the cities themselves, particularly with regard to the stability of the neighborhoods. In the early part of this century rapid urbanization was already under way. Cities were being fed population from the rural areas and from European immigration. Population growth in the cities far outstripped the nation's ability to construct new housing, and it was not unusual to find three and four generations in a single household. We have idealized this pattern over the years, but it is highly likely that these three- and four-generation households resulted less from choice than from the fact that there was no other housing available.

Neighborhoods in cities tended to remain stable for several reasons: once lodging was found it was not likely to be given up, children were forced to remain in their parents' household, and once jobs were found, they were kept. These factors produced neighborhoods with many long-term residents. Older people in this type of neighborhood often enjoyed the prestige of being such residents. They were regular gold mines of information about everything and everybody in the neighborhood. Often they were family patriarchs or matriarchs of considerable influence.

Today's big city neighborhood is a much different place. The housing squeeze is gone for the majority of our population. When children grow up, they move out into their own households. With the availability of newer housing, older people themselves are also moving in increasing numbers. The result is a constant state of flux in the urban neighborhood with a sizable annual turnover. In this kind of situation the positions of older people are very much altered. The prestige of long-term residency loses some of its weight, and family members have scattered to the suburbs, usually taking with them the older person's possibility of being an active family head.

In short, the changes in the urban neighborhood have created a situation in which older people have become detached from the neighborhood. It should be noted that older people are not alone in this respect. The closest thing to neighborhood in most of our cities is a group of several couples and their children who get together twice a year for a "neighborhood" picnic. Sustained, regular interaction with people who live near you is fast being replaced by interaction with people met through work or other activities, particularly for those in the middle class.

Along with changes in the neighborhood, important and fundamental changes have occurred in the family as urbanization increased. It is doubtful if three- or four-generation families were ever typical in this country except perhaps among the European immigrants and long-time city-dwellers. In frontier days the trek across the country by wagon would have been too much for older people. The answer is, of course, that in those days there were very few older people and they were usually left behind with children who did not choose to migrate. Those people who did live to become older people became part of three- or four-generation households, but there were so few of them that such households made up a very small proportion of the total.

With the gradual increase in both the numbers and proportion of older people in the population, the small family has gradually become typical. The average family in the U. S. today consists of a husband and wife and their children living together in a single dwelling unit. Older people expect and are expected to maintain a household separate from their married children.

At one time older people in the family usually owned the property, and therefore had economic power. Nowadays very few people make their living from property, and very few own any property other than the lot where they live. Most people get money by trading for it in the job market. Therefore the economic power of older people is diminished. The information explosion has occurred so rapidly in recent years that the historical perspective of older people is sometimes too hastily judged as being of little value. Even babysitting is not really needed, since the trend toward early child-bearing patterns and small families has produced a situation in which grandchildren are often grown by the time the grandparents reach retirement age.

Nothing can be gained by pining for the "good old days." As a matter of fact, the old days may not have been quite so good as we would like to believe they were. In the family, relations were often based on tyranny rather than affection, and the power and influence of older people were not always cheerfully accepted by adult children. The point is not whether the older person's position has been downgraded, but rather that there has been a change. And older people's problems are caused at least partly by the difficulties associated with adjusting to this change.

Industrialization

Industrial societies are characterized by their great per capita productivity and their tendency to use machine labor to replace human labor.

One of the greatest challenges in a capitalist society is to sustain a rate of growth that will keep everybody working who should work and at the same time to maintain a reasonably stable wage-price structure. One way of stabilizing wages, or at least preventing them from falling, is to reduce the size of the work force. This will keep the supply of labor from exceeding the demand. In recent years two patterns have been employed which have tended to reduce the work force. Retirement policies have been introduced into almost every realm of labor and the period of pre-work preparation (schooling) required to get the average job has been prolonged. Whether or not they were intended to do so, both of these patterns have reduced the size of the labor force competing for the available jobs and have kept worker incomes at unprecedented highs.

Since it directly concerns older people, retirement is of great interest to the gerontologist. The national interest may require retirement at age sixty-five or seventy, but what are its costs and who pays them? In many cases they are paid by the older person alone. Retirement will be examined in detail in later chapters.

The Stigma

From a purely practical point of view, old age is in itself a stigma. This stigma is often the unjust and unearned result of false stereotypes, but sometimes it results from an adequate and necessary evaluation of actual capabilities. Regardless of source, however, the stigma of old age is important because it influences the way older people live. It influences what they expect of themselves, and it influences what others think about them. Understanding older people demands that one understand this stigma: its grounds in fact, if any; its effects; and remedies for its unwanted effects.

By far the most important aspect of the stigma of old age is its negative, disqualifying character. On the basis of their age, older people are usually relegated to a position in society in which they are no longer judged to be of any use or importance. Like most other expendable elements in society, older people are subjected to poverty, illness, and social isolation.

The Pace of
Social Change

When the pace of change in a society is slow, most people are able to keep abreast of what is expected of them. For the most part, the norms they learned early in life remain appropriate, and unprecedented situations are few enough to not cause major problems.

In a rapidly changing society, however, many people often find themselves in unprecedented positions for which norms are not yet specified. These people face the dilemma of having to play a role for which the dialogue and action are either missing or only partly there.

When changes are few and far between, the various parts of society can adjust easily because it is usually necessary to accommodate only a few changes at a time. Rapid change alters this strategy because many changes must be accommodated simultaneously.

Furthermore, the various parts of society do not change at the same rate. Any single change is like a rock thrown into a pond. The spot where the rock hits is changed very quickly, but the ripples reach the bank only gradually. Social change usually starts by affecting a subgroup within the whole, and slowly the other parts of society adapt until eventually the entire society feels the effects of the change. A particularly difficult period occurs just after the change begins, when the rest of society has not yet recognized or accepted a change within a subgroup. For example, older people often experience problems because other parts of society have not yet recognized or accepted the fact that chronological age is not a reliable indicator of an individual's capabilities. Compounding this problem even further is the fact that a rapidly changing society is more like a pond with a hundred rocks being thrown into it at the same time.

Hence, the impact of population growth, urbanization and industrialization on the lives of older people has been heightened by the fact that these changes are occurring rapidly. For example, the norms are still evolving for the position *retired person,* and this creates difficulties for older people both in the way they see themselves and in the ability of others to respond to them. The retired person is not always sure what he should expect of himself, and other people may avoid him simply because they are not sure how to behave toward him. In addition, there are usually people who do not yet recognize retirement as legitimate, and the retired person may have difficulty in his relationships with such people. Finally, efforts to mount a concerted societal effort to meet the needs of retired people are hindered by the fact that retirees are not by any means the only group whose problems have been increased by rapid population growth, urbanization, and industrialization. The poor, the blacks, the Indians, and women have all recently made loud claims to first priority in terms of the need for social adjustments.

At the risk of considerable oversimplification, the social problems of aging can be perhaps best seen in terms of changes in what happens to the individual as he goes through the life cycle. In the early part of this century American society was almost completely oriented around bringing people into the system and keeping them there. Childhood was a period of preparation for the tasks of adulthood. Family, church, and school all combined to instill the skills, competitive spirit, and achievement motivation that are prime requisites of the economic and social system. Adulthood was a period characterized by increasing involvement in the system. Most young people began their occupational careers as they do today in positions with minimal responsibility, and gradually they were incorporated fully into the economic system. Promotions came slowly for most people, and in general the older the person the more responsible and secure his position. Keep in mind that age fifty in 1900 was about the equivalent of age seventy today in terms of distance from the end of the life cycle. Accordingly, the latter part of the life cycle was expected to be more or less a continuation of the middle years.

Since World War II we have seen a significant change in the social definition of the life cycle. As society became more complex, there was an increase in the length of preparation for adulthood. Whereas 50 percent of young men were in the labor force by age fifteen in 1910, a negligible percentage was in the labor force by that age in 1970.

For reasons mentioned earlier, policies have developed which arbitrarily disqualify people from economic participation once they reach a given retirement age. While most other institutions in society do not phase out older people in quite this rigid a fashion, there are nevertheless norms which downgrade the value of the older person's contribution to the family, the church, the neighborhood, and voluntary associations. Only in politics and government, and in the arts and certain professions like medicine and law, have older people been able to keep positions earned earlier in life more or less intact.

Thus, since World War II there has been a significant change in society's response to the later stages of the life cycle. Youths are still courted eagerly by the system, and adults still become increasingly involved in society as they get older, but toward the end of the life cycle society has gradually turned away from the older individual. His participation is no longer sought or even desired, and he is left to his own devices for getting satisfaction from life. His meaningful contacts are increasingly restricted to people his own age, and his power in the social system is limited.

In large measure, the problems of aging relate to the fact that the preparation for young adulthood, particularly for work and child rearing, is an institutionalized part of the system, while the preparation for later adulthood is left to the individual, and as a result is haphazard and often incomplete. Add to this the problems associated with a rapidly changing situation, and it becomes a wonder that older people are able to cope with aging at all. As we shall see, however, most of them do, and many cope quite well. The ones who do not are understandably a source of concern, and it is primarily they who have created the heightened interest in aging as a social problem.

This book is not about social problems. Problems of aging will be considered only as a part of the overall picture of aging in urban-industrial societies. What we will attempt to do is to present as much knowledge as possible about older people, in the hope that this knowledge will lead to a better understanding of the normal, as well as those aspects that make aging a social problem.

Some Important Gaps in Knowledge

While most aspects of later life have been researched far more than one might expect, there are nevertheless two very important gaps in our present knowledge: the lack of cross-national data, and the lack of data on older minority group members. Both of these gaps stem at least in part from the research priorities in the United States, where a significant proportion of the research in social gerontology goes on. Since research funds for social gerontology have never been generous, investigators have usually chosen to study white, middle- or working-class older Americans rather than attempt the more difficult task of drawing cross-national samples or samples from minority groups.

There is a great need for more cross-national data in social gerontology. Since aging becomes a visible social problem primarily in industrial societies, there is pitifully little research data on social gerontology in the nonindustrial nations of the world. In addition, the data for industrial nations are quite variable, with the United States being by far the most widely researched. For example, the proceedings of the Seventh International Congress of Gerontology, held in 1966 in Vienna, show that *half* of all of the research reports in social gerontology concerned the United States only.[6] The other half were widely scattered over Western Europe with a few from Eastern Europe and Japan. There was a conspicuous absence of papers from Central and South America, the Middle East, Africa, and Asia. And this situation has prevailed thus far at all of the International Congresses.

Thus, the body of knowledge we call social gerontology is heavily biased in terms of the American situation, and this book of necessity reflects this bias. However, the pioneering work of Ethel Shanas and her associates has shown that the situations of older people are remarkably similar in the United States, Great Britain, and Denmark.[7] Therefore, biased as it is at this point, the knowledge we have of social gerontology is probably reasonably representative of industrial societies.

Despite the fact that older Americans have been researched far more than any other older population in the world, very little is known about significant subgroups of older Americans. Not only are there individual differences which produce heterogeneity in the older population, but there are subgroup differences in culture and behavior which also create diversity among older people. A sixty-five-year-old American cannot be understood apart from his earlier life, and if he is a minority group member, his experience has probably been quite different from that of most of his fellow older Americans. Thus, older people who happen also to be black, poor, Appalachian, foreign-born, or members of an ethnic minority probably face a different situation in old age as compared with the majority of the older population. But as yet we are in an incredibly poor position to say exactly how minority group elders differ from the majority. This is a

---

[6] International Congress of Gerontology, *Proceedings of the 7th International Congress of Gerontology, Vol. VI: Psychology and the Social Sciences, Vol. VII: Applied Social Research (Social Welfare)* (Vienna, Austria: Wiener Medizinischen Akademie, 1966).

[7] Ethel Shanas, Peter Townsend, Dorothy Wedderburn, Henning Friis, Paul Milhøj, and Jan Stehouwer, *Older People in Three Industrial Societies* (New York: Atherton Press, 1968).

significant research need which is only beginning to be met, and as a result of this gap in our knowledge, most of what we have to say about older people in this book will not necessarily apply to older members of minority groups.

Summary

Gerontology is a complex enterprise which is comprised of the efforts of all areas of study as they apply to describing and understanding older man. Social gerontology is a subfield of gerontology which deals primarily with the nonphysical aspects of aging.

Our definition of "older person" is based on the life cycle more than on chronological age. The criteria that define entry into the category "older people" include a greater awareness of aging, drastic reductions in available energy, and awareness of failing senses and declining biological and psychological resiliency. Social changes such as retirement and widowhood may also occur at the onset of this period.

Ideally, people would be categorized as "older" only if they exhibited these symptoms, but since it is difficult to measure such symptoms we rely on the fact that there is a rough correlation between aging and chronological age, particularly during the period of old age. For our purposes, then, "older people" refers to those in their very late fifties and older.

Bear in mind as we use this term that it applies *in general* to people in their late fifties or more, but it may not apply very well at all to a *particular* person in his late fifties or even in his late seventies.

Aging has emerged as an important area of study because it has come to be viewed as a social problem and because there are people who are interested in it. It has come to be viewed as a social problem because older people became more visible as their numbers increased, urbanization and industrialization produced changes which undercut the traditional position of the older person in society, and the fast pace of change in urban-industrial societies created obstacles to social adjustment in terms of accommodating an increased number and proportion of older people.

Since World War II, society has increasingly withdrawn from its older members. The labor of older people is neither sought nor desired. They are left primarily on their own, particularly in terms of social contacts and life satisfactions. Compounding this problem is the fact that preparation for the "freedom" of later life is largely left up to the individual and as a result is often inadequate.

The emphasis in this book will be on overall patterns of aging in modern societies. Its aim is to provide perspectives on *all* aspects of aging, including both normal and problem situations.

Bibliography

Beale, Calvin L., "Rural Depopulation in the United States; Some Demographic Consequences of Agricultural Adjustments," *Demography*, 1:264–272, 1964.

Beattie, Walter M., Jr., "The Place of Older People in Different Societies," in *Age with a Future*, ed. P. From Hansen. Copenhagen: Munksgaard, 1964, pp. 44–47.

Birren, James E., "The Aged in Cities," *Gerontologist*, 9:(3, part 1), 163–169, 1969.

Blau, David and Martin A. Berezin, "Some Ethnic and Cultural Considerations in Aging," *Journal of Geriatric Psychiatry*, 2:3–5, 1968.

Bowles, Gladys K. and James D. Tarver, "The Age-Sex-Color Composition of Net Migration in the United States, 1950–1960," *Population Index*, 30:307–308, 1964.

Brotman, Herman B., *Who Are the Aged: A Demographic View*. Ann Arbor, Michigan: University of Michigan-Wayne State University Institute of Gerontology, 1968.

———, "Trends in Life Expectancy, 1900–1962," *Welfare Review*, 3:6–7, 1965.

Eisenstadt, S. N., *From Generation to Generation: Age Groups and Social Structure*. Glencoe, Illinois: Free Press, 1956.

Goldscheider, Calvin, "Differential Residential Mobility of the Older Population," *Journal of Gerontology*, 21:103–108, 1966.

Havighurst, Robert J., "Social Class Perspectives on the Life Cycle," *Human Development*, 14:110–124, 1971.

Henry, William E., "The Role of Work in Structuring the Life Cycle," *Human Development*, 14:125–131, 1971.

Hickey, Tom, Louise A. Hickey and Richard A. Kalish, "Children's Perceptions of the Elderly," *Journal of Genetic Psychology*, 112:227–235, 1968.

Jackson, Jacquelyne J., "Social Gerontology and the Negro; A Review," *Gerontologist*, 7:(3)168–178, 1967.

———, "The Blacklands of Gerontology," *Aging and Human Development*, 2:156–171, 1971.

———, "Negro Aged: Toward Needed Research in Social Gerontology," *Gerontologist*, 11:(1, part II) 52–57, 1971.

Kalish, Richard A. and Sam Yuen, "Americans of East Asian Ancestry: Aging and the Aged," *Gerontologist*, 11:(1, part II) 36–47, 1971.

Kent, Donald P., "Aging within the American Social Structure," *Journal of Geriatric Psychiatry*, 2:19–32, 1968.

———, "The Elderly in Minority Groups: Variant Patterns of Aging," *Gerontologist*, 11:(1, part II) 26–29, 1971.

———, "The Negro Aged," *Gerontologist*, 11:(1, part II) 48–51, 1971.

Kutner, Bernard, "The Social Nature of Aging," *Gerontologist*, 2:(1)5–8, 1962.

Lawton, M. Powell, Morton H. Kleban and Maurice Singer, "The Aged Jewish Person and the Slum Environment," *Journal of Gerontology*, 26:231–239, 1971.

Maddox, George L., "Growing Old: Getting Beyond the Stereotypes," in *Foundations of Practical Gerontology*, eds. Rosamonde R. Boyd and C. G. Oakes. Columbia, South Carolina: University of South Carolina Press, 1969, pp. 5–16.

Metropolitan Life Insurance Company, "International Gains in Longevity after Midlife," *Statistical Bulletin of the Metropolitan Life Insurance Company,* 45:1–3, April, 1964.

———, "International Trends in Survival After Age 65," *Statistical Bulletin of the Metropolitan Life Insurance Company,* 46:8–10, January, 1965.

Moore, Joan W., "Mexican-Americans," *Gerontologist,* 11(1, part II):30–35, 1971.

National Urban League, *Double Jeopardy: The Older Negro in America Today.* New York: The League, 1964.

Neugarten, Bernice L. and Joan W. Moore, "The Changing Age-Status System," in *Middle Age and Aging,* ed. Bernice L. Neugarten. Chicago: University of Chicago Press, 1968, pp. 5–21.

Niebank, Paul L. and John B. Pope, *The Elderly in Older Urban Areas.* Philadelphia: Institute for Environmental Studies, University of Pennsylvania, 1965.

Parsons, Talcott, "Age and Sex in the Social Structure of the United States," *American Sociological Review,* 7:604–616, 1942.

Rosenfelt, Rosalie H., "Elderly Mystique," *Journal of Social Issues,* 21:37–43, 1965.

Seltzer, Mildred M. and Robert C. Atchley, "The Concept of Old: Changing Attitudes and Stereotypes," *Gerontologist,* 11:(3, part I) 226–230, 1971.

Simmons, Leo W., *The Role of the Aged in Primitive Society.* New Haven: Yale University Press, 1945.

———, "Aging in Preindustrial Societies," in *Handbook of Social Gerontology,* ed. Clark Tibbitts. Chicago: University of Chicago Press, 1960, pp. 62–91.

Smith, Stanley H., "The Older Rural Negro," in *Older Rural Americans,* ed. E. Grant Youmans. Lexington, Kentucky: University of Kentucky Press, 1967, pp. 262–280.

Statistical Office of the European Communities, *Basic Statistics of the Community: Comparison with Some European Countries, Canada, the United States of America, and the Union of Soviet Socialist Republics.* Brussels: The Office, 1971.

Streib, Gordon F. and Harold L. Orbach, "Aging," in *The Uses of Sociology,* eds. P. E. Lazarsfeld, *et al.* New York: Basic Books, 1967, pp. 612–640.

Townsend, Peter, "The Place of Older People in Different Societies," *Lancet,* 1:159–161, 1964.

United States Bureau of the Census, "Projections of the Population of the United States, by Age and Sex (Interim Revisions): 1970 to 2020," *Current Population Reports,* Series P-25, Number 448, 1970.

———, "Lifetime Migration Histories of the American People," *Current Population Reports,* Series P-23, Number 25, 1968.

———, "Projections of the Population of the United States, by Age and Sex: 1970 to 2020," *Current Population Reports,* Series P-25, Number 470, 1971.

Zelinsky, Wilbur, "Toward a Geography of the Aged," *Geographical Review,* 56:445–447, 1966.

2

Approaches to the Study of Social Gerontology

Characteristics of Social Gerontology as a Discipline

There are two essential areas within any discipline: language and knowledge. Language provides a set of symbols which promote efficient communication and which allow adequate description of what people see. Language also contains systems of classification which can be used to diagnose and to attach labels to the phenomena people observe. An area of study which is a subfield of a larger discipline will usually have available to it all of the language of the larger field, plus a specialized language of its own. Students of social gerontology, for example, use the term "social role" from sociology, but at the same time they use the term "disengagement," which as a term is almost unknown outside social gerontology.

Language also tells us where to look for additional factors of interest. For example, an observer might see an object which he labels as "retired man." He would also probably look for a phenomenon which he could type "working man," since his language also provides a relationship between the symbols "retired man" and "working man." The language of a discipline thus can be expected to provide a group of *definitions* and a *system of classification* which connects these definitions.

As with the language, knowledge has many facets. In its simplest form, knowledge is the *systematic description* of the world we live in. This type of knowledge answers the questions what, when, and where. An example of this type of knowledge is the statement, "When an employee reaches thirty-five years of service with the company, he retires." "An employee retires" tells *what* happens; "when he reaches thirty-five years of service" tells *when* it happens; and "with the company" tells *where* it happens.

As you have no doubt noticed, two important questions—how and why—are omitted. Answering these questions is a more complex aspect of knowledge, and the operation involved in gaining this type of knowledge is called *explanation*. Explanation builds upon description, for in order to explain a phenomenon, something must be known about it and other surrounding phenomena. To expand our earlier description into explanation we might say, *"In order to make room for incoming personnel and to expand opportunities for promotion,* when an employee reaches thirty-five years of service with the company, he is *forced to* retire." Of course, a single short statement of this type is seldom a complete description or explanation.

Knowledge in social gerontology thus aims at making *explicit* the systematic and predictable elements of the world around us. It seeks to describe and explain the structure of the social world of older people and how they are influenced by it. The ideas that go to make up social gerontology are a hodge-podge of social criticism, impressionistic observations and scientifically developed facts and theories, and the test of any particular idea is not its source or the prestige of its proponents, but its ability to help people understand and cope better with their world.

At the outset it should be understood that we are not concerned with all of man's ideas about the how and why of the social world of older people. We are only concerned with explanations and descriptions that can be *empirically verified.* This automatically rules out many magical, mystical, and religious explanations, not because these ideas are necessarily wrong, but because they cannot be *proved* one way or the other. Thus, an important criterion for evaluating a proposed explanation or description is whether it can be established or refuted by direct observation. If so, then it can be evaluated. If not, then it must simply be accepted or rejected as the spirit moves us, so to speak.

Because the discipline includes only those ideas which can be tested, it is possible to set up procedures for refining and accumulating both descriptions and explanations, all firmly founded in the world of concrete observation. Thus, the social gerontologist uses his observations and ideas about society to invent explanations for what he observes. But he uses still more observations to try to disprove the explanations he has invented. The more times he has tried to disprove an explanation and failed, the more confident he can be that it will lead to successful decisions (i.e., predictions about what will happen). We call explanations that have withstood innumerable tests *laws* and those which have not been tested so many times *theories,* and the predictions we make from our theories and laws are called *hypotheses.* These terms are important only insofar as they constitute an evaluation of how sure we are of various ideas. Hypotheses we may not be sure of at all; theories we feel more comfortable about (depending on how many tests they have withstood); and laws we sometimes literally stake our lives on (such as the law that when we push our foot on the brake, the force will be transmitted to the wheels, stopping the car).

Most explanations in social gerontology are either theories or hypotheses. We simply haven't had time yet to develop many laws because so many tests are required. In fact, because tests must be carried out under similar conditions to be comparable, and the social environment usually cannot be controlled very well, many people question whether there ever will be very many laws concerning the operation of complex social structures.

Because a given description or explanation of a social setting has not yet been widely tested does not mean that it is false. It merely means that we should expect less accurate results from untested facts and theories than from tested ones.

Whenever possible we will rely on the descriptions and explanations developed from controlled observation, because like everyone else we play the percentages. Moral philosophy may lead you to some right answers, but it is effective much less often than controlled observation.

Scientific Knowledge

Scientific ideas are developed from structured direct observation. By structured direct observation we mean that the procedures used to make the observations are explicit enough that they can be exactly repeated. This is necessary, of course, in order to make comparable, repeated tests.

Figure 1 shows a model for the development of scientific knowledge. What distinguishes scientific knowledge from other types is a reliance for

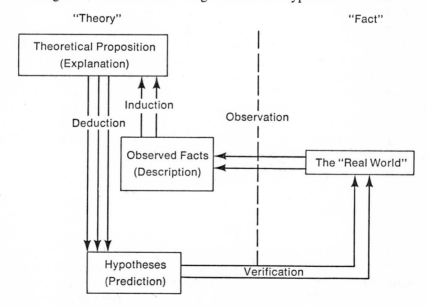

Figure 1. Development of Scientific Knowledge

description on observations which can be repeated, the development of explanations only from empirically grounded description, and the use of observation again to verify and refine scientific explanations and predictions.

Scientific ideas are also characterized by what happens to them after they are developed. Whereas mystical ideas are accepted on faith and tend to remain static, scientific ideas are continually being classified, tentatively substantiated, reconsidered, and corrected. This tentative nature of scientific ideas means that they are seldom viewed as "truths" but are more like road maps—they'll do for the present, but when a better one comes along we don't hesitate to use it. In terms of emphasis, social gerontology puts the highest premium on scientifically developed ideas.

Impressionistic Knowledge

While the greatest emphasis may be placed on scientific ideas, impressionistic ideas are also quite common in social gerontology. Whereas scientific ideas are developed from direct and repeated observations, impressionistic ideas are often based on the unverified work of a single observer. Because each one of us has his own unique biases, none of us sees exactly the same thing when we observe the world; and while the training of the scientist stresses unbiased observation, a certain amount of bias is unavoidable. Thus, the more observers who give the same report, the more sure we can be that we are getting an accurate picture, and the weakness of impressionistic ideas is that they present a less firm foundation for making valid inferences than do scientific ideas. Yet in many important areas of social life we simply have not yet conducted enough scientific studies, and in these cases we make use of impressionistic ideas because they show us where our scientific efforts need to be directed. Also, impressionistic ideas are not necessarily wrong. They may produce useful decisions. Scientific ideas are preferable only because they generally have a lower probability of being wrong.

Social Criticism

Social criticism arises in social gerontology from the fact that scientists are always more than that. They are also fathers or mothers, children of their parents, members of a political party, church, or civic association, amateur artists, music lovers, and so on. As a full-fledged member of society, the scientist takes on certain values and shares most of them with the people around him. The dominant values, those that people are willing to base decisions upon, are usually widely shared and serve as the basis for defining what is good, true, and beautiful. Thus, values are translated into behavior, and they serve as the underpinnings for the society. People want to know whether or not their values are being served by the social world they are participating in, and the social scientist is in a good position to tell them because he himself understands and often holds these same values, and he knows how to find out whether social reality is matching up to them. Furthermore, because he is armed with explanations for some of the things that happen in the social world, he can often explain how reality comes to fall short of desirable goals and suggest changes in society that might improve society's direction toward these goals.

Consequently, the social scientist is often tempted, not only within himself but also by those around him, to become actively involved in the continuous process of evaluating what is going on in society. Everyone else does it, and often with less knowledge and skill than the social scientist commands; therefore, why shouldn't he get into the act? As long as he remains as accurate as possible in his descriptions and explanations, the social scientist need not jeopardize his position as a respected social analyst.

The content of social criticism usually consists of attacks on popular myths which are used as guides for behavior; statements identifying social situations that tend to lead away from the goals society desires; and suggestions for how to get back on the right track.

There is disagreement among social scientists over just how much they should get involved in social criticism. Some say that any social criticism is inappropriate because it takes the social scientist away from an "objective" search for "truth" and because the public may misunderstand and hold all social science responsible for inept criticisms. Opponents of this view reply that objectivity and truth are relative concepts that can be used in social criticism as well as in "hard science"; that social science knowledge is going to get into the public domain no matter what; and that it is to the advantage of social scientists to do it themselves so that it gets done right.

Arguments aside, however, social criticism is here to stay because it is *valued*. Not only does it perform a valuable function of self-analysis for the society as a whole, it points to areas of social life in need of more rigorous inquiry. Social criticism can be very useful to the social gerontologist, provided he keeps in mind that the social critic has a message to deliver which might possibly be interfering with the accuracy of his analysis.

The Role of Methodology

Methodology refers to the *procedures* used to develop knowledge. It includes the analysis of the basic assumptions of science, the process of theory construction, the interrelationship of theory and research, and the procedures of empirical investigation. As such it is at the heart of any discipline. The scientific method of collecting knowledge is characterized by a preoccupation with the *design of research* and with the rigorous identification and control of *error*. Error can get into research results from a number of sources: 1) from the fact that the observer is not conscious of everything that goes on around him and is thus apt to miss something; 2) from his not knowing where to look; 3) from his rationalizing or repressing what he sees; 4) from his looking at a part of the social world that is unrepresentative; 5) from his asking the wrong questions; 6) from his asking questions in the wrong ways; or 7) from his using faulty measurement. Research design aims to identify and control these sources of error.

Hundreds of books have been written on social research and how it should be done, and anyone who intends to do research in social gerontology must be thoroughly familiar with general research procedures.[1] However, there are also several methodological problems which are unique to the study of older people.

Methodological Problems in Social Gerontology

Defining "older people"

Chapter One concludes that a *symptomatic* approach to defining the stages of later life is preferable to a chronological approach. Yet we are forced to continue to use chronological age as the operational definition of these stages because no one has come up with a satisfactory way of identifying older people symptomatically. It is conceivable that a scale could be constructed which, in addition to chronological age, would take energy availability, health, social roles, awareness of death, degree of

---

[1] Some good books on research methods are: Julian L. Simon, *Basic Research Methods in Social Science* (New York: Random House, 1969); Claire Selltiz, *et al.*, *Research Methods in Social Relations* (New York: Holt, Rinehart and Winston, 1959); and John Lofland, *Analyzing Social Settings* (Belmont, California: Wadsworth, 1971).

future-orientation, mental slow-down, activity restriction, and loneliness and boredom into account. Yet even should an operational definition by symptoms be possible, much of the data on older people would still be accessible only in terms of chronological age.

Heterogeneity of the Study Group

In the literature of social gerontology one constantly finds the terms *the aged* or *older people* being used as if they identified a single, homogeneous category of people. In reality, however, the older population in many ways exhibits a greater variety of personalities, life styles, and life chances than any other category in society. Race, religion, social class, education, occupation, and many other social characteristics often produce differences among people that can all but completely obscure the influence of aging. A crucial methodological issue is the problem of holding these factors constant so that the impact of aging can be observed.

In addition, the older population is a composite of many groups of people who were born and reared in quite different times. Thus, the characteristics people attribute to aging are often actually the result of differences in experience, and this produces heterogeneity in the older population. It is therefore important to recognize that the historical era in which one enters various phases of the life cycle may also obscure the influence of aging.

Nevertheless, while it is good to be aware that all older people are to some extent individual, this in no way denies the fact that people have certain characteristics and situations in common as a result of being old. Our job is to identify this communality and at the same time to respect individual uniqueness.

Sampling

A crucial problem in social gerontology involves *sampling*. Very seldom is it necessary to examine an entire population to answer a given research question. Instead, a representative sample can be examined and the results generalized to the entire population. But adequate sampling requires some sort of *concrete* representation of the population, such as a list of names and/or addresses. For the general population, addresses can be used, because the U. S. Bureau of the Census maintains a file of addresses for residences throughout the country. But for subgroups within that population the task is more difficult. How would you locate a list of all older people in Atlanta? Social Security is out because they are forbidden by law to release the names of their pensioners. Besides, there are many older people who never established entitlement to Social Security. Internal Revenue and the Census Bureau are out for the same reasons. These are the most inclusive lists, but even less inclusive lists are hard to get because people do not like to have their names and addresses given out. They only sure-fire way to sample the older population of Atlanta would be to conduct your own census to locate and list all of the older people and then draw a sample from the list. This is obviously an expensive project, and as a result it is almost never done.

Sampling difficulties have often obliged the social gerontologist to settle for the sample he can get rather than the sample he needs.

For example, a researcher studying retirement needs a sample which represents *all* retired people, from former Pullman porters to former bank executives. Yet because there is no listing available, the typical retired sample is drawn from the retirement rolls of a particular company or union. Obviously, if the investigator attempts to generalize about all retired people from a sample of this type, he will be on shaky ground indeed. It is precisely because of such problems that our knowledge of the effects of retirement is not very firm at this point, and the same can be said for many other aspects of social gerontology as well.

Research Design

Most research on older people is cross-sectional. This means that the research is conducted in a short time, and inferences as to the effect of aging *per se* are made by comparing people of different ages at the time the research was conducted. For example, people sixty-five to seventy-four might be compared with those seventy-five and over, and the differences attributed to the influence of aging. This procedure is based on the assumption that observing different people at successive points in the life cycle produces the same result as observing a single group of people as they move through the life cycle.

While a great many of the generalizations in social gerontology are based on this assumption, it is still questionable. The most serious flaw in the cross-sectional approach is that people in different phases of the life cycle at the same point in calendar time differ in other ways than simply the impact of aging. For example, in a cross-sectional sample of retired women teachers the older the women were, the higher they scored on a scale designed to measure the extent to which they thought work should be considered an end in itself rather than simply a means to an end. Using cross-sectional logic, it might be inferred that aging produced an increase in this kind of orientation toward work. The problem is that there is another possible explanation: namely, that women reared later were taught a different attitude toward work. With cross-sectional data it is literally impossible to tell which of these explanations is the correct one.

A good example of the power of longitudinal research occurred in the area of voting patterns. It had been widely assumed that as people grow older, their interest in voting declines, and most cross-sectional studies showed just such an age pattern. Yet when a group of people was traced through the life cycle, it was found that people remain relatively constant over their adult lives in terms of interest in voting. Thus, what appeared to be the result of aging when only cross-sectional data were used turned out to be the result of differences between people who became politically active in different eras. (See Chapter 15 for a more detailed discussion of this research.)

Longitudinal research is the only way that ongoing events in the world can be held reasonably equal so that the impact of aging can be observed. But longitudinal research requires observing the same people over a period of years, and thus it is expensive and difficult to conduct.

In addition, it is not enough to follow only one group through the life cycle. This must be done for several groups, so that we can see the changes, if any, that are occurring in the impact of aging.

Social gerontology is in its infancy in terms of developing and accumulating knowledge through longitudinal studies, and the difficulties of conducting longitudinal research plus the research priorities of the agencies which pay for research will probably retard its development.

Measurement

Measurement involves translating observations into meaningful numbers. The adequacy of the procedures we use to measure social variables is judged by two important criteria, *validity* and *reliability*. Validity refers to the correspondence between what the measurement process is supposed to measure and what it actually measures. The closer the correspondence, the more valid the measure. Validity is usually assessed by comparing the results of the measure in question with an accepted measure of the same characteristic. Most of the time, however, there is no other accepted measure, and the researcher has to guess what the validity of his measure is. Since validity often cannot be concretely established, the investigator must therefore be constantly on the alert for impressionistic data concerning validity.

Reliability refers to the extent to which a given measure gives stable results over successive trials. For example, a test may be given to the same people more than once, and the results compared. This is called the test-retest method of assessing reliability. A measure can be reliable without being valid, but it cannot be valid without being reliable.[2]

Problems of validity and reliability are important for gerontological research because the validity and reliability of many of the measures we want to use were established for young subjects but not for older ones. It is quite possible for a test to be valid and reliable for college students but not for retired professors. The investigator who wants to use an already established measure will ordinarily want to reestablish the validity and reliability of the measure when it is used with older people. Too little attention has been paid to this problem by gerontological researchers.

The Role of Theory

Many of the inadequacies of social gerontology are methodological, but this is important only because methodology is a partner to theory. It is theory that gives integrity to any body of knowledge.

A theory is a set of interrelated principles and definitions that serves to organize conceptually selected aspects of the empirical world. The process of theory building is shown in Figure 1, p. 23. "The essence of theory is that it attempts to explain a wide variety of empirical phenomena in a parsimonious way."[3]

Accordingly, the job of the theorist is to invent explanations, and if he wants to be successful, he uses all of the tools available to him. He uses any system of classification that works, and he borrows from various theories freely in his attempts to fashion explanations that make sense and that will stand the test.

The remainder of this chapter is concerned with current theories in social gerontology. Throughout the book research illustrations show how knowledge is accumulated in social gerontology, and it is important to be familiar with the theories that form the underpinnings of this research. We will thus concentrate on several prominent theoretical perspectives that will be encountered throughout the rest of the book.

---

[2] For a detailed discussion of problems of validity and reliability see Claire Selltiz, *et al.*, *Research Methods in Social Relations* (New York: Holt, Rinehart, and Winston, 1959), Chapter 5.

[3] George A. Theodorson and Achilles G. Theodorson, *A Modern Dictionary of Sociology* (New York: Thomas Y. Crowell Co., 1969), p. 436.

Prominent Theories in Social Gerontology

There are a great many theories in social gerontology, but we shall concentrate on three of the major ones: disengagement theory, activity theory, and continuity theory. This is not to imply that the others are not useful, but rather that they are less frequently encountered than the three presented here.

Disengagement Theory

Possibly the most controversial theory in social gerontology has been the theory of disengagement.[4] As defined by the proponents of the theory, disengagement is an inevitable process in which the individual reduces the number of his interpersonal relationships and alters the quality of those that remain. Since it appeared in 1961, the disengagement theory has been the source of a great deal of controversy and a flurry of research. For this reason it will be analyzed in some detail.

The fundamental basis for the theory of disengagement is the mortality of man. All men must eventually die, and in order for society to outlive its individual members, some means must be found to carry out an orderly transition of power from older members to younger. This need is satisfied by the disengagement process. As one grows older the probability that death will occur increases, and at some point it no longer pays society to rely on the services of those who are about to die. For this reason it is profitable for society to phase out those whose possible contributions are outweighed by the possible disruption their deaths would cause to the smooth operation of society.

As man grows older, a reduction in production efficiency is quite probable. For this reason society may at some point feel justified in replacing an inefficient functionary with a better one.

When it becomes possible to categorize the people to be disengaged as is done with the old, the disabled, and so on, the machinery for accomplishing the process becomes *institutionalized*. This means that a set of norms is generated to provide the group with criteria for selecting those to

---

[4] For a more complete treatment see Elaine Cumming and William E. Henry, *Growing Old: The Process of Disengagement* (New York: Basic Books, 1961), Elaine Cumming, "New Thoughts on the Theory of Disengagement" in *New Thoughts on Old Age,* ed. Robert Kastenbaum (New York: Springer, 1964), William E. Henry, "The Theory of Intrinsic Disengagement" in *Age With a Future,* ed. P. From Hansen (Copenhagen: Munksgaard, 1964), and Arnold Rose, "A Current Theoretical Issue in Social Gerontology," *The Gerontologist* 4: 46–50, 1964.

be disengaged and to provide individuals with guidelines for behavior during the disengagement process. Thus, we have rules which demand retirement at a particular age, and we have rudimentary rites of passage like retirement ceremonies to indicate the transition from working to retirement.

This sounds as if disengagement were a single event, but in fact the process is a gradual one which involves separation of the individual from a great many of his positions and roles. For each role in which separation occurs regularly in a group, a set of institutionalized norms could be expected to appear.

The theory of societal disengagement is functionalist. It assumes that society must constantly seek equilibrium, and that to maintain such an equilibrium, a set of absolute needs for survival must be met. To meet these functional requirements, the society must have people in key positions who will be able to carry out their jobs without interruption. It is therefore a functional requirement that society restrict eligibility for key positions to those who have a high probability of being able to carry through. This leads to the institutionalization of disengagement, a mechanism whereby those who are incapable of filling key positions either because of inability or because of a high probability of death are shifted out of these positions and into less important ones.

A serious difficulty arises when we examine the political institution in the United States. If societal disengagement were a functional necessity, then we would expect it to apply to the political institution perhaps more than to any other. Yet when we examine the key positions in American politics we are forced to conclude that the norms of societal disengagement are clearly inoperative. The average age of Senators, for example is around fifty-eight, and many are over seventy.

Obviously societal disengagement is not a functional necessity because politics is quite able to survive without it. Perhaps it would be more accurate to say that societal disengagement is a tendency more *possible* to realize in some institutions than in others. Thus, the theory of societal disengagement is better at explaining some parts of society than others. It would appear that societal disengagement is more limited in its possible applications than its original formulation indicates.

Thus far we have considered disengagement only from the point of view of society, but there is also an individual side.

Individual disengagement is usually selective; that is, the individual withdraws from some roles but not from others. With each withdrawal from a role, the individual becomes increasingly preoccupied with himself. The upshot of this process is that the individual equilibrium achieved in middle age and oriented toward society is replaced through the process of disengagement by a new equilibrium centered around the individual himself in old age.

It is held that the reduced frequency of interaction weakens the hold of norms over the individual. Thus, the disengaged individual becomes a free individual. Freed from the constraint of norms, the disengaged individual with his declining physical energy is content to live with symbols from the past. To the extent that roles are available to allow the disengaged individual to live in his own self-centered world, his morale will remain high, but if he cannot find roles which allow this, his morale will decline with increasing disengagement.

The individual is said to be ready for disengagement when (1) he becomes aware of the short amount of life remaining to him, (2) he perceives his life space as shrinking, and (3) his ego-energy is lessened.

The first point at which this theory of individual disengagement seems questionable concerns the effect of norms on individual behavior. The theory assumes that the withdrawal of reinforcement for an internalized norm will result in the withering away of that norm as far as the individual is concerned. This assumption is not supported by the evidence. For example, people who had been retired for more than twenty years were found to be still very positively oriented toward the norm of getting intrinsic satisfaction from work. Once a norm has been internalized, something more than an absence of interaction seems to be required to eliminate that norm.

Another difficulty with the theory of individual disengagement is its assumption that desire for disengagement encounters no competition from desires that would dispose the individual toward continued engagement. For example, it has been found that among people in attractive occupations such as teaching, a high potential for disengagement can be overcome by an even higher predisposition to continue receiving the satisfactions that come from continued engagement.

A further difficulty with individual disengagement is its simplicity. The study of social psychology requires models even more complex than those required to study society alone. The compound influences of biology, sociology, and psychology which come together to produce individual disengagement will eventually require a much more sophisticated theory than has been presented to date.

Nevertheless, the theory of individual disengagement can be an important tool in explaining and predicting the behavior of older people. Some questions which need to be answered now are: 1) What is the impact of several intersecting roles on the individual's ability to disengage? 2) If mere lack of interaction does not produce a reduction of psychological commitment, what does? 3) What part do others play in facilitating disengagement?

At some point the paths of society and of the individual cross with respect to disengagement. At this point there is interaction between the societal and individual mechanisms of disengagement. The most obvious point where the two paths cross is in initiating disengagement. With increased age there often comes a reduction of knowledge and skill. In an industrial society with a growing population, success depends on knowledge and skill. Therefore disengagement is initiated by the individual because he recognizes his lack of knowledge and skill, by society because it recognizes his lack, or by both simultaneously. In the last instance, *mutually satisfactory* disengagement occurs. If, however, the individual desires disengagement and society does not, *forced engagement* will result. And if society desires disengagement and the individual does not, the result is *forced disengagement*. Only in the first case can the individual be satisfied with the outcome, while in either of the latter cases, his morale will be seriously lowered.

Society and the individual are *both* responsible for disengagement. Society creates the *situation* in which disengagement takes place, and the individual attitude toward disengagement can determine the *form* the process will take.

Despite its failings, disengagement is one of the most important theories in social gerontology. Throughout this book, we will constantly be making reference to it, expanding on it, and examining efforts to improve on it. This theory is particularly difficult for many students because it is hard to respond to it in intellectual rather than emotional terms. It is difficult for highly engaged people to accept the possibility that some day engagement will no longer be attractive, and that they may in fact desire disengagement. To the young person full of life and energy it is difficult to imagine not wanting to be "in the swing of things," but for the old person, particularly one in ill health, the sum total of his available energy may be wrapped up in mere survival with little left over for engagement.

Activity Theory

The *activity theory* is perhaps the commonest in terms of serving as a guide for action; yet is the theory which has received the least amount of formal consideration. It holds that the norms for old age are the same as those for middle age, and that the older person should be judged in terms of a middle aged system for measuring success.[5] The greatest compliment someone can be paid in this framework is "My, she certainly doesn't look her age." This theory holds that older people try to deny the existence of old age as long as possible. Older people are said to be disorganized if they exhibit behavior other than that appropriate for the middle-aged person, and low morale is expected. Thus, according to this theory, successful

---

[5] Robert J. Havighurst, "Successful Aging," in Richard H. Williams, Clark Tibbitts, and Wilma Donahue (eds.) *Processes of Aging* (New York: Atherton Press, 1963) Vol. 1, pp. 299–320.

aging consists in being as much like the middle-aged person as possible. "Act your age!" for the older person means to act like a middle-aged person. It is assumed that if older people are to relinquish useful roles, they must be given new useful roles to take their place. This theory assumes that aging is a continuous struggle to remain middle-aged.

This theory is not without its support. For example, it was found in a large sample of retired women[6] that very few described themselves as old or very old, but rather as middle-aged or just past middle age. This was true of women who were over seventy. This would seem to suggest the possibility that many people view middle-aged characteristics as being highly desirable in old age. There is also a denial of old age in a great many cases. Therefore, the activity theory of aging seems to serve as a source for the attitudes of these older women, at least insofar as life-cycle identity is concerned.

The prime difficulty with this theory is that it says nothing about what happens to people who cannot maintain the standards of the middle-aged. Obviously, many cannot. The solution here seems to be that the people who fit the implicit model are in fact symptomatically middle-aged rather than old. The average age at which physical deterioration sets in is increasing, and this means, among other things, that sixty-year-olds forty years ago *acted* old, while today most sixty-year-olds are still quite active and vigorous. We must therefore guard against using chronological age as the sole criterion for determining whether or not a person is in fact old. The activity theory could thus be expected to apply quite accurately to the chronologically old but still healthy and energetic person. In terms of disengagement theory, this person would not yet be ready for disengagement. This would mean, for example, that when society forces a man not yet ready for disengagement to retire, he might fit the activity theory of aging by attempting to replace the lost role. The theory of societal disengagement would explain why he might be unsuccessful, but the activity theory would explain why he would keep trying.

Continuity Theory

A third major theory has begun to emerge in social gerontology in recent years.[7] As developmental psychologists have turned their attention

---

[6] Fred Cottrell and Robert C. Atchley, *Retired Women: A Preliminary Report* (Oxford, Ohio: Scripps Foundation, 1969).

[7] Bernice Neugarten, *Personality in Middle and Late Life* (New York: Atherton Press, 1964); Robert C. Atchley, "Retirement and Leisure Participation: Continuity or Crisis," *The Gerontologist*, 11: (1, part I) 29–32, 1971.

to aging, more attention has been paid to continuity between phases in the life cycle as well as change.

Continuity theory holds that in the process of becoming an adult, the individual develops habits, commitments, preferences, and a host of other dispositions that become a part of his personality. As the individual grows older, he is predisposed toward maintaining continuity in his habits, associations, preferences, and so on. Unlike the activity theory, the continuity theory does *not* assume that lost roles need be replaced.

Continuity theory holds that the individual's reaction to aging can be explained by examining the complex interrelationships among biological and psychological changes; the person's habits, preferences, and associations; situational opportunities for continuity; and actual experience. The person's life-long experience thus creates in him certain predispositions that he will maintain if at all possible. These predispositions include such things as brushing one's teeth right-handed, shopping at a particular department store, living in a certain neighborhood, having certain friends, and working at a particular job. At all phases of the life cycle these predispositions constantly evolve from interactions among personal preferences, biological and psychological capabilities, situational opportunities, and experience. Change is thus an adaptive process involving interaction among all of these elements.

Both the disengagement and activity theories posit a single direction that the individual's adaptation to aging will take. Continuity theory, on the other hand, holds that adaptation can go in any of several directions. For example, if the individual did not like retirement, he might respond less favorably to aging than he would otherwise. A person who was favorably disposed toward retirement might later change his mind as the result of unfavorable experience.

There are literally hundreds of *possible* combinations of reactions to aging, according to continuity theory, because each individual has a slightly different combination of factors to adjust to. This immense complexity is mitigated a great deal, however, by the fact that many people share roughly the same status with respect to various factors. Nevertheless, continuity theory implies that there are many possible adaptations to aging rather than just a few. This complexity gives continuity theory the advantage of coming perhaps the closest to explaining the full reality of aging. But this same complexity has the disadvantage of being difficult to conceptualize, measure, and analyze. While research on disengagement has been widespread, research on continuity theory is just beginning, and for this reason it will probably be some time before the full impact of continuity theory on social gerontology can be assessed.

Other Theories

There are several other theories that deserve mention, although they have not generated as much research as have the preceding three. The theory of *older people as a subculture* holds that by virtue of their shared characteristic of old age, and society's categorical negative response to anyone old, older people are being forced to interact with each other.[8] This forced interaction is seen as a forerunner of the development of a genuine group. Perhaps the critical flaw in this theory is that it has yet to be demonstrated that any significant interaction among older people is occurring across social class lines. Social class is still apparently a force strong enough to prevent the development of an old-age subculture.

Closely related to the subculture theory is the theory that *older people are a minority group*.[9] According to this theory, older people, like the blacks, are discriminated against because they share a common biological characteristic. Like racial discrimination, age discrimination depends on the visibility of the undesired trait, and older people who "do not look their age" escape the effects of age discrimination. This theory has a lot of truth in it. The negative evaluation and prejudice against old age is used as a criterion for discrimination. There are certainly parallels between the situations of many older people and those of various minority groups: low income, low status, self-hatred, and unequal opportunity. Yet there are also large numbers of older people for whom these parallels do not apply. Thus, the major limitation of this theory is its inability to explain why discrimination against older people applies in some situations and not in others. For example, why do older people face discrimination in office-holding everywhere but in political offices?

The *identity crisis theory*[10] also relates to the older person's view of himself. This theory states that involuntary changes in social position occurring in later life produce a crisis in the individual's ability to achieve a satisfactory identity in his new position. It applies well to the people whose problems it was designed to explain, namely, those who were forced to retire. It is limited in application because it applies to only a minor segment of the older population, since most people retire voluntarily.[11]

---

[8] Arnold Rose, "The Subculture of the Aging: A Framework for Research in Social Gerontology" in *Older People and their Social World*, eds. A. Rose and W. Peterson (Philadelphia: F. A. Davis, 1965), pp. 3–16.

[9] Gordon F. Streib, "Are the Aged a Minority Group?" in *Applied Sociology*, eds. A. W. Gouldner and S. M. Miller (New York: The Free Press of Glencoe, 1965).

[10] Stephen J. Miller, "The Social Dilemma of the Aging Leisure Participant," in Rose and Peterson, *op. cit.*, pp. 77–92.

[11] This theory is discussed in greater detail in the chapter on Recreation and Leisure.

By this time it should be clear that none of the existing theories can completely explain aging in modern society. The responsible investigator must constantly compare the situation he is attempting to explain with the existing theories and be ready to invent a new explanation if none of the ready-made ones works.

Summary

Like all other sciences, gerontology is a complex of ideas comprised of language and knowledge. The goal of gerontology is to make descriptions, explanations, and predictions about older man. To accomplish this task the gerontologist uses theories and systems of classification to make deductions about older man. He then tests these deductions through research. In the absence of scientific theories, the researcher may also use common-sense or impressionistic theories as the basis for hypotheses.

Knowledge in social gerontology consists of scientific ideas, impressionistic ideas, and social criticism.

Adequate methodology is crucial to the development of any discipline, but social gerontology faces particularly difficult problems in such areas as definition, handling the heterogeneity of the older population, sampling, research design, and measurement.

The three most prominent thories in social gerontology are disengagement theory, activity theory, and continuity theory.

Disengagement theory is actually two theories, one applying to society and the other applying to the individual. Society is said to disengage from older people in order to replace its inefficient members and avoid disruption as the probability of death increases. The individual is said to disengage out of a desire to turn his attention inward. Both types of disengagement are held to be inevitable and mutually desired. Disengagement theory is more limited to particular situations than its original framers supposed, and this is perhaps its major drawback. Yet this theory has generated more research than any other in social gerontology.

Activity theory holds that older people should be just like middle-aged people, and that successful adjustment means replacing lost roles. The problem with this theory is that it is limited to the small proportion of people who are chronologically old, but symptomatically still middle-aged. This theory has not fostered much research, but decisions concerning programs for older people are often based on it.

Continuity theory is founded on the premise that people will stay the same unless there is a reason for change. Reasons for change should be sought in the relationships among the individual's biological and psychological capabilities, his personal habits, preferences, and associations, his experiences, and his situational opportunities. Continuity theory is one of the most complex in social gerontology, and it is backed by much less research evidence than is disengagement. Nevertheless, it is a promising theory.

Other theories that provide useful perspectives, but which have fostered little research, include the subculture of the aging, the aging as a minority group, and the identity crisis theories.

Bibliography

Albrecht, Ruth E., *Aging in a Changing Society*. Gainsville, Florida: University of Florida Press, 1962.

Anderson, John E., "A Development Model for Aging," *Vita Humana*, 1:5–18, 1958.

Anderson, Nancy N., "The Significance of Age Categories for Older Persons," *Gerontologist*, 7:164–167, 1967.

Atchley, Robert C., "Respondents vs. Refusers in an Interview Study of Retired Women: An Analysis of Selected Characteristics," *Journal of Gerontology*, 24:42–47, 1969.

———, "Disengagement among Professors," *Journal of Gerontology*, 26:476–480, 1971.

Back, Kurt W. and K. J. Gergen, "Cognitive and Motivational Factors in Aging and Disengagement," in *Social Aspects of Aging*, eds. Ida H. Simpson and John C. McKinney. Durham, North Carolina: Duke University Press, 1966, pp. 289–295.

Barron, Milton L., "Minority Group Characteristics of the Aged in American Society," *Journal of Gerontology*, 8:477–482, 1953.

Bloom, Martin, "Life-Span Analysis; A Theoretical Framework for Behavioral Science Research," *Journal of Human Relations*, 12:538–554, 1964.

Bultena, Gordon L., "Life Continuity and Morale in Old Age," *Gerontologist*, 9:(4, part I) 251–253, 1969.

Cumming, Elaine *et al.*, "Disengagement—A Tentative Theory of Aging," *Sociometry*, 23:23–35, 1960.

———, "New Thoughts on the Theory of Disengagement," in *New Thoughts on Old Age*, ed. Robert Kastenbaum. New York: Springer, 1964, pp. 3–18.

Hayflick, Leonard, "Quantity, Quality, and Responsibility in Aging Research," *Gerontologist*, 11:(1, part I) 68–73, 1971.

Havighurst, Robert J., Bernice L. Neugarten and Sheldon S. Tobin, "Disengagement and Patterns of Aging," in *Middle Age and Aging*, ed. Bernice L. Neugarten. Chicago: University of Chicago Press, 1968, pp. 161–172.

———, "Disengagement, Personality and Life Satisfaction in the Later Years," in *Age with a Future*, ed. P. From Hansen. Copenhagen: Munksgaard, 1964, pp. 419–425.

Henry, William E., "The Theory of Intrinsic Disengagement," in *Age with a Future*, ed. P. From Hansen. Copenhagen: Munksgaard, 1964, pp. 415–418.

Maddox, George L., Jr., "Disengagement Theory: A Critical Evaluation," *Gerontologist*, 4:80–82, 1964.

———, "Disengagement among the Elderly; How Common and with What

Effect?" in *Duke University Council on Gerontology Proceedings of Seminars, 1961–1965,* ed. Frances C. Jeffers. Durham, North Carolina: Duke University Regional Center for the Study of Aging, 1965, pp. 317–323.

———, "Themes and Issues in Sociological Theories of Human Aging," *Human Development,* 13:17–27, 1970.

McTavish, Donald G., "Perceptions of Old People: A Review of Research Methodologies and Findings," *Gerontologist,* 11:(4, part 2), 90–101, 1971.

Mercer, Jane R. and Edgar W. Butler, "Disengagement of the Aged Population and Response Differentials in Survey Research," *Social Forces,* 46:89–96, 1967.

Neugarten, Bernice L., "A Developmental View of Adult Personality," in *Relations of Development and Aging,* ed. James E. Birren. Springfield, Illinois: Charles C. Thomas, 1964, pp. 176–208.

Riley, Matilda W., "Social Gerontology and the Age Stratification of Society," *Gerontologist,* 11:(1, part I) 79–87, 1971.

Roman, Paul and Philip Taietz, "Organizational Structure and Disengagement: the Emeritus Professor," *Gerontologist,* 7:(3)147–152, 1967.

Rose, Arnold M., "Class Differences among the Elderly; A Research Report," *Sociology and Social Research,* 50:356–360, 1966.

———, "Group Consciousness among the Aging," in *Older People and Their Social World,* eds. Arnold M. Rose and Warren A. Peterson. Philadelphia: F. A. Davis, 1965, pp. 19–36.

———, "The Subculture of the Aging; A Framework for Research in Social Gerontology," in *Older People and Their Social World,* eds. Arnold M. Rose and Warren A. Peterson. Philadelphia: F. A. Davis, 1965, pp. 3–16.

Rosow, Irving, "Old Age: One Moral Dilemma of an Affluent Society," *Gerontologist,* 2:182–191, 1962.

Seltzer, Mildred M. and Robert C. Atchley, "The Impact of Structural Integration into the Profession on Work Commitment, Potential for Disengagement, and Leisure Preferences among Social Workers," *Sociological Focus,* 5:9–17, 1971.

Streib, Gordon F., "Are the Aged a Minority Group?" in *Applied Sociology,* ed. Alvin W. Gouldner. New York: The Free Press of Glencoe, 1965.

———, "Disengagement Theory in Sociocultural Perspective," *International Journal of Psychiatry,* 6:(1),69–76, 1968.

Tallmer, Margot and Bernard Kutner, "Disengagement and the Stresses of Aging," *Journal of Gerontology,* 24:70–75, 1969.

Tissue, Thomas L., "A Guttman Scale of Disengagement Potential," *Journal of Gerontology,* 23:513–516, 1968.

———, "Disengagement Potential: Replication and Use as an Explanatory Variable," *Journal of Gerontology,* 26:76–80, 1971.

Wershow, Harold J., "The Older Jews of Albany Park—Some Aspects of a Subculture of the Aged and Its Interaction with a Gerontological Research Project," *Gerontologist,* 4:198–202, 1964.

Youmans, E. Grant, "Family Disengagement among Older Urban and Rural Women," *Journal of Gerontology,* 22:209–211, 1967.

Part Two

The Aging Individual

Beliefs about the presumed biological and psychological changes that aging brings are used to formulate and justify the social behavior of the aged themselves and of others toward them. Throughout this book we will be constantly seeking to determine whether various social patterns exist because of the *actual* limitations imposed by aging, or because of *presumed* limitations that have no basis in fact. To do this we must have "the facts" about the actual physical limits caused by aging. The chapters on the biology and psychology of aging help to provide some of these facts. While every effort has been made to make these chapters as accurate as possible, they are limited, nevertheless, by the scarcity of scientific studies on many aspects of aging. These chapters are intended only as background for a detailed examination of the social aspects of aging, and those who are strongly interested in the physical aspects of aging should certainly consult more complete sources.

The chapter on the psychological foundations of behavior deals with the psychological processes and factors which mediate between the outside world and what goes on inside the individual.

3

Biological Aging

Sooner or later we must all face the progressive loss of our energies and our ability to resist disease. Eventually, no matter how well we look after ourselves, this loss will become so great that we will die. For most of us it is decidedly unpleasant when we discover that we must decline in this way, that even if we escape wars, accidents, and diseases we will still die from old age. Most people tend to ignore these unpleasant facts until they are forced to face them, and even then they tend to search for fountains of youth. But aging and eventual death are human verities which have haunted poets and philosophers since the beginning of human history.

Biological aging is called senescence by biologists. It has been described as "a deteriorative process. What is being measured, when we measure it, is a decrease in viability and an increase in vulnerability. . . . Senescence shows itself as an increasing probability of death with increasing chronological age: the study of senescence is the study of the *group* of processes, different in different organisms, which lead to this increase in vulnerability."[1]

Senescence does not appear to be characteristic of an entire species, but rather of individual members of all species. There is no known animal species whose individual members do not at some time grow old and die. However, the length of time this requires varies greatly.

One of the startling facts about senescence is that although it is a phenomenon that will occur in each of us, we know very little about it. This is not to say that no research has been done on senescence. Over half a dozen different major theories of senescence are currently being pursued in biology; yet none of them seems to have produced firm results.

While the causes of senescence may have eluded us, it is nevertheless possible to pinpoint some criteria which differentiate senescence from other

---

[1] Alex Comfort, *Aging: The Biology of Senescence* (New York: Holt, Rinehart and Winston, 1964), p. 22.

biological processes. To begin with, its characteristics must be *universal;* that is, they must eventually happen to *all* people. Thus, the fact that older people show a higher prevalence of some condition does not necessarily make that condition part of senescence. For example, more older people than young ones get lung cancer; but for this to be accepted as part of senescence, *all* older people would have to get lung cancer. Second, the changes which constitute senescence come from *within the organism.* Thus, cosmic radiation would not be a part of senescence, since it is a part of the outside environment and can be modified. Third, the process associated with senescence *occur gradually* rather than suddenly. This rules out accidental changes. Finally, the processes of senescence contribute to the decline in function and consequent increased mortality which we observe as the organism ages. The changes which mark senescence thus have a *deleterious* effect on the organism.[2]

One point should stand out here. Senescence is not one process, but many. This may account for the large number of theories of biological aging. A cataloging of the theories of senescence will give some idea of the range of these processes.[3]

Probably the most frequently propounded theory is the "wear and tear" theory based on a mechanical analogy. The idea here is that the body is like a machine, and eventually its parts wear out and the machine breaks down. This theory seems logical, since we have so many organs performing highly specific functions in our bodies. And in a limited sense this theory is true. For example, the valves of the heart perform a mechanical function, and some forms of heart disease result from calcification of these valves. However, this theory is vulnerable to the universality criterion. It is difficult to show that any specific organ or system consistently goes bad or wears out in *all* older people. It also fails to take into account the fact that the body can repair itself.

Another popular theory is that we all have a certain fixed amount of life to live, and the faster we use it up, the faster it is gone. This "rate of living" theory leads to the conclusion that those who lead vigorous lives should die young. Unfortunately for the theory, but fortunately for active people, the evidence seems to indicate that exercise prolongs life. This would seem to dispose of the "rate of living" theory.

The "waste product" theory gives accumulated waste products in the body a key role in the process of senescence. While it is true that various chemical wastes do collect in some tissues, no evidence has been found that these wastes interfere with cell functioning in any important way.

---

[2] Bernard L. Strehler, *Time Cells and Aging* (New York: Academic Press, 1962), pp. 12–17.

[3] For more details see Howard J. Curtis, *Biological Mechanisms of Aging* (Springfield, Ill.: Charles C Thomas, 1966) and Nathan W. Shock, ed., *Perspectives in Experimental Gerontology* (Springfield, Ill.: Charles C Thomas, 1966).

More promising is the "collagen" theory. Collagen is a substance associated with connective tissue. It is present in most organs, tendons, skin, blood vessels, and so on. Collagen gets stiffer with age, and as a result, the tissues containing collagen lose elasticity. This increased stiffness is due to change over time in the cross-linkages between the strands of the collagen molecules.[4] Curtis says, "It seems quite likely that this will cause a deterioration of function in the organs affected and may well lead to some signs and symptoms of aging."[5] Excess collagen in tissues is associated with aging, but it is apparently not a basic cause of aging.

An interesting theory of senescence is the "autoimmunity" theory. Stated as simply as possible, this theory holds that as age increases, mutations cause some of the cells of the body to produce proteins which are not recognizable as part of "self" and are thus responded to as if they were foreign substances. When foreign substances appear in the body, antibodies are produced which attempt to neutralize the effect of the foreign substance. This is called an immune reaction. When antibodies respond to mutations within the body, this is called an *autoimmune* reaction.

Evidence for the autoimmunity theory comes from diverse sources. For example, McKay severely underfed rats during the first third to half of their lives, and he found that this greatly increased their ultimate longevity. The organs which showed the greatest weight loss were precisely those which produce antibodies. The results of McKay's experiment can thus be interpreted as showing that increased longevity is associated with a slow-down in the development of the ability to produce immune reaction.[6]

Several diseases of older people, such as rheumatoid arthritis, are known to be caused by autoimmune reactions. Autoimmunity is therefore a promising theory. Yet there are many "diseases of the aging," such as diabetes, which have not been linked with autoimmune reactions.

The "mutation" theory relates to the fact that the functioning of the cells in our bodies is controlled by the genetic material (DNA) which can be found within each of them. Once mutations in DNA occur, subsequent cell divisions will perpetuate them. As more and more cells develop mutations, an appreciable fraction of the cells of any given organ may become mutated. Since most mutations are deleterious, mutated cells function less efficiently, and organs made up of these cells become inefficient and senescent.

This theory has received perhaps the greatest support from scientific research. Rates of genetic mutation have been shown to increase steadily with age. When genetic material is artificially damaged by radiation, it

---

[4] Curtis, *op. cit.*, p. 19.

[5] Howard J. Curtis, "A Composite Theory of Aging," *The Gerontologist,* 6: 143–149, 1966.

[6] Roy L. Walford, "The Immunologic Theory of Aging," *The Gerontologist,* 4: 195–197, 1964.

shortens the life span of the organ in direct proportion to the amount of genetic damage that has been produced. Animals with shorter life spans have a less stable genetic structure than animals with longer life spans. In addition, the autoimmune reaction discussed earlier has been shown to be associated with genetic mutation. Even so, geneticists are reluctant to accept this theory wholeheartedly because it still contains significant gaps. For example, genetic mutations can increase many times over, with, in some cases, only a small reduction in life expectancy. There is evidently some mediating factor which minimizes the effects of genetic mutations in these cases. Because this and many other questions remain unanswered, the mutation theory of aging remains promising but nevertheless tentative.

A more complex variant of mutation theory is called "error" theory. Whereas the mutation theory concentrates on the cumulative effects of mutations in DNA, the error theory broadens this concern to include the cumulative influence of "mistakes" in RNA synthesis, protein synthesis, enzymic reactions, and so on. Because error is such a broad concept, there are literally scores of causes which may produce molecular and genetic errors. As a result, while this is a promising theory, research evidence on error theory is sparse.

In short, we have a number of promising notions concerning *why* human cells age, but much work remains to be done before we will have a well-developed answer. It is clear that so far none of the current theories has produced a body of concepts which fits the criteria of senescence mentioned earlier.

The single most difficult criterion to meet in isolating the causes of senescence appears to be *universality*. There are many conditions which appear to originate from within the body and which seem to gradually have a harmful result. But as yet we have found no conditions which *always* occur in older man but not in younger man.

One of the biggest stumbling blocks for biological theories of aging is the fact that aging is extremely variable among human beings. The quest for universal factors associated with senescence is very much complicated by the fact that even if they exist, they will probably not show up in all people at the same chronological age, or even within a ten-year range of chronological age. Such a degree of variability is likely to make trouble for the purely biological theories for many years to come.

The variability of human aging may be due partly to *heredity*. It is an inescapable fact that each of us is born with a slightly different program for development which we inherit from our parents and the generations before them. It is highly probable that heredity is a significant determinant of the aging process. There is moderate correlation between the longevity of parents and that of their children. Among twins, even those who have been separated and thus exposed to environmental differences show marked similarities in longevity and bodily characteristics. One-egg twins show more similarities than two-egg twins. These facts point to the conclusion that aging is definitely influenced by heredity. If people of similar heredity were examined, some of the foregoing theories might fare better.

Results of Senescence

Although we may not know precisely *why* the body ages, we cannot very well escape the fact that it does. It might be good at this point to consider some of the important bodily changes that occur as chronological age increases. These changes are important for social gerontology because they represent the concrete physiological limits around which social arrangements are built.

The easiest way to tell an older person when you see one is by his skin. It tends to be wrinkled and rough, and spots of dark pigment can usually be observed. It is more vulnerable than the skin of younger people to malignancies, bruises, loss of hair, and dryness. It heals slowly. Because it symbolizes many other biological changes, which are generally defined in negative terms, the skin of an older person becomes a badge of inferiority.

With age, the older person's joints tend to stiffen, particularly the hips and knees. Compressed spinal discs produce the shorter, bent posture which characterizes many older people.

Loss of muscular strength is commonly thought to be a characteristic of aging. It is true that older people show some loss of muscle tissue, but at high work rates there is virtually no difference between older and younger people in terms of muscular efficiency. It is only at low work rates that older people show a decline in muscular performance, and this is thought to be more a function of declines in coordination than of declines in muscular efficiency.

Two important changes occur in the nervous system as age increases. Hardening of blood vessels creates circulatory problems in the brain, and aging reduces the speed of impulses travelling through nerve tissues. An adequate blood supply is crucial to an efficiently functioning brain, but fortunately most people are not bothered by this problem until well past age seventy-five. Declines in the speed of nerve impulses are a more widespread problem even at the beginning of later life. Most people begin to notice lagging reflexes and reaction time in their late forties. Changes in the nervous system also influence most psychological processes, and these will be dealt with in succeeding chapters.

Failure of the circulatory system is the most common cause of death for people over forty. Heart disease or interrupted blood flow to the brain or heart are prevalent among older people as a result of reduced cardiac output, reduced elasticity of the large arteries, and general deterioration of blood vessels. At age seventy-five the probability of death from cardio-vascular disease is 150 times higher than at age thirty-five.

Of the major systems in the body, the kidneys show the greatest decline in function with increasing age. The kidneys of people over eighty perform only half as well as those of people in their twenties.

The respiratory, digestive, reproductive, and temperature control systems all decline with age, but only rarely do these systems decline enough to produce disability in older people.

Nutrition has an important influence on biological aging. The food requirements of older people are not significantly different from those of younger people. The daily food intake must simply be enough to supply the needed vitamins and energy, but because they engage in less vigorous activity, most older people must gradually reduce their calorie intake or get fat. Unfortunately, too many older people are like the elderly grandmother who stated, "I watch everything I eat very carefully—then I eat it."

Older people need a greater *proportion* of protein in their diets, even if their overall intake is reduced. Otherwise, fatigue, swelling, or lowered resistance to infection may result. And as with the general population, older people should restrict the amount of saturated fat in their diets. These factors make adequate nutrition slightly more expensive for older people than for others.

The importance of good nutrition to the maintenance of the biological systems of older people cannot be overstressed. Unfortunately, as we shall see later, the incomes of most older people are such that malnutrition is rampant among this group. And under these circumstances it is often difficult to tell exactly what part of an individual's biological decline with age is inevitable, and what part is simply due to poor nutrition.

Conclusion

In summary, the aging of the human body manifests itself in three ways, only two of which are probably based on things that happen within the body. Perhaps most important is the deterioration of the irreplaceable organs and systems of the body. The heart, lungs, nervous system, liver, kidneys, and digestive system all show a loss of function as the organism ages. This factor is very much related to a second, the loss of the ability to withstand disease. A strong, efficiently functioning human body has an amazing capacity to ward off disease. With advancing age, however, the body becomes less efficient and less capable of resisting disease. These two factors in combination make up what we have called *senescence*. It should be emphasized that it is not merely the failure of major systems that produces aging. Even one-celled organisms grow old and die. The problem is rather that the cells making up these systems undergo the processes of aging. There seem to be no exceptions to this rule.

The accumulation of unrepaired injuries is not strictly a biological process, since its source is from outside the body. Nevertheless it contributes to the decline in function and may therefore also contribute to the decline in ability to resist disease.

It is very important to remember that these biological aspects of aging do not take place in a vacuum. There appear to be major social factors which operate alongside the process of senescence to produce the results we see in the older person. The assumption that human aging is purely a biological problem should be avoided. Nothing could be further from the truth.

It is also important to remember that biological aging occurs at different rates in different people. The result is an older population that is very heterogeneous in terms of symptoms of senescence. This is an important reason why a symptomatic definition of aging is preferable to a purely chronological one.

Bibliography

Bakerman, Seymour, ed., *Aging Life Processes.* Springfield, Illinois: Charles C Thomas, 1969.

Blumenthal, H. T. and Aline W. Berns, "Autoimmunity and Aging," in *Advances in Gerontological Research,* Volume I, ed. Bernard L. Strehler. New York: Academic Press, 1964, pp. 289–342.

Botwinick, Jack, "A Crude Test of a Hypothesis Relating Rate of Growth to Length of Life," *Gerontologist,* 8:(3)196–197, 1968.

Comfort, Alex, "The Causes of Aging," *Science Journal,* March, 1965, pp. 71–75.

————, *The Process of Aging.* New York: New American Library, 1964.

————, "Theory and Research in the Biology of Aging," *Geriatric Focus,* 8:1; 3; 5–6, 1969.

Curtis, Howard J., *Biological Mechanisms of Aging.* Springfield, Illinois: Charles C Thomas, 1966.

Hayflick, Leonard, "Human Cells and Aging," *Scientific American,* 218:(3), 32–37, 1968.

Krohn, Peter L., ed., *Topics in the Biology of Aging.* New York: Interscience Publishing Company, 1966.

Rockstein, Morris, "The Biological Aspects of Aging," *Gerontologist,* 8:(2) 124–125, 1968.

Shock, Nathan W., ed., *Biological Aspects of Aging.* New York: Columbia University Press, 1962.

————, ed., *Perspectives in Experimental Gerontology.* Springfield, Illinois: Charles C Thomas, 1966.

Strehler, Bernard L., *Time, Cells, and Aging.* New York: Academic Press, 1962.

Verzar, F., "The Aging of Connective Tissue," *Gerontologia*, 1:363–378, 1957.

Walford, Roy L., "The Immunologic Theory of Aging," *Gerontologist*, 4:(4) 195–197, 1964.

————— and Gary M. Troup, "Auto-Immunity Theories," in *Perspectives in Experimental Gerontology*, ed. Nathan W. Shock. Springfield, Illinois: Charles C Thomas, 1966, pp. 351–358.

4 The Psychology of Aging

The psychology of aging is a wide realm which encompasses the sensory and psychomotor processes, perception, and mental ability. While the various aspects of psychology may be dealt with separately, it must be remembered that the human mind as a whole is more than just the sum of its various functions. The importance of age-related psychological changes to social gerontology lies in the impacts these changes have on the *social functioning* of the individual, and not on the drama these changes may introduce to an age graph of a particular psychological function.

Sensory Processes

The senses are the means through which the human mind experiences the world both outside and inside the body. In order to adapt to and interact with his environment, the individual must be able to find out something about this environment, and he depends upon his senses to gather information.

The sensory process is not particularly complex. Sensory organs pick up information about changes in the internal or external environment and pass this information on to the brain. All of the input from the sensory organs is collected and organized in the brain, and the result is what we call *sensory experience*.

The minimum amount of stimulation a sensory organ must experience before sensory information is passed to the brain is called a *threshold*. Each individual has his own threshold for each sense, and the higher the threshold, the more stimulus there must be to get information to the brain. For example, some people require very little noise before they begin to hear while others require a considerable amount. In studying the operation of the sensory processes as a function of age, we will be concerned both with changes in threshold that occur with increasing age and with the complete failure of a particular sensory process.[1]

Vision and hearing are the major sensory processes. Both are very flexible and both can sense objects from a distance. Between them, they do most of the information gathering for the individual.

Vision

Vision is particularly adaptable. It can record experience over a wide range of colors, intensities, distances, and widths of field. The eye has an iris which controls the amount of light that can get to the optic nerve (retina) and a lens which bends the light pattern entering the pupil (the opening surrounded by the iris) so as to focus the pattern of light on the optic nerve.

The lens must change shape in order to be able to focus on both near and distant objects. As age increases, the ability of the eye to change shape and therefore to focus on very near objects decreases. For this reason many older people find glasses necessary for reading if for nothing else. The tendency toward farsightedness increases about tenfold between age ten and age sixty, but after age sixty it does not appear to increase much more.

The size of the opening (pupil) of the eye is also influenced by age. The size of the pupil is important because it controls the amount of light that gets into the eye. In one study, 37 percent of those over sixty-five showed no change in pupil size in response to changes in light intensity. Fifty-six percent showed no change in pupil size in response to changes in lens shape. These two factors are important because proper focusing of an image on the retina requires both the proper quality of light (controlled by the lens) and the proper quantity of light (controlled by the iris). Since both the lens and the iris show a decline in function with increasing age, the results for sight are obvious.

The average diameter of the pupil also declines with age. This reduction in diameter has great influence on the amount of light entering the eye. The eye of the average sixty-year-old admits only about one-third as much light as the eye of the average twenty-year-old.

In general, the visual acuity of young children starts off relatively poor and increases in quality until it hits its peak at about age twenty. After that it remains relatively constant for most people until somewhere in the early forties, when a slow decline begins. Senile changes in the eye do not

---

[1] For a more detailed discussion of aging and sensory processes see James Birren, *The Handbook of Aging and the Individual,* Chapters XV and XVI; James Birren, *The Psychology of Aging,* Chapter 4; Alastair Heron and Sheila Chown, *Age and Function,* Chapter 6; and A. T. Welford and James Birren, *Behavior, Aging, and the Nervous System,* Chapter 16.

occur until around age seventy, and until then there is relatively little deterioration in visual acuity. However, there are many exceptions to this general trend because visual acuity is one of the most variable of human senses. Figure 2 shows the changes in the percent of the population with normal vision as age increases.

Adaptation to dark takes longer as age increases, and it also becomes more difficult to distinguish between levels of brightness. In addition, the threshold of the optic nerve increases with age.

Color vision also changes as the individual grows older. The lens gradually yellows with age and filters out the violet, blue and green colors

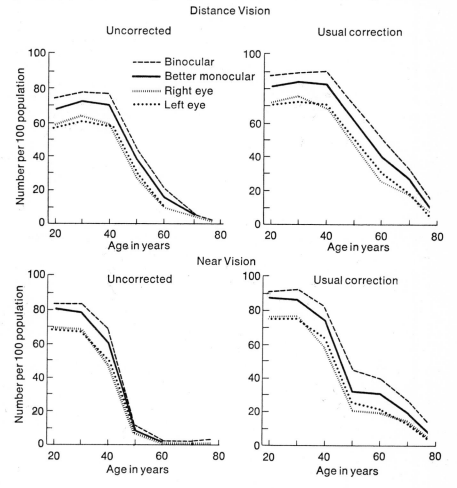

Figure 2. Proportion of American Adults with Monocular and Binocular Visual Acuity of 20/20 or Better at Distance and 14/14 or Better at Near: U.S., 1961–1962.
Source: National Center for Health Statistics, *Vital and Health Statistics,* Series 11, No. 30, April, 1968, p. 3.

toward the dark end of the spectrum. The threshold for these colors increases significantly as people grow older; and for this reason it is much easier for older people to see yellow, orange and red as compared with the darker colors.

In summary, there is a general decline with age in visual capability beginning somewhere in the forties. This decline involves increasing farsightedness, decreasing sensitivity to light, and declining visual acuity. There is a decline with age in the amount of light which can get into the eye, an increase in the time required to get used to darkness, and an increase in threshold for the darker colors. Accordingly, older people need either glasses or large print books for reading, and close work of all kinds becomes more difficult. General levels of illumination must be significantly higher for older people to get the same visual result as young people. The increasing amount of time required for adapting to darkness means that older people have difficulty driving at night because they can be literally blinded for several seconds by the lights of oncoming cars. This does not mean that older people should not drive, merely that they must exercise extra care when driving at night. Finally, changes in color vision mean that for older people to get the same satisfaction from looking at colors in their surroundings that young people get, their environment must present more yellow, orange and red, and less violet, blue and green.

Only a small percentage of older people are blind, yet these people constitute a large proportion of the blind population. In one California study it was found that 55 percent of the blindness in that state occurred after age sixty-five, and 85 percent occurred after age forty-five. Thus, while the number of blind people is relatively small, blindness definitely appears to be age-related.

Hearing

Hearing is the second major sense. Hearing is made up of many kinds of reactions, but the most essential ones are the detecting of the frequency (pitch) of a sound, its intensity, and the time interval over which it occurs.

As the person grows older, his reactions to frequency and intensity change, but there is no evidence to indicate that ability to distinguish time intervals changes significantly with age.

Hearing loss begins about age twenty, and very gradually, as they get older, people lose their ability to hear certain frequencies. This type of hearing loss is very slight for low-pitched sounds, but the loss for high-pitched sounds tends to be considerable. Thus, as age increases, sounds in the higher range become relatively harder to hear.

There is also a change in intensity threshold with advancing age. There are some frequencies that older people cannot hear no matter how loud, but even within the range of pitch that they can hear, the intensity level necessary to produce hearing is greater than among the young.

Older people are also more susceptible to ear damage than the young. For example, industrial noise produces a greater hearing loss among older workers than among younger ones.

Older people, even those with relatively little hearing loss, have greater difficulty in making the fine distinctions required to hear speech than do younger people.

After about age fifty-five, a consistent sex difference appears in hearing ability. Up to that point, the prevalence of hearing loss is about equal for men and women, but after age fifty-five men show considerably greater incidence of hearing loss than do women.

In summary, as people grow older it becomes more difficult for them to hear high-pitched sounds and sounds of low intensity. Older men have greater hearing difficulty than do older women.

As a result, older people enjoy music with more low-pitched sounds and with uniform intensity. Organ music is popular among older people because of the richness of its lower tones. Older people must play radios and television sets louder in order to hear them, and many older wives can be irritated by the fact that their husbands play everything so loud.

Hearing loss is not as easy to measure as visual acuity, and for this reason it makes more sense to talk in terms of *impaired hearing* rather than "normal hearing." Impaired hearing is a hearing loss of sufficient magnitude to reduce the individual's capacity for interacting successfully with his environment. Impaired hearing does not always result when the sense of hearing declines. For example, if the individual still has good eyesight, he may be able to compensate for hearing loss by reading lips.

As we noted earlier, however, eyesight too begins to decline in the early forties. The incidence of impaired hearing therefore increases sharply after age forty-five and it increases even more rapidly thereafter.

A decline of either sight or hearing can be partly compensated by the other, but when both decline simultaneously, as is so often the case among older people, a serious problem of adaptation to the environment occurs. Not only is the individual's ability to earn a living adversely affected, but those who deal with him on a personal basis must learn to take these new limitations into account if they are to help him make maximum use of his capabilities and opportunities.

Other Senses

Within the ear is the inner ear. This apparatus consists of tiny hair-like projections suspended in a fluid environment inside a structure that looks like a horn of plenty. These hair-like projections are sensory receptors which pick up and pass on to the brain information about changes in body position and orientation in space that constitutes our sense of *balance*.

The inner ear is very important in maintaining an upright posture. Its action is not usually a conscious process; balance is normally maintained by unconscious reflex movements.

The efficiency of the sense of balance is difficult to measure. One way is to spin a person around several times and then observe how long it takes him to reestablish his orientation. Maximum sensitivity of the sense of balance appears to occur between ages forty and fifty, later than most other senses; nevertheless, older people take longer to reorient themselves than do younger people.

It has not been established that aging causes a decline in the tissues of the inner ear, yet older people characteristically tend to fall oftener. It is thought that the difficulties in maintaining balance experienced by older people may result more from a failing blood supply than from a failing inner ear. Part of the problem may also be that the central nervous system's ability to coordinate the balance reflexes declines with age, particularly in terms of the speed with which corrections are applied.

Whatever the cause, older people have difficulty in maintaining their balance. They tend to fall more than young people, and for them falls can be more serious.

As a sense, *taste* has less importance for individual's survival, but it certainly can have a good deal to do with his satisfaction. The evidence indicates that all four taste qualities—sweet, salt, bitter, and sour—show an increase in threshold after age fifty. Women remain much more sensitive to taste than men. Not only do individual taste buds become less sensitive with aging, but also the number of taste buds declines. It is estimated that a man in his seventies has only about one-sixth the number of taste buds that a young man in his twenties has. Nevertheless, it is unlikely that *large* changes in taste sensitivity occur before age seventy.

People in old age are apt to require more highly seasoned food to receive the same taste satisfactions they received when they were twenty. They also seem to prefer tart tastes and to show less interest in sweets.

We do not know how or even whether the sense of *smell* changes with age.

From the lack of research in these areas, it appears that taste and smell are the "poor relations" of the senses. This is unfortunate, because these two senses are capable of giving great satisfaction, and compensation for declines in taste and smell could be very important to the individual.

The so-called general body sensations include touch, pain, muscle movement, and vibration. Sensitivity to touch appears to increase from birth to about age forty-five. From that point on the threshold increases sharply.

Pain is an important sense which alerts the body to a state of emergency, some state either within or outside the body which threatens its well-being. There appears to be a decline with increasing age in sensitivity to pain, particularly pain sensed by nerves in the skin. There are also nerves which pick up sensations of pain within the body, but no studies could be found of this aspect of pain in relation to increasing age.

As people grow older, they increasingly make errors in estimating the direction of muscle motion. The ability to detect vibrations appears to be a function of age only for the lower extremities of the body.

Perceptual Process

The senses provide the means for assembling and classifying information, but they do not evaluate it. The process of evaluating the information gathered by the senses and giving it meaning is called *perception.*

Not all sensory input is perceived, for perception is a conscious process and some senses, such as the sense of balance, may be mainly unconscious. But for every sense in which there is consciousness of the stimulus received, there is an evaluative perception.

In perception not all of the information collected may be given equal weight. In visual perception, for example, shape appears to be a more important characteristic than color when it comes to evaluation of an object.

Older people tend to underestimate the passage of time much more than younger people do. Thus, they are very likely to let time "slip by." They are also less capable of judging the speed of a moving object than are younger people.

Closure is the ability to come to a decision concerning the evaluation of a stimulus. People are thought to become more cautious and less capable of closure as they grow older. This may partly account for what many interpret as the indecisiveness of some older people.

As for speed of perception, people appear to suffer a decline with age in the general speed with which they can organize and evaluate stimuli.

A word of warning is appropriate here, however. The available evidence concerning perceptual processes is far less conclusive than that concerning sensory processes.

For many of the sensory and perceptual processes, it would appear that declines in function do not often seriously hamper behavior until after age seventy. "Until that time, disease and other unique circumstances would appear to be more relevant than an intrinsic age-related change would be."[2]

---

[2] James Birren, *The Psychology of Aging* (Englewood Cliffs, N. J.: Prentice-Hall, 1964), p. 107.

Psychomotor Performance

Psychomotor performance[3] refers to a complex chain of activity beginning with a sensory mechanism and ending with some sort of reaction, usually through a muscle. When a muscle acts as a part of the stimulus-response chain of events, it is called an *effector*. In between the sense organs and the effectors lies a chain of brain mechanisms which are called *central processes*. In the ideal situation, psychomotor performance involves taking sensory input, attaching meaning to it through perception, incorporating the perceived information into the mind alongside other ideas (integration), making a decision concerning the action, if any, required by this new information, sending instructions to the appropriate effector, and activating the effector's response. This is indeed a much more complex process than simple sensation of perception.

Psychomotor performance is limited in its abilities by the capacities of the various parts of the system.

In most cases the sensory and effector mechanisms are more than capable of handling the task to be done. Hence, the limits on performance are usually set by "the central mechanisms dealing with perception, with translation from perception to action, and with the detailed control of action."[4]

Performance capacity is a function not only of the available pathways in the brain, but also of the strength of the sensory "signal" and its relative strength compared with other signals entering the brain at the same time.

A decline in absolute or relative signal strength can be partially offset by taking more time to integrate incoming data. This may explain much of the slowness of performance associated with aging. Errors are likely to result if the older individual cannot take the extra time needed to process all the data. In this sense, errors result from the fact that too little information can be processed between the time the sensory input is received and the time action must be taken.

> Adequate functioning of peripheral organs is a prerequisite for adequate performance, but the subtleties of timing, grading, and patterning included in the term "skill" are obviously dependent upon central factors. All we can ask is what function in any given circumstances *sets limits* to the performance. Any link in the chain from receptor to affector and any mechanism concerned in the serial characteristics of performance may in certain circumstances limit the level of achievement.[5]

---

[3] This discussion is based largely on Alan T. Welford, "Psychomotor Performance," in *The Handbook of Aging and the Individual,* ed. James Birren (Chicago: University of Chicago Press, 1961).

[4] *Ibid.,* p. 563.

[5] *Ibid.,* p. 664.

The most serious sensory limitation on psychomotor performance is the general rise in sensory threshold. Once sensory response is triggered, however, the senses do not pose much problem. Research findings suggest that changes in performance would remain even if there were some way to completely eliminate sensory decline. There is also only a negligible change in the speed of nerve conduction as age increases.

The effectors can be a prime weakness in the psychomotor chain. Maximum strength, regardless of how it is measured, declines sharply in the later years. From the twenties to the seventies there is about a 45 percent decline in muscular strength. A similar decline is observed in the endurance of the muscular structure. Nevertheless, recovery time from exertion and the mechanical efficiency of muscles are not the only factors influencing effectors. In fact, poor muscular performance in old age may be due more to poor coordination than to decline in muscular strength or endurance. Since coordination is the result of control by the central processes, the inefficiency of effectors in old age could be looked upon as a result rather than a source of poor psychomotor performance.

From the point of view of psychomotor performance, then, the important limitations would appear to come from the central processes. But regardless of where the limitations come from, there are definite changes in observed psychomotor performance as the individual ages. The most important differences are in reaction time, speed and accuracy of response, and inability to make complex responses.

Reaction Time

Reaction time is usually defined as the period that elapses between the presentation of the stimulus and the beginning of the response to that stimulus. Reaction time has traditionally been considered a measure of the time used by the central processes.

Reaction time increases with age. This increase is very slight for simple tasks, but it becomes greater as the tasks get complex. Oddly enough, however, the more complex the task, the better older people tend to look in relation to the young. If the task is increased in complexity, older people do not take much more time to accomplish it. This is not the case with younger people. For them, the more complex the task, the longer it takes. Given a large age gap for simple tasks, these two separate age trends in reaction time mean that as the complexity of the task *increases,* the reaction time the older person relative to that of the younger may actually *improve.*

The only cases where this is not true are those where the magnitude of the stimulus is at or near the sensory threshold. Here, as would be expected, a marginal signal creates many obstacles to psychomotor reaction time.

The slowing of reactions in older people may result mainly from a tendency toward care and accuracy which seems to characterize this group. They tend to spend more than the average amount of time checking their results; therefore, part of their slowness may be the difference between the time required for *accuracy* and the time required for *certainty*.

The slowing of reaction time is thus mainly in the central processes. Neither the speed of input nor the speed of output is responsible, and in fact, slowing probably results primarily from a desire for certainty rather than a physical inability to act quickly. The slower reaction times of older people are a fact, but the reason for this fact is far from clear.

Speed and Accuracy

Not only the reaction time, but also the speed of movement, tends to decline with increasing age. Again the evidence seems to point to the central processes as the source of slowing rather than to any loss of ability to move quickly. In fact, when older people try to hurry, their control capabilities are often so poor that their movements appear jerky in comparison with the more fluid motions of younger people.

Another factor pointing to the central processes as the source of slowing is that for simple movements the slowing with age is very slight, whereas for complex movements where the same muscles must be more controlled, the slowing with age is more marked.

These same comments apply to *accuracy*. Accuracy declines as the individual grows older unless more time is taken to compensate for the greater difficulty in controlling the response.

Complex Performance

Complex performance involves a series of actions in response to a complex stimulus. It has been found that the brain operates on data serially —that is, it deals with stimuli as they arrive—and if the "old" response is not completed when the "new" stimulus arrives, then the new stimulus must wait its turn. It may be that processing takes older people longer. Certainly the research data point in this direction. If this is true, then it would explain why response time increases with age.

Another factor that seems important in producing age differences in complex response is the strategy used to organize a complex problem for solution. It appears that young people, knowing that they are capable of quick response, use the trial-and-error method extensively when trying to solve a complex problem. On the other hand, older people, knowing that they cannot respond quickly, tend to think the problem through and try to solve it in the fewest tries. The result is that when unlimited time is available, older people do about as well as their younger counterparts in solving complex problems. When time is limited, however, and reflection on the problem is not feasible, older people do much worse because they are forced to use the trial-and-error method. Trial-and-error methodology is only fruitful if a large number of trials can be made. The slowness of the older person makes such a task very difficult.[6]

In summary, it would appear that the psychomotor performance of older people is limited more by the central processes than by any other factor. These central processes appear to have definite limits in terms of the amount they can do in a given time. A loss in capacity can be offset by taking longer, but when this is not possible, a much larger percentage of errors will be observed among older people than among the young.

The more complex the integrating and controlling functions must be, the more aging slows down performance. Older people thus shift their emphasis from speed to accuracy.

The implications of these factors are important. First, factors other than changes in the central processes have relatively little influence on psychomotor response. Also, the central processes are very difficult to offset mechanically, as we can do with glasses or hearing aids for poor sensory processes. Reaction time, speed and accuracy of movement, and organization of complex performance all suffer as a result of the decline in integrating and controlling ability which occurs in the central processes in the later years. However, in situations where these characteristics are important, the older person can still do about as well as anyone else if given enough time.

Mental Functioning

Sensation, perception, and psychomotor performance are all very important for the functioning of the individual, yet in man as in no other animal these processes must take a back seat to what we will call mental functioning. *Mental functioning* is an overall term that refers to a large group of complex processes, subdivided for convenience into intelligence, learning, memory, thinking, problem-solving, and creativity.

---

[6] The conclusion is suggested by the material in Birren, *Handbook of Aging and the Individual,* pp. 600–602.

Intelligence

When we think of intelligence, we usually imply both a *potential* and an *actual* ability. In practice, however, we always deal with *measured* ability. Thus, conceptually intelligence as it is studied by psychologists has three aspects: potential intelligence, actual intelligence and measured intelligence. Our discussion will center around age changes in measured intelligence.

Measured intelligence is actual mental ability defined in terms of responses to items on a test. Yet no matter how extensive or well-prepared a test is, there is always a margin of error in its measurement of actual

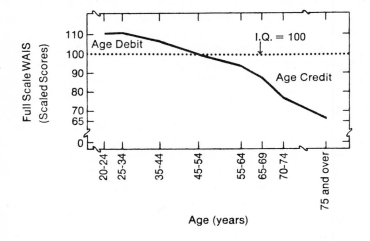

Figure 3. Full Scale WAIS Scores as a Function of Age.
Source: Jack Botwinick, *Cognitive Processes in Maturity and Old Age* (New York: Springer, 1967), p. 3. Reprinted by permission.

mental ability. Perhaps the most frequently used test in studies of adult intelligence and age-related changes is the Wechsler Adult Intelligence Scale (WAIS)

I.Q. (intelligence quotient) is a number established by test performance which is taken as a point of comparison with the "normal" or average score of 100. When the WAIS is used for adults aged twenty to seventy-five and over, *there is an age factor built into the determination of what is normal.* In Figure 3 the heavy black line indicates the mean raw scores on the WAIS by age. Note that measured performance peaks about age twenty-five and declines thereafter, particularly after age sixty-five. The shaded area on Figure 3 represents the handicap or advantage that is built into the WAIS I.Q. score to control for age. There could be 40 points difference between the score at age twenty-five and the score at age seventy-five, and yet the I.Q. score would be the same. The importance of this is that the most frequently used test of mental ability incorporates an assumption that a 40-point drop in score from age twenty-five to age seventy-five is normal.

In practical terms, however, the *average* decline with age in WAIS scores masks a large amount of individual variation. Any given older person might have an extremely high I.Q. even when compared to the young. In fact, the correlation between age and I.Q. is not particularly high, only around −.40. This means that if the odds against predicting the I.Q. score were 10 to 1, then knowledge of age would reduce these odds to 6 to 1, not a particularly stunning reduction.

Table 3. Rank Order of WAIS Subtests with Elderly Subjects Based on Several Studies

	Subtests	Average Rank of Score
Verbal Subtests	Information	1.85
	Vocabulary	2.33
	Comprehension	2.75
	Arithmetic	4.40
	Similarities	5.60
	Digit Span	6.50
Performance Subtests	Picture Completion	6.65
	Object Assembly	7.00
	Block Design	8.55
	Picture Arrangement	9.85
	Digit Symbol	10.85

Intelligence is not a single ability; it is a set of abilities. Table 3 shows the various ability measures that have been combined in the WAIS. The subtests are arranged in order of performance by elderly subjects in ten different studies.[7] These people did best on the information subtest and worst on the digit symbol subtest. As Table 3 shows, the subtests can be broken into two sets, one set dealing with verbal ability and the other dealing with performance ability. It has come to be a classic pattern that older people do better on the verbal tests and worse on the performance tests.

[7] Jack Botwinick, *Cognitive Processes in Maturity and Old Age* (New York: Springer, 1967), p. 9. Reprinted by permission.

The rankings in Table 3 lead to the conclusion that stored information and verbal abilities are sustained in old age at a much higher level than are psychomotor-perceptual-integrative skills.[8]

There are a number of factors which influence age changes in I.Q. Perhaps the most important is the individual's initial level of functioning. People in the 95th percentile, that is, people with scores high enough that 95 percent of all scores would fall below theirs, show a leveling off in vocabulary score between ages twenty and thirty. But rather than showing a decline thereafter, these people show a plateau or slight rise in score with advancing age.[9] On the other hand, people in the 25th percentile show a marked decline in vocabulary score after about age thirty. These results suggest that with regard to verbal ability, the rich get richer and the poor get poorer as the years go by.

Performance on an intelligence test is closely related to such factors as motivation, anxiety, and cooperation. If the test is given in an atmosphere where anxiety is very high or where cooperation and motivation are very low, then these factors will prevent the test from measuring what the subject knows and can do.

The higher the level of education, the higher will be the performance on an intelligence test. We do not know which comes first, however, intelligence or education. We simply know that they are highly correlated.

Health is also very closely related to I.Q. Even a slight reduction in optimum health can negatively influence intelligence scores, and serious disorders such as arteriosclerosis markedly reduce such scores. We can go so far as to say that very rapid declines in I.Q. after age sixty-five or seventy are usually the result of changes in health.

Most studies of intelligence and age utilize test scores of people of different ages and assume that the only factor that varies among these people is age. This assumption is obviously difficult to defend. Most older people have lived through a different era and use a slightly different body of symbols than their younger counterparts. Thus, most studies have examined age *differences* rather than age *changes* in intelligence.

The examination of age changes in intelligence requires a longitudinal study in which the subject is followed along through life with periodic measures of intelligence. Such studies have been conducted and have shown the same patterns that were mentioned above except that the declines observed in overall scores were much smaller. This would suggest that *at least part of what appears to be the decline in intelligence of older people is actually a change in the skills that are being emphasized by the culture.*

---

[8] *Ibid.,* p. 10.

[9] Harold Jones, "Intelligence and Problem-Solving," in *Handbook of Aging and the Individual,* ed. James E. Birren (Chicago: University of Chicago Press, 1961), p. 715.

I.Q. tests tend to emphasize contemporary skills and therefore to de-emphasize the skills of people educated in earlier eras.

Memory is also a factor influencing older people's performance on intelligence tests. Studies have shown that it is short-term memory that tends to lose efficiency with advancing age. Since perceptive and integrative skills depend heavily on short-term memory, and vocabulary and information skills depend mainly on long-term memory, these findings may account for much of the observed difference in I.Q. test performances between older and younger people.

But what do I.Q. test scores mean for real life situations? Within wide limits, age-related declines in measured intelligence probably have very little to do with the individual's ability to perform everyday tasks. Unless there is a drastic decline in mental ability, such factors as perseverance, sense of responsibility and responses to group pressure are probably at least as important as mental ability in the social functioning of the individual.

Learning

Learning means the acquisition of information or skills, and it is usually measured by looking for improvements in task performance. When someone improves his performance at a given intellectual or physical task, we say he has learned. All studies of performance indicate a decline with age.

Clearly, however, there are a number of factors other than learning ability which affect performance. These include motivation, speed, and physiological states. In practice it is extremely difficult to separate the components of performance in order to examine the influence of learning ability, although a number of studies have attempted to do so. Yet despite the evidence that other factors contribute to the decline in task performance, part of this decline must still be attributed to a decline with age in the ability to learn.

From a practical point of view it seems that learning performance tends to decline as age increases, although the declines are not noticeable until past middle age. All age groups *can* learn. Older people can usually learn anything anyone else can if given a bit more time. Tasks that involve manipulation of distinct objects or symbols, distinct and unambiguous responses, and low interference from prior learning are particularly conducive to good performance by older people.

Memory

Memory is intimately related to both intelligence and learning, since remembering is a part of the evidence of learning and learning is part of the measurement of intelligence. For example, if a man does not learn, he has nothing to remember. Conversely, if he cannot remember, there is no sign of his having learned.[10]

There are essentially four types of memory. *Short-term* or immediate memory involves recall after very little delay, from as little as five seconds up to thirty seconds. *Recent* memory involves recall after a brief period, from one hour to several days. *Remote* memory refers to recall of events which took place a long time in the past, but which have been referred to frequently throughout the course of a lifetime. *Old* memory refers to recall of events which occurred a long time in the past and which have not been thought of or rehearsed since.

Regardless of type, there are three *stages* of memory. *Registration* refers to the "recording" of learning or perceptions. In concept it is analogous to the recording of sound on a tape recorder. *Retention* refers to the ability to sustain registration over time. *Recall* is retrieval of material that has been registered and retained. Obviously in any type of memory, a failure at any of these stages will result in no *measurable* memory.

It is commonly believed that all kinds of memory show a decline with advancing age. However, studies do not overwhelmingly support this idea. While it is true that there is an age deficit in recall of various types, it is not clear whether this results from declining memory or declining ability to learn in the first place. "Nevertheless, if we take the position of being interested only in whether or not there is a decline with age in the ability to reproduce previously exposed material, regardless of what the basis for the decline may be, the evidence seems to point to an age deficit in the performance of both immediate and delayed recall."[11]

There appears to be a greater loss with age in short-term and recent memory than in remote or old memory, and the decline with age in memory function is less for rote memory than for logical memory. As age increases, the retention of things heard becomes increasingly superior to the retention of things seen, and use of both gives better results than the use of either separately.

Bright people are less susceptible to memory loss with increasing age than are their less intelligent counterparts, and some older people escape memory loss altogether. This suggests that the memory loss which is asso-

---

[10] Botwinick, *op. cit.*, p. 107.
[11] *Ibid.*, p. 116.

ciated with age may not in fact be due to processes of senescence. In fact, people who exercise their memories tend to maintain both remote and recent memory.

Any attempt to try to reverse or compensate for a decline in memory functions must obviously depend on some notion of why people forget. There are a number of theories of forgetting, and each has implications for various treatment solutions.

One theory holds that forgetting results from faulty registration at the beginning. Studies supporting this theory have shown that when older people are not hurried in their learning or perception, recall is improved. It has also been held that retention declines with age, and there is some support for this idea. But perhaps the most widely supported theory of forgetting states that new material learned interferes with the recall of old material. Numerous studies have supported this idea, although the results to date are far from clear-cut.

One biological theory which may hold promise is that memory is located in RNA (ribonucleic acid). This theory states that forgetting is the result of a loss of RNA with age due to the influence of certain enzymes.

The RNA theory has great practical promise, for if it is true, then at least some of the memory loss in older people might be treatable. Experiments with humans to date suggest that severe cases of memory decline are improved by administering RNA either orally or by intravenous injection.[12] Researchers indicate that "this procedure [RNA therapy] constitutes the only methods which in our experience has produced a halting and, in favorable cases, a reversal of deterioration in [memory] function in organic brain syndromes."[13]

If the interference theory is true, then about all that could be done to ward off memory decline would be periodic rehearsal, a highly impractical method. Faulty registration could be at least partly countered by allowing plenty of time for learning and/or perception to take place. Not much could be done about a decline in ability to retain material that has been registered.

Thinking

As a result of intelligence, learning, and memory, the human being has at his disposal a great many separate mental images. Thinking, problem-

---

[12] *Ibid.*, p. 146.

[13] D. E. Cameron *et al.*, "Ribonucleic Acid in Psychiatric Therapy," in *Current Psychiatric Therapies*, ed. J. H. Masserman. (New York: Grune and Stratton, 1964), p. 132.

solving and creativity are all terms which apply to the manipulation of ideas and symbols.

Thinking can be defined as the process of developing new ideas. It helps bring order to the chaos of data brought into the mind by learning and perception by *differentiating* and *categorizing* these data into constructs that psychologists call concepts. Thus, thinking is the process we use to form concepts.

Differentiation occurs at two separate levels. The first is the level of sensation, perception, or learning. These processes were discussed earlier, and obviously declines in these functions with age would serve as effective barriers to concept formation. A second level of differentiation is in a process psychologists call stimulus generalization. Stimulus generalization makes different stimuli functionally equivalent, and the more similar the stimuli, the more nearly equal the responses. For example, most oranges are unique. They vary according to weight, thickness of skin, number of seeds, number of bumps on their skins, and enough other characteristics to give an almost infinite set of possible combinations. Yet we have the mental capacity to treat all oranges alike. This is stimulus generalization, and it is an essential prerequisite for the process of categorization.

It is thought that the ability to perform stimulus generalization declines as age increases, and early experiments have tended to confirm this supposition. When declines in speed were accounted for, it was found that most older people produce more accurate and specific differentiations and thus have less ability for stimulus generalization than their younger counterparts. Thus, when not given enough time, older people tend to be confused by tasks which require stimulus generalization and to be less capable of concept formation than the young.

Once mental data have been differentiated, they must be categorized. This allows data to be dealt with in general terms, which is much easier than trying to deal with everything in specifics. Thus, when we encounter a stop sign we can deal with it as a member of a class of objects rather than trying to figure out why it is there, who put it there, and so on. The assumptions we make when we encounter a stop sign are the result of stimulus generalization and categorization.

Older people seem to be particularly poor at forming concepts. As a matter of fact, the age curve for conceptualization ability is very nearly the same as the one shown earlier for the WAIS (Figure 3). Concept formation often involves making logical inferences and generalizations. Older people have been found to resist forming a higher order generalization and to refuse to choose one when given the opportunity. All studies seem to agree that as age increases, ability at concept formation and its components declines.

Yet common sense tells us that older people form concepts and that some do it exceedingly well. What does it mean when we say that older

people consistently show a decline in performance on tests of differentiation and categorization? At this point it appears that at least part of this
result may be attributed to the characteristics of the tests used. Two types
of items are generally used: abstract and concrete. When an item requires
generalization from a single case and inference beyond the specific details
of that case, the item is said to be abstract. When the specific case need
not be put into a broader framework and not much more than literal
recognition is involved, then the item is said to be concrete. The idea has
been advanced that the past training and experience of older people leaves
them ill prepared to deal with the high proportion of abstract items found
on most tests of thinking. Where today's schools encourage generalization
and inference, the schools of fifty years ago are said not to have emphasized these skills.

Longitudinal data could give some key answers to these questions, but
unfortunately very little is available. Data from studies where education
level was controlled suggest that both level and type of education may
modify, but not eliminate, the relationship between age and measured
thinking ability.

Likewise, studies which have held I.Q. constant have shown a reduction in the age-thinking association, but not completely. Studies have also
shown that declines in memory function do not account for the age decline
in ability to form concepts. There have also been studies which suggest
that those who retain the greatest degree of verbal facility in old age are
also those who retain the greatest amount of skill in concept formation.

In their entirety, these data suggest that concept formation is not completely independent of other skills such as learning and intelligence, but
at the same time is not completely dependent on them either. A substantial
part of the decline with age in measured ability to form concepts appears
to be genuine, and not due to artifacts of the measurement process or the
influence of intervening variables.

Problem-solving

Problem-solving means the development of decisions out of the processes of reason, logic, and thinking. Whereas thinking involves the differentiation and categorization of mental data, problem-solving involves
making logical deductions about these categories, their properties, and
differences among them. Problem-solving differs from learning in that
learning is the *acquisition* of skills and perceptions, while problem-solving
is *using* these skills and perceptions to make choices.

In solving problems, older subjects are at a disadvantage if many items
of information must be dealt with simultaneously. They have more diffi-

culty giving meaning to stimuli presented and more trouble remembering this information later when it must be used to derive a solution. The number of errors in solving problems rises steadily with age.

Older people take a long time to recognize the explicit goal of a particular problem. Their search for information is thus characterized by haphazard questioning rather than by concentration on a single path to the goal. They attain information randomly, have trouble separating the relevant from the irrelevant, and thus tend to be overwhelmed by a multitude of irrelevant facts. They also tend toward repetitive behavior, which can be disruptive in situations where the nature of problems and their solutions is constantly and rapidly changing. Repetition can be an advantage, however, in situations which are changing slowly or not at all.

In general, the same trend of decline is observed with regard to problem-solving that was observed in the other mental processes. There just may be some truth in the old saying that championship chess players are finished at forty.

Creativity

Creativity is unique, original, and inventive thinking. It is usually identified by its concrete results. Studies of creativity indicate that creativity reaches its peak in the thirties and very gradually declines thereafter. Why the decline? It seems to be more a matter of quantity than of quality. Studies show that as age increases, the amount of creative working time available decreases, presumably due to a declining level of energy.

Conclusion

There can be little doubt that all of the psychological processes examined in this chapter show declines in function as the age of the individual increases. As they get older, most people begin to notice impairments in their sight and hearing. Their other senses also become less efficient. Due to declines in the efficiency of the central processes, perception, reaction time, speed and accuracy of response, and complex task performance all suffer as aging progresses. Likewise, loss of brain tissue, changes in the metabolic rate of the brain, and loss of circulatory capacity in the brain all produce changes in mental functioning. Intelligence, learning, memory, thinking, problem-solving, and creativity all show reductions with advancing age.

Yet these losses seldom hamper the activities of older people until quite late in life, and most older people maintain their psychological skills at levels quite acceptable for adequate everyday functioning. In addition, the extent to which chronologically old people exhibit declines in function varies considerably. Some people at age sixty-five show very few signs of loss of function. As long as they stay out of very volatile situations, older people are usually capable of solving most problems that arise. And while the energy needed to work declines, the ability to do creative work in later life seems to remain for most people who were capable of it when they were young. The most serious deficit which apparently cannot be corrected is in the ability to coordinate bodily movements, but in industrial societies little premium is put on exceptional skill in this area. Overall, then, the picture is relatively positive for older people in terms of psychological functioning. The most important factor in maintaining mental skills into old age seems to be an environment which allows the mental faculties to be constantly exercised.

Bibliography

Bayley, Nancy, "Cognition and Aging," in *Theory and Methods of Research on Aging,* ed. Klaus W. Schaie. Morgantown, West Virginia: West Virginia University, 1968, pp. 97–119.

———— and Melita Oden, "The Maintenance of Intellectual Ability in Gifted Adults," *Journal of Gerontology,* 10:91–107, 1955.

Birren, James E., ed. *Handbook of Aging and the Individual.* Chicago: University of Chicago Press, 1960.

————, *The Psychology of Aging.* Englewood Cliffs, New Jersey: Prentice-Hall, 1964.

————, ed., *Relations of Development and Aging.* Springfield, Illinois: Charles C Thomas, 1964.

————, Henry A. Imus and William F. Windle, eds., *The Process of Aging in the Nervous System.* Springfield, Illinois: Charles C Thomas, 1959.

Blumenkrantz, Jack, "Assessment of Higher Mental Functions in the Aged: Proposals for Research," *Gerontologist,* 7:(2, part II), 55–60, 1967.

Botwinick, Jack, *Cognitive Processes in Maturity and Old Age.* New York: Springer, 1967.

Bromley, Dennis B., *The Psychology of Human Ageing.* Baltimore: Penguin Books, 1966.

Chown, Sheila and Klaus F. Reigel, eds., *Psychological Functioning in the Normal Aging and Senile Aged.* New York: S. Karger, 1968.

Fisher, Jerome and Robert C. Pierce, "Dimensions of Intellectual Functioning in the Aged," *Journal of Gerontology,* 22:166–173, 1967.

Gilbert, Jeanne G., "Memory Loss in Senescence," *Journal of Abnormal and Social Psychology,* 36:3–54, 1941.

Heron, Alastair and Sheila Chown, *Age and Function.* Boston: Little, Brown and Co., 1967.

Hulicka, Irene M., "Age Changes and Age Differences in Memory Functioning," *Gerontologist,* 7:(2, part II), 46–54, 1967.

Jones, Harold E., "Intelligence and Problem-Solving," in *Handbook of Aging and the Individual*, ed. James E. Birren. Chicago: University of Chicago Press, 1959, pp. 700–738.

Klonoff, Harry and Margaret Kennedy, "Memory and Perceptual Functioning in Octogenarians and Nonagenarians in the Community," *Journal of Gerontology*, 20:328–333, 1965.

Koyl, Leon F. and Pamela Marsters Hanson, *Age, Physical Ability, and Work Potential*. New York: National Council on the Aging, 1969.

McFarland, Ross A., "The Sensory and Perceptual Processes in Aging," in *Theory and Methods of Research on Aging*, ed. Klaus W. Schaie. Morgantown, West Virginia: West Virginia University, 1968, pp. 9–52.

Owens, William A., "Age and Mental Abilitites: A Longitudinal Study," *Genetic Psychology Monographs*, 48:3–54, 1953.

————, "Age and Mental Abilities: A Second Adult Follow-up," *Journal of Educational Psychology*, 57:311–325, 1966.

Talland, George A., ed., *Human Aging and Behavior*. New York: Academic Press, 1968.

Welford, Alan T., *Ageing and Human Skill*. London: Oxford University Press, 1958.

————, "Psychomotor Performance" in *Handbook of Aging and the Individual*, ed. James E. Birren. Chicago: University of Chicago Press, 1959, pp. 562–613.

———— and James E. Birren, eds., *Behavior, Aging and the Nervous System*. Springfield, Illinois: Charles C Thomas, 1965.

———— and ————, eds., *Decision Making and Age*. Basel, Switzerland: S. Karger, 1969.

5

The Psychological Foundations of Behavior

At the root of most human behavior is a complex mental structure which is made up of drives, motives, emotions, expectancies, knowledge, and attitudes, plus various psychological skills such as perception, intelligence, and the like. When a person behaves, he is generally responding to a drive, motive, or emotion. Expectancies and attitudes, on the other hand, influence the *nature* of his response. This structure is welded into a more or less organized and interdependent system by the personality. As a system, the personality *is* the individual in that therein lies his humanity.

This chapter deals with the impact of aging on drives, motives, emotions, expectancies, and attitudes; and with the influence of aging on personality.

Drives

Drives are unlearned bodily states that are frequently experienced as feelings of tension or restlessness which make people want to act. When a person is hungry, for example, feelings of tension and restlessness do not have to be learned, they just appear. The primary drives which have been studied from the point of view of age changes include hunger, sex, and activity.

Hunger　There has been little systematic study of age changes in hunger in humans, but data from animal studies indicate that older animals are less driven by food deprivation and can withstand greater food deprivation than younger animals. However, the literature on the food habits of older people does not exactly fit this picture. Some older people appear to have less appetite than their younger counterparts, but many older people also enjoy eating and do not reduce their food intake appreciably with age.

This seeming enigma raises an interesting point. Past learning associated with the satiation or reduction of drives is frequently overlooked as a factor influencing responses to drives. Certain drives appear regularly, and human culture contains patterns for satisfying them. These cultural patterns become ingrained in the individual as habits. Habits have a way of acting like drives, and a reduction in the physiological state (drive) need not necessarily lead to a change in behavior. Hence, eating habits may persist even though the physiological basis for eating has diminished. If food consumption remains constant or increases as age increases, then the source of this behavior is probably a result more of culture than of the hunger drive.

Another facet of this same question concerns the fact that behavior can serve more than one function. In measuring the hunger drive, we observe behavior toward food. However, this behavior can result from habit, from a desire for taste sensations, or from a desire to socialize at mealtime, as well as from hunger. These dilemmas are present in the study of human drives, regardless of which one we study.

Sex   Next to hunger, the *sex drive* is perhaps the most important drive in man. If frequency of sexual outlet is taken as an indicator of the drive state, then among males there appears to be a marked decline in the sex drive as age increases. (See Figure 4.) These findings remain fairly stable regardless of the sexual outlet, and it has been found that as men get older, they become more and more alike in terms of the frequency of their sexual behavior, or rather the infrequency of it. The sexual capacities of women change very little with age. If masturbation is taken as the indicator of sexuality, then women show a very slight decline with age as compared to a much larger decline among men.

While sexual behavior declines with age, it does not disappear—all the jokes to the contrary notwithstanding. Continued sexual activity in later life is associated with the capacity for orgasm, the age of the partner, and health. Once they have discovered their capacity for sexual response, women are apt to seek sexual gratification after the death of their spouse, and the same is true of men; but for men the problem is less acute because at later ages there are many more single women than there are single men.

Masters and Johnson,[1] in their pioneering study of human sexual response, studied the sexual activities of a limited number of older people in great detail. They found that in aging women steroid starvation and hormone imbalance following menopause often lead to changes in the sex organs which result in painful coition and orgasm. Masters and Johnson consider pain a primary cause of reduced sexual activity in the older woman; and they contend that hormone therapy in women is effective in

---

[1] William H. Masters and Virginia Johnson, *Human Sexual Response* (Boston: Little, Brown and Co., 1966).

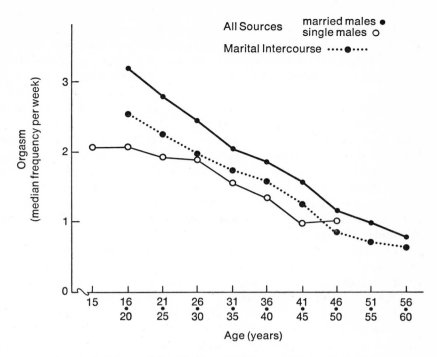

Figure 4. Age and the Median Frequency of Orgasms per Week for Men. Orgasms from All (Six) Sources Include Marital Intercourse.
Source: A. C. Kinsey, W. B. Pomeroy, and C. E. Martin. *Sexual Behavior in the Human Male* (Philadelphia: W. B. Saunders Company, 1948).

increasing sexual capacity primarily because it eliminates pain rather than because it stimulates the sex drive, as had been widely thought. Even in spite of steroid and hormone problems, most older women who maintain a regular outlet for their sexual drives are able to retain a much higher capacity for sexual performance than their counterparts who do not have a regular outlet.

Masters and Johnson conclude that the sexual responsiveness of the male wanes as he ages. This appears to be true no matter what measure of response is used. After about age sixty there is a loss of maintained levels of sexual tension and reduced reactive intensity during sexual expression. Masters and Johnson's data sustain the commonly held notion that the sexual performance of the male declines with age; but except in cases of drastic physical infirmity they contend that the greatest causative factor in this change is socio-psychological rather than biological in nature. Boredom with one's partner, preoccupation with career or economic pursuits, mental or physical fatigue, overindulgence in food or drink, physical and mental infirmities, and fear of failure are all held to be more important in the sexual performance decline in the older male than aging *per se*. Masters and Johnson found that as in the case of older women, one of the biggest factors associated with maintenance of effective sexuality in the older male was a continuing regular outlet for active sexual expression.

Activity   In most animals there appears to be a drive toward undirected, spontaneous activity (sometimes called curiosity). In animal studies it has been found that this drive first increases with age and then decreases. In rats, for example, spontaneous activity increases from birth to puberty, and declines from then on. This drive has not been studied in humans, but at least part of the lethargy to be found in some older people probably results from a decline in the drive toward activity. Nevertheless, the decline in available energy is probably more important than any decline in drive in reducing the spontaneous activity of older people.

In summary, it appears that drives do wane as age increases, but because there are a good many factors which intervene between drives and overt behavior, drives play a relatively small part in explaining behavior changes that occur as aging progresses.

Motives are closely related to drives. Drives are very generalized dispositions toward action. Superimposed on these generalized states are patterns of learned behavior which give specific direction to these general tendencies to act. Motives are thus specific, goal-directed, and learned.

Motives intervene between biological drives and human behavior. "Virtually all behavior that is distinctively human has little in the way of simple one-to-one connections with . . . primary drives. The same drive may be involved, for example, in many different motives. Although the hunger drive usually leads directly to food-getting behavior, it may also instigate behavior directed toward injuring others (aggressiveness), toward hoarding (acquisitiveness), or toward competing or cooperating with others."[2]

For obvious reasons, motives are an important aspect of human behavior, but we know very little about them. What evidence there is indicates that age changes in capacity for motivation are very slight. Botwinick suggests that the role of motivation in the behavior of older people cannot be understood outside the specific situation in which it occurs.

Since motives are learned, even relatively satiated human desires can be aroused given a sufficient amount of stimulus, and motives can disappear if there is little opportunity to satisfy or reinforce them. As Kuhlen has stated, "A society or culture decrees in many subtle ways, and in some not so subtle, that certain types of stimulation will be brought to bear on certain age groups and largely withheld from those of other ages. . . . Moreover, since the motivational tendencies of people are very largely

---

[2] Theodore M. Newcomb, Ralph H. Turner and Philip E. Converse, *Social Psychology* (New York: Holt, Rinehart, and Winston, 1965), p. 25.

learned as a result of the reward and punishment systems to which they are exposed during the course of early development, it is reasonable to expect that motives may be *changed* during adulthood if the individual is exposed to a new set of punishment and reward patterns."[3]

Kuhlen has also advanced the notion that growth-expansion motives dominate the early adult years, while anxiety and threat represent primary motivators in the later years. Needs for achievement, power, creativity, self-actualization, and affiliation are said to give rise in early adulthood to growth-expansion motives, with behavior resulting from such motivation centering around family and work. As the person moves into later adulthood, however, Kuhlen sees work and family as becoming less and less capable of providing continued satisfaction, whereupon interests shift to other kinds of activity. Studies indicate that this process of forced reorientation in major goals is likely to result in considerable stress. This stress is most often felt as a general sensation of anxiety or threat.[4] "This anxiety may not only generate constructive efforts to reduce it, sometimes through education or therapy, but is especially important as a generator of defensive and handicapping behavior patterns. . . . Various personality changes, such as conservatism, intolerance of ambiguity, and rigidity are construed as ego defenses, or maneuvers utilized to control the anxiety. . . ."[5]

Research Illustration 1
Motivation of Aged Persons*
Richard N. Filer and Desmond O. O'Connell

Working under the assumption that motivation for improvement is a big factor in any rehabilitation program, Filer and O'Connell investigated two methods of influencing the attainment of rehabilitative goals by older patients in a Veterans Administration home.

Attention was directed toward a group of goals: (a) self-management of medication, (b) dependability in keeping appointments, (c) participation in some productive, constructive work, (d) housekeeping

---

[3] Raymond G. Kuhlen, "Developmental Changes in Motivation During the Adult Years," *Relations of Development and Aging,* ed. James E. Birren (Springfield, Ill.: Charles C Thomas, 1964), pp. 210–211.

[4] *Ibid.,* pp. 209–246.

[5] *Ibid.,* pp. 224–225.

* Based on Richard N. Filer and Desmond O. O'Connell, "Motivation of Aging Persons," *Journal of Gerontology,* 19:15–22 (January, 1964).

maintenance of their own living area, (e) personal appearance and
hygiene, (f) responsibility for maintenance of their clothing, (g) management of their own finances, and (h) not being a disciplinary problem.

Based on interviews with patients, five rewards were selected which
were important to them: (a) more privacy and a more pleasant appearance in the ward environment, (b) monetary pay for work in adapted
workshops, (c) membership in a club, limited to members who maintain
a high level of behavior, (d) increased privileges, (e) eligibility to
participate in ward self-government.

Two matching groups of forty-four elderly male patients each
(average age over seventy) were then formed, using degree of disability
(Severe, Moderately Severe, and Moderate) as the criterion for matching.
Group A was to receive immediate and definite reinforcement and
Group B was to receive no differential reinforcement. Both groups were
then told about the behavior standards and informed that they would
be evaluated every two weeks and that they would receive "report cards"
telling them whether or not they had succeeded in meeting the standards.

Group B was not told what would happen should they meet or fail
to meet the standards. The implication was that they would continue
to be treated like any other patients. They were given no indication that
they would be rewarded for satisfactory performance.

On the other hand, Group A was carefully informed of the five
rewards for which they would be eligible if they performed satisfactorily
on all eight behavior categories for two successive rating periods.

As expected, Group A's performance was much superior to Group B's,
particularly with regard to keeping appointments, personal appearance,
and work participation. Both groups improved during the study, and
Filer and O'Connell attribute the improvement in Group B to the
opportunity for participation, the clearly defined staff expectations,
knowledge of staff approval or disapproval, and increased attention by
the staff. Although both groups improved, the group that received the
multiple rewards (Group A) attained satisfactory levels more often
and more quickly, and maintained them longer than did the control group.
One important implication of this study is that motivation is very much
dependent on specific goals, and that the more explicit the goal and its
reward, the greater the motivation.

Filer and O'Connell conclude that their results may apply to many
institutional settings, including those where efforts to control a large
mass of residents by focusing on preventing "bad" behavior have failed
or have produced only token compliance. They observe that "some of
the deterioration of behavior observed in aging, institutionalized
persons seems to be fostered by the institutional climate and is not merely
the result of the aging process. Elderly, disabled persons in such a setting
may be functioning far below their capacity. When exposed to greater
opportunity and increased expectancy for performance and increased

attention and knowledge of approval or disapproval from the staff, functional levels rise. When additional incentives are consistently offered for specific behavior performances, further significant improvement of performance may be made."

Expectancies are mental sets. They can also be anticipations which predispose the individual to respond in a particular way. Mental sets are a very important aspect of human behavior. Without them we would have to relearn almost everything we do every time we wanted to do it. Yet a very important element of mental flexibility seems to be the ability to inhibit, to ignore, or to modify our mental sets in situations where they are not appropriate. This ability appears to decline with increasing age, and this decline is an important factor determining the nature of response in older people.

Emotions are strong mental states, often of an agitated nature, that are frequently accompanied by physiological changes in the gastrointestinal system or in the vasomotor system. They include such things as fear, anger, anxiety, disgust, grief, joy, or surprise, and are usually a response to an external situation. Emotions often lead to observable behavior, but this is not one of their necessary characteristics. There is, however, always an internal state which arises as part of the emotional response.

Studies have shown that as people move into old age they show a decline in their ability to show emotional response. For example, the ability to experience irritation and anger has been shown to decline with increasing age. Yet older people are also under a great deal of social pressure against showing emotions such as anger, and at least part of the observed decline with age in emotionality may be due to changing social demands rather than changing capacity to feel emotion.

Research Illustration 2
Aging and the Decline of Emotional Response*
Lois R. Dean

Dean dealt with four specific emotions: anger, irritation, boredom, and loneliness. Her research was designed to answer two questions:

* Based on Lois R. Dean, "Aging and the Decline of Affect," *Journal of Gerontology,* 17:440–446, 1962.

(1) As people move from middle to old age do they report a higher or a lower incidence of these four emotions? and (2) As people grow older, do they attribute any different meanings to these four emotions?

The subjects were 200 men and women who were periodically interviewed over a six-year period as a part of the Kansas City Study of Adult Life. Table 4 shows a summary of the results.

Table 4. Age and Reported Incidence of Affective States

		50–59	60–69	Age 70–79	80–	Total
How often do you find yourself feeling						
Irritated	*Never, hardly ever*	*34%*	*42%*	*54%*	*66%*	*57%*
	Sometimes or oftener	*66%*	*58%*	*46%*	*34%*	*43%*
	N	*(64)*	*(48)*	*(67)*	*(29)*	*(208)*
Angry	*Never, hardly ever*	*46%*	*78%*	*78%*	*69%*	*66%*
	Sometimes or oftener	*54%*	*22%*	*22%*	*31%*	*34%*
	N	*(63)*	*(49)*	*(66)*	*(29)*	*(207)*
Bored	*Never, hardly ever*	*61%*	*64%*	*63%*	*63%*	*65%*
	Sometimes or oftener	*39%*	*36%*	*37%*	*37%*	*35%*
	N	*(61)*	*(50)*	*(66)*	*(29)*	*(206)*
Lonely	*Never, hardly ever*	*74%*	*65%*	*71%*	*47%*	*68%*
	Sometimes or oftener	*26%*	*35%*	*29%*	*53%*	*32%*
	N	*(60)*	*(52)*	*(66)*	*(30)*	*(208)*

Source: Lois R. Dean, "Aging and the Decline of Affect," *Journal of Gerontology*, 17:441, (October, 1962). Reprinted by permission.

The results for intensity of emotions were as follows:
—There was a steady decline in felt irritation with each decade from the fifties through the eighties.
—There was also a decline in felt anger, but in this case the decline was very abrupt and occurred in the sixties.
—There was a slight decline in felt boredom as age increased (a result opposite that predicted by Dean).
—There was an increase in felt loneliness over the age range from the fifties to the eighties.

Irritation appeared to be the only emotion that the subjects were willing to admit to in large numbers, and the meaning of irritation tended to remain consistent as age increased.

Anger dropped very abruptly in the sixties, and Dean found this to be closely related to the absence of a work situation. The only case where those not working showed more anger than those who were was for respondents in their seventies. Dean hypothesized that this resulted from the fact that inactivity leads indirectly to frustration and, in turn, to anger. This would mean a change in the meaning of anger, for in the middle-aged anger resulted from resistance to domination by others or blocked instrumentality, while in old age anger would result from the frustrations and inactivity.

Boredom defied Dean's predictions. It had been expected that boredom would be a passive emotion which would increase as the more active emotions of anger and irritation declined. But Dean found that boredom declined right along with anger and irritation. On closer examination it turned out that most people in all age groups defined boredom not as lethargy or ennui, but rather as an irritation at having to accommodate others by putting up with them. The following comment is a typical answer to the question: "What is the most boring thing that happens to you, would you say?"

"To be with people who talk about themselves and the wonderful things they've done. Maybe I'd rather talk about myself!"

Invasion of privacy by others and interference by others with self-expression or self-assertion are the main sources of the irritation most people call boredom. Since boredom turned out in fact to be an active emotion, it is not surprising that it should show a decline with age.

Loneliness conformed to Dean's expectations in that it increased with age, but it also changed meaning with increasing age. To the middle-aged loneliness meant an absence of *interaction,* while among the old loneliness meant an absence of *activity.*

Interestingly, Dean's findings lead to the hypothesis that anger, irritation, boredom, and loneliness among the old would all be reduced by an environment which emphasized activity and *deemphasized* interaction with others.

Attitudes

A single attitude represents an organization of positive or negative cognitions directed toward some object. An individual's attitude toward something may also represent his predisposition to be motivated in relation to it. "The fact that meaningful definitions of 'attitude' may be made from both a cognitive and a motivational point of view is a simple reflection of the location of attitudes at a crucial intersection between cognitive processes (such as thought and memory) and motivational processes (involving emotion and striving)."[6]

It turns out that almost the only attitudes of older people that have been studied in any depth are attitudes toward death.[7] None of the studies that have been done has involved enough subjects to allow adequate control of age, but some general statements may still be made.

The tendency seems to be to either look forward to death or to evade the issue. Avoidance of the thought of death is a common reaction among older people, but younger people tend to accept or neutralize it. Some investigators even contend that dread of death in older people is a neurotic symptom. Older people in poor health and those living in institutions tend to have a positive attitude toward death, and those who have deep religious convictions are the least likely to fear it.

It has often been said that the topic of death is as taboo today as was the topic of sex during the nineteenth century. However, it has been found that most patients are willing and sometimes even relieved to discuss their feelings about death. In fact, fear of discussing death and feelings about it may reflect the orientation of the professional person rather than that of the patient.

Since a person's attitudes dispose him to act in certain ways, it is important that we learn much more about age changes in attitudes. Even the limited knowledge we have of attitudes toward death suggests the practical importance of such knowledge for the care and treatment of the aged. Studies have shown that attitudes vary with age; it now remains for research to document these variations.

Personality

Personality is a complex and interdependent system of mental faculties* and behavior patterns characteristic of a person, and recognized as such by himself and others. The term "individual" implies discreteness. This discreteness results from the fact that personality is so complex and is shaped by so many different forces that it is unique for each human being.

Yet, because people share a similar biological and social heritage, a

---

[6] Theodore M. Newcomb, *et al., op. cit.,* p. 40.

[7] Robert Havighurst and Bernice Neugarten, eds., "Attitudes Toward Death in Older Persons: A Symposium," *Journal of Gerontology,* 16:44–66, 1961.

* Mental faculties include such things as drives, motives, emotions, expectancies, attitudes, knowledge, psychomotor performance, perception, intelligence, sensation, memory, learning, creativity, and the like.

great many aspects of personality are shared by large groups of people; thus one can make some generalizations about age-related changes in personality.

Personality arises out of the need to relate what goes on inside our minds to what goes on outside. Birren distinguishes between the two as follows:

> There are two broad categories of responses that the individual makes, an inner, or covert, response and an outer, or overt, response. Inner responses consist of the ways in which we see ourselves, other people, and events; our thoughts and associations about them; and the meanings we read into them. We also respond in terms of moods. Our perceptions and motivations may lead to actions controlled in a way typical of us. Our overt actions involve other people; e.g., whether we characteristically move toward or away from others. Among other traits, whether we are friendly and interested in other persons or are suspicious and withdrawing, whether we are disposed to action or passivity, characterize our styles of responding and acting and are elements of our personality.[8]

Many approaches have been used to study the human personality, and for this reason it is difficult to present a unified picture of our knowledge in this area.

One of the most useful approaches to personality from the point of view of aging has been the developmental approach used by Bernice Neugarten and her colleagues.[9] This view sees personality not as a rigid or fixed entity but rather as an ongoing system that is continuously changing in response to events both internal and external to the individual. In this view, changes in personality related to chronological age would be expected.

Neugarten and her associates undertook a comprehensive series of studies of adult personality, with particular emphasis on the effects of age. She reports that in those cases where the investigator was concerned with *intrapsychic processes,* or more exclusively internal processes, significant and consistent age differences emerged.[10] For example, "forty-year-olds see the environment as one that rewards boldness and risk-taking and too see themselves possessing energy congruent with the opportunities presented in the outer world. Sixty-year-olds seem to see the environment as complex and dangerous, no longer to be reformed in line with one's own wishes, and to see the self[11] as conforming and accommodating to

---

[8] James E. Birren, *The Psychology of Aging* (Englewood Cliffs, N. J.: Prentice-Hall, 1964), p. 223–224.

[9] Bernice L. Neugarten and Associates, *Personality in Middle and Late Life* (New York: Atheron Press, 1964).

[10] This discussion of Neugarten's findings is based on pp. 188–200 of *Personality in Middle and Late Life.*

[11] A definition of self will be given later in this chapter

outer-world demands."[12] This change is generally described as a change from an active to a passive orientation in terms of mastery of the environment.

As age increases, preoccupation with the inner life becomes greater, ability to relate emotionally to people or objects declines, readiness to perceive people as active and as experiencing emotions is reduced, and there is movement away from outer-world to inner-world orientations.

The ability to integrate a wide range of stimuli becomes constricted, and along with it comes an unwillingness to deal with complicated and challenging situations. Older people "tend less often to perceive affect [the subjective experiencing of emotions] as an important part of life; and tend toward inactivity or passivity rather than toward more active, assertive forms of behavior."[13]

Neugarten interprets her data as supporting the notion that as age increases, "there is less energy available . . . for responding to, or maintaining former levels of involvement in, the outside world. The implication is that the older person tends to respond to inner rather than outer stimuli, to withdraw emotional investments, to give up self-assertiveness, and to avoid rather than embrace challenge."[14]

Sex differences were found with regard to the influence of age on the intrapsychic processes. Older men are more willing to accept their impulses to like and be with other people, to help others, and to gratify their senses than are younger men. Older women are more willing to accept their aggressive and egocentric impulses than are younger women. "Men appear to cope with the environment in increasingly abstract and cognitive terms; women, in increasingly affective and expressive terms. In both sexes, however, older people seem to move toward more eccentric, self-preoccupied positions and to attend increasingly to the control and the satisfaction of personal needs."[15]

On the other hand, adaptational patterns showed no significant changes as age increased. The adaptive, goal-directed, and purposive qualities of personality, areas where control of the self and of the life situation are conspicuous elements, seem to be relatively unaffected by age. Neugarten draws the implication from various studies, in addition to their own, that factors such as work status, health, financial resources, and marital status are more important than chronological age in influencing the *social* adaptation of people over fifty.[16]

Neugarten found that with age there was an increase in the saliency to

---

[12] Neugarten, *op. cit.,* p. 189.

[13] *Ibid.,* p. 99.

[14] *Ibid.*

[15] *Ibid.,* p. 190.

[16] *Ibid.,* p. 193.

the individual of his inner life and a decrease in the efficiency of certain cognitive processes. In fact, many older people who were given psychological tests showed what would be defined in younger persons as "pathological" patterns of thought and affect, a finding frequently encountered by other investigators not only in tests but through other techniques as well. At the same time, Neugarten found no relationship between social adaptation and age. The same people who showed "pathological" affect and thought patterns showed no changes in the competence of their social role[17] performance or in interpersonal skills. This seeming contradiction led Neugarten to ask: "How is it that individuals, as they age, continue to function effectively in their social environments despite not only increased interiority but also decreased efficiency in certain cognitive processes? How do those men and women who give evidence of ineffective thought processes continue to appear integrated?"[18]

Neugarten concludes that the answer lies in the stability of patterns for coping with the external environment. This stability develops over a period of time.

In a sense, the self becomes institutionalized with the passage of time. Not only do certain personality processes become stabilized and provide continuity, but the individual builds around him a network of social relationships which he comes to depend on for emotional support and responsiveness and which maintain him in many subtle ways. It is from this point of view that the typical aging person may be said to become, with the passage of years, a socio-emotional institution with an individuated structure of supports and interactional channels and with patterns which transcend many of the intrapsychic changes and losses that appear.

Along with increased interiority there seems to go a certain reduction of the complexity of the personality. With the shrinkage in psychological life space and with decreased ego energy, an increasing dedication to a central core of values and to a set of habit patterns and a sloughing off of earlier cathexes [likes or dislikes] which lose saliency for the individual seem to occur.

The direction of personality change, then, from middle to old age, seems to be one of increased inner orientation; increased separation from the environment; a certain centripetal movement which leads to increased consistency and decreased complexity and in which the synthesizing and executive qualities, in maintaining their centrality, maintain also the continuity of the personality.[19]

Other investigators have also encountered a long-range continuity and consistency in personality. For example, Smith and Hall found that the

---

[17] *Social roles* will be defined later in this chapter.

[18] Neugarten, *op. cit.*, p. 197.

[19] *Ibid.*, pp. 198–199. Reprinted by permission of Atherton Press, Inc. Copyright © 1964 Atherton Press, Inc. New York. All Rights Reserved.

unconscious remains relatively stable throughout life.[20] Dennis found that verbal communications, a measure of thought structure, remained remarkably consistent over a period of six decades.[21] Thaler observed that the cognitive rigidity so often found among older people results at least in part from an extremely consistent way of looking at things.[22]

Neugarten's findings would seem to indicate that there are three sets of variables in the aging personality which merit study: the intrapsychic structure, the cognitive structure, and the interpersonal structure. We have already documented the changes with age in cognitive functioning in Chapter 4. Just as older people compensate for losses in hearing and so forth, they also compensate for losses in cognitive functions. For example, many older people compensate for a declining memory by keeping notes. The overall decline with age in cognitive functioning must be considered as a limiting factor in terms of changing either the intrapsychic or interpersonal structures, but it will not be considered in detail here. Discussion will center on the intrapsychic structure (the self) and on the interpersonal structure (social roles and social interaction).

The Self

Human beings are unique in their ability to think about themselves. Man's ability to utilize language and to form abstract ideas allows him to think about his own body, his own behavior, his own mind, and his own appearance to other people. The *interpretation* of perceived feedback from within ourselves and from others defines the self. Carl Rogers has theorized that as a result of interactions with the environment, the individual gradually differentiates a *part* of his total body of ideas as pertaining to his *self*. The self is characterized as being organized but flexible. The person strives to integrate all of his experiences, perceptions, and ideas into the structural system of his self.[23] Thus, the self is an intrapsychic system which depends in part on feedback from others, but which also feeds back upon *itself*.

The self is comprised of both cognitive and emotional elements. The cognitive element is called the *self-concept*. It is basically the individual's

[20] Madorah E. Smith and Calvin Hall, "An Investigation of Regression in a Long Dream Series," *Journal of Gerontology,* 19:66–71, 1964.

[21] Wayne Dennis, "Long Term Constancy of Behavior," *Journal of Gerontology,* 15:195–196, 1960.

[22] Margaret Thaler, "Relationships among Wechsler, Weigl, Rorschach, EEG Findings, and Abstract-Concrete Behavior in a Group of Normal Aged Subjects," *Journal of Gerontology,* 11:404–409, 1956.

[23] Klaus F. Riegel, "Personality Theory and Aging" in *Handbook of Aging and the Individual,* ed. James E. Birren (Chicago: University of Chicago Press, 1959).

description *to himself* of who he is and what he is like. The emotional element of the self is called *self-esteem*. It is basically how the individual feels about his self-concept in comparison with some ideal—whether he likes or dislikes it, is proud or ashamed of it, and so on. Both self-concept and self-esteem represent a synthesis of data about the self which derive from both inside and outside the individual.

Social Roles

A key social factor related to the development of the self is the complement of social roles the person plays. What is expected of us depends in large part on the positions we occupy (mother, friend, baseball player, astronomer, waitress, judge, and so on) and the behavior *expected* of someone in those positions. The expectations associated with a position form what is called a *social role*.

Each position has attached to it personal qualities and behavior which others *expect* of a person filling that position, and which any person filling that position can lay claim to. Together with the position's title (if any), these expectations provide the person filling the position with a *self-concept* and with a basis for imagining the concept others will have of him.

> It is important to note that in performing a role the individual must see to it that the impressions that are conveyed in the situation are compatible with role-appropriate personal qualities effectively imputed to him: a judge is supposed to be deliberate and sober; a pilot, in a cockpit, to be cool; a bookkeeper to be accurate and neat in doing his work. These personal qualities . . . provide a basis of [self] for the incumbent and a basis for the image . . . others will have of him. A self, then, virtually awaits the individual entering a position; he need only conform to the pressures on him . . .[24]

Age Changes in Self-Concept

Neugarten's findings cited earlier suggest that as people move into later life, the self-concept becomes dependent less on external factors than on an inner orientation which stresses consistency in self-concept. My own research supports this idea in that a sizeable proportion of retired women in one sample appeared to have self-concepts which depended very little on

---

[24] Erving Goffman, *Encounters* (New York: Bobbs-Merrill Co., 1961), p. 87.

feedback from other people.[25] But rather than leading to a change in self-concept, this trend could be expected to introduce stability.

Role changes play a part in developing the self, and many role changes accompany later life. Widowhood, disability, retirement, dependency, and sickness all involve changes in position and role that are associated with age. Yet these changes bring about less change in self-concept than we would expect. The reason for this is that the older person tends to retain roles he formerly played as part of his self-concept. For example, the retired railroader still sees himself as a railroader, and the older widow still sees herself as the wife of so-and-so. Thus, our concepts of who we are, being based primarily on the social roles we play, often remain reasonably stable in later life because roles we no longer play can still be drawn on as sources for identity.

This may not always be good, however, since roles such as mental patient or sick person may also become a durable part of the self-concept.

Social interaction is the major external source of information about individual characteristics and qualities. We find out whether we are smart or stupid, kind or cruel, from observing the ways others behave toward us. The impact of aging on this process depends largely on the style the person develops in making use of such information. Some people develop a concept of their personal characteristics and qualities early in adulthood. They say to themselves, "So that's the way I am and will always be, and that's that." Once he reaches closure, this type of person is not likely to be greatly influenced by interaction at any stage of adulthood. And the inner orientation brought on by aging would seem to reduce this likelihood still further.

Other people never quite reach closure concerning their personal qualities. These people constantly seek more information about themselves, and they are likely to seek interaction actively throughout their lives. They may even seek interaction and at the same time want very much to turn their attention inward. What prevents them from doing so is insecurity. In fact, a good definition of insecurity might be the inability to come to closure concerning one's self-concept.

In summary, the inward orientation of older people and the relative stability of the set of roles they use as the basis for their self-concepts promote stability of self-concept in later life.

The older people of whom this is not true are primarily those who have never reached any appreciable degree of closure concerning their concept of themselves. For these people the self-concept is still relatively responsive to social interaction.

---

[25] Robert C. Atchley, "Respondents vs. Refusers in an Interview Study of Retired Women," *Journal of Gerontology*, 24:42–47, 1969.

Age Changes in Self-Esteem

When a person compares what he is like and who he is (self-concept) with what he seriously wishes he were like and who he seriously wishes he could be (self-ideal) the feelings he gets as a result constitute his *self-esteem*.

Inner feelings, social roles, and social interaction function in developing self-esteem much as they do in developing the self-concept. Yet there are some important differences.

For one thing, self-esteem is much more volatile than self-concept. Since it is emotional in content, it can be more responsive to moods and bodily states, while our knowledge of ourselves (self-concept) tends to be more consistent and stable.

As the individual grows older, his inner orientations tend to shift from seeing himself as the captain of his fate to seeing himself as primarily responsive to other people's demands. How he reacts to this depends on his vision of the ideal. If he sees the rugged individualist as the ideal, then the result for his self-esteem will probably be negative. If, on the other hand, he sees the ideal as accepting one's allotted part in life and playing it to the hilt, then the results could be positive.

Role performance is important to self-esteem because the prescriptions and proscriptions that make up the social role serve as one of our major sources of self-ideal. People who perceive themselves as having done well in the past are also more likely to perceive themselves as doing well in old age than are people who come to old age feeling that they have not done well in the past.[26] Thus, the key to positive self-esteem in old age may in some cases reside in the past.

The various role changes encountered by older people tend to introduce a certain amount of fluidity in self-esteem. It is primarily the current roles one plays that generate the external information used to establish self-esteem. As older people pick up new roles, such as great-grandparent, widow, sick person, they must rely on others, at least at first, to establish entitlement to self-esteem. For example, Anderson's research showed that high self-esteem among newly admitted nursing home patients was directly related to a high frequency of social interaction.[27] But Davis found that the influence of interaction on self-concept depended on the nature of the interaction. Those who were reacted to favorably by their peers had favor-

---

[26] Suzanne Riechard, F. Livson and P. Peterson, *Aging and Personality*. New York: John Wiley and Sons, 1962.

[27] Nancy N. Anderson, "Effects of Institutionalization on Self Esteem," *Journal of Gerontology*, 22:313–317, 1967.

able self-concepts, while those who were not reacted to favorably had less favorable self-concepts.[28]

Yet research results show less instability in self-esteem than could be expected. Secord and Backman have presented a theory of the self which helps explain this seeming paradox.[29] According to this theory, the individual may be pressured by circumstances to change, but he will *actively* attempt to maintain stability of self and behavior. He will not sit idly by and permit negative reactions from others to destroy this concept of himself. In this theory, self-stability relies on congruency among three components: 1) a given aspect of the individual's self, 2) the individual's perception of his behavior relative to that aspect, and 3) his beliefs about how other people behave toward him and feel toward him with regard to that aspect. Faced with a changing situation, the individual "actively uses techniques or mechanisms for maintaining his interpersonal environment so as to maximize congruency."[30] Such mechanisms include refusal to perceive negative feedback, avoidance of people apt to give negative feedback, devaluation of people apt to give negative feedback, downgrading that particular aspect of the self, and several others.[31] In one study, for example, a majority of people over seventy were found to identify with "middle-aged" rather than "old."[32] In another, perceptions of shortcomings in the self were consistently less prevalent among older people than among younger people.[33] These findings are both examples of selective perception of negative feedback.

This theory is important for social gerontology because, if true, it would help explain how some older people can undergo significant reductions in their field of potential roles, and dramatic changes in their life situations—often changes most of us would label "bad"—and still come out of it all with a positive opinion of themselves. It would help also to explain some of the long-term consistency of personality mentioned earlier.

---

[28] Robert Davis, "The Relationship of Social Preferability to Self-Concept in an Aged Population," *Journal of Gerontology,* 18:431–436, 1963.

[29] Paul F. Secord and Carl Backman, *Social Psychology* (New York: McGraw-Hill Book Co., 1964), pp. 583–592.

[30] *Ibid.,* p. 584.

[31] *Ibid.,* pp. 587–591.

[32] Raymond G. Kuhlen, "Changes in Self Concept" in *Relations of Development and Aging,* ed. James E. Birren (Springfield, Ill.: Charles C Thomas, 1964), pp. 226–230.

[33] Matilda W. Riley and Ann Foner, *Aging and Society,* Vol. I, *An Inventory of Research Findings.* (New York: Russel Sage Foundation, 1968), p. 291.

Summary

Drives are unlearned, internal tensions that predispose the organism to act. Hunger, sex, and activity drives are examples. Drives appear to diminish as age increases. But because many factors intervene between drives and overt behavior, drives play a relatively small part in explaining age-related changes in behavior.

Motives are learned predispositions that translate drives into specific goals, such as looking for food. Motivation is highest for specific goals with explicit rewards which are periodically achieved. Goals which are not achievable are not apt to be high motivators. Thus, motivation in later life can be expected to be a product of reduced drives and changes in opportunities for goal attainment. There is some evidence that the structure of motives does change in response to changes in social situation.

Expectancies are learned mental sets that simplify life by creating near-automatic reactions to familiar situations. Equally important, however, is the ability to override expectancies when they do not apply, and this ability appears to diminish as age increases.

Emotions are strong mental responses to stimuli, either internal or external, although for most people emotions are triggered by external events. Studies show that observed emotional response diminishes as age increases, and this is apparently true for all types of emotions.

Attitudes are positive or negative orientations toward particular objects, persons, or ideas. They represent a readiness to be motivated in a particular direction, and are products of both thought and emotion. Attitudes become slightly more pessimistic as age increases, and attitudes toward death become slightly more favorable.

Personality is the complex mental system through which a person is identified as an individual and through which he responds to the world around him. While there are elements of personality that are unique to the individual, there are also elements of personality that are common to large numbers of people. Social gerontology is concerned with the impact of aging on the common elements of personality.

Using the developmental approach, Neugarten found that the inner life of the individual became more important to him as he aged, that cognitive processes declined with age, and that competence in role performance and interpersonal skills showed little or no change with age. With advancing age there was an increasing separation from the environment, and an increasing continuity, consistency, and simplicity of the personality.

The self is the intrapsychic aspect of personality which comprises the individual's thought and emotions about himself. The self has two elements, the *self-concept,* which relates to knowledge about oneself, and *self-esteem,* which relates to feelings about oneself. *Social roles* are the expectations associated with a position in society, such as judge or mother. These expectations often become a part of the self-concept of the role player.

The self-concept tends to remain stable in later life. This is due to the inward orientation the personality typically takes, and the fact that former roles can still be used as part of the self-concept. The major exceptions to this trend are highly insecure older people who have never come to a significant degree of closure concerning their self-concept.

Self-esteem is more volatile among older people than among younger ones, but it is much more stable than might be expected. Although role changes in later life force older people to rely on social interaction to establish self-esteem, any negative impact this might have is probably largely offset by the defense mechanisms, such as selective perception, that older people use to protect their vulnerable self-esteem. Since self-esteem is the product of a comparison between self-concept and self-ideal, the older person can manipulate it by controlling the extent to which social interaction is allowed to influence self-concept.

Thus, while there are significant changes in self and personality in later life, they tend to be of consequence mainly for the person's inner orientations and have little influence on his social functioning.

Based on the conclusions of the various chapters in Part Two, it seems apparent that while older people do undergo certain significant physical and psychological changes with age, most older people find these changes more an inconvenience than a true handicap. Keep in mind that these observations represent the "typical" case, and that chronologically old people vary widely in terms of the symptoms of psychological aging. In terms of adequate social functioning, most people do not find themselves physically or psychologically disabled until the late seventies. Social disability is an entirely different matter, however, and it is the subject of the remainder of this book.

Bibliography

Aaronson, Bernard S., "Personality Stereotypes of Aging," *Journal of Gerontology,* 21:458–462, 1966.

Anderson, Barbara G., "Bereavement as a Subject of Cross-Cultural Inquiry: An American Sample," *Anthropological Quarterly,* 38:181–200, 1965.

Anderson, Nancy N., "Institutionalization, Interaction, and Self-Conception in Aging," in *Older People and Their Social World,* eds. Arnold M. Rose and Warren A. Peterson. Philadelphia: F. A. Davis, 1965, pp. 245–257.

———, "Effects of Institutionalization on Self-Esteem," *Journal of Gerontology,* 22:313–317, 1967.

Back, Kurt W., "Transition to Aging and the Self-Image," *Aging and Human Development,* 2:296–304, 1971.

Becker, Howard S. and Anselm Strauss, "Careers, Personality, and Adult Socialization," in *Middle Age and Aging,* ed. Bernice L. Neugarten. Chicago: University of Chicago Press, 1968, pp. 311–320.

Berezin, Martin A., "Sex and Old Age: A Review of the Literature," *Journal of Geriatric Psychiatry,* 2:131–149, 1969.

Bloom, Kenneth L., "Age and Self-Concept," *American Journal of Psychiatry,* 118:534–538, 1961.

Bortner, R. W., "Personality and Social Psychology in the Study of Aging," *Gerontologist,* 7:(2, part II), 23–36, 1967.

Botwinick, Jack, "Drives, Expectancies, and Emotions," in *Handbook of Aging and the Individual,* ed. James E. Birren. Chicago: University of Chicago Press, 1959, pp. 739–768.

Brim, Orville G. and Stanton Wheeler, *Socialization After Childhood.* New York: John Wiley, 1966.

Butler, Robert N., "The Life Review: An Interpretation of Reminiscence in the Aged," *Psychiatry,* 26:65–76, 1963.

Carp, Frances M., "Attitudes of Old Persons Toward Themselves and Toward Others," *Journal of Gerontology,* 22:308–312, 1967.

———, "The Psychology of Aging," in *Foundations of Practical Gerontology,* eds. Rosamonde R. Boyd and C. G. Oakes. Columbia, South Carolina: University of South Carolina Press, 1969, pp. 100–116.

Christenson, Cornelia V. and John H. Gagnon, "Sexual Behavior in a Group of Older Women," *Journal of Gerontology,* 20:351–356, 1965.

Clark, Margaret, "The Anthropology of Aging, A New Area for Studies of Culture and Personality," *Gerontologist,* 7:(1)55–64, 1967.

Coe, Rodney M., "Self-Conception and Institutionalization," in *Older People and Their Social World,* eds. Arnold M. Rose and Warren A. Peterson. Philadelphia: F. A. Davis, 1965, pp. 225–243.

Davis, Robert W., "Social Influences on the Aspiration Tendency of Older People," *Journal of Gerontology,* 22:510–516, 1967.

Dean, Lois R., "Aging and the Decline of Affect," *Journal of Gerontology,* 17:440–446, 1962.

Filer, Richard N. and Desmond D. O'Connell, "Motivation of Aging Persons in an Institutional Setting," *Journal of Gerontology,* 19:15–22, 1964.

Friedman, Alfred S. and Samuel Granick, "A Note on Anger and Aggression in Old Age," *Journal of Gerontology,* 18:283–285, 1963.

Fulton, Robert, ed., *Death and Identity.* New York: John Wiley, 1965.

Gergen, Kenneth J. and Kurt W. Back, "Cognitive Constriction in Aging and Attitudes Toward International Issues," in *Social Aspects of Aging,* eds., Ida H. Simpson and John C. McKinney. Durham, North Carolina: Duke University Press, 1966, pp. 322–334.

Gutman, David L., *The Country of Old Men: Cultural Studies in the Psychology of Later Life.* Ann Arbor, Michigan: University of Michigan, Wayne State University Institute of Gerontology, 1969.

Handal, P. J., "The Relationship Between Subjective Life Expectancy, Death Anxiety, and General Anxiety," *Journal of Clinical Psychology,* 25:39–42, 1969.

Hansen, G. D., S. Yoshioka, M. J. Taves, and F. Caro, "Older People in the Midwest, Conditions and Attitudes," in *Older People and Their Social World,* eds. Arnold M. Rose and Warren A. Peterson. Philadelphia: F. A. Davis, 1965, pp. 311–322.

Heyman, Dorothy K. and Frances C. Jeffers, "Study of the Relative Influence of Race and Socio-Economic Status upon the Activities and Attitudes of a Southern Aged Population," *Journal of Gerontology,* 19:225–229, 1964.

Jeffers, Frances C., Claude R. Nichols, and Carl Eisdorfer, "Attitudes of Older Persons Toward Death," *Journal of Gerontology,* 16:53–56, 1961.

Kaplan, Howard B., "Age-Related Correlates of Self-Derogation: Contemporary Life Space Characteristics," *Aging and Human Development,* 2:305–313, 1971.

Kastenbaum, Robert and Nancy Durkee, "Elderly People View Old Age," in *New Thoughts on Old Age,* ed. Robert Kastenbaum. New York: Springer, 1964, pp. 250–262.

———, "Is Old Age the End of Development?", in *New Thoughts on Old Age,* ed. Robert Kastenbaum. New York: Springer, 1964, pp. 61–71.

Kelly, E. Lowell, "Consistency of the Adult Personality," *American Psychologist,* 10:659–681, 1955.

Kogan, Nathan and Michael A. Wallach, "Age Changes in Values and Attitudes," *Journal of Gerontology,* 16:272–280, 1961.

Kuhlen, Raymond G., "Motivational Changes During the Adult Years," in *Psychological Backgrounds of Adult Education,* ed. Raymond G. Kuhlen (Chicago: Center for the Study of Liberal Education for Adults, 1963), pp. 77–113.

———, "Developmental Changes in Motivation During the Adult Years," in *Relations of Development and Aging,* ed. James E. Birren. Springfield, Illinois: Charles C Thomas, 1964, pp. 209–246.

———, "Personality Change with Age," in *Personality Change,* eds. Philip Worchel and D. Byrne. New York: John Wiley, 1964, pp. 524–555.

Kutscher, Austin H., ed., *Death and Bereavement.* Springfield, Illinois: Charles C Thomas, 1969.

Lakin, Martin, and Carl Eisdorfer, "A Study of Affective Expression among the Aged," in *Social and Psychological Aspects of Aging,* eds. Clark Tibbitts and Wilma Donahue. New York: Columbia University Press, 1962, pp. 650–654.

Lehr, Ursula, "Attitudes Towards the Future in Old Age," *Human Development,* 10:230–238, 1967.

Levin, Sidney, "Depression in the Aged: The Importance of External Factors," in *New Thoughts on Old Age,* ed. Robert Kastenbaum. New York: Springer, 1964, pp. 179–185.

Lewis, Charles N., "Reminiscing and Self-Concept in Old Age," *Journal of Gerontology,* 26:240–243, 1971.

Ludwig, Edward G. and Robert L. Eichhorn, "Age and Disillusionment: A Study of Value Changes Associated with Aging," *Journal of Gerontology,* 22:59–65, 1967.

Mason, Evelyn, "Some Correlates of Self-Judgments of the Aged," *Journal of Gerontology,* 9:324–337, 1954.

Masters, William H. and Virginia E. Johnson, *Human Sexual Response.* Boston: Little, Brown and Co., 1966.

Neugarten, Bernice L., "Personality Changes During the Adult Years," in *Psychological Backgrounds of Adult Education,* ed. Raymond G. Kuhlen. Chicago: Center for the Study of Liberal Education for Adults, 1963, pp. 43–76.

——— and Associates, eds., *Personality in Middle and Late Life.* New York: Atherton Press, 1964.

Peters, George R., "Self-Conceptions of the Aged, Age Identification, and Aging," *Gerontologist,* 11:(4, part II), 69–73, 1971.

Preston, Caroline E. and Karen S. Gudiksen, "A Measure of Self-Perception among Older People," *Journal of Gerontology,* 21:63–71, 1966.

Reichard, Suzanne K., Florine Livson, and Paul G. Peterson, *Aging and Personality.* New York: John Wiley, 1962.

Riegel, Klaus F., "Personality Theory and Aging," in *Handbook of Aging and the Individual,* ed. James E. Birren. Chicago: University of Chicago Press, 1959, pp. 797–851.

Robin, Ellen Page, "Discontinuities in Attitudes and Behaviors of Older Age Groups," *Gerontologist,* 11:(4, part II), 79–84, 1971.

Schwartz, Arthur N. and Robert W. Kleemeier, "The Effects of Illness and Age upon Some Aspects of Personality," *Journal of Gerontology,* 20:85–91, 1965.

Shanas, Ethel, "A Note on Restriction of Life Space; Attitudes of Age Cohorts," *Journal of Health and Social Behavior,* 9:86–90, 1968.

Shenkin, A., "Attitudes of Old People to Death," in *Current Achievements in Geriatrics,* eds. William F. Anderson and B. Isaacs. London: Cassell, 1964, pp. 171–177.

Shukin, Alexey and Bernice L. Neugarten, "Personality and Social Interaction," in *Personality in Middle and Late Life,* eds. Bernice L. Neugarten, *et al.* New York: Atherton Press, 1964, pp. 149–157.

Slater, Philip E. and Harry A. Scarr, "Personality in Old Age," *Genetic Psychology Monographs,* 70:229–269, 1964.

Swenson, Wendell M., "Attitudes Toward Death in an Aged Population," *Journal of Gerontology,* 16:49–52, 1961.

Thune, Jeanne M., "Racial Attitudes of Older Adults," *Gerontologist,* 7:(3) 179–182, 1967.

Tuckman, Jacob and Irving Lorge, "Classification of the Self as Young, Middle-Aged, or Old," *Geriatrics,* 9:534–536, 1954.

——— and ———, and F. D. Zeman "The Self-Image in Aging," *Journal of Genetic Psychology,* 90:317–321, 1961.

Walker, J. V., "Attitudes to Death," *Gerontologia Clinica,* 10:304–308, 1968.

Welford, Alan T., "Aging and Personality: Age Changes in Basic Psychological Capacities," in *Age with a Future,* ed. P. From Hansen. Copenhagen: Munksgaard, 1964, pp. 60–66.

White, Robert W., "Motivation Reconsidered: The Concept of Competence," *Psychological Review,* 66:297–333, 1959.

Wylie, R. W., "Attitudes Toward Aging and the Aged among Black Americans: Some Historical Perspectives," *Aging and Human Development,* 2:66–70, 1971.

Zola, Irving K., "Feeling about Age among Older People," *Journal of Gerontology,* 17:65–68, 1962.

Part Three

Age Changes in Situational Context

While the psychological and biological changes that accompany old age are important, they are translated into an immediate reality in the various ongoing situations the individual finds himself in. The social situation is the total configuration of social factors influencing an individual's behavior or experience at a given point in time.

His situation determines how he fits into society. The social situation *is* society from the individual's point of view, and the picture is greatly complicated by the fact that most people move in and among several different social situations.

Our concern is with situational changes that come with growing old. Since changes in social roles play a key part in this process, Chapter 6 presents an overview of role changes which normally occur in later life. Subsequent chapters deal with situational changes in health, financial status, occupational roles, recreation and leisure, and personal independence. The final chapter in Part Three deals with personal adjustment to these changes.

6

Role Changes in Later Life

Social roles are very important in everyone's life, for the individual defines himself in terms of these roles, and his place in society is determined by them. Between them, social roles and personality set the limits for most individual behavior. They are the means through which society is recreated in the individual and through which the individual functions in society. Accordingly, it is as important to understand the role changes related to growing old as it is to understand personality changes.

As we move into the discussion of social roles, our focus shifts from the individual to the *social situation* the individual finds himself in. Social roles are a key element of that situation.

Positions

Positions are categories of individuals which are collectively recognized in the society. They are based on common attributes, as in the case of Negroes or youngsters, or on similarities in behavior, as in the case of judges. *Older person* is a position based on a common attribute, age. By contrast, the position *computer operator* is based on behavior computer operators have in common.

Social Roles

A *social role* can mean any one of three things: 1) what is *expected* of a person in a given position, 2) what *most* people *do* in a given position, or 3) what a *particular* person does in a given position. For any given position these three aspects of the social role may coincide or differ depending on hundreds of factors. The first meaning is by far the most frequently used, but the gap between the ideal (first meaning) and behavior (second and third meanings) is usually great enough to be significant. The reason most discussion of roles centers around expectations is that they are more general and therefore easier to discuss.

Roles are not free-floating. They are attached to positions. What is expected of us depends in large part on the *positions* we occupy (everyone occupies many positions, often simultaneously). Thus, we often need not know much about an individual to be able to predict his behavior; we need only know his position. For example, it does not require a psychoanalyst to predict at least 80 percent of the on-the-job behavior of a baseball umpire. Not many positions must be adhered to *that* rigidly; nevertheless, the fact that we all play our roles within certain bounds gives a comfortable predictability to human behavior.

The importance of any position and its role depends upon the status[1] or prestige, the wealth, or the influence attached to the position. Most positions have some degree of at least one of these elements; and some positions have a great deal of all three. Positions such as physician, state governor, or U.S. Supreme Court Justice tend to possess all three elements to a high degree, while positions such as sharecropper, shoeshine boy, or bartender tend to possess these elements to a very slight degree, if at all.[2]

In American society, the positions of older person, older man, or older woman do not in themselves enjoy much prestige, status, wealth, or influence. This is not to say that no older people have these characteristics; it merely means that when an older person has wealth or prestige or influence it is because he simultaneously occupies *some other position* to which these benefits are attached. Former President Eisenhower enjoyed a great deal of prestige and influence in his old age, but these qualities adhered to him not because he was old, but because he was a former president and revered military chief.

To put the position of older person into proper perspective, one need only to ask: do people get wealthy, revered, or influential simply by growing old? The answer must be a resounding "no." As a matter of fact, if anything happens to a person as a result of getting old, it will probably be that the wealth, influence, or prestige of his other positions will *decrease*. Being defined as old may even cause him to be *removed* from some of his other positions.

In America today, older people generally occupy a position of lower

---

[1] *Status* is used here in a social stratification context rather than in a role theory context.

[2] For a more detailed discussion of role theory see Bruce J. Biddle and Edwin J. Thomas, *Role Theory: Concepts and Research* (New York: John Wiley, 1966).

status than the middle-aged. In many ways older persons are accorded little prestige or deference. As a category they possess less economic and political power than the middle-aged. The position of the old in America has often been compared unfavorably with that of the old in other societies. In Imperial Chinese society, for example, individuals as they aged were said to have been given more and more respect and deference. There is reason to doubt, however, that in earlier times, either in Western or non-Western societies, the aged were uniformly valued as a category. Their status has probably always had both positive and negative elements, as shown in a recent study of three traditional villages in India[3] where the position of the aged was analyzed with regard to prestige, authority, power, and security. A wide gap was found to exist between the ideal norms and actual practices. The old lost status with the death of a spouse; many older people felt neglected; only a very few old people of the upper class played leadership roles in the village; and control of family affairs and participation in community affairs was generally relinquished after middle age. This picture is not unlike descriptions of the status of the aged in contemporary Western societies.

Most people consider the twenties and thirties to be "the best years" of their lives, and both old and young people attach a negative value to the concept "old age," although the old themselves are not quite so negative as the young. The older person thus occupies a position that tends to be downgraded by everyone.

The influence of the relatively low status of older people might be felt in several ways. The individual's opinion of himself might be lowered—but many older people avoid this possibility by not seeing themselves as old. Also, the people the individual interacts with may react to him differently once he becomes old—but older people who do not consider themselves old usually do not see others perceiving them as old. Thus, selective perception tends to minimize some of the impact of the status loss associated with moving from middle age to later maturity.

But the older person cannot very easily misperceive the fact that *being old may cause him to lose his eligibility to occupy positions he values.* This is perhaps the most important impact that aging has on the set of positions a person occupies. And this, in turn, is very significant to the individual, because the positions he occupies determine the roles he plays and the roles he plays have a lot to do with what kinds of things he *does.*

Age is important in role behavior because it acts as one of the primary rules of eligibility for various positions. We do not simply occupy or take over positions. They are usually assigned to us as a result of our having

---

[3] Bernice L. Neugarten, "The Aged in American Society," in *Social Problems,* ed. Howard S. Becker (New York: John Wiley, 1966), p. 173.

met certain entry criteria. In most societies there are particular positions, rights, duties, privileges, and obligations that are assigned to children, adolescents, young adults, the middle-aged and the old; and certain behavior is regarded as appropriate for each age group. In our culture the primary entry criteria are health, age, sex, color, experience, and educational achievement. Novelists have built many plots around girls who pass themselves off as boys and boys who pass themselves off as men in order to be allowed to do something otherwise denied to them, but in everyday life, most people abide by the rules.

Thus, as we pass through the life cycle, the field of positions for which we are eligible keeps changing as our age changes. As children we can legitimately be members of the neighborhood gang, pupils, and unemployed—all things we cannot be as adults. As young adults we can be auto drivers, barflies, and voters—all things we cannot be as children. As older adults we can be retired, be great-grandmothers, or pretend to be deaf— all things we cannot do as young adults. Of course age works negatively too. For example, older people are often prevented from working, even if they want to.

In addition to making people eligible for positions, age is important as a position in itself, and certain expectations are associated with it. Thus, an "older person" is expected to behave differently from a "younger person." For example, an elderly matron who attempted the latest teen-age dance at a party of youngsters she was chaperoning would be regarded with dismay; primarily because she would have behaved contrary to the expectations of "dignity and refinement" we hold for elderly matrons. Thus, aging changes not only the roles we are expected to play, but also the *manner* in which we are expected to play them.

Retirement

Most people experience a number of role changes as they pass middle age. Perhaps the first, and for some the most important, change occurs at *retirement*. Retirement is the institutionalized separation of an individual from his occupational position. Age is usually the prime consideration in such separation, although health may also be a big factor, and the commonest retirement age is sixty-five. Usually a certain latitude is given to allow the individual to choose the point at which he retires, sometimes as early as fifty and often as late as 70. Over age 65, about 70 percent of men and about 90 percent of women do not have an occupational position.

When an individual leaves his occupation, many changes occur in his life regardless of whether he retired voluntarily or was forced to retire. In fact, many gerontologists feel that retirement is prehaps the most crucial life change requiring a major adjustment of the older person. The changes can involve not only a time void which must be filled, but a change in other roles the individual plays as well. Miller puts the matter as follows:

The urban-industrial society of today has developed a policy for old age which provides pensions, housing, and medical care when the worker, due to his advanced years, is no longer required to trade the major part of his time spent in labor for the necessities of subsistence. The implication of such a policy is that the worker, by his lengthy labor, has earned the right to rewards which will make his remaining years comfortable. However, it is tacitly understood, the worker is allowed to retire and receive the accompanying benefits in order to facilitate his removal from a role which he is arbitrarily considered no longer capable of playing. In these terms, retirement is not so much a system of rewards as it is the instrumentality by which the removal of those persons perceived as useless is accomplished. The older persons who are so removed suffer a debilitating social loss—the loss of occupational identity and a functional role in society.

Though the occupational identity and role of each person, as well as the succession of other conventional roles, are taken very much for granted and are a matter of little conscious concern, nevertheless, they are the crucial elements which facilitate the varying social role performances demanded of each person. Work not only provides the individual with a meaningful group and a social situation in which to develop a culturally approved and personally acceptable self-concept, it also provides an identity with an accompanying rationale for his performance in other social situations. The individual's occupational identity establishes his position in the social system at large, allowing others to evaluate his status and role and providing a context within which his social activity can be interpreted. For example, the occupational identity of a working male places him in relationship to other members of his family and supports his roles in that social system. Before retirement, the role of "husband," as mediated by occupational identity, supports the various roles that the person is expected to assume in the family system. It is extremely difficult to maintain the role as "head of the family" if an occupational identity is lacking. The occupational identity may provide the social substance by which other identities are maintained, various roles are coordinated, and the appropriateness of social activity is substantiated. In other words, the retired person may find himself without a functional role which would justify his social future, and without an identity which would provide a concept of self tolerable to him and acceptable to others.[4]

---

[4] Stephen J. Miller, "The Social Dilemma of the Aging Leisure Participant" in *Older People and Their Social World*, ed. Arnold Rose (Philadelphia: F. A. Davis, Co., 1965), p. 78. Reprinted by permission.

Although we shall see later that Miller's analysis applies to only a relatively small proportion of older people, those it does describe graphically illustrate the disruptive potential of retirement.

As Miller implies, retirement appears to be a bigger problem for men than for women. Although most women have had work experience, their orientation toward work is apparently not strong enough to cause any significant problems in retirement. On the other hand, numerous investigators have described the crisis that retirement represents to men, although this assertion is still open to challenge.

Research Illustration 3
The Role Count*
Elaine Cumming and William E. Henry

As a part of the Kansas City Study of Adult Life, Cumming and Henry reported age differences in the number of active roles played.

Their subjects consisted of a random sample of 104 Kansas City men and women aged fifty or over and a quasi-sample of 107 men and women aged seventy or over.

Interviews were used to establish the number of active roles for each subject. Each respondent got one score each for being a household member (if he did not live alone), kinsman (one score for each category of kinsmen interacted with regularly), friend, neighbor, worker, churchgoer, organization or club meeting attender, or a specific role player such as shopper or customer. The scores ranged from 1 to 9, and were distriubted as follows:

Number of Roles	Number of Respondents	Percent
1–2	8	3.8
3–4	60	28.4
5–6	93	44.1
7–8	46	21.8
9	4	1.9
Total	211	100.0

---

* Based on Elaine Cumming and William E. Henry, *Growing Old: the Process of Disengagement* (New York: Basic Books, 1961), pp. 38–45 and pp. 248–250.

Table 5A shows the percentages by age and sex for those who scored 6 or more on the role count. The pattern for the total is quite stable until age sixty-five, when a sharp and significant decline in role count begins, and this general pattern holds for both men and women.

Table 5B shows percentage of those interviewed who hold various types of roles, classified by age and sex.

Table 5A. Percent with a Large Number of Roles, by Age and Sex

Age	N	Total % with a Large Number of Roles	N	Males % with a Large Number of Roles	N	Females % with a Large Number of Roles
50–54	36	61.1	19	68.4	17	52.9
55–59	34	61.8	18	61.1	16	62.5
60–64	34	58.8	19	47.4	15	73.3
65–69	31	38.7	12	50.0	19	31.6
70–74	50	22.0	25	20.0	25	24.0
75 and over	26	7.7	14	7.1	12	8.3
Total	211	41.7	107	42.0	104	41.2

Table 5B. Percent with Various Active Roles, by Age and Sex

					Roles			
Age and Sex	N	Spouse	House-hold	Kin	Friend	Neigh-bor	Worker	Organ-ization
Males	107							
50–54	19	89.5	100.0	68.4	73.7	68.4	94.7	36.8
55–59	18	88.9	94.4	61.1	50.0	66.7	100.0	55.6
60–64	19	84.2	84.2	63.2	73.7	47.4	78.9	21.1
65–69	12	91.7	100.0	83.3	83.3	66.7	33.3	33.3
70–74	25	64.0	76.0	76.0	72.0	48.0	24.0	20.0
75 and over	14	78.6	85.7	71.4	71.4	35.7	21.4	7.1
Females	104							
50–54	17	82.4	82.4	64.7	70.6	58.8	82.4	35.3
55–59	16	62.5	87.5	87.5	75.0	75.0	31.3	43.8
60–64	15	60.0	86.7	80.0	66.7	73.3	53.6	53.3
65–69	19	36.8	57.9	52.6	63.2	57.9	26.3	36.8
70–74	25	28.0	52.0	56.0	60.0	52.0	16.0	32.0
75 and over	12	16.7	50.0	50.0	83.3	50.0	16.7	25.0

As expected, roles became fewer with age for both men and women. For men, loss of formal roles such as worker or organization member accounted for most of the reduction. Women tended to lose these roles *plus* their roles as spouse and household member. From these data it appears that women compensated for widowhood by increasing their contacts with friends, while men compensated by remarrying. Older women were much more likely to live alone than older men.

Widowhood

Widowhood is another role change that is commonplace among older people. In 1960 more than half the women and 20 percent of the men over sixty-five were widows or widowers. Widowhood appears to be for many women what retirement is for many men—the conclusion of the central task of adult life. The role of widowhood is completely unlike the marriage role. Unlike marriage, widowhood is a position which allows no fulfillment of sexual needs, an important item to many older people. It also diminishes the possibility of gaining identity through the accomplishments or positions of the spouse. Widowhood also marks the loss of intimate give-and-take based on mutual interests. For example, the widow often replaces one intimate, extensive, and interdependent relationship with her husband by adding several transitory and independent relationships with other widows. The case of Mrs. Willoughby is reasonably typical.

Mrs. Willoughby is having problems adjusting to widowhood and compensating for restrictions in her social, as well as physical, life space after three decades of marriage and joint employment with her husband. Together, they managed an apartment building. She has no children. Today, her most regular contacts are with a younger sister, but there is little comfort in the relationship, for the sister is condescending toward Mrs. Willoughby and her abilities. Mrs. Willoughby feels she thinks too much about herself: "I just think about sitting here and vegetating. I didn't used to have time to think of myself before. I had my husband and we were busy taking care of the apartment house we managed." With the loss of her husband, Mrs. Willoughby's financial situation as well as her health began to deteriorate. She could not continue to manage the apartment building without her husband, and so she is now living on her savings and some Social Security benefits. She would like to work and try to find companionship, perhaps with a man, but her sister has persuaded her she could probably not succeed at either endeavor. She does have misgivings about her sister's wisdom in these things, but not enough self-confidence to act on her own initiative, for she is used to depending on the judgments of others: "I had to do everything my husband said because he was the boss, although I did resent it deeply." In near desperation, she seems to feel there *must* be a way for her to get some of the most pressing needs met; that somewhere, close at hand, there must be a new way of life—if only she could discover it. She would like to make a grasp at it: "I want to do something, but I don't know just what it is or how to go about it." She constantly chides herself for minutes spent in late-morning sleep when she could be doing other things, but she admits frankly she does not know what those things might be.[5]

The role changes which occur with retirement and widowhood are not necessarily unwelcome to the individual. Often the responsibilities of work are given up happily and retirement is viewed as a period of increased fulfillment. Likewise, after the initial shock of grief wears off, many widows enjoy the sense of freedom and relief from responsibility that comes with widowhood. For many, widowhood means a reunion with friends who have been widowed for some time. In fact, a frequent complaint of married older women is that their family obligations shut them out of many of the activities their widowed friends enjoy. Nevertheless, these changes still require that the individual adjust.

Perhaps the most significant factor influencing the adjustment of widows relates to the number of other roles available to widows in a given society. Lopata[6] found that the more densely settled and the more urbanized the area of residence, the larger the field of available women's roles and the more freedom widows had in choosing among them.

Dependency

Perhaps one of the most dreaded role changes accompanying old age is the shift from the role of independent adult to that of dependency.[7] Older people, both in the community and in institutions, fear becoming dependent, whether physically or financially—either way it is a difficult position for most adults to accept. This is easy to understand. We are taught from birth that man's goal in life is to become independent and self-sufficient. This is a deeply ingrained value for most people, and it is not surprising that they are hostile to the idea of giving up their autonomy and becoming dependent on others.

---

[5] Margaret Clark and Barbara Anderson, *Culture and Aging* (Springfield, Ill.: Charles C Thomas, 1967), p. 408. Reprinted by permission.

[6] Helena Z. Lopata, "Social Relations of Widows in Urbanized Countries," *Sociological Quarterly* (forthcoming).

[7] While psychologists use dependency to refer to a psychological state, the usage here refers to a position and role characterized by the necessity to rely on others for one's livelihood.

Dependency is all the more difficult to accept because of the changes it brings in other roles. For example, older people are sometimes forced by necessity to fall back on their married children. This produces a strain on the parent-child relationship for a number of reasons. The parent sometimes resists and often resents having to depend on his child. He may become angry and frustrated by the changes in interaction brought on by the reversal of positions. He may feel guilty because he feels he shouldn't be dependent. The child, now an adult, may also resent having to provide for both his own children and his parent, yet he may feel guilty for having this resentment. And finally, the child's spouse may not willingly accept the diversion of family resources to the aged parent.

What makes the position "dependent" especially difficult is the set of expectations attached to it. Dependent people in our society are supposed to defer to their benefactors, to be eternally grateful for what they receive, and to give up their rights to lead their own lives. This is what we demand of our children, the poor, or any other dependent group. Is it any wonder, then, that an older person, often having spent as many as fifty years as an independent adult, rebels at the idea of assuming the dependent position? Yet about a third of older Americans find themselves having to ask their children for some kind of help at one point or another.[8]

Disability and Sickness

Disability is another new role that older people are likely to experience. There are varying degrees of disability, and when disability becomes extreme, it usually turns into dependency. But there are many older people whose disabilities have not reached that stage, and for them disability brings with it a restriction in the number of roles one can play and a change in other people's reactions. Over a third of the older population has some disability serious enough to limit their ability to work, keep house, or engage in other major activities.[9]

Sickness is similar to disability in that its influence is felt mainly through a limitation of role-playing. Good health, or absence of sickness or disability, operates alongside age and sex as a major criterion for eligibility for various positions. Most positions outside one's circle of family and friends require activity that is impossible for severely sick or disabled people.

It has long been recognized in our society that the sick person occupies

---

[8] Matilda W. Riley and Ann Foner, *Aging and Society.* Vol. I, *An Inventory of Research Findings.* (New York: Russell Sage Foundation, 1968), p. 309.

[9] *Ibid.,* p. 214.

a unique position. He is not expected to work, go to school, or otherwise meet the obligations of his other positions, and he is often dependent on others to care for him. If he plays the sick role long enough, he may be permanently excluded from some of his other positions, such as his job, his office in a voluntary association, or his position as the family bread-winner.

The sick person is usually exempt from social responsibilities, is not expected to care for himself, and is expected to need medical help. The more serious the prognosis, the more likely he is to find himself being treated as a dependent.

Whether a person is defined as sick partly depends on the seriousness

Table 6. Percent with a Specified Number of Chronic Conditions (Including Chronic Diseases and Impairments), by
Age, United States, 1957 to 1958

No. of conditions	All ages	Age under 15	Age 15–44	Age 45–64	Age 65+
Males					
1 or more chronic conditions	39	19	39	58	75
Only 1 chronic condition	23	15	26	30	26
2 chronic conditions	9	3	9	16	21
3 or more chronic conditions	7	1	4	12	28
Females					
1 or more chronic conditions	44	16	45	63	81
Only 1 chronic condition	23	13	26	27	27
2 chronic conditions	11	2	11	18	20
3 or more chronic conditions	10	1	8	18	34

Source: United States National Health Survey, 1959, *Health Statistics*. Series B., No. 11. p. 2.

and certainty of the prognosis. Even if he has a functional or physical impairment, the individual is less likely to be allowed to play the sick role if his prognosis is known not to be serious. Yet the sick person is often ex-pected to want to get well, and actually to do so, regardless of the prog-nosis.

The importance of aging to sickness and disability is of course the fact that as age increases, the probability of disease, illness, or disability be-comes greater. For example, as Table 6 shows, people aged sixty-five and over have one or more chronic conditions at almost twice the incidence of those aged fifteen to forty-four.

The Role of the Institutional Resident

When illness and disability become a serious handicap, many older people take up residence in nursing homes and homes for the aged. While only about 4 percent of the older population lives in institutional facilities, for those who do, entering an institution usually involves important role changes.

In the institutional setting, opportunities for useful activity, leisure activities, contacts with the outside world, and privacy are all somewhat less frequent than they are outside. Coupled with the extremely negative attitude of most older people toward living in an institution, these changes create significant obstacles to continuity of role playing.

Other Important Changes

There are also changes with age in roles that continue into later life. For example, there is a decline in religious participation as age increases. Overall participation in voluntary associations declines in terms of number of memberships held *and* in terms of meetings attended. Contacts with friends appear to be maintained until about age seventy-five, but after that there is a decline.

Thus far, the changes in position and role that we have found to be associated with aging would be defined by most people as changes for the worse. They represent a constriction of the individual's life-space, a diminution of the number of positions he can legitimately occupy, and changes from positively valued positions such as breadwinner, husband, or employee to negatively valued positions such as widow, dependent, or sick person. While these changes are not without their positive aspects, they still come out negative overall in the minds of most people.

Are there no positive changes in position as one grows older? The answer is, yes, there are a few. For one thing, people appear to take a stronger interest in politics in their later years. Voting percentages peak at about age sixty-two, and people over seventy as a group turn out over 75 percent to vote in presidential elections as compared with about 60 percent for those aged twenty-five. This same pattern exists with regard to party identification, or interest in political affairs. Older people have substantially higher representation among public officials in the United States (both elected and appointed) than among the rank and file of occupations. Thus, while only a small fraction of the population engages actively in politics, opportunities for increased participation seem to be present *for a few* older people in this area.

Older people may join special clubs such as Golden Age Clubs or Senior Centers. Yet seldom more than 3 percent of the older people in a given community join such organizations. There appears to be a widespread reluctance on the part of older people to identify themselves as being old. One seventy-year-old, when asked if she belonged to the local Senior Center, told me, "Who wants to be with those old fogies all the time?" This reluctance is likely to hamper attempts to form any kind of organization that is widely regarded as being for older people. Thus, while membership in such clubs is a position that opens up to people as they grow older, it is also a position that most older people tend to reject.

In their later years, people have much more time to devote to leisure participation. Most older people spend more time in leisure activity than on daily maintenance activities such as grooming, housekeeping, and cooking. Specific leisure activities that increase as age increases are television watching, visiting, reading, and gardening. Television watching occupies more of the older person's time than any other single activity, and this is particularly true of those who live alone. Older people in general have a positive attitude toward television. Most older people spend about two hours a day visiting, either inside or outside their own household. Time spent with friends tends to decline from the teens through the fifties, but tends to rise again after age sixty. Reading is a more important activity to the old than to the young. As an activity, gardening tends to increase from the teens through the sixties. In one survey 42 percent of older people said they had been working around the yard the previous day.

Generally speaking, the increase in time available for leisure practically forces a role change in this area. The general trends in leisure participation of older people will be considered at greater length in Chapter Ten.

Summary

In general, social roles are comprised of the rights and duties of persons who occupy a given position. The role specifies not only what is expected of the role player, but also what he can expect in return.

The position of older person in urban-industrial societies is a negatively valued one. That is, no highly desirable rewards are gained by occupying the position. Yet it is impossible to live a long life without eventually becoming an "older person."

Age is a prime criterion of eligibility for entry into and maintenance of most desirable positions in urban-industrial societies. This fact represents the strongest single link between aging and an individual's social roles.

In addition, as the individual enters the latter part of the life cycle, he finds that he is expected to change the manner in which he plays even the most familiar roles.

Retirement, widowhood, dependency, disability, sickness, and institutionalization are some major role changes that accompany later life. Each of these plus many other role changes will be discussed in more detail in Part IV. Taken together, they represent very significant changes in the situation the individual confronts as he grows old.

Bibliography

Clark, Margaret and Barbara G. Anderson, *Culture and Aging.* Springfield, Illinois: Charles C Thomas, 1967.

Cox, Peter R. and J. R. Ford, "The Mortality of Widows Shortly After Widowhood," *Lancet,* 1:163–164, 1964.

Cumming, Elaine and William E. Henry, *Growing Old: The Process of Disengagement.* New York: Basic Books, 1961.

Gordon, Gerald, *Role Theory and Illness.* New Haven, Connecticut: College and University Press, 1966.

Gorer, Geoffrey, *Death, Grief and Mourning.* Garden City, New York: Doubleday & Co., 1965.

Heilbrun, Alfred B., Jr. and Charles V. Lais, "Decreased Role Consistency in the Aged," *Journal of Gerontology,* 19:325–329, 1964.

Lopata, Helena Z., "Social Relations of Widows in Urbanized Countries," *Sociological Quarterly,* (forthcoming).

Miller, Stephen J., "The Social Dilemma of the Aging Leisure Participant," in *Older People and Their Social World,* eds. Arnold M. Rose and Warren A. Peterson. Philadelphia: F. A. Davis, 1965, pp. 77–92.

Starkey, P. D., "Sick-Role Retention as a Factor in Nonrehabilitation," *Journal of Counseling Psychology,* 15:75–79, 1968.

Stern, Karl, Gwendolyn M. Williams, and Miguel Prados, "Grief Reactions in Later Life," *American Journal of Psychiatry,* 108:289–294, 1951.

Williams, Richard H., "Changing Status, Roles, and Relationships," in *Handbook of Social Gerontology,* ed. Clark Tibbitts. Chicago: University of Chicago Press, 1960, pp. 261–297.

For additional bibliography, see also Chapters Nine through Eleven and Thirteen through Eighteen, as well as the general bibliography.

7 Health

Health is a central factor in everyone's life, but most people are fortunate enough to be able to take good health for granted. However, health affects participation in most social roles, life satisfaction, and the way we are treated by others. It would be difficult to overstate the importance of good health for a successful and satisfying life.

In later life declining health cuts across all social, political, and economic lines. Health becomes a major influence on participation in the family, the job, the community, and in leisure pursuits, and health needs absorb a larger amount *and* proportion of a person's income as he grows older. In fact, a large proportion of the medical industry's facilities and services are geared toward meeting the needs of people with disease and infirmities characteristic of old age.

Health is obviously a major influence on the older person's situation. Social gerontology is therefore concerned with the continuum of health all the way from good to bad, with programs for health improvement and rehabilitation, and with the importance of health to the life situations of older people.

Health is a complex term and difficult to define. It refers not merely to the absence of disease or disability, but also to more positive things, such as mental, physical, and social well-being. It is most useful to look at health as a continuum. At the one end is complete social, physical, and mental well-being and at the other end is death. Figure 5 shows several stages along the health continuum.

Ideally, good health would be measured in terms of social, physical and mental well-being, but since these conditions are very difficult to measure, good health is operationally defined as the absence of disease or infirmity. This operational definition is placed just short of the good health pole of the continuum in Figure 5 to indicate that it falls short as a true indicator of good health.

A *condition* is defined as a departure from physical or mental well-

Good   Poor
Health   Health

Absence	Presence	Seeks	Restricted	Restricted	Institutionalized	Illness
of	of a	treat-	activity	in major		Death
disease	condition	ment		activity		
or						
impair-						
ment						

Figure 5. Stages of the Health Continuum

being. It has its onset when it is first noticed either by the individual or by a physician. Conditions obviously vary in many important ways. *Chronic* conditions are long-term conditions that either are permanent, or leave residual disability, or require special training for rehabilitation, or may be expected to require a long period of supervision, observation, or care. Chronic conditions include diseases such as asthma, high blood pressure, diabetes, heart trouble, or arthritis; and impairments such as deafness, paralysis, or permanent stiffness in joints. *Acute* conditions are expected to be *temporary* and may be as mild as a bruised foot or as serious as pneumonia. *Injuries* constitute the third and final major category of conditions. Within these categories, conditions can be discussed in terms of incidence (number of *new* cases per year), or of prevalence (average number of *existing* cases per year).

Once a condition becomes known, it may simply be ignored. Or either self-treatment or professional treatment may be sought.

The next phase of illness is the *restriction of activity*. The restriction in this phase, however, does not prevent the individual from carrying out his major activities.

Restriction of major activity is more serious. It means that the individual is unable to carry out his most necessary activities, such as work or housework. This phase is commonly called disability.

When a condition becomes medically demanding or very serious, or when disability reaches the point where the individual cannot care for himself, the phase of *institutionalization* usually begins.

It should be recognized that these phases of illness are very arbitrary, but they provide a number of useful reference points which can be used to compare the health of older people with that of younger ones.

General

On the average, older people are comparatively less often afflicted than the young with conditions classified as *acute* (such as infectious diseases or common colds). They are more often afflicted with *chronic* conditions (such as heart trouble or deafness), and more likely to suffer *disability* restrictions on their activity.

The extreme variability in the health status of older people definitely shows that poor health is by no means necessarily associated with old age. But *as a group* older people do appear to suffer increasingly from chronic conditions.

Chronic Conditions

Most older people have one or more chronic conditions. In fact, three out of four older people have at least one chronic condition. This compares to one in three in the fifteen to forty-four age group. Table 7 shows the incidence of chronic conditions by age and sex.

For older people, the most prevalent chronic conditions are arthritis and rheumatism, heart disease, and high blood pressure, and the prevalence of these conditions rises with age after about age fifty. Other conditions appear to remain fairly stable, in terms of prevalence, as age increases. (See Figure 6, on p. 117.)

Acute conditions, on the other hand, appear to *decline* in incidence as age increases. Table 8 shows that the total incidence of acute conditions declines with each succeeding age interval. Respiratory conditions have the highest incidence at all ages for both sexes. Young children experience an average of four acute conditions per year, while the average is about 1.6 for older people.

Duration

The duration of conditions increases with age. People sixty-five and over report twice as much time restricted due to illness as do people aged forty-five to sixty-four, and although older people experience acute conditions less often, they take longer to recover from them. "There is a definite increase in the duration per *case* from about ten days per year in the forties to about twenty to twenty-five days per year in the late seventies, probably due to declining recuperative powers in the older years."[1]

---

[1] Eugene A. Confrey and Marcus S. Caldstein, "The Health Status of Aging People," in *Handbook of Social Gerontology,* ed. Clark Tibbitts (Chicago: Univ. of Chicago Press, 1960), p. 173.

Table 7. Percent Distribution of Persons, by Chronic Condition and Activity Limitation Status, by Age and Sex: United States: July 1963—June 1965

Age and Sex	Total	Persons with no chronic conditions	Persons with 1 or more chronic conditions		
			Total	Limitation in major activity	Total Disability
All Ages					
Both Sexes	100.0	54.2	45.8	6.6	2.2
Male	100.0	56.0	44.0	6.2	3.1
Female	100.0	52.6	47.4	6.9	1.4
Under 45					
Both Sexes	100.0	64.8	35.2	2.5	0.4
Male	100.0	65.8	34.2	2.5	0.5
Female	100.0	63.8	36.2	2.6	0.3
45–64					
Both Sexes	100.0	34.2	65.8	11.6	2.8
Male	100.0	36.4	63.6	11.1	4.5
Female	100.0	32.1	67.9	12.0	1.2
65–74					
Both Sexes	100.0	19.6	80.4	25.3	9.7
Male	100.0	21.3	78.7	26.4	16.3
Female	100.0	18.3	81.7	24.3	4.3
75 and Over					
Both Sexes	100.0	12.6	87.4	29.9	23.7
Male	100.0	14.4	85.6	27.2	32.5
Female	100.0	11.3	88.7	31.9	17.1

Source: National Center for Health Statistics, *Vital and Health Statistics*, Series 10, Number 32, p. 46

Mental Illness

Mental illness is a special category of condition. It can be chronic or acute; most often it is chronic. "When various types of mental disturbance are examined by age, certain ones, particularly psychoses and various psychiatric symptoms experienced as bodily illness, appear to be more prevalent among older than among younger people. Other types, such as

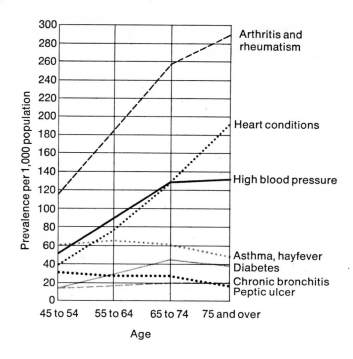

*Figure 6. Prevalence of Selected Chronic Illnesses among
Persons Forty-Five and Over.*
Source: United States National Health Survey, 1960, *Health
Statistics,* Series C, No. 4, pp. 31, 35.

neuroses, do not appear to increase by age. . . ."[2] In one study, the incidence of psychosis ranged from 3.5 cases per 1000 people age fifteen to
thirty-four to *40.0* cases per 1000 people aged sixty-five or over.[3] In another, the rates of psychosis were found to increase with age beyond age
sixty-five, and over 30 percent of the men age eighty-five or more were
classified as psychotic.[4] Caution should be used in interpreting these data,
however, since we do not know how much mental illness exists purely as
a result of the definition of psychosis that is used. A good case can be made
assuming that anyone who can function adequately in a community setting
is not psychotic, no matter *how* he answers the psychologists' questions.

---

[2] Matilda Riley and Ann Foner, *Aging and Society,* Vol. I, *An Inventory of
Research Findings.* (New York: Russell Sage, 1968), p. 370.

[3] *Ibid.*

[4] *Ibid.,* p. 371.

Table 8. Incidence of Acute Conditions, by Age
(per 100 Persons per Year)

Condition	All ages	Age under 5	Age 5–14	Age 15–24	Age 25–44	Age 45–64	Age 65+
Males							
Total	248	406	347	251	194	157	155
Infectious and parasitic	22	56	41	14	13	7	1
Respiratory	158	260	218	144	124	106	114
Digestive	13	20	17	20	11	5	13
Injuries	34	36	40	52	31	28	14
All other acute	21	34	31	21	15	11	13
Females							
Total	272	402	355	291	247	194	169
Infectious and parasitic	24	51	51	18	16	9	4
Respiratory	179	273	237	183	163	131	98
Digestive	15	27	15	20	13	10	14
Injuries	23	22	24	22	19	25	32
All other acute	31	29	28	48	36	19	21

Source: United States National Health Survey, 1958, *Health Statistics*, Series B, No. 6, p. 19.

Research Illustration 4
Social Isolation and Mental Illness in Old Age*
Marjorie Fiske Lowenthal

As a part of an overall study of social isolation and mental illness, Lowenthal examined the relationship between age-linked isolation and mental illness.

Her subjects were 534 persons age sixty or over admitted to the psychiatric screening wards of the San Francisco General Hospital and 600 community residents in the same age category drawn on a stratified random basis from eighteen San Francisco census tracts. The base year was 1959.

* Based on Marjorie Fiske Lowenthal, "Social Isolation and Mental Illness in Old Age," *American Sociological Review*, 29:54–70 (1964).

With regard to social isolation, the subjects were separated into *pure isolates*—people who had no friends or relatives involved in the decision to enter the hospital and for whom no friends or relatives could be located after hospitalization, and community people who had had no contacts with friends or relatives within the past three years; *semi-isolates*—hospitalized people who resembled pure isolates but for a few casual and infrequent social contacts prior to admission; *social interactors*—people in both samples who had attended a social function or visited friends within the two-week period prior to the interview; and a *remainder* category that fell somewhere between the isolates and semi-isolates on the one hand, and the interactors on the other.

The following is a breakdown of the samples by type of social isolation.

Hospital Sample	N
"Pure" Isolates	52
Semi-isolates	56
Interactors	39
Remainder	387

Community Sample	
Isolates	30
Interactors	417
Remainder	144
Unclassifiable	9

Isolates were also differentiated into lifelong isolates and those whose isolation had developed relatively late in life.

Mental illness was defined in terms of a phychiatrist's rating of the subjects as showing a high degree of psychiatric impairment, and was differentiated into psychogenic disorders, alcoholism, and organic disorders. The distribution of the 525 impaired subjects was as follows:

Diagnosis	"Pure" Isolates %	Semi-isolates %	Inter-actors %	Remainder %
Psychogenic alone or in combination with organic	22	25	44	23
Alcoholism alone or in combination with organic	20	21	15	15
Organic alone	58	54	41	62
Total	100	100	100	100
N	(50)	(52)	(39)	(384)

The psychiatrist also rated the subjects as to their physical health at the time of the interview.

Lowenthal found that organic disorders were more common among late isolates, and that psychogenic disorders were twice as prevalent among interactors as among isolates. Yet those with organic disorders showed no more social changes, such as death of a spouse or relative, change in living arrangements, or retirement, than did those with psychogenic disorders.

As Lowenthal remarked, "This leaves us with the rather obvious conclusion that the interactors' superior physical condition and lack of intellectual deterioration permit them to maintain their comparatively high degree of interaction, and that the generally poor physical condition and greater intellectual deterioration of the organics . . . has resulted in their greater isolation. *Relative isolation, then, may be more a consequence than a cause of mental illness in old age, and the consequences for psychogenics may be less severe than for organics because of their generally superior physical condition*" (p. 70, emphasis added).

In short, Lowenthal concluded that social isolation in old age results from mental illness, and that since organic mental illness is related to poor physical health, social isolation should be more prevalent among organics than among psychogenics.

Treatment

No data are available on the extent of age changes in self-treatment, but the available evidence suggests that as age increases, so does the average number of trips to the doctor. One study showed an increase from five per year at ages forty-five to fifty-four to about seven per year after age sixty-five. Women average about one more visit per year than men.[5] As age increases, the tendency to see a doctor about physical illness seems to increase, while the tendency to see a doctor about mental illness seems to decline. In a study done in New York City it was found that among people with impaired mental health, 34 percent of those between twenty and twenty-nine had seen a doctor, while only 21 percent of those between fifty and fifty-four had done so.[6]

Impairment and Disability

Impairment and disability often result from chronic conditions. Table 9 shows the prevalence of various types of impairments among people of various ages.

Table 9. Type of Impairment among Persons Forty-Five and
Over, United States, 1967 to 1968
(Rate per 1,000)

Type of impairment	Age 45–64	Age 65–74	Age 75+
All impairments	212.4	376.6	615.0
Blindness	5.9	25.9	83.3
Other visual impairment	18.5	48.8	74.3
Hearing impairments	52.2	129.2	256.4
Speech defects	3.7	6.8	6.1
Paralysis	8.8	15.9	34.4
Absence, fingers, toes, only	15.9	22.6	17.4
Absence, major extremities	3.3	4.4	7.0
Impairment,* lower extremities	26.5	37.1	39.7
Impairment,* upper extremities	17.6	24.6	26.6
Impairment,* limbs, back, trunk, except extremities only	48.7	49.7	61.6
All other impairments	11.2	11.6	8.2

* Except paralysis and absence.
Source: United States National Health Survey, 1959, Health Statistics, Series B., No. 9.

Note the marked differences between the age group sixty-five to seventy-four and the group seventy-five and over with respect to blindness, hearing impairment, and paralysis. Between ages sixty-five and seventy-four, 40

---

[5] Ibid., p. 217.
[6] Ibid., p. 383.

percent of all people have some impairment, while after age seventy-five, this figure rises to 60 percent.

Loss of teeth is also related to age. By age seventy-five, two-thirds of the population have lost all of their natural teeth as compared with about one-fifth of the population aged forty-five to fifty-four.[7] This pattern may change significantly in the future, however, since dentists today are much more reluctant to pull teeth than they were in the past.

Along with the rise in chronic disease and impairments, disability increases steadily with age for both sexes. Yet despite the reported prev-

Table 10. Degree of Limitation of Activity Due to Chronic Conditions, by Age, 1961 to 1963 (Percentage Distribution)

			Persons with one or more chronic conditions				
Age	All persons	Persons with no chronic conditions	Total	With no limitation of activity	With limitation, but not in major activity*	With limitation in amount or kind of major activity*	Unable to carry on major activity*
All ages	100.0	55.9	44.1	31.9	3.4	6.6	2.3
Under 17	100.0	80.1	19.9	17.8	1.1	0.8	0.2
17–44	100.0	52.5	47.5	39.3	3.1	4.5	0.6
45–64	100.0	35.9	64.1	43.7	5.9	11.6	2.8
65+	100.0	19.0	81.0	32.3	7.3	25.9	15.5

* Major activity refers to ability to work, keep house, or engage in school or preschool activities.
Source: National Center for Health Statistics, 1965, *Vital and Health Statistics*, Series 10, No. 17, p. 26.

alence of chronic conditions, only small proportions of older people seem severely handicapped. While 81 percent of older people suffer some chronic condition, more than half of all older people are not limited in any way due to chronic conditions, and only 15 percent are unable to carry on their major activity [8] (See Table 10).

Thus, while the expected disability and illness exist among older people, the proportion who escape limitation by these factors is surprisingly large. Even among those who are disabled by illness or injury, most are not permanently bedridden.

This is not to say that chronic illness and disability are not serious

[7] *Ibid.,* p. 209.
[8] *Ibid.,* p. 214.

problems among older people. Clearly, they are. The point is that for many people old age is not accompanied by illness and disability. There are millions of older people in our society who consider themselves to be in good health and to have no serious limitations on their normal activities.

Institutionalization

Less than 4 percent of all people sixty-five or over live in institutions, but as age increases after sixty-five, so does the percentage. For example, *14* percent of those age eighty-five or over are institutionalized. Of those who are institutionalized, most are in nursing and personal care homes. Table 11 shows the rates of residency in various types of institutions by age, sex, and color.

Various studies have shown that while many older people in institutions are mentally and physically impaired, impairment is not necessarily related to institutionalization. Thus, the rates of institutionalization present an inaccurate picture of the health of the older population because they include people who live in homes for the aged but who are not impaired, disabled, or ill. In nursing homes, about half the older patients are ambulatory and continent; while in mental hospitals the proportion reaches upwards of 80 percent.

Perhaps a better indicator of the extent to which health is seriously impaired is short-term hospitalization. From July, 1965 to June, 1966, *87 percent of the 17.5 million older people in the United States had no hospital episodes.* This is not significantly different from the 90 percent figure for the total population.

Taking institutionalization as an indicator of poor health, then, we can say that even if we consider the entire institutionalized population of older people as being extremely ill, we can still only account for less than 4 percent of all older people. The absence of age changes in the utilization of short-term hospitals is probably due to the fact that the increase in chronic conditions and the decrease in acute conditions tend to cancel each other out. From the standpoint of seriousness, we can probably safely say that many older people have serious illnesses and disabilities, but that these are not yet so serious as to require hospitalization.

A key factor in institutionalization appears to be the residential setting and family system. Older people in nursing and personal care homes tend not to have a spouse or children. They also tend to be those who have lived alone. Indications are that many older people are able to avoid institutionalization if they have relatives to help care for them and adequate financial resources. In fact, the breakdown in this support system appears to be the primary cause of institutionalization among older people.

Table 11. Rates of Residency in Institutions of Various Types by Age, Sex, and Color, United States, 1963 (per 1,000)

Age	Total			White			Nonwhite		
	Total	Male	Female	Total	Male	Female	Total	Male	Female
(a) Nursing and personal care homes									
All ages, 20+	4.5	3.2	5.6	4.8	3.4	6.0	1.7	1.8	1.7
20–64	0.6	0.7	0.6	0.6	0.7	0.6	0.6	0.7	0.5
65–74	7.9	6.8	8.8	8.1	6.9	9.1	5.9	6.2	5.6
75–84	39.6	29.1	47.5	41.7	30.5	49.9	13.8	12.4	15.0
85+	148.4	105.6	175.1	157.7	111.9	185.8	41.8	40.4	42.9
(b) Geriatric and chronic disease "hospitals"*									
All ages, 20+	0.7	0.8	0.6	0.7	0.8	0.6	0.6	0.8	0.5
20–64	0.2	0.3	0.1	0.2	0.3	0.1	0.3	0.4	0.2
65–74	1.7	2.5	1.1	1.6	2.4	1.0	2.3	3.3	1.5
75–84	4.4	4.5	4.4	4.5	4.5	4.5	3.5	4.6	2.6
85+	13.6	12.4	14.3	14.2	13.2	14.8	6.7	4.7	8.2
(c) Long-stay mental hospitals									
All ages	4.4	4.9	3.9	4.1	4.4	3.7	7.0	8.9	5.3
15–44	2.4	3.1	1.8	2.1	2.6	1.6	4.9	6.8	3.2
45–54	5.0	5.6	4.6	4.6	5.0	4.3	8.8	11.0	6.9
55–64	6.7	7.0	6.3	6.3	6.5	6.0	10.7	12.1	9.4
65–74	8.8	9.7	8.0	8.4	9.3	7.7	12.7	14.6	11.1
75+	10.8	10.2	11.3	10.5	9.7	11.1	14.8	16.1	13.7

* "Hospitals" include only geriatric and chronic disease hospitals and chronic disease wards and nursing home units of general hospitals.
Source: National Center for Health Statistics, 1965, *Vital and Health Statistics*, Series 12, No. 2, pp. 4, 13; No. 3, p. 5.

Another important factor is loss of residence. Many moves to homes for the aged are precipitated by urban renewal, changes in apartment ownership, and so on.

Older people do not end up in institutions overnight. Usually a series of measures is taken which attempt to solve the person's problem short of institutionalizing him, and the nursing home is often viewed as a last resort. The fact that admission to a nursing home so often comes at the end of a long string of disappointments is bound to have its effect on the patient and his family.

Most older people look on nursing homes in a very negative way. These views result partly from the person's desire to remain in familiar surroundings and near his relatives, but they are also partly influenced by the concept of the poorhouse which has come down from another era. In terms of preference, in fact, the nursing home is about the *last* place most older people would prefer to go, although many of them recognize that this may be the best living arrangement for people who can no longer take care of themselves. Most of the fear that leads older people to reject the idea of living in a nursing home is related to a perceived loss of independence, a perception that the nursing home represents formal proof that death is near, and a fear of rejection by their children. Older people who live with their spouses, with their children, or in an owned home are the most resistant to the idea of living in a Home.[9] But these negative attitudes do not prevent older people from moving into nursing homes.

The facts of life in long-term care facilities often justify the negative view most older people have of them. Many Homes lack physical facilities, staff, and provision for activities. Seldom is any effort made to prepare either the patient or his family for life in the Home. Many Homes have over-restrictive institutional rules, and useful occupations and leisure activities are often completely lacking. Most nursing homes also tend to be completely cut off from the community, making little or no use of community resources for the benefit of their patients. Finally, there is far less privacy in most nursing homes than the patients would like.

Older people fear nursing homes largely because they fear the influence of the home on their chance for survival—and, it appears, with good reason. Mortality rates for older people in institutions are higher than for those outside, particularly during the first year. This is partly because sickness often prompts the move to a nursing home in the first place. Nevertheless, this alone cannot explain the higher mortality rate in such homes. There is some evidence to suggest that a certain amount of bodily

---

[9] In this section Home is capitalized to differentiate the nursing or personal care facility from an independent household.

stress is associated with a move of any kind, and one could expect this stress to be higher in a move to a nursing home.

Living in a nursing home does not appear to have any direct influence on life satisfaction or self-image, but no doubt it has indirect effects via family and other relationships. A key factor determining satisfaction with the Home was its overall rating in the community. Regardless of the objective facts, Homes that are more positively viewed in the community produce more satisfaction in their patients.

The new resident in the Home often faces several simultaneous changes that can make it hard for him to adjust to his new circumstances. Illness, dependency, widowhood, and loneliness are the changes most frequently encountered.

Illness can bring important changes for two reasons. First, it puts the individual in a position where he is *forced* to become dependent. Second, it creates internal states within the individual that make it difficult for him to maintain a reasonable perspective on the outside world. When a person is in pain, or under medication, or just plain fatigued from fighting illness, it is much easier to allow himself to become irritable and depressed. There can be little doubt that for some people a long-term illness can produce profound personality changes.

In addition to the unfamiliar surroundings, the shock of moving, and often the depressing influence of illness, the patient also finds that he has lost his independence. He has lost personal control over many of the simplest everyday functions. When to get up, when to go to sleep, when to eat and what, whom to associate with, whether the TV will be on or off, whether the windows will be open or closed, whether to use a heavy or a light blanket—these and a host of other seemingly trivial decisions are often now out of the patient's hands.

Widowhood often precipitates a move into an extended care facility. The newly widowed person faces a great many problems: grief, homesickness, loss of outside contacts, financial insecurity, and a feeling of uselessness. It is hard to overestimate the impact of moving into a Home on a woman who has been a housewife for most of her adult life. She has lost her husband, who was more than likely the most important person in the world to her. She has lost her useful function of keeping a house, and what's more, she *misses* the physical surroundings.

Thus, the new Home resident often faces difficult changes in addition to his institutionalization. But the nursing home can seldom help him deal with these very personal concerns.

Most extended care facilities are not oriented toward the *patients;* instead the organization revolves around instrumental tasks such as making beds or giving medication. It is not that these tasks are unimportant, it is just that they often seem to be the staff's reason for being—to the total exclusion of contact with the patient as a person.

The following incidents reported by Henry illustrate this emphasis on the mechanistic to the total exclusion of the human element.[10]

—Patients' being bathed in assembly-line fashion in order to get the task done quickly with no thought to the patient's privacy or modesty.
—Inability to call patients by name who have been in the facility several months.
—Patients not spoken to except to issue directions such as "turn over," "sit down," etc.
—Complete and continuous disregard of patients' requests to contact relatives to bring them things.
—Several patients being bathed in the same water.
—Patients who cause trouble being tied to the bed.

A final example:
(Nurse) Beck came into the room and went over to one of the beds and turned the patient on her side without saying anything. . . . She pulled up the gown exposing the patient's buttocks and gave her an injection. I glanced back at the patient as Beck left the room and saw that the patient was still on her side, buttocks exposed, blood oozing from the injection site.[11]

The dehumanization of the patient is usually excused on the grounds of administrative and medical necessity. However, it is important to note that patients judge the adequacy of the care they receive as much in terms of its humanitarian effectiveness as of its medical effectiveness.

Bureaucratic structure is a system of organization which supposedly utilizes institutional rules to enhance the operating efficiency of the organization. Too often, however, people working in bureaucratic organizations lose sight of the goals beyond the rules and set the rules up as ends in themselves. The result is a stifling and dehumanizing rigidity which prevents the institution from being able to deal with each individual as a unique person with a unique set of problems.

In most cases we tolerate the depersonalization of bureaucracy because it does not intrude into our primary relationships. In the case of the Home resident, however, the Home *is* the setting for his most important relationships and associations. Its bureaucratic rules need to be flexible enough so as not to interfere with them.

One of the biggest problems patients have is that they cannot find anyone who will tell them honestly what is the matter with them. This problem is particularly acute among the victims of cancer or heart disease. Even the physician often has a difficult time being honest with seriously ill

---

[10] Jules Henry, *Culture Against Man* (New York: Alfred A. Knopf, 1963), pp. 391–474.
[11] *Ibid.*, p. 395.

patients, simply because it is sometimes very hard to admit that medical science has its limits. Another factor which compounds the problem is the increasing depersonalization of medicine. With the rise of the specialist and the demise of the family GP, there is a tendency for the doctor to look at his patient as a collection of physical symptoms and to know very little of his personal history. This also makes it easier for the physician to kid the patient along. Finally, some patients want to know what is wrong with them and some do not. The end result is that very often the physician simply cannot be relied upon to discuss the patient's diagnosis with him, to lay out his options, and to answer his questions.

Nor are relatives very good at talking honestly with patients about such taboo topics as terminal cancer or impending death. They, more than anyone else, often attempt to keep up a sham that everything will turn out all right, that the patient may get well and come home again, or that the situation will improve to the point where the Home resident can once again be self-sufficient. Usually the patient knows that this is mostly sham, and it puts a strain on him to have to keep up the farce for the benefit of his relatives. Many patients express relief at finding someone they can talk to without having to keep up a front.

From the standpoint of communication, the terminal patient is the biggest problem. At the point where the case becomes absolutely hopeless we tend to write off the patient and to begin to treat him as if he were an object. Usually the surest way for a patient to know when the end is near is to observe how other people behave toward him. When the staff starts talking openly about the case in the patient's presence—with each other as if the patient were not there—it is usually a sure sign that death is just around the corner.

Given the shortage of staff in most facilities, the temptation to concentrate efforts on the "salvageable" cases is understandable. Then too, many terminal patients, particularly cancer victims, are so preoccupied with the pain they are experiencing that they are oblivious of anything else. Yet is this a good enough excuse to treat people as objects, no matter how hopeless their case?

Death

Death is the ultimate in poor health, and every year about 6 percent of the total population of older people in the United States can be expected to die. It is obvious that older people die at a much greater rate than young ones, but the *causes* of death at various ages differ in important ways. For example, older people most frequently die from heart disease, cancer, strokes, influenza, and pneumonia. In contrast, people between twenty-five and forty-four most frequently die from accidents, heart disease, cancer, suicide, and cirrhosis of the liver. For all ages, infectious diseases have declined in importance in recent years, while chronic diseases have taken over as the leading causes of death.

In 1900 the list of leading causes of death among older people was exactly the same as it is today. The main difference now is that more people live to reach the ages where these diseases become prevalent.

The age trend in suicide deserves some comment here. Figure 7 shows that among American women the age curve for suicide rates is nearly flat, indicating stability, while for American men, on the other hand, suicide rates increase with age. A comparison with the Japanese data, which show the same trend for both sexes, indicates that suicide is a cause of death which responds to social and cultural factors. This presents a strong case for including social well-being in with physical and mental well-being in the definition of health.

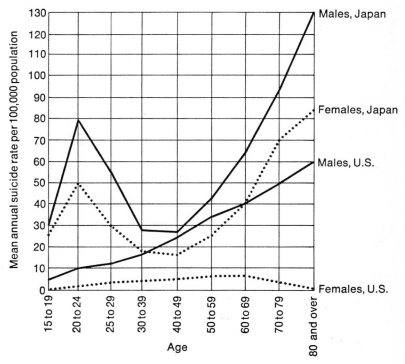

*Figure 7. Suicide Rates, United States and
Japan, 1956–1958*
Source: Riley and Foner, *op. cit.,* p. 393.

Variations

Thus far only general trends in health for the older population have been considered. However, within this population there is a great deal of systematic variation.

Sex   Older women differ significantly from older men in terms of health, but the data present an enigma. In terms of death rates, males die at a faster rate than females at *all* ages, even in the fetal period. Among all causes of death common to both sexes, men have higher rates than women. As age increases, the size of the differential in death rates between men and women also increases until about age seventy-five, after which it decreases.

In terms of trends in mortality, the outlook for the future is for a further decline in death rates for older women and stable or increasing death rates for older men. The principal cause of this trend is a growing differential in deaths from heart-kidney ailments, influenza and pneumonia, and diabetes. Death rates from all of these causes are declining for older women, but are stable or increasing among older men.

In terms of social impact, these data suggest that the proportion of single women in the older population is likely to continue to increase for the forseeable future.

Based on mortality we would expect older males to show higher rates of physician visits, disability, and hospitalization. In fact, the reverse is true. Older women show consistently higher rates of morbidity (illness) than older men, even if we take into account the fact that there are more women in the older population. This puzzling relationship between sex differences in illness and in deaths has not yet been satisfactorily explained, but its implications are clear: older women predominate among the sick, and older men predominate among the dead.

Race   The nonwhite population in the United States has always experienced higher morbidity rates[12] than the white population, but in recent years these differences have been declining. Death rates among older non-whites for such diseases as cancer and diabetes are increasing rapidly, while the rates for whites are stable or declining. As a result of the generally higher rates, sex differences in mortality are less significant among older nonwhites as compared to older whites.

For the immediate future relatively high mortality and morbidity rates for the nonwhite population can be expected, mainly due to their comparatively low socio-economic position. The long-term prospects are better.

---

[12] A morbidity rate is a measure of the prevalence of illness in the population.

As the economic position of the older nonwhite population improves, gradual declines in differential mortality and morbidity between white and nonwhite older people will probably occur.

Marital status   Married people have lower death and morbidity rates than do single people, and the differential is greater among the old than among the young. Older single people tend oftener to be malnourished and to be without the necessary emotional support—both important elements in recovery from disease.

Economic status   Morbidity and mortality for older persons of lower economic status are considerably higher than for the more economically advantaged groups. Unfortunately, most older people fall into the lower economic category; therefore, those who most need health care are among those least capable of paying for it. Medicare and other state and Federal programs take up some of the slack, but the fact remains that a very large proportion of long-term health care patients are welfare cases. This not only governs the quality of care given, but the duration of the illness and the prospects for recovery. These facts are all the more significant when one considers that only about 12 percent of the general older population receives public assistance, while *over half* of the institutionalized older people do so. Economic status, then, is very much related to health, and more so among older people than in any other group.

Retirement   One of the commonest stereotypes about aging is that upon retirement, many older people become sick and die. This is definitely untrue. There is absolutely no evidence that retirement has *any* deleterious effects on health. If anything, people show a tendency toward *improved* health upon retirement.

Stress   Gray[13] found that those older people with severe illness or disability are more likely than others to have been exposed to unusually large amounts of stress prior to illness or injury. Stress in a variety of roles was considered. Even among those who were ill or disabled, those who had earlier been exposed to unusual stress were more seriously afflicted.

Helping the Chronically Ill or Disabled Older Person

While most older people are reasonably healthy, there are still a good many who are chronically ill or disabled. These people must be cared for.

---

[13] Robert M. Gray, *et al.,* "Stress and Health in Later Maturity," *Journal of Gerontology,* 20:65–68, January, 1965.

Health programs   For the general older population the following measures can improve health:

Periodic Health Examination: early detection is often valuable for the treatment of chronic diseases.

Accident Prevention: programs to design safer housing for older people and to alert them to potential hazards in the home can prevent many of the accidents that so often lead to more serious complications.

Nutrition: common causes of poor nutrition among the elderly include inadequate income, living alone (fixing meals for one is too much trouble), loss of teeth, difficulty in food shopping, and long-standing poor eating habits. Meals-on-wheels is a good example of a public program designed to provide better nutrition for older people by serving home-delivered meals.

Exercise: this is particularly important in warding off cardio-vascular diseases. Even diabetes is helped by exercise.

Rehabilitation: a major aspect of health care, rehabilitation is geared toward relieving or controlling clinical symptoms, strengthening and retraining the capacities remaining, creating motivation, or giving self-care training. Only a small proportion of mental health care facilities now in existence use rehabilitation programs as part of their care for older people. However, studies have shown that such programs can be extremely successful in making older people self-sufficient, and much more effort along the lines of rehabilitation is needed.

Summary

Conditions of ill health can be chronic or acute, depending on the duration of the condition. Older people show an increased prevalence of chronic conditions and a decreased prevalence of acute conditions in comparison with the young. However, when acute conditions do strike older people, they tend to linger twice as long as among the middle-aged. Rates of mental illness increase sharply with age if psychiatric definitions are used, but in functional terms the increase is much smaller.

As age increases, people are more likely to see a doctor about physical illness and less likely to see one about mental illness.

The morbidity and mortality statistics indicate that the age group sixty-five-to-seventy-four differs significantly with regard to health from the seventy-five-and-over age group. In general, health declines do not become precipitous until after age seventy-five. This is no doubt related to the fact that biological declines in function do not become marked until about this time. Most older people consider themselves to be in reasonably good health, and most are not limited in their activities by illness or injury.

Only about 4 percent of the older population resides in institutions of various types, and many of them are there for reasons other than health.

Older people with spouses or living children and adequate financial resources can usually avoid entering a nursing or personal care facility. Loss of residence and widowhood are two events which often precipitate a move into an institution. Most older people view nursing homes negatively, but enter them if necessary. The inability of our system to come up with a way to finance genuinely adequate long-term health care means that most nursing homes are lacking in staff and facilities. It also results in an organizational structure which must stress efficiency and which often neglects the socio-emotional needs of the residents.

Adjustment to nursing homes is made difficult by the negative stereo-type most people hold, the isolation of the Home from the community, the weakened condition of the residents, loss of independence, and often widowhood. Yet residence in a Home apparently has few direct effects on life satisfaction or self-image.

The gap in mortality rates between older men and women can be expected to widen in the future because the rates for the leading causes of death are going down for older women but staying the same or going up for older men.

Differences in sex, color, marital status, stress, and financial status all apparently produce differences in mortality among older people. Retirement has *no* impact.

Health programs for older people stress periodic examinations, accident prevention, nutrition, and exercise. At this point, rehabilitation appears to be a neglected aspect of mental health programs. The single factor which appears to offer the most for improving the health of older people is an increase in income.

For most older people, health is not a seriously limiting factor, but for those who *are* seriously affected by chronic illness or disability, it can be central to their situation.

Bibliography

A. General

Anand, M. P., "Accidents in the Home," in *Current Achievements in Geriatrics,* eds. W. F. Anderson and B. Isaacs. London: Cassell, 1964, pp. 239–245.

Bell, Benjamin, Charles L. Rose, and Albert Damon, "The Veterans Administration Longitudinal Study of Healthy Aging," *Gerontologist,* 6:179–184, 1966.

Busse, Ewald W., "The Aging Process and the Health of the Aged," in *Duke*

University Council on Gerontology: Proceedings of Seminars, 1961–1965, ed. Frances C. Jeffers. Durham, North Carolina: Duke University Regional Center for the Study of Aging, 1965, pp. 220–225.

Butler, Robert N., "Patterns of Psychological Health and Psychiatric Illness in Retirement," in *The Retirement Process,* ed. Frances M. Carp. Washington: U. S. Government Printing Office, 1968, pp. 27–41.

Cain, L. S., "Determining the Factors That Affect Rehabilitation," *Journal of the American Geriatrics Society,* 17:595–604, 1969.

Chase, Helen C., "White-Nonwhite Mortality Differentials in the United States," in *Health, Education and Welfare Indicators.* Washington: U. S. Government Printing Office, 1965, pp. 27–36.

Clausen, John A., "Methodological Issues in the Measurement of Mental Health of the Aged," in *Colloquium in Health and Aging of the Population,* eds. Marjorie F. Lowenthal and Ariv Zilli. New York: S. Karger, 1969, pp. 111–127.

Coe, Rodney M. and Elizabeth Barnhill, "Social Participation and Health of the Aged" in *Older People and Their Social World,* eds. Arnold M. Rose and Warren A. Peterson. Philadelphia: F. A. Davis, 1965, pp. 211–223.

Cohen, Burton H., "Family Patterns of Mortality and Life Span," *Quarterly Review of Biology,* 39:130–181, 1964.

Denney, Duane, Delbert M. Kole, and Ruth G. Matarazzo, "The Relationship Between Age and the Number of Symptoms Reported by Patients," *Journal of Gerontology,* 20:50–53, 1965.

Donahue, Wilma, "Rehabilitation of Long-Term Aged Patients," in *Processes of Aging,* eds. Richard H. Williams, Clark Tibbitts, and Wilma Donahue. New York: Atherton Press, 1963, I, 541–565.

Ekblom, B., "Significance of Sociopsychological Factors with Regard to Risk of Death among Elderly Persons," *Acta Psychiatri Scandanavia,* 39:627–633, 1963.

Geltner, Luzer, "Somatic Illness: Prevention and Rehabilitation," in *Colloquium on Health and Aging of the Population,* eds. Marjorie F. Lowenthal and Ariv Zilli. New York: S. Karger, 1969, pp. 76–87.

Haymes, D. E., "Psychological Factors in Rehabilitation of the Elderly," *Gerontologia Clinica,* 11:129–126, 1969.

Kaplan, Jerome A., Caroline S. Ford, and Harry Wain, "Assessing the Impact of a Gerontological Counseling Service on Community Health Resources," *Geriatrics,* 22:150–154, 1967.

Kaplan, Oscar J., ed., *Mental Disorders in Later Life.* Palo Alto, California: Stanford University Press, 1956.

Kay, David W., K. P. Bamish, and Martin Roth, "Old Age Mental Disorders in Newcastle-upon-Tyne, Part I: A Study of Prevalence," *British Journal of Psychiatry,* 110:146–158, 1964.

——, ——, and ——, "Old Age Mental Disorders in Newcastle-upon-Tyne, Part II: A Study of Possible Social and Medical Causes," *British Journal of Psychiatry,* 110:668–682, 1964.

Kutner, Bernard, "Aging and Disability," in *Duke University Council on Gerontology: Proceedings of Seminars, 1961–1965,* ed. Frances C. Jeffers. Durham, North Carolina: Duke University Center for the Study of Aging, 1965, pp. 40–50.

Lawton, Alfred H., "Accidental Injuries to the Aged," *Gerontologist,* 5:(2), 96–100, 1965.

Lawton, M. Powell and Fay G. Lawton, eds., *Mental Impairment in the Aged.* Philadelphia: Philadelphia Geriatrics Center, 1965.

————, "Social Rehabilitation of the Aged: Some Neglected Aspects," *Journal of the American Geriatrics Society,* 16:1346–1363, 1968.

Lowenthal, Marjorie F., "Social Isolation and Mental Illness in Old Age" *American Sociological Review,* 29:54–70, 1964.

————, "Antecedents of Isolation and Mental Illness in Old Age," *Archives of General Psychiatry,* 12:245–254, 1965.

———— et al., *Aging and Mental Disorder in San Francisco.* San Francisco: Jossey-Bass, 1967.

Marden, Parker G. and Robert G. Burnight, "Social Consequences of Physical Impairment in an Aging Population," *Gerontologist,* 9:39–46, 1969.

Metropolitan Life Insurance Company, "Accidental Injury and Death at the Older Ages," *Statistical Bulletin of the Metropolitan Life Insurance Company,* 46:6–8, February, 1965.

————, "Health Characteristics of the Elderly," *Statistical Bulletin of the Metropolitan Life Insurance Company,* 49:2–4, August, 1968.

National Center for Health Statistics, *The Change in the Mortality Trend in the United States.* Washington, D. C.: Government Printing Office, 1964.

————, "Chronic Conditions and Activity Limitation, United States, July, 1961 to June, 1963," *Vital and Health Statistics.* Series 10, Number 17, 1965.

————, "Disability Days, United States, July, 1961 to June, 1962," *Vital and Health Statistics,* Series 10, Number 4, 1963.

Newman, H. F., "The Impact of Medicare on Group Practice Prepayment Plans," *American Journal of Public Health,* 59:629–634, 1969.

Palmore, Erdman and Frances C. Jeffers, "Health Care in a Longitudinal Panel before and after Medicare," *Journal of Gerontology,* 26:532–536, 1971.

Reynolds, Frank W. and Paul C. Barsam, *Adult Health: Services for the Chronically Ill and Aging.* New York: Macmillan Co., 1967.

Rice, Dorothy P. and Barbara S. Cooper, "Medical Care Outlays for Aged and Nonaged Persons, 1966–1968," *Social Security Bulletin,* 32:3–11, September, 1969.

————, Arne Anderson, and Barbara S. Cooper, *Personal Health Care Expenditures of the Aged and Nonaged, Fiscal Years 1966 and 1967.* Washington, D. C.: Department of Health, Education and Welfare, 1968.

Richardson, Ian M., "Occupation and Health," in *Processes of Aging.* eds. Richard H. Williams, Clark Tibbitts, and Wilma Donahue. New York: Atherton Press, 1963, II, 459–477.

Rose, Arnold M., "Physical Health and Mental Outlook Among the Aging," in *Older People and Their Social World,* eds. Arnold M. Rose and Warren A. Peterson. Philadelphia: F. A. Davis, 1965, pp. 201–209.

————, "Mental Health of Normal Older Persons" in *Older People and Their Social World,* eds. Arnold M. Rose and Warren A. Peterson. Philadelphia: F. A. Davis, 1965, pp. 193–199.

Rothenberg, Robert E., *Health in the Later Years.* New York: New American Library, 1964.

Sainsbury, Peter, "Social and Epidemiological Aspects of Suicide with Special Reference to the Aged," in *Processes of Aging,* eds. Richard H. Williams, Clark Tibbitts, and Wilma Donahue. New York: Atherton Press, 1963, II, 153–175.

Shanas, Ethel, "Health Care and Health Services for the Aged," *Gerontologist,* 5:240; 276, 1965.

————, "Measuring the Home Health Needs of the Aged in Five Countries," *Journal of Gerontology,* 26:37–40, 1971.

Spear, Mel, "Paramedical Services for Older Americans," *Journal of the American Geriatrics Society,* 16:1088–1094, 1968.

Szewczuk, Wlodzimierz, "Rehabilitation of the Aged by Means of New Forms of Activity," *Gerontologist,* 6:93–94, 1966.

Travis, Georgia, *Chronic Disease and Disability.* Berkeley, California: University of California Press, 1966.

United States Department of Health, Education, and Welfare, *Health Manpower and Health Facilities, 1970.* Washington, D. C.: U. S. Government Printing Office, 1971.

United States Public Health Service, "Older Persons, Selected Health Characteristics, United States, July, 1957 to June, 1959," *Health Statistics,* Series C, Number 4, 1960.

United States Senate, Special Committee on Aging, *Health Aspects of the Economics of Aging.* Washington, D. C.: U. S. Government Printing Office, 1969.

Van Zonneveld, Robert J., *The Health of the Aged.* Baltimore, Md.: Williams and Wilkins, 1962.

Walker, D. W., "A Study of the Relationships Between Suicide Rates and Age in the U. S. (1914 to 1964)," *Proceedings of the Social Statistics Section,* American Statistical Association, Washington, D. C., 1968, pp. 408–420.

White, E. L. and T. Gordon, "Related Aspects of Health and Aging in the United States," in *Colloquium on Health and Aging of the Population,* eds. Marjorie F. Lowenthal and Ariv Zilli. New York: S. Karger, 1969, pp. 27–44.

World Health Organization, "Mental Health Problems of Aging and the Aged. Sixth Report," *World Health Organization Technical Report Series,* 171: 3–51, 1959.

B. Institutions for the Aged

American Association of Homes for the Aged, *The Social Components of Care.* New York: The Association, 1966.

Bell, Tony, "The Relationship Between Social Involvement and Feeling Old Among Residents in Homes for the Aged," *Journal of Gerontology,* 22:17–22, 1967.

Bennett, Ruth, "The Meaning of Institutional Life," *Gerontologist,* 3:(3, part I), 117–125, 1963.

———— and Lucille Nahemow, "Institutional Totality and Criteria of Social Adjustment in Residences for the Aged," *Journal of Social Issues,* 21:44–76, October, 1965.

Brody, Elaine M., "Follow-Up Study of Applicants and Nonapplicants to a Voluntary Home," *Gerontologist,* 9:187–196, 1969.

———— and Geraldine M. Spark, "Institutionalization of the Aged: A Family Crisis," *Family Process,* 5:76–90, 1966.

Coe, Rodney M., "Self-Conception and Institutionalization," in *Older People and Their Social World,* eds. Arnold M. Rose and Warren A. Peterson. Philadelphia: F. A. Davis, 1965, pp. 225–243.

Donahue, Wilma, "Rehabilitation of Long-Term Aged Patients," in *Processes of Aging,* eds. Richard H. Williams, Clark Tibbitts, and Wilma Donahue. New York: Atherton Press, 1963, I, 541–565.

Droller, H., "Institutionalisation," in *Colloquium on Health and Aging of the Population,* eds. Marjorie F. Lowenthal and Ariv Zilli. New York: S. Karger, 1969, pp. 103–110.

Gelfand, Donald E., "Visiting Patterns and Social Adjustment in an Old Age Home," *Gerontologist,* 8:272–275, 1968.

Henry, Jules, *Culture Against Man.* New York: Alfred A. Knopf, 1965, pp. 391–474.

Jacobs, R. H., "One-Way Street: An Intimate View of Adjustment to a Home for the Aged," *Gerontologist,* 9:(4, part I), 268–275, 1969.

Lieberman, M. A., "Institutionalization of the Aged; Effects on Behavior," *Journal of Gerontology,* 24:330–340, 1969.

National Center for Health Statistics, "Characteristics of Residents in Institutions for the Aged and Chronically Ill, U. S., April–June, 1963," *Vital and Health Statistics,* Washington, D. C.: U. S. Government Printing Office, 1965.

Townsend, Peter, *The Last Refuge.* New York: Rutledge, 1964.

Wessen, A. F., "Some Sociological Characteristics of Long-Term Care," *Gerontologist,* 8:72–75, 1968.

8

Finances

Financial security is extremely important because it largely determines the range of alternatives people have in adjusting to aging. Older people with adequate financial resources can afford to travel, to go shopping, to entertain friends, to seek the best in health care, and to keep a presentable wardrobe and household. Older people without money can do none of these things, and herein lies perhaps the single most demoralizing fact of life for most older people, for most older people are poor.

The median income for people sixty-five or over was $1,828 in 1967. If the poverty level is taken as $3,000 for married couples and $2,000 for single individuals, then *60 percent of the older people in the United States are poor.*[1]

In this chapter the financial aspects of growing old are detailed, first by establishing what is meant by a minimum financial *need,* and then by examining the financial resources of older people in relation to this need. Changes in level of living that occur as one grows old and the prospects for the future financial security of older people are also considered.

The Financial Need

It is difficult to determine the financial needs of older people in general because the older population varies so. Some older people own their homes, have their own cars, or have financial assets to supplement their retirement

---

[1] This chapter is based primarily on income data from the United States. Shanas and her associates found that the relative income deprivation of older people was typical of industrial societies. The only significant divergence from the U. S. pattern was in Denmark where the *average* was about the same but the range of the inequality around this average was somewhat smaller. (See Ethel Shanas, *et al., Older People in Three Industrial Societies* [New York: Atherton Press, 1968].)

incomes. Others have neither assets nor income. Certainly no single "financial requirement" could fit the needs of both groups. Also the situation is markedly different for couples than for single individuals.

Epstein has estimated that a "modest but adequate" budget for older people would be about $2,100 a year for a single older person and $2,900 for a retired couple.[2] Steiner and Dorfman have estimated that home ownership is worth about $400 per year to an older couple and about $225 to a single individual.[3] All of these estimates are for older people living in cities; these figures would probably be somewhat lower for rural dwellers. The picture we get in terms of financial need is thus as follows:

Table 12. Annual Financial Requirement, Couples and Single Individuals Age sixty-five and Over: United States, 1969.

	Couples	Individuals
Own Home Free and Clear	$2,500	$1,875
Do Not Own Home	$2,900	$2,100

All estimates of this variety tend to fall short of the actual requirements because they do not include any slack for "contingencies." For example, slightly more than one out of every ten older people will end up in a hospital this year and the average stay will be *fourteen days.* The cost of this unhappy event will run about $700 for the hospital alone. It is not difficult to see what such an expenditure would do to an annual budget of $2,000. Even if the individual has hospitalization insurance (and only about half of the older population does), and Medicare pays part of the cost, the individual will still have to cover about half of the cost of his health care himself.[4] Thus, the figures given in Table 12 can be considered conservative.

By these standards, over 40 percent of older couples and over 70 per-

---

[2] Matilda W. Riley and Ann Foner, *Aging and Society.* Vol. I, *An Inventory of Research Findings.* (New York: Russell Sage Foundation, 1968), p. 104. Figures inflated to reflect 1969 value of the dollar.

[3] Peter O. Steiner and Robert Dorfman, *The Economic Status of the Aged* (Berkeley, Calif.: University of California Press, 1957). Estimate adjusted to reflect 1969 value of the dollar.

[4] In 1966, government was paying 24.8 percent of health care costs, private insurance was paying 23.4 percent, and philanthropic agencies were paying 1.9 percent. Private individuals were paying the rest (49.9 percent).

cent of single older individuals have financial resources below the "modest but adequate" level.

Income   Money comes from two major sources, income and assets. Figure 8 shows the sources of aggregate *income* for older people.

From the figure it would appear that earnings are the major source, followed closely by Social Security (technically called Old Age, Survivors, Disability and Health Insurance).

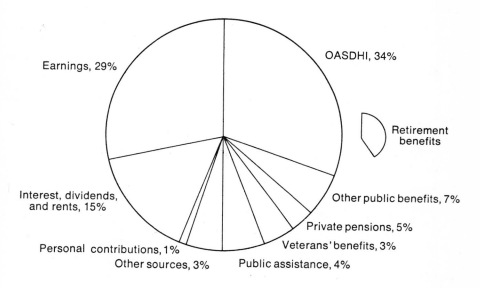

Figure 8. Shares of Aggregate Money Income of Persons sixty-five and Over (including their spouses), by source, United States, 1967.
Source: Lenore A. Bixby, "Income of People Aged 65 and Older," *Social Security Bulletin,* April, 1970, p. 10.

These data are somewhat misleading, however, since only three out of eighteen million older people are in the labor force. The percentage of the aggregate income accounted for by earnings is inflated by the fact that older people who work have average incomes much higher than those who do not work.

For the fifteen million who do not work, Social Security is the major source of income. In 1967 Social Security paid a median annual amount of $2,187 to married couples, $1,368 to single men, and $1,044 to single women; considerably less than the "modest but adequate" figures given above. In many cases Public Assistance, technically called Aid for the Aged, is used to help fill the gaps left by Social Security. Over four-fifths of the older people in the United States collect Social Security, Aid for the Aged, or both, and for about half the older people in America these are the *only* sources of income.

Dismal as the income picture is for older people in general, it is even worse for older Negroes. In 1968, the median annual income for white older males was $2,789, but for Negro older males it was $1,470! About one-third of white older men had annual incomes of less than $2,000, but nearly two-thirds of Negro older men had incomes this low. For older females the situation was even worse, with 78 percent of the white and 90 percent of Negro older females having annual incomes of less than $2,000.[5] Older Mexican-Americans are similarly worse off in relation to the majority of older people.[6]

As a source of income, Social Security has the advantages of being as reliable as insurance (which is what it is technically supposed to be) yet flexible, since the benefits can be increased by Congressional action. Historically, standard insurance has provided *fixed* payments that tended to be eroded by inflation, while Social Security payments have tended to be periodically *increased* to offset the effects of inflation. The disadvantages of Social Security include the fact that adjustments needed to offset inflation often lag behind inflation itself and, more important, the fact that the level of payments is very inadequate as a sole source of income.

For those older people who work (about one-sixth of the total), the situation is quite different. In 1967, the average income of married couples who worked and did not collect Social Security was $6,470 per year as compared with $3,480 per year for couples who received Social Security benefits. Obviously the financial picture is better for those who work, but older people seldom have much choice about retiring, particularly after age seventy.

Interest, dividends, and rents form another large source of the aggregate income for older people, but here the proportion who do the receiving is very small. While two-thirds of older Americans report income from this source, the median amount is less than $200 per year. For most older people, this is an unimportant source of income.

Few older people are receiving private pensions—only 12 percent in 1967—and only about 5 percent of the aggregate income of older people comes from this source. This is largely because private pension plans are a relatively new development. Most of the older people who are presently retired did not work under pension plans or, if they did, they did not work under them long enough to receive any significant benefits. This picture may

---

[5] Donald P. Kent, "The Negro Aged," *Gerontologist,* 11: (1, part II), pp. 49–50, 1971.

[6] Joan W. Moore, "Mexican-Americans," *Gerontologist,* 11: (1, part II), p. 31, 1971.

gradually improve as the number of workers covered by private pension plans increases and the pensions of those retiring increase. Nevertheless, private pensions are not a significant source of income for older people now, nor are they likely to become so in the near future, except as a supplement to Social Security.

Schulz[7] concludes that private pensions grew primarily out of a need for additional retirement income to supplement Social Security. A dramatic increase in new private pension plans covering large numbers of workers took place shortly after the 1947 Supreme Court ruling that pensions were a proper issue for collective bargaining. Feelings of social obligation on the part of industry, wage stabilization policies associated with the Korean War, favorable tax treatment for industries setting up pensions, and the development and expansion of negotiated multi-employer pension plans combined to open up coverage to millions of workers. However, a slow-down in rates of growth in private pension coverage since 1960 indicates that those segments of the labor force still not covered by private pensions are having trouble securing coverage. The most accessible groups are already covered, and the next likely target, small business, will probably remain an area of the economy with relatively poor access to private pensions.

Even for those covered by private pensions there are problems. For example, employees of Studebaker had what they thought was an excellent pension plan; but the company went out of business before the pension fund was filled. The result was that those over sixty-five received a reduced pension, and those not yet sixty-five lost the money they had paid in.

Another problem is nontransferability. In most private plans, retirement credits cannot be transferred to another plan. This means that if the worker changes jobs, he stands to lose all of his retirement credits because he can never accumulate enough to entitle him to a pension.

These and similar problems led one Labor Department official to state: "In all too many cases the pension promise shrinks to this: 'If you remain in good health and stay with the same company until you are sixty-five years old, and if the company is still in business, and if your department has not been abolished, and if you haven't been laid off for too long a period, and if there is enough money in the fund, and if that money has been prudently managed, you will get a pension.' "[8]

The major virtue of private pension plans is held to be their flexibility, their ability to deal with the unique situation of the particular worker and his

---

[7] James H. Schulz, "Pension Aspects of the Economics of Aging: Present and Future Roles of Private Pensions," a special report to the Special Committee on Aging, U. S. Senate, January, 1970.

[8] *Ibid.*, p. 39.

particular company. This is an especially attractive feature for managers who use pension plans as a tool in meeting labor problems. Yet private pensions also serve the public interest by providing income maintenance for older people.

Schulz concludes that the advantages of flexibility must be weighed against what it does to the interests of the employee and of the general public. "For example, is it in the employee's and public interest that a large proportion of workers who build up credits under private pension plans never qualify for an eventual pension because of insufficient periods of service with any one company? Is it in the employee's and public interest that the final pensions earned by short-term workers are so much less than those earned by career employees because there are few provisions for transferring and accumulating pension credits from a host of jobs? Is it in the employee's and public interest that private funds be permitted to promise the payment of future benefits without providing sufficient guarantees that the money will be there when needed? In short, to what extent can it be assumed that pension plan provisions geared to meet the special problems of individual firms are also of maximum benefit to the worker, the public, and the economy?"[9]

Contrary to the popular stereotype, only about 1 percent of the aggregate income of older people comes from cash contributions from relatives. Since many states have laws requiring children to support needy parents, this small figure would seem to suggest that these laws are not being enforced. Older people themselves feel in general that the government rather than their children should bear the burden of supporting them.

Hidden by the above data, however, is a small but significant number of older people who live with relatives, and who have extremely low incomes. It is this latter factor more than any other which brings older people to move in with relatives.

Overall, the income picture for older Americans is not bright. Compulsory retirement policies plus longer life mean that a progressively smaller proportion of older people will be able to stay in the labor force. Social Security benefits have increased, but at about the same pace as the cost of living. Under present levels of Social Security those who have no other source of income can do little more than manage to stay alive.

Assets

Many would argue that income need not support older people because they have other financial assets that can be used for this purpose.

---

[9] *Ibid.,* p. 49.

The rationale here is that older people should gradually liquidate their personal assets to supplement their money incomes.

Financial assets are things like automobiles, homes, insurance policies (only the kind with cash value), stocks, bonds, and cash savings. Such assets can provide housing and directly contribute to income via rents, interest, and dividends. Perhaps the most important points about older people's assets are the following:

> On the average, older people, with their years of asset accumulation behind them, tend to own more and owe less than younger people (under fifty-five). Yet assets tend to be correlated with income, so that those families with the highest incomes are most likely to have substantial assets; whereas those with the lowest incomes are least likely to have any assets.[10]

Equity in a home is the most common asset among older people, yet more than half own *no* equity in a home. Among unmarried older people this proportion rises to over two-thirds; for older couples it is slightly less than half. Equity in a home is important in determining the adequacy of receipts *only* if the home is owned free and clear. Mortgage payments look no different from rent in a monthly budget.

Among older people home equity tends to be modest, and savings in rent tend to be partially offset by the cost of insurance, taxes, and upkeep. As we noted earlier, home ownership is worth only $400 per year in out-of-pocket costs.

Because home equity is not readily converted into cash, it makes a poor contingency reserve. This is perhaps its greatest disadvantage. Many older people might be better off to pay the extra 30 percent for rental housing in order to be able to convert their assets into usable cash. Certainly if financial assets are viewed as a means of expanding the alternatives for adjusting to aging, home ownership can be more constraining than liberating.

Once home equity is accounted for, the proportion of older people with additional assets drops. Home equity aside, well over half of all older people have less than $1,000 in assets, and these are the same people who have incomes below the poverty level.

Thus, the argument that older people can use their liquid assets to supplement their incomes is not valid, particularly for those older people who need supplemental incomes the most.

---

[10] Riley and Foner, *op. cit.*, p. 85.

Level of Living

At this point an examination of spending patterns may be useful to illustrate the practical impact of income on level of living. Table 13 shows the expenditures for various items at various age and income intervals.

First let us compare people aged forty-five to fifty-four having $5,000 per year income with those seventy-five or over having $1,000 per year. This comparison comes closest to the facts of life, since well over half

Table 13. Consumer Expenditures for Households by Age and Annual Income of Head: United States, 1960

| Item | Income of $1,000 | | Income of $5,000 | |
	Age 45–54	Age 75+	Age 45–54	Age 75+
Food	311	389	1460	1615
Housing	224	316	755	750
Household				
Operations	43	54	215	235
Furnishings	46	26	340	295
Clothing	81	41	615	560
Transportation	89	38	665	565
Medical Care	73	73	245	370
Personal Care	20	17	115	100
Recreation	27	21	280	290
Miscellaneous	85	25	310	220

Source: Adapted from Sidney Goldstein, *Consumption Patterns of the Aged* (Philadelphia: Univ. of Pennsylvania Press, 1960).

of those in the first age group have incomes of $5,000 or more, and well over half of those in the second have incomes of $1,000 or less.

The difference in terms of food is staggering. The younger household with the larger income spends nearly four times as much on food as the older household with the lower income. This cannot be attributed to a larger household at a younger age, either, since the older household with the higher income spends *over* four times as much on food as its poorer counterpart. For a lot of people this means a dramatic decline in the level of nutrition between age fifty and age seventy-five. This fact has particular relevance to the health of older people, since malnutrition is a significant contributing factor in disease. With an average of $32.42 per month to spend on food, the older poor household is bound to concentrate on foods with more starch and less protein or vitamins than it would buy if $121.66 per month were available for food.

Going down the line, the average older household has half as much for housing, one-quarter as much for household operations, one-thirteenth as much for furnishings and recreation, one-fifteenth as much for clothing, one-seventeenth as much for transportation, one-third as much for medical care, and one-seventh as much for personal care as has the average younger household. Those are among the most important "facts of life" that confront many older people.

Other comparisons are also instructive. For example, expenditures within income groups are more consistent than are expenditures within age groups. While expenditures do change with age, these changes are relatively minor. Changes in income obviously have more important results.

Medical care is a good case in point. In the $1,000 income group the health expenditure is a consistent $73 across the age groups, while in the higher income group the figure increases from $245 to $370 with increasing age. This is a good example of the type of constraint low income places on the alternatives people have in adjusting to aging. Although all people suffer some decline in health as they get older, those with low incomes are unable to increase the level of medical attention to compensate for this, while those with higher incomes can. In practical terms, those with money can afford the option of better health, while those without it cannot.

In summary, then, we find that lowered income produces critical deficiencies in level of living, particularly with regard to food and medical care. All of the basic needs—food, clothing, and shelter—tend to become more difficult to meet with increasing age. At a time in life when expenditures for recreation naturally tend to go up, the older poor are forced to reduce expenditures for recreation. What kind of recreation can be bought for $21 *per year?* It hardly allows for maintaining a TV set, much less buying one. In addition, most older people have no other assets to fall back on. The result is a level of financial support that barely meets physical needs and leaves psychological needs almost totally neglected.

The Future

The prospects for the future are not encouraging. The incomes of older people have increased over time, but *relative* to the general rise in income throughout the country, they have remained at a standstill. Little or no progress has been made in bringing retirement incomes more closely into line with pre-retirement levels.

In the future we can expect to see a continuation of the trend toward early retirement. This will reduce even further the number of older people in the labor force and cut aggregate income even further. We can expect that earnings will occupy a progressively less important place as a source of income for older people.

Social Security, on the other hand, stands to become even more important as a source of income in the later years. As coverage becomes more complete, Social Security plus Medicare will no doubt become the leading financial resources for older people. In practical terms, these programs offer the greatest promise of an adequate income, particularly if the level of minimum benefits can be raised above the bare subsistence level, and if cost-of-living increases can be made automatic.

Private pension plans will become increasingly important as a source of supplementary income in retirement. Estimates for 1980 indicate that by that time 25 to 30 percent of older people will be receiving payments from this source. In addition, over the years the paid-in shares of private pension holders will probably result in a significantly higher average benefit than is the case now.

Old Age Assistance will probably be gradually eliminated as an income source for older people. As Social Security and Medicare assume an increasingly larger share of the public benefits, Old Age Assistance can be expected to decline accordingly, even though many older people's incomes will still fall far short of their needs.

Compounding the problem is the fact that many older people will be relying on fixed or semi-fixed (OASDHI) sources. For these people inflation would be disastrous. An individual can currently expect to live about twenty years after retirement. In that length of time inflation can significantly reduce the purchasing power of a dollar. For example, a couple with an income of $2,400 per year could buy more than twice as much in 1940 as they could in 1960.

Income from interest, rents, and dividends can be expected to increase, but the proportion of older people getting more than a token payment from these sources is apt to remain quite small.

Conclusion

As people grow old, their income drops. Even before retirement, many older people need some sort of supplementary income. At retirement, income usually drops by 50 percent or more, and during the years that follow, it deteriorates even further.

Income for older people comes primarily from earnings, assets, and Social Security. Only one-sixth of the older population has earnings, and only a very small proportion has any appreciable income from assets. Social Security provides the only income of any consequence to the vast majority of older people. As a result, over 60 percent of the older people in the United States are poor.

Possible strategies for attacking this problem include opening up more employment opportunities for older people, encouraging people to save more, expanding private pension coverage, and expanding Social Security. While all of these strategies can be used to some extent, it is probably fair to say that the only one that holds genuine promise for the vast majority of older people is the development of more adequate Social Security benefits.

The primary importance of financial resources to older people lies in the influence of money on the range of alternatives an individual has in attempting to adjust to aging. For most older people the financial factor sharply limits the available options even in such basic areas as food and medical care. For most older people, poverty is like a vise—it holds them down and leaves them no room to maneuver. In this regard freedom from work and family is more than offset by the constraints of poverty. The end result is often a hopeless, stifling existence in place of what might be the most satisfying period of human life.

Bibliography

Aaron, Henry, "Social Security: International Comparisons," in *Studies in the Economics of Income Maintenance,* ed. Otto Eckstein. Washington, D. C.: Brookings Institution, 1967, pp. 13–48.

Beresford, John C. and Alice M. Rivlin, "Privacy, Poverty, and Old Age," *Demography,* 3:247–258, 1966.

Bernstein, Merton C., *The Future of Private Pensions.* New York: Free Press, 1964.

Blackburn, John O., "Pensions, the National Income, and the National Wealth," in *Employment, Income, and Retirement Problems of the Aged,* ed. Juanita M. Kreps. Durham, North Carolina: Duke University Press, 1963, pp. 178–198.

Brady, Dorothy S., *Age and Income Distribution.* Washington, D. C.: U. S. Government Printing Office, 1965.

Brennan, Michael J. *et al., The Economics of Age.* New York: W. W. Norton & Co., 1967.

Brinker, Paul A., *Economic Insecurity and Social Security.* New York: Appleton-Century-Crofts, 1968.

Carroll, John J., *Alternative Methods of Financing Old-Age, Survivors, and Disability Insurance.* Ann Arbor, Michigan: University of Michigan Press, 1960.

Chandler, Suzannah, *Home Maintenance and Repair Program for the Older Poor.* New York: National Council on the Aged, 1968.

Chen, Y., "Economic Poverty; The Special Case of the Aged," *Gerontologist,* 6:39–45, 1966.

———, "Low Income, Early Retirement, and Tax Policy," *Gerontologist,* 6:35–38, 1966.

Cole, Dorothy and John E. G. Utting, *The Economic Circumstances of Old People.* London: Codicate Press, 1962.

Corson, John J. and John W. McConnell, *Economic Needs of Older People.* New York: Twentieth Century Fund, 1956.

David, Z. M., "Old-Age, Survivors, and Disability Insurance: Twenty-five Years of Progress," *Industrial and Labor Relations Review,* 14:10–23, October, 1960.

Dyer, J. K., "Private Pension Legislation—Existing, Pending, and Proposed," *Pension and Welfare News,* 4:24–27, April, 1968.

Ferber, Robert, "A Study of the Comparative Financial Position of Older People in the United States," in *Age with a Future,* ed. P. From Hansen. Copenhagen: Munksgaard, 1964, pp. 526–544.

Ferguson, Elizabeth, *Income, Resources and Needs of Older People: Selected Supplementary References.* New York: National Council on the Aging, 1965.

Gordon, Margaret S., "Aging and Income Security," in *Handbook of Social Gerontology,* ed. Clark Tibbitts. Chicago: University of Chicago Press, 1960, pp. 208–260.

———, "Income Security Programs and the Propensity to Retire," in *Processes of Aging,* eds. Richard H. Williams, Clark Tibbitts, and Wilma Donahue. New York: Atherton Press, 1963, II, 436–458.

Greenfield, Margaret, *Property Tax Exemptions for Senior Citizens.* Berkeley, California: University of California Institute for Governmental Studies, 1966.

Kreps, Juanita M., ed., *Employment, Income, and Retirement Problems of the Aged.* Durham, North Carolina: Duke University Press, 1963.

Krislov, Joseph, "Four Issues in Income Maintenance for the Aged During the 1970's," *Social Service Review,* 42:335–343, 1968.

Lamale, Helen H. and Ewan Clague, "Standard Budgets for Elderly Persons," in *Processes of Aging,* eds. Richard H. Williams, Clark Tibbitts and Wilma Donahue. New York: Atherton Press, 1963, II, 526–542.

Lewis, Doris K., "Guaranteed Income for the Aged in Belgium," *Social Security Bulletin,* 32:30–32, September, 1969.

Lubove, Roy, *The Struggle for Social Security: 1900–1935.* Cambridge, Massachusetts: Harvard University Press, 1968.

Merriam, Ida C., "Implications of Technological Change for Income," in *Technology, Manpower and Retirement Policy,* ed. Juanita M. Kreps. New York: World Publishing Co., 1966, pp. 166–174.

Morgan, James N., "Measuring the Economic Status of the Aged," *International Economic Review.* 6:1–17, 1965.

Murray, Roger F., *Economic Aspects of Pensions: A Summary Report.* New York: Columbia University Press, 1968.

Palmore, Erdman, "Work Experience and Earnings of the Aged in 1962: Findings of the 1963 Survey of the Aged," *Social Security Bulletin,* 27:3–14, June, 1964.

Polinsky, Ella J., "The Position of Women in the Social Security System," *Social Security Bulletin,* 32:3–19, July, 1969.

Schottland, C. I., "Poverty and Income Maintenance for the Aged," in *Poverty in America,* ed. Margaret S. Gordon. San Francisco: Chandler Publishing Company, 1965, pp. 227–239.

Schulz, James H., "Some Economics of Aged Home Ownership," *Gerontologist,* 7:73–74, 1967.

———, *The Economic Status of the Retired Aged in 1980: Simulated Projections.* Washington, D. C.: U. S. Government Printing Office, 1968.

———, *Pension Aspects of the Economics of Aging: Present and Future Roles of Private Pensions.* Washington, D. C.: U. S. Senate, Special Committee on Aging, 1970.

Shulman, Harry, "Beneficiaries with Minimum Benefits; Their Characteristics in 1967," *Social Security Bulletin,* 32:3–20, October, 1969.

Steiner, Peter O. and Robert Dorfman, *The Economic Status of the Aged.* Berkeley, California: University of California Press, 1957.

Tissue, Thomas, "Old Age, Poverty and the Central City," *Aging and Human Development*, 2:235–248, 1971.

Turnbull, John G. *et al., The Changing Faces of Economic Insecurity*. Minneapolis, Minnesota: University of Minnesota, 1966.

United States Bureau of the Census, "Income of the Elderly in 1963," *Current Population Reports*, Series P-60, Number 46, 1965.

————, "Characteristics of the Low-Income Population, 1970," *Current Population Reports*, Series P-60, Number 81, 1971.

United States Department of Labor, *Retired Couple's Budget*. Washington, D. C.: U. S. Government Printing Office, 1966.

United States Senate, Special Committee on Aging, *Economics of Aging: Toward a Full Share of Abundance*. Washington, D. C.: U. S. Government Printing Office, 1969.

Wedderburn, Dorothy, "Cross-National Studies of Income Adequacy," in *Methodology Problems in Cross-National Studies in Aging*, eds. Ethel Shanas and John Madge. New York: S. Karger, 1968, pp. 61–74.

————, "Economic Circumstances of Old People," *Gerontologia Clinica*, 7:69–77, 1965.

Wendell, Richard F., "The Economic Status of the Aged," *Gerontologist*, 8:(2, part II), 32–36, 1968.

Williams, Walter and James M. Lyday, "Income Sufficiency and the Aged Poor," *Quarterly Review of Economics and Business*, 8:19–25, 1968.

9

Retirement

Retirement is the separation of an individual from a work role, a role performed for pay. While people can indeed give up such nonpaying positions as scoutmaster, church deacon, or volunteer worker, the term *retirement* is generally reserved for separation from those positions that bring monetary rewards.

Retirement has also been used to describe "the people who are living out the last ten or twenty years of their lives without working for a living."[1] It has also been said that retirement is socially approved unemployment.[2] A more comprehensive definition states that:

> Retirement represents the creation in modern society of an economically nonproductive role for large numbers of persons whose labor is not considered essential or necessary for the functioning of the economic order . . . retirement is the prescribed transition from the position of an economically active person to the position of an economically nonactive person in accordance with the norms through which society defines and determines the nature of this change.[3]

People may approach retirement gradually, reducing their commitments slowly; or they may retire suddenly and without preparation. Regardless of the individual pattern, however, retirement involves changes that somehow result in the separation of the individual from a work role for which he received pay.

Retirement marks the end of what is generally thought to be a close

[1] Eugene A. Friedmann and Robert J. Havighurst, *The Meaning of Work and Retirement* (Chicago: University of Chicago Press, 1954), p. 1.

[2] *Ibid.,* p. 185.

[3] Harold L. Orbach, "Normative Aspects of Retirement," in *Sociological and Psychological Aspects of Aging,* eds. Clark Tibbitts and Wilma Donahue (New York: Columbia University Press, 1962), p. 53.

relationship between the kind of work an individual does and the kind of life style and livelihood he enjoys. This relationship results, of course, from the fact that for most people in American society, the only fully acceptable way of getting money is by working for it. Americans come to identify a person's work with his style of life, and this way of assessing a person's status is usually correct, for job usually determines income and income sets limits on life style.

Another factor in the relationship between man and his work is the idea that work can be pursued as an end in itself, purely for the satisfaction of doing a workmanlike job. This idea springs from the notion that work can give man his greatest opportunities for creation, and in this way can become his entire life. Mills incorporates these ideas into his concept of craftsmanship.

> Craftsmanship as a fully idealized model of work gratification involves six major features: There is no ulterior motive in work other than the product being made and the processes of its creation. The details of daily work are meaningful because they are not detached in the worker's mind from the product of the work. The worker is free to control his own working action. The craftsman is thus able to learn from his work; and to use and develop his capacities and skills in its prosecution. There is no split of work and play, or work and culture. The craftsman's way of livelihood determines and infuses his entire mode of living.[4]

Mills also says,

> Work may be a mere source of livelihood, or the most significant part of one's inner life; it may be experienced as expiation or as exuberant expression of self; as bounden duty, or as the development of man's universal nature. Neither love nor hatred of work is inherent in man, or inherent in any given line of work. For work has no intrinsic meaning.[5]

The Link Between Man and His Work

Understanding retirement thus involves understanding the nature of the link between man and his work. It can be said with some certainty that this relationship has changed over the years. In the days of the medieval guilds the idea of work as a way of life was generally accepted. Not many people lived to become old in those days, but those who did continued to

---

[4] C. W. Mills, *White Collar* (New York: Oxford University Press, 1956), p. 220.
[5] *Ibid.*, p. 215.

work until they grew too feeble or died. Since work was a major satisfaction in life, it was engaged in as long as possible. Then too, there were no provisions for gaining income in any other way. The industrial revolution, assembly line production, and automation have made some important changes in this picture.

To begin with, our productive system has increased in power to the point where relatively few people are required to produce the nation's increasing output. This was made possible largely by the switch from low energy power converters such as animals, wind, and water to high energy converters such as steam and electricity. Also, the demographic revolution reduced death rates and prolonged life. The eventual result was a significant proportion of old people in the population. Declining birth rates meant a smaller proportion of young dependents to support, and this opened up the possibility of supporting older dependents.

The rise of industrial systems of production increased the need for planning and coordination within the economic system. Mechanisms such as the corporation and the bureaucracy were introduced into the economic system and gradually became dispersed throughout society. Government bureaucracy grew to become the political counterpart of the economic corporation, and once the state became a large-scale organization, it was capable of pooling the nation's resources and allowing a segment of society to be supported in retirement. It was thus no accident that the first retirement program, inaugurated in 1810, consisted of pensions for civil service workers in England. America's failure to introduce civil service pensions until 1920 can be partly explained by the slow development of our national government.

The rise of industrialism brought with it urbanization and extensive physical mobility. These two factors combined to weaken the traditional ties to family and local community that had been the source of a great many different kinds of services. These trends resulted in a redefinition of the relationship between the individual and the government. At the same time, the wage system was putting an end to the traditional economic functions of the family. All of these trends combined to increase individualism in the relationship between the person and society.

The Evolution and Institutionalization of Retirement

Accordingly, the link between man and his work came to be separated from his political and family life. One important result was to reduce the amount of cohesion that people could gain in their lives through work. Another was that with the new relation between the individual and the state, the stage was set for establishing an institutionalized *right* to support in one's old age. This is how Social Security came about, and with its introduction the institution of retirement came of age in the United States. As it has continued to mature, the concept of retirement has come to embody the idea that by virtue of a long-term contribution to the growth and prosperity of society, its individual members earn the *right* to a share of the nation's prosperity in their later years without having to work for it. Thus, the concept of retirement included the right to at least a partial continuance of *income* without the necessity of work. The idea that the right must be earned is related to the fact that retirement is reserved for only older *workers*.

The foregoing factors constitute the social evolution and justification for retirement. There is, however, also a rationale for retirement that assumes that the older worker is no longer capable of doing his job, and it is this rationale which forms the basis for the compulsory retirement policies that now pervade society.

The Retirement Concept

Before examining retirement in detail, it might be useful to refine the concept. Retirement can be viewed as an event, as a process, or as a social role. Viewing retirement as an event focuses attention on the actual point of separation, but this point is not always clear-cut. Many people leave one job only to take up another—or only to find that they cannot get another. Operationally, retirement as an event is probably best defined in terms of the point at which the individual separates himself or is separated from a job and has no *intent* to seek another job.

Focusing on the point of separation, however, produces a somewhat artificial picture of the nature of retirement. Retirement is not usually an all-or-nothing phenomenon with two states: retired or not retired. Instead, it tends to be a continuous *process* that begins when the individual recognizes that some day he will leave the work force, and ends when he leaves it for good. In between there are gradual stages of withdrawal. Considering this aspect of retirement means concentrating on preparation for retirement, attitudes toward retirement, conditions leading to retirement—including retirement policies, and adjustment to retirement.

Finally, it is possible to view retirement as a position in society with rights and duties accompanying it, just as they accompany such positions as child, mother, or judge. Viewed in these terms, retirement often appears to be what E. W. Burgess called "the roleless role." That is, retirement is definitiely a position in society, but—as is not true of most other positions—there is little agreement about the behavior that *should be* associated with being retired. If adjustment to retirement is likened to becoming socialized into a social role, then the lack of anticipatory socialization and the difficulties of learning the role "on-the-job" become significant factors to be examined. Also it is necessary to consider the *consequences* of the change in role from worker to retired person.

The relationship among these various ways of looking at retirement may be easier to understand if presented graphically.

Figure 9. The Retirement Process

In this chapter retirement will be examined from each of these perspectives. The relationship between the job and the individual is discussed, as are the ways in which changes in this relationship influence both the individual and society. The chapter also discusses the future of retirement.

Retirement as Process

As a process, retirement begins when the individual recognizes that some day he will retire. Attitudes toward retirement and preparations for retirement are two factors which greatly influence the pre-retirement segment of the total process.

How younger people view the prospect of retirement has a bearing on how they assess their retired friends and, more importantly perhaps, on how they fare when retirement comes. In a real sense, one's attitudes about retirement can become a self-fulfilling prophecy; that is, the older person who looks forward to enjoying retirement is much more likely to do so than someone who dreads it.

In general, people's ideas about retirement seem to be vague but favorable. Since they know very little about its realities, younger adults are more favorably disposed toward retirement than those who are approaching retirement age. Most adults expect to retire (less than 10 percent do not), and most of them expect to retire *before* age sixty. Only a very few say they dread retirement.

Generally the individual's attitude toward retirement is closely allied to his financial situation. The higher the expected retirement income, the more favorable the attitude. About two-thirds of working adults envision no financial troubles in retirement, although most expect retirement to reduce their incomes by 50 percent from their preretirement levels.

The relationship between income, education, and occupation on the one hand and attitudes toward retirement on the other is complex.

People with high incomes realisticially expect to be financially secure in retirement, although they tend to estimate their income requirements at a level substantially below their present incomes. People with college education are more likely than others to plan an early retirement, and those at higher occupation levels, with the exception of professionals, executives, and government officials, tend to see retirement more favorably than people in lower occupational groups.

Workers at the higher occupation and education levels not only have higher earnings and more favorable attitudes toward retirement, but they also find their jobs more interesting and in actual practice are less prone to retire.[6] Those who feel they achieved what they wanted in life are very likely to favor retirement, but those who still feel *committed* to their work seldom seek retirement, although they may not be antagonistic toward it.

Those at lower occupational levels have less income and anticipate more financial insecurity in retirement. These people do not favor retirement. Notice that here the question is money. Apparently, few people at the lower occupational levels continue to work because they love their jobs.

At the middle occupational level, positive orientation toward retirement is at its peak. These people anticipate sufficient retirement income and at the same time have no lasting commitment toward the job.

At the upper occupational level the picture is mixed. Income is no problem. The only factor which produces attitudes against retirement appears to be commitment to work. In terms of proportions, the evidence indicates that more than half of the people who occupy upper-level occupations have a high work commitment.

Age is also related to attitudes toward retirement. The older the worker gets, the more likely he is to dread retirement. This is largely due to the fact that with increasing age the proportion of workers that anticipate financial difficulties in retirement increases. That finances are all-important in the relationship between age and attitude toward retirement is illustrated by the fact that if adequate income could be assured, the proportion who

---

[6]Matilda W. Riley and Ann Foner, *Aging and Society,* Vol. I, *An Inventory of Research Findings.* (New York: Russell Sage Foundation, 1968), p. 445.

would retire increases steadily with age from twenty-one to sixty-four.[7]

Overall, except for a relatively large proportion of those who occupy upper-level occupations, retirement appears to be attractive to most people, provided that they have some assurance of maintaining an adequate income.

Retirement Preparation

Since almost everyone expects to retire, it may be useful to examine the planning and preparation that precedes the event. Very few people make plans for retirement, and very few are exposed to retirement counseling programs. Yet favorable attitudes toward retirement are associated with planning retirement activities, company counseling, personal discussions of retirement, and exposure to news media presentations about retirement. It would appear, then, that some type of anticipatory program is needed.

That retirement involves a change in position, and that one of the elements of this change is learning what to expect, has already been established. *Socialization* is the technical term for the process whereby people learn the attitudes, values, beliefs, knowledge, and skills that allow them to become more or less able members of society. Socialization can mean learning an orientation, or a particular pattern of behavior, or a *manner* of acting. Socialization may also involve discarding old ways and learning new ones.

Much socialization takes place in childhood, but obviously it would not be possible or even desirable to teach a child to fill all of the roles he will play throughout his entire life. Therefore much socialization also takes place *after* childhood. It can be anticipatory or concurrent; anticipatory socialization is the type related to preparation for retirement. Just as the child learns to be a mother by playing with dolls, an adult may learn *in advance* how to retire.

Perhaps the most important facet of any counseling program should be a very early exposure to the facts of life concerning retirement income. Some employers or unions will be able to point with pride to programs providing a retirement income high enough to meet the individual's needs. Others will have to spell out the shortcomings of their programs and the steps individual workers can take to guarantee their own financial security in retirement. Professional associations should also make it a point to provide realistic retirement information to their members, particularly to those just entering the profession. It is imperative for the individual to know as

---

[7] *Ibid.*

soon as possible precisely where he stands with regard to retirement income. For example, many younger workers will receive only Social Security upon retirement; they do not know specifically what benefits they will receive; they only feel vaguely that Social Security will somehow take care of them. A direct comparison between the average salary of a mature worker in a given occupation and the Social Security benefits he would receive is probably the quickest way to illustrate the need for additional individual financial planning. And this should be done before it is too late for the individual worker to do anything about it. The income picture may improve in the future. But at present the most important element of retirement preparation is certainly teaching people how to assure their own financial security.

Nevertheless retirement preparation can have other desirable features. Learning how to take care of one's health in the later years and developing interests outside work are two important aspects of successful retirement. The aging worker needs to be taught that continued activity is the best way to retain the capacity for activity.

Gradually increasing the time spent in roles other than work and gradually decreasing the time spent working can be particularly useful. This has been done by gradually increasing the length of the annual vacation, but perhaps a method more in tune with the physical decline in energy is to gradually reduce the length of the work day. This proposal would only apply if the transition were to be begun after age sixty. Before that, the declines in energy are probably not great enough to matter.

Right now most people retire suddenly, usually because of health, or because their jobs disappear due to transfer of a firm, business failure, reductions in personnel and so on. Only one in ten is forced to retire by reaching a mandatory retirement age. In the future, however, as the usual retirement age is lowered, more and more people can be expected to benefit from a gradual transition.

Education, above all, determines the need for retirement preparation. Generally, the higher the level of formal education, the less retirement preparation is needed. However, the high correlation among income, education, and occupation means that those who need retirement preparation the most are at income and occupational levels where they are least likely to get it.

Retirement preparation programs are few and far between. Most are offered by companies whose workers are covered by a private pension and by government agencies. These retirement preparation programs fall into two categories. *Limited* programs do little more than explain the pension plan, the retirement timing options, and the level of benefits under various options. *Comprehensive* programs attempt to go beyond financial planning and deal with such topics as physical and mental health, housing, leisure activities, and legal aspects of retirement. Research indicates that only 20 to 30 percent of preretirement programs are comprehensive.[8]

Yet these programs pay off. People who are exposed to preretirement counseling programs have done more planning for retirement and have higher retirement incomes, more activities after retirement, and less belief in the stereotypes concerning retirement in comparison with peers who have not had preretirement counseling. Surprisingly, exposure to these programs produces results even if the participants see the program as not being very helpful.[9] Thus, whether he knows it or not, heightened sensitivity to his needs in retirement probably has beneficial long-range results for the individual exposed to preretirement counseling.

However, preretirement programs cover at most only about 10 percent of the labor force. In addition, most programs should begin sooner, especially if they are to succeed in encouraging development of activities and interests and adequate financial planning. Thus far, the need for retirement preparation is not being met for the vast majority of people.

The Retirement Decision

Both attitudes toward retirement and planning or preparation for it have an impact on the decision to retire. Other important factors include the hiring and retirement policies of employers and individual factors such as health.

First, an individual may decide to retire because he cannot find a job. Particularly in manufacturing there tends to be discrimination against hiring older workers. About the only jobs which grow no harder to find as one grows older are those that pay badly, or those in areas where there is a chronic labor shortage.

When asked to defend their hiring policies, employers usually say that older people cannot meet the physical or skill requirements of the jobs. There is apparently no foundation for these allegations; nevertheless, they are acted upon as if they were true.

A case illustration may make clear just how this kind of hiring discrimination can influence decisions to retire.

In December of 1956 a large printing company that published several wide-circulation magazines ceased operations and closed down its nine-story plant. Over 2,500 workers were left jobless.

---

[8] Mark R. Greene, *et al., Preretirement Counseling, Retirement Adjustment, and the Older Employee,* (Eugene, Oregon: Graduate School of Management and Business, 1969), pp. 4–5.

[9] *Ibid.,* pp. 239–243.

Among those affected was Mr. John Hilary, age fifty-nine, who was a master printer with forty-two years of experience. Mr. Hilary was put in a real bind by the shutdown. He could have secured employment elsewhere, but it would have meant a move of over a thousand miles for himself and his family. Mr. Hilary was reluctant to leave his home town. He had been born there and many of his relatives and all of his friends were there. He was active in his church and in local politics. In short, his ties to the community were too strong to make it worth his while to uproot himself completely in order to continue his chosen trade.

Instead, Mr. Hilary tried to find employment outside his profession. His age prevented him from being hired by any of the many local manufacturing concerns, even though his skills were easily adaptable to any situation requiring skill in running or repairing machinery. Even though he was willing to work for less than he had made as a printer, he was unable to get a job. He finally decided to retire from the labor force.

Now seventy-three, Mr. Hilary supplements his union and Social Security retirement incomes by doing carpentry work for relatives and neighbors. He says bluntly that he is not really sorry he was forced to retire, but that if he could have found a job he would have continued to work for another ten years. He is bitter that in order to get any kind of job that would allow him to maintain his self-respect, he would have had to leave everything else that had any meaning to him.

It is clear that Mr. Hilary's decision to retire was precipitated prematurely by the fact that employer hiring policies prevented him from gaining employment.

A second factor involved in the retirement decision is employer retirement policies. Only a small proportion of workers is forced to retire by mandatory retirement policies, but this proportion is increasing. Many firms have such policies, and mandatory retirement is universal within the realm of government employment. While the worker's seniority usually protects him until the mandatory retirement age, the fact that the mandatory policy *is there* probably has an influence on voluntary retirement prior to the mandatory age.

The age specified for retirement can range from fifty-five to seventy; but retirement before sixty-five usually means taking reduced benefits.

The overall effect of mandatory retirement policies is to convince the worker that retirement is inevitable and to make it easier to justify early retirement. Donahue, Orbach, and Pollak have cataloged the case for and against compulsory retirement:[10]

---

[10] Wilma Donahue, Harold Orbach and Otto Pollak, "Retirement: The Emerging Social Pattern," *Handbook of Social Gerontology,* ed. Clark Tibbitts (Chicago: University of Chicago Press, 1960), pp. 355–356. Reprinted by permission.

The Case for Compulsory Retirement

—It permits an orderly separation and transition from employment to retirement when declining health and productibility make it timely and appropriate [if they ever do].

—It provides a practical administrative procedure that is objective, impersonal, and impartial, and which avoids charges of discrimination, favoritism, and bias.

—It maintains open channels of promotion, insures more upward mobility, and strengthens incentive of younger persons as well as helps make a more efficient, effective, and adaptive organization.

—It encourages the individual to plan and prepare for his own retirement, and it makes it necessary for the organization to make plans for adequate reserves and replacements for those who have retired.

The Case Against Compulsory Retirement

—The sharp reduction in income and the downward adjustment in living standards occasioned by retirement create undue hardship and resentment.

—Compulsory retirement tends to disregard important individual differences in capacity as well as differences in job requirements. It ignores the productive potential of people and deprives them of the social and occupation significance which accrues from work.

—The argument that compulsory retirement is a convenient and practical administrative procedure for separating older employees and for maintaining channels and opportunities for promotion of younger employees overlooks the effective alternatives of flexible retirement and the advantages of selective employment and utilization of older persons.

—Compulsory retirement is costly and wasteful for the company, the individual, and the economy.

Actually, when the individual approaches retirement age, the course of action he takes is not entirely predetermined. Compulsory retirement policies, hiring discrimination, and health do impose certain limitations, but within these boundaries, most older people still have some leeway.

Most people retire voluntarily—about two-thirds of the wage and salary workers who retired between 1958 and 1963 did so, and this proportion is increasing. Among those who voluntarily retire, however, poor health has been by far the major reason given historically (see Table 13). This factor can be mitigated somewhat by a less physically demanding occupation. Despite its importance in the past, however, health seems to be declining as a factor influencing the decision to retire.

Research Illustration 5
Health as an Early Retirement Factor*
A. William Pollman

Retirement research in the 1950s established that poor health was the most prevalent reason for early voluntary retirements. Most investigators agreed that the low level of benefits at that time produced pressure against early retirement that only very poor health could overcome.

Pollman sought to examine the relationship between health and early retirement when a reasonable retirement income was assured. To do this he took a sample of 725 male auto workers who in 1965 retired early from the Chrysler Corporation with incomes of around $400 per month. Using a mail questionnaire, Pollman asked the subjects to rank job satisfaction, fellow workers, supervision, retirement benefits, health, and desire for free time in terms of their influence on their retirement decisions. Questionnaires were returned from 60 percent, about average for research on older people.

Table A shows the percentage of respondents citing various factors as the *primary* reason they retired early.

Only a quarter of these early retirees cited poor health as their pri-

Table A. Primary Reason for Early Retirement

Retirement Reason	% of Subjects Citing as Primary Reason
Adequate Retirement Income	47.34
Poor Health	24.49
Wanted More Free Time	19.49
Dissatisfied with Job	5.52
Didn't Like the Boss or the People on the Job	3.16

mary reason, and nearly 70 percent retired early either because they felt they could afford it or because they wanted more free time. Thus, when retirement income was perceived as adequate, poor health assumed a rela-

---

* Based on A. William Pollman, "Early Retirement: A Comparison of Poor Health and Other Retirement Factors," *Journal of Gerontology,* 26:41–45 (1971).

tively minor role in the decision to retire voluntarily. If adequate retirement benefits become the rule rather than the exception, then health will probably assume a minor role in voluntary decisions to retire among the older population in general.

Table 14. Reasons for Retirement* Given by Men Aged Sixty-five and Over, United States, 1963

Reason for retirement	Total	OASDI bene-ficiaries	Non-bene-ficiaries
Number (in thousands)			
Not employed full time, 1962	6,009	4,707	1,303
Reporting on retirement	5,329	4,302	1,029
Retired in 1957 or earlier†	3,362	2,561	802
Retired since 1957	1,967	1,741	227
Wage and salary workers retired since 1957			
Number (in thousands)	1,509	1,332	178
Total per cent	100	100	100
Own decision	63	62	65
Poor health	35	35	36
Preferred leisure	19	19	22
Other reasons	9	9	7
Employer's decision	37	38	35
Compulsory retirement age	19	20	17
Poor health	6	5	6
Laid off or job discontinued	8	8	8
Other reasons	4	4	4
Self-employed retired since 1957			
Number (in thousands)	441	394	47
Total per cent	100	100	—‡
Poor health	53	53	—‡
Preferred leisure	29	31	—‡
Business went bad	5	4	—‡
Other reasons	13	12	—‡

* "Retirement" is defined here to mean not working at a regular, full-time job (35 hours or more a week for 6 months or more).
† Includes a few who never held regular, full-time jobs.
‡ Percentage not shown where base is less than 50,000.
Source: Erdman Palmore, "Retirement Patterns among Aged Men: Findings of the 1963 Survey of the Aged," *Social Security Bulletin*, August, 1964, pp. 3–10.

People who voluntarily retire tend to be dissatisfied with their jobs and less likely to view work as an end in itself. More and more people are citing a preference for leisure as their reason for retirement.

Most people who would rather work than retire give financial reasons, and the higher the individual's earnings, particularly in relation to expected retirement income, the less likely he is to retire.

This general analysis of decisions to retire is based primarily on research from the United States. Shanas and her associates found that Americans were more likely to retire voluntarily than either Danes or Britons.[11] These data give the impression that the cross-national sample showed a more traditional approach to retirement and work than has been found in recent studies in the United States.

Retirement as Event

Retirement as an event takes on the characteristics of a rite of passage. That is, the event of retirement marks the ends of productive economic life and the beginning of life outside the system of economic production. It marks the passage from one role to another. Retirement rites are largely informal; in fact, except in the case of some V.I.P.'s, the event is usually approached as if it were one that people would like to forget rather than remember.

The object of a rite of passage is to call attention to the fact that the individual has left one position and entered another. For the individual it emphasizes the fact that the behavior appropriate to his former position is no longer appropriate. For example, the ritual of the wedding ceremony is designed to reinforce in the minds of both partners the idea that neither of them is free to make decisions which exclude the other. The obligations of marriage are also stressed, and even in civil ceremonies there tends to be this specifying of the demands of marriage.

Retirement as an event is a poorly developed rite of passage. The ceremony usually stresses past success and seldom deals with the facts of life in terms of separation from work or the obligations of retirement. Retirement is not made visible by a rite of passage—partly, at least, because it is a status change that our society teaches people to keep quiet about. This negative orientation toward retirement ceremonies is widely held in our society.

---

[11] Ethel Shanas, *et al., Older People in Three Industrial Societies* (New York: Atherton Press, 1968), p. 436.

Retirement as a Role

After the event, be it formalized or not, the individual is expected to assume the role of "retired person." In gerontology there has been a long and loud debate over the nature of the retirement role; and, in fact, over whether such a role even exists. Part of the confusion stems from the fact that various definitions of *social role* are possible.

Most people would agree that there is a position, *retired person,* that the individual enters when he leaves his job under given circumstances. The disagreement comes when an attempt is made to specify the *role* associated with that position. A social role can mean either (1) what is *expected* of any person in a given position, (2) what *most people do* in a given position, or (3) what *a particular person does* in a given position. The discussion of retirement will concentrate on the first two aspects.

The greatest disagreement centers around the nature of the cultural expectations concerning retirement behavior. Some people say that there are no rules to tell the person what he should do in retirement. Others hold that there are plenty of rules; they are simply on a different dimension than those associated with work.

Work roles are usually instrumental—that is, the rules specify actions to be done. The worker must be in a certain place at a certain time and perform certain functions while he is there. In addition, he often belongs to various organizations as a result of his job: union, professional association, and so on. The most significant expectation the retiree faces is that he will drop not only his work role but work-related roles as well. Thus, the retirement role is largely a set of norms governing the types of roles an individual can legitimately play.

There is no specific activity expected of a retired person just as there is no specific activity expected of a child. The expectations exist purely as a set of rules specifying how an individual should occupy himself.

Thus, when the individual retires, he is expected to spend more time at home with his family if he has one, he is expected to expand the amount of time he spends at leisure, he is expected to drop his memberships in work-related organizations, he is expected to give up work, he is expected to get by on less income, he is expected to spend more time with his friends, and he is expected to increase his involvement in nonwork-related organizations. These expectations apply regardless of the age at which the individual retires. Expectations other than these are more often the result of aging than of retirement.

The facts indicate that most retired people conform to these expectations. In our retired sample, for instance, we found that upon retirement most people interact more with their families, they spend as much or more time with their friends, and they take a bigger part in any nonwork-related organizations they are affiliated with.[12] Leisure participation increases after retirement but not dramatically. Apparently such activities as participating in organizations, hobbies, and reading begin a gradual increase at about age thirty and continue to increase into retirement.

The Consequence of Retirement

In addition to affecting the individual's other role-playing, retirement and the loss of work have various effects on the individual himself. Perhaps the most important of these concerns the individual's self-concept. Back and Guptill report on one study of the effect of retirement on the self:

> The overriding point of interest has been that retirement leads to a feeling of loss of involvement for males in this study. Without the job around which their life had been built for some forty or fifty years, these retired men were unable to avoid feeling less useful, less effective, and less busy than the men who were still employed. Different conditions of life in retirement did little to alter these findings.
>
> Our findings indicate that if the retiree were healthy, had had a middle or upper-stratum occupation, and was highly involved, especially in personal interests, he would feel less of a loss in the activity dimensions (of self). Yet even these retirees did not successfully plug the gap left by the loss of their job; they felt less active than the pre-retirees. This self-rating of loss contrasts with the objective determination of actual attitudes and activities, and seems to depend on comparison with an ideal standard. This difference may account for several discrepancies found in the literature concerning factors in the morale of the aged. Impressionistic and clinical studies based mainly on complaints of the aged show a great loss of morale due to retirement itself. On the other hand, studies based on survey analysis indicate that this loss is mainly a function of the general life style of the retiree, and only incidentally is it a result of the retirement process.[13]

It is important to note that involvement was the only dimension of the self that Back and Guptill found affected by retirement. Optimism and autonomy were not affected.[14] Data from other sources indicate that, in

---

[12] W. Fred Cottrell and Robert C. Atchley, *Women in Retirement: A Preliminary Report* (Oxford, Ohio: Scripps Foundation, 1969).

[13] Kurt W. Back and Carleton S. Guptill, "Retirement and Self Ratings," in *Social Aspects of Aging,* eds. Ida H. Simpson and John C. McKinney (Durham, North Carolina: Duke University Press, 1966), p. 129.

[14] Back and Guptill, *op. cit.,* p. 125.

general, negative orientations toward the self tend to decrease with an increase in age. The higher the occupational status, the less likely the individual will be to miss his job.[15]

Other research found that retirement as such had little influence on variables such as depression, anxiety, anomie, or self-stability.[16] In addition, loss of involvement was not associated with a loss of morale. In short, the only influence of retirement on the self appears to be with regard to involvement, and this factor is related to cognitive aspects of the self and unrelated to self-esteem or morale.

The popular stereotype holds that retired people get sick and die at a rapid rate once they retire. The facts, however, are that retirement results in *as good or better health* for the retired person *despite* the fact that poor health is a major cause of retirement. Likewise, there is no evidence that retirement has any effect on mortality. When one views only those who were forced to retire by reaching retirement age, and whose retirements, therefore, are largely unrelated to health, there is no significant difference between pre- and post-retirement mortality rates, if age is controlled.

There is little evidence that retirement *per se* has any necessary relationship to problems frequently found among individual older people. Certainly the commonest effect of retirement is the limitation it places on income. It is the sharp loss of income and the change in life style associated with it that has the most significant influence on the individual. For people with enough money, the theories which link unhappiness in retirement to the need to work appear ludicrous. In my own studies of retirement, only a minute proportion of those with moderate incomes missed their jobs.

Research Illustration 6
The Effect of Retirement on Personal Adjustment*
Wayne E. Thompson, Gordon F. Streib, and John Kosa

Thompson, Streib, and Kosa sought to examine the influence of retirement on the personal adjustment of older men. They began with a group of 1,559 men, all gainfully employed, who were between sixty-five and

---

[15] Riley and Foner, *op. cit.,* p. 290.

[16] Cottrell and Atchley, *op. cit.*

* Based on Wayne E. Thompson, Gordon F. Streib, and John Kosa, "The Effect of Retirement on Personal Adjustment: A Panel Analysis," *Journal of Gerontology,* 15:165–169 (1960).

sixty-eight in 1952. By 1954, 477 of these men had retired. While the sample overrepresented large, affluent, and progressive organizations and prosperous and better educated individuals, it did represent most major industries, all walks of life, and all parts of the country.

The study was designed to answer the question: given a certain personal adjustment score in 1952, when all of the subjects were still on the job, are there differential changes in personal adjustment score among those who subsequently retired as compared with those who continued on the job?

Personal adjustment was measured by three indices which ranged from "satisfaction with life" through "dejection" to "hopelessness" in terms of decreasing adjustment. Table A shows the impact of retirement on personal adjustment.

In general, the view that retirement has negative effects on personal adjustment was not supported by these findings. In fact, Table A shows that retirees were consistently more likely to show *gains* in personal adjustment.

Thompson, Streib, and Kosa also classified their subjects as "willing" and "reluctant" based on their preretirement attitudes toward retirement. "Reluctants" were those who viewed retirement as mostly bad for people, who disliked the idea of retirement, and who, if given a choice, would have continued to work.

Reluctant retirees were more likely to become dissatisfied and dejected, while the willing retirees were no more likely to become dissatisfied than those who stayed on the job and were the *least* likely to become dejected. There were no differences in terms of hopelessness.

Thompson, Streib, and Kosa state, "In all it would appear that the negative effects of retirement have largely been overestimated. Changes in the direction of maladjustment occur only when the retirees hold an unfavorable preretirement attitude toward retirement and then only as indexed by the two less extreme indices of personal adjustment." In further analysis, they found that this pattern held even among those who were not economically deprived, who were in good health, and who did not have trouble keeping occupied. In other words, even when the effects of other major causes of maladjustment were controlled, there was still this slight tendency toward maladjustment among the reluctant retirees.

From their findings, Thompson, Streib, and Kosa conclude that "In all, retirement appears to have a negative effect upon personal adjustment only insofar as it has an effect upon economical wherewithal . . . and upon difficulty in keeping occupied. Also, as indexed by the least extreme of the indices . . . , reluctance to retire evidently plays an independent part in changes in personal adjustment. However, there is no evidence that extreme maladjustment is a typical result of retirement, even among those who are economically deprived, are in poor health, or are finding it difficult to keep occupied."

*Table A. Changes in Personal Adjustment between 1952 and
1954 among Those Who Stayed on the Job and
Those Who Retired*

	Stayed on the Job Throughout (N = 1082)	Retired between 1952 and 1954 (N = 477)
Satisfaction with Life		
% Satisfied in 1952 who became dissatisfied	*34% (550)**	*44% (238)*
% Dissatisfied in 1952 who became satisfied	*22% (532)*	*26% (239)*
Dejection		
% Not dejected in 1952 who became dejected	*14% (810)*	*19% (349)*
% Dejected in 1952 who ceased being dejected	*49% (272)*	*51% (128)*
Hopelessness		
% Hopeful in 1952 who lost hope	*10% (1003)*	*12% (416)*
% Without hope in 1952 who became hopeful	*62% (79)*	*77% (61)*

* The number in parenthesis is the percentage base. The percentages represent "changers." For example, the top left-hand cell shows that of the 550 persons on the job throughout who were satisfied with their life in 1952, 187 or 34 percent became dissatisfied between 1952 and 1954.

Apparently, then, retirement has very little psychological effect on the individual. Nevertheless, some meaningful changes in behavior take place as a result of assuming the retirement role. To begin with, the individual may shift his point of reference with respect to his behavior. During the working years he tends to orient himself toward his occupational peers as a source of norms and guidance for a wide variety of behavior—ranging from styles of dress to where to go on vacation. In retirement this reference point very often shifts to his retired peers, and often the retirement variable somewhat transcends the occupational variable.

It is also important to note that any type of role behavior is at least partly the result of negotiations between the role player and the other role players to whom his behavior relates. In these terms, retirement changes the set of people with whom one negotiates. At work one negotiates behavior in the work role with one's peers, superiors, subordinates, and audiences. One's family and friends are involved only on the extreme periphery of work role negotiations. In retirement, the people associated with one's former work drop out of the picture almost entirely (except for friends who also were work associates); and one negotiates primarily with family and friends in order to translate the general demands of retirement into particular behavior.

Most people seem able to make these transitions reasonably smoothly. A major influence on this transition is the generally held stereotype of the retired person. The fact that both the retired person and the people with whom he interacts share at least to some extent a common idea of the nature of the retired role gives everyone a place to begin the interaction. Very quickly, however, the individual retired person learns how to manipulate this interaction in the direction he wants by virtue of his more detailed knowledge of the retirement situation—unless the other person is retired too. In that case, the interaction is based on a deeper understanding resulting from both the stereotype and an intimate knowledge of the actual retirement situation.

The Future of Retirement

The future of retirement seems assured. Increasingly larger proportions of our labor force can be expected to retire and at increasingly earlier ages. In all probability the commitment to work as an end in itself will continue to decline. There is no indication at present that the nature of jobs in American society will change in any way that would reverse this trend.

Compulsory retirement policies will also probably be extended to a larger segment of the labor force, but an ever-decreasing proportion of the labor force will remain in it long enough to be pushed out. Thus, compulsory policy will become increasingly prevalent and increasingly irrelevant.

The retirement income picture should improve somewhat, but there is little to indicate that Social Security will rise above the bare subsistence level any time soon. The prospects for individual planning to bridge the gap left by inadequate Social Security payments are poor because information programs tend to be too little—too late, and because the people who need self-planning the most are the least likely to grasp its importance on their own. Thus, during the next two decades inadequate income is likely to remain the major problem associated with retirement.

Summary

Retirement means the legitimate separation of the older individual from a job he performed for pay. It evolved as a response to the labor needs of advanced industrial societies.

Retirement can be viewed as a process, as an event, or as a social role. The process of retirement begins when the individual realizes that some day he will leave his job for good. Most adults look forward to retirement, but as retirement and the financial insecurity it brings grow nearer, this eagerness diminishes. However, provided that there is some assurance of adequate retirement income, retirement appears attractive to most people, regardless of income, education, or occupation.

Most people do very little specifically to prepare for retirement, and those who need the most preparation generally prepare the least. Such preparation should emphasize the financial facts of life, health care information, and ways to develop interests other than work.

Most people voluntarily retire, most frequently because of poor health. However, preference for leisure is gaining as a reason for voluntary retirement, while the need for income is by far the most prevalent reason for continuing to work. As a rite of passage, retirement is a minor event in life.

Retirement *per se* apparently has little psychological effect on the individual, although this is still the subject of a great deal of research. Nor has it any appreciable effect on health or mortality. Some important changes in situation are related to retirement, however. The fact that one's point of reference for guidance often shifts away from the world of work toward the family is probably the most important of these.

Reduced income will probably remain the most serious problem accompanying retirement for some time to come.

Bibliography

"Poor Health Not Result, But Cause of Retirement, Missouri Study Finds," *Aging,* 173–174, 11–12, 1969.
Atchley, Robert C., "Retirement and Leisure Participation: Continuity or Crisis?" *Gerontologist,* 11: (1, part I), 13–17, 1971.
———, "Retirement and Work Orientation," *Gerontologist,* 11: (1, part I) 29–32, 1971.
Barfield, Richard and James Morgan, *Early Retirement: The Decision and the*

Experience. Ann Arbor, Michigan: Institute for Social Research, 1969.

Bixby, Lenore E. and E. Eleanor Rings, "Work Experience of Men Claiming Retirement Benefits, 1966," *Social Security Bulletin,* 32:3–14, August, 1969.

Bortz, Edward L., "Retirement and the Individual," *Journal of the American Geriatrics Society,* 16:1–15, 1968.

Bultena, Gordon and Vivian Wood, "Normative Attitudes Toward the Aged Role among Migrant and Nonmigrant Retirees," *Gerontologist,* 9: (3, part I), 204–208, 1969.

Carp, Frances M., ed., *The Retirement Process.* Washington, D. C.: United States Department of Health, Education, and Welfare, 1968.

Charles, Don C., "Effect of Participation in a Pre-Retirement Program," *Gerontologist,* 11: (1, part I), 24–28, 1971.

Chen, Yung-Ping, "Low Income, Early Retirement, and Tax Policy," *Gerontologist,* 6:35–38, 1966.

Cottrell, W. Fred and Robert C. Atchley, *Women in Retirement: A Preliminary Report.* Oxford, Ohio: Scripps Foundation, 1968.

Cottrell, W. Fred, *Technological Change and Labor in the Railroad Industry.* Lexington, Massachusetts; D. C. Heath & Co., 1970.

Davidson, Wayne R. and Karl R. Kunze, "Psychological, Social, and Economic Meanings of Work in Modern Society; Their Effects on the Worker Facing Retirement," *Gerontologist,* 5:129–133, 1965.

Ellison, David L., "Work, Retirement and the Sick Role," *Gerontologist,* 8:189–192, 1968.

Epstein, Lenore A., "Early Retirement and Work-Life Experience," *Social Security Bulletin,* 29:3–10, March, 1966.

———— and Janet H. Murray, "Employment and Retirement," in *Middle Age and Aging,* ed. Bernice L. Neugarten. Chicago: University of Chicago Press, 1968, pp. 354–356.

Fillenbaum, Gerda H., "On the Relation Between Attitude to Work and Attitude to Retirement," *Journal of Gerontology,* 26:244–248, 1971.

Friedmann, Eugene and Robert A. Havighurst, *The Meaning of Work and Retirement.* Chicago: University of Chicago Press, 1954.

Gallaway, Lowell E., "The Retirement Decision: An Exploratory Essay," Social Security Administration *Research Report No. 9.* Washington, D. C.: U. S. Government Printing Office, 1965.

Gordon, Margaret S., "Work and Patterns of Retirement," in *Aging and Leisure,* ed. Robert W. Kleemeier. New York: Oxford University Press, 1961, pp. 15–53.

————, "Income Security Programs and the Propensity to Retire," in *Processes of Aging,* eds. Richard H. Williams, Clark Tibbitts, and Wilma Donahue. New York: Atherton Press, 1963, II, 436–458.

Great Britain Ministry of Pensions and National Insurance, *Reasons for Retiring or Continuing to Work.* London: HMSO, 1954.

Havighurst, Robert J., Bernice L. Neugarten, and Vern L. Bengston, "A Cross-National Study of Adjustment to Retirement," *Gerontologist,* 6:137–138, 1966.

————, ————, and ————, *et al., Adjustment to Retirement, A Cross-National Study.* Assen, The Netherlands: VanGorcum, 1969.

Heron, Alastair, "Retirement Attitudes among Industrial Workers in the Sixth Decade of Life," *Vita Humana,* 6:152–159, 1963.

Heyman, Dorothy K. and Frances C. Jeffers, "Wives and Retirement; A Pilot Study," *Journal of Gerontology,* 23:488–496, 1968.

Jaffe, A. J., "Differential Patterns of Retirement by Social Class and Personal

Characteristics," in *The Retirement Process,* ed. Francis M. Carp. Washington, D. C.: United States Department of Health, Education and Welfare, 1968, pp. 105–110.

Kerckhoff, Alan C., "Husband-Wife Expectations and Reactions to Retirement," *Journal of Gerontology,* 19:510–516, 1964.

King, Charles E. and William H. Howell, "Role Characteristics of Flexible and Inflexible Retired Persons," *Sociology and Social Research,* 49:153–165, 1965.

Kreps, Juanita M., *Employment, Income, and Retirement Problems of the Aged.* Durham, North Carolina: Duke University Press, 1963.

———, "Employment Policy and Income Maintenance for the Aged," in *Aging and Social Policy,* eds. John C. McKinney and Frank T. deVyver. New York: Appleton-Century-Crofts, 1966, pp. 136–157.

———, ed., *Technology, Manpower, and Retirement Policy.* Cleveland, Ohio: World Publishing Co., 1966.

———, "Comparative Studies of Work and Retirement," in *Methodology Problems in Cross-National Studies in Aging,* eds. Ethel Shanas and John Madge. New York: S. Karger, 1968, pp. 75–99.

Lambert, Edouard, "Reflections on a Policy for Retirement," *International Labor Review,* 90:365–375, 1964.

Laurence, Mary W., "Sources of Satisfaction in the Lives of Working Women," *Journal of Gerontology,* 16:163–167, 1961.

Maddox, George L., "Retirement as a Social Event in the United States," in *Middle Age and Aging,* ed. Bernice L. Neugarten. Chicago: University of Chicago Press, 1968, pp. 357–365.

Martin, John and Ann Doran, "Evidence Concerning the Relationship Between Health and Retirement," *Sociological Review,* 14:329–343, 1966.

McEwan, Peter J. M. and Alan P. Sheldon, "Patterns of Retirement and Related Variables," *Journal of Geriatric Psychiatry,* 3:35–54, 1969.

Monk, Abraham, "Factors in the Preparation for Retirement by Middle-Aged Adults," *Gerontologist,* 11: (4, part I), 348–351, 1971.

Morse, Nancy C. and Robert S. Weiss, "The Function and Meaning of Work and the Job," *American Sociological Review,* 20:191–198, 1955.

Myers, Robert J., "Factors in Interpreting Mortality after Retirement," *Journal of the American Statistical Association,* 49:499–509, 1954.

Nadelson, Theodore, "A Survey of the Literature on the Adjustment of the Aged to Retirement," *Journal of Geriatric Psychiatry,* 3:3–20, 1969.

Orbach, Harold L., *et al., Trends in Early Retirement.* Ann Arbor, Michigan: University of Michigan, Wayne State University Institute of Gerontology, 1969.

Owen, John P. and L. D. Belzung, "Consequences of Voluntary Early Retirement; A Case Study of a New Labour Force Phenomenon," *British Journal of Industrial Relations,* 5:162–189, 1967.

Palmore, Erdman B., "Differences in the Retirement Patterns of Men and Women," *Gerontologist,* 5:4–8, 1965.

———, "Retirement Patterns among Aged Men: Findings of the 1963 Survey of the Aged," *Social Security Bulletin,* 27:3–10, August, 1964.

———, "Why Do People Retire?" *Aging and Human Development,* 2:269–283, 1971.

Pollak, Otto, *The Social Aspects of Retirement.* Homewood, Illinois: R. D. Irwin, 1956.

Pollman, A. William, "Early Retirement: Relationship to Variation in Life Satisfaction," *Gerontologist,* 11: (1, part I), 43–47, 1971.

————, "Early Retirement: A Comparison of Poor Health to Other Retirement Factors," *Journal of Gerontology,* 26:41–45, 1971.

Powers, Edward A. and Willis H. Goudy, "Examination of the Meaning of Work to Older Workers," *Aging and Human Development,* 2:38–45, 1971.

Reichard, Suzanne, Florine Livson, and Paul G. Petersen, "Adjustment to Retirement," in *Middle Age and Aging,* ed. Bernice L. Neugarten. Chicago: University of Chicago Press, 1968, pp. 178–180.

Simpson, Ida H. and John C. McKinney, eds., *Social Aspects of Aging.* Durham, North Carolina: Duke University Press, 1966.

————, Kurt W. Back, and John C. McKinney, "Orientation toward Work and Retirement, and Self-Evaluation in Retirement," in *Social Aspects of Aging,* eds. Ida H. Simpson and John C. McKinney. Durham, North Carolina: Duke University Press, 1966, pp. 75–89.

————, ————, and ————, "Exposure to Information on, Preparation for, and Self-Evaluation in Retirement," in *Social Aspects of Aging,* eds. Ida H. Simpson and John C. McKinney. Durham, North Carolina: Duke University Press, 1966, pp. 90–105.

————, "Problems of the Aging in Work and Retirement," in *Foundations of Practical Gerontology,* eds. Rosamonde R. Boyd and G. C. Oakes. Columbia, South Carolina: University of South Carolina Press, 1969, pp. 151–166.

Slavick, Fred and Seymour L. Wolfbein, "The Evolving Work-Life Pattern," in *Handbook of Social Gerontology,* ed. Clark Tibbitts. Chicago: University of Chicago Press, 1960, pp. 298–329.

————, *Compulsory and Flexible Retirement in the American Economy.* Ithaca, New York: Cornell University Press, 1966.

Stokes, Randall G. and George L. Maddox, "Some Social Factors in Retirement Adaptation," *Journal of Gerontology,* 22:329–333, 1967.

Streib, Gordon F. and Wayne E. Thompson, issue eds., "Adjustment in Retirement," *Journal of Social Issues,* 14: (2), 1958.

———— and ————, "Situational Determinants: Health and Economic Deprivation in Retirement," *Journal of Social Issues,* 14:18–34, 1958.

Thompson, Wayne E., "Pre-Retirement Anticipation and Adjustment in Retirement," *Journal of Social Issues,* 14:35–45, 1958.

————, Gordon F. Streib, and John Kosa, "The Effect of Retirement on Personal Adjustment: A Panel Analysis," *Journal of Gerontology,* 15:165–169, 1960.

Tuckman, Jacob and Irving Lorge, *Retirement and the Industrial Worker; Prospect and Reality.* New York: Columbia University Teacher's College, 1953.

Tyhurst, James S., Lee Salk, and Miriam Kennedy, "Mortality, Morbidity, and Retirement," *American Journal of Public Health,* 47:1434–1444, 1957.

Wentworth, Edna C., *Employment after Retirement: A Study of Post-entitlement Work Experience of Men Drawing Benefits under Social Security.* Washington, D. C.: U. S. Government Printing Office, 1968.

10

Recreation and Leisure

Recreation refers to activities such as sports, games, vacations, and hobbies that aim to renew mind and body by either relieving them of tension or delivering them from boredom. Recreation is primarily a reaction to some state of body or mind.

Leisure activities are pursued as ends in themselves. They are unplanned and unrequired. Leisure is primarily action, directed generally toward self-development.

Recreation and leisure aim primarily at relaxation, entertainment, and personal development. As such, they are institutions that are oriented around the needs of individuals, particularly the needs for tension management, enhancement of self-esteem, and identity.[1]

For simplicity we will lump recreation and leisure together under the general label of leisure.

Information about patterns of leisure among older people is essential in examining the nature of growing old. People gradually expand the time they spend at leisure as age increases.[2] Upon retirement, leisure pursuits occupy a great deal of the individual's time, but there is some question whether leisure roles can fill the void left by work. There is little doubt that leisure can fill the *time* formerly occupied by work, but the problem is whether leisure is capable of giving the individual the kind of *self-respect* and identity that he got from the job.

Perhaps the most articulate and repeatedly quoted spokesman on the negative side is Miller,[3] who has taken the following position:

---

[1] Robert C. Atchley, *Understanding American Society* (Belmont, California: Wadsworth, 1971), p. 325.

[2] Matilda N. Riley and Ann Foner, *Aging and Society*, Vol. I, *An Inventory of Research Findings.* (New York: Russell Sage Foundation, 1968), p. 513.

[3] Stephen J. Miller, "The Social Dilemma of the Aging Leisure Participant," in *Older People and Their Social World,* eds. Arnold Rose and Warren Peterson (Philadelphia: F. A. Davis, 1965), pp. 77–92. The analysis of Miller's theory which

1. Retirement is basically degrading because, although there is an implication that retirement is a right that is earned through life-long labor, there is also a tacit understanding that this reward is being given primarily to coax the individual from a role he is no longer able to play.

2. Occupational identity invades all of the other areas of the person's life. Accordingly, the father and head of household roles, the friend role, and even leisure roles are mediated by the individual's occupational identity.

3. Among all roles which could be used as a source of identity, work is the one people are taught to prefer.

4. The leisure role cannot replace work as a source of self-respect and identity because it is not supported by norms that would make this legitimate. That is, the retired person does not *feel justified* in deriving self-respect from leisure because leisure is not defined as a legitimate source of self-respect by the general population.

5. Beyond the simple need to be doing something there is a need to do something that most people define as utilitarian or gainful in some way. Thus, the stamp collector must emphasize the financial rewards, paintings are offered for sale, or woodworking is confined to immediately "useful" objectives. In short, the only kind of leisure that can provide identity is the work-substitute.

6. A stigma of "implied inability to perform" is associated with retirement and is carried over into all of the individual's remaining roles, resulting in an identity breeakdown.

7. Identity breakdown is a process whereby the individual's former claims to prestige or status are invalidated by the implied inability to perform, and this proves embarrassing for the stigmatized person. Miller calls this result "the portent of embarrassment."

8. Embarrassment leads the individual to withdraw from the situation or prevents him from participating to begin with.

9. The answer lies not in inventing new roles for the aging, but rather in "determining what roles presently exist in the social system . . . , offering vicarious satisfactions that can reduce the socially debilitating loss accompanying occupational retirement."[4]

10. Miller implies that creating an ethic which would make full-time leisure an acceptable activity for a worthwhile person is a possible way to resolve the dilemma of the retired leisure participant.

Miller's analysis of the situation contains many insights. Nevertheless it rests on the assumption that prior to retirement the individual derived his

---

occupies the next several pages is a revised version of my paper, "Retirement and Leisure Participation: Continuity or Crisis?" which first appeared in *The Gerontologist,* 11:13–17 (1971).

[4] Miller, *op. cit.*

identity primarily from his job. Also implied in Miller's identity crisis theory is the assumption that most people want to stay on the job, since this is their main identity, and that therefore most retirement is involuntary. This is no doubt because Miller does not discuss those who retired voluntarily. Miller also implies that he subscribes to the activity theory of adjustment to aging, since he assumes that lost roles need to be replaced.[5]

Several questions thus emerge from an examination of Miller's identity crisis theory. First, in his portrayal of the relationship between involuntary retirement and leisure an accurate one? Second, is the pattern, even if accurate, typical of most older leisure participants? Third, what is the pattern among those who are voluntarily retired? Data from recent studies of retired people can shed some light on these questions.

Some of these data will be drawn from the Scripps Foundation studies in retirement, a series that has produced several published reports and which is still continuing.[6]

1. Retirement has been found to result in a loss of a sense of involvement, *but this was unrelated to other self-concept variables of optimism and autonomy.*[7]

Disengagement theory tells us to expect some withdrawal from involvement, and it is noteworthy that this loss of involvement does not appear to have adverse results for other aspects of the self-concept. This makes one skeptical about Miller's "portent of embarrassment."

2. Strong work-orientation *is* frequently found among retired people, but this is *not* accompanied by anxiety, depression, dislike of retirement, or withdrawal from activity.[8]

Cottrell and Atchley's findings indicate that a strong positive orientation toward work *"exists apart from the job itself but . . . has no import*

---

[5] Robert J. Havighurst, "Successful Aging," in *Processes of Aging,* eds. Richard H. Williams, Clark Tibbitts, and Wilma Donahue (New York: Atherton Press, 1963), pp. 299–320.

[6] Robert C. Atchley, *Retired Women: A Study of Self and Role,* Unpublished Doctoral Dissertation, The American University, 1967; Fred Cottrell and Robert C. Atchley, *Women in Retirement: A Preliminary Report* (Oxford, Ohio: Scripps Foundation, 1969); Robert C. Atchley, "Respondents vs. Refusers in an Interview Study of Retired Women," *Journal of Gerontology,* 24:42–47 (1969); Fred Cottrell, *Technological Change and Labor in the Railroad Industry* (Lexington, Massachusetts: D. C. Heath, 1970); Robert C. Atchley, "Retirement and Work Orientation," *The Gerontologist,* 11:29–32 (1971); Robert C. Atchley, "Potential for Disengagement among Professors," *Journal of Gerontology,* 26:476–480 (1971); Mildred M. Seltzer and Robert C. Atchley, "Work Commitment, Potential for Disengagement and Leisure Preferences among Social Workers," *Sociological Focus,* Autumn, 1971.

[7] Kurt W. Back and C. S. Guptill, "Retirement and Self-Ratings," in *Social Aspects of Aging,* eds. I. H. Simpson, K. W. Back, and J. C. McKinney (Durham, North Carolina: Duke University Press, 1966).

[8] Cottrell and Atchley, *op. cit.*

for the individual apart from the job."[9] In terms of adjustment, carrying a positive orientation toward work into retirement apparently had *no* negative result.

3. When men retired from upper-white-collar, middle-status, and semi-skilled jobs were compared, it was found that the upper-white-collar people had internalized, occupationally oriented norms. Middle-status workers were oriented toward specific tasks and situations, often giving them skills that were transferable to leisure situations. Semi-skilled workers were engaged mainly in activities oriented toward *things.*[10]

Of these occupational strata, the upper-white-collar stratum comes closest to Miller's model of the retired person. These are work-oriented people. However, neither of the other two strata fits the work-oriented model. Middle-status people develop skills on the job that carry over into other roles. Thus, the salesman may carry his smooth-talking style over into his leisure roles. Semi-skilled people are oriented around the job, but not necessarily because they have any deep, abiding commitment to it. For them it may be purely a matter of not having been trained for anything else.

4. The *style* of work activities tends to remain dominant in retirement.

Simpson, Back, and McKinney[11] found that upper-white-collar jobs were oriented around *symbols,* middle-status jobs were oriented around *people,* and semi-skilled jobs were oriented around *things.* The middle-status people showed the greatest continuity in style from pre- to post-retirement. This suggests that retirement, and leisure roles in particular, offer greater opportunities for practicing interpersonal skills than for practicing skills oriented around symbols of things.

The implication of this finding is that it is not so much the *ethic* learned on the job that interferes with successful pursuit of leisure in retirement as it is the *skills.* Those who learn job skills that cannot be readily used in leisure pursuits have a hard time adjusting to an increase in leisure unless they have had the opportunity to learn these skills elsewhere. This notion is reinforced by the finding that middle-status people who had thing-oriented jobs resembled the semi-skilled more than they did their middle-status peers in terms of retirement activities.

5. In addition, data from retired railroaders indicates that there are continuities in the situations people face that minimize the impact of retirement.[12] Family, friends, church, and other roles continue despite retire-

---

[9] *Ibid.,* p. 49.

[10] Ida H. Simpson, Kurt W. Back, and John C. McKinney, "Continuity of Work and Retirement Activities," in *Social Aspects of Aging, op. cit.,* pp. 106–119.

[11] *Ibid.*

[12] Cottrell, 1970, *op. cit.*

ment. Cottrell's data suggest that the import of embarrassment and loss of identity is minimized by the tendency to select friends on the job from among those of one's own age. The end result of this process is to create *retirement cohorts* of people who have known each other on the job and who retire together. In the Scripps Foundation studies of retirement this phenomenon has been observed in retirement from occupations as diverse as teacher, railroader, and telephone operator. It results in a group of retired friends who have known each other for years and whose concepts of each other involve a great deal more than the mere playing of an occupational role. Nevertheless, this group is also capable of sustaining the prestige gained on the job because they know how this prestige was generated.

To the extent that older people are geographically mobile, they might tend to lose these continuities, but most retired people, particularly the semi- or unskilled, do not move away from their place of long-term residence.[13]

6. Cottrell's data[14] also indicate that as the concept of retirement is incorporated into the culture, the tendency to look upon work as a temporary part of life increases.

The implication here is that if work is not viewed as a permanent part of life, one puts greater emphasis on other parts of life that are more permanent. For example, if a man knows the day he begins working that he will work twenty-five years and then quit, he is very likely to avoid letting work become an all-consuming part of his life.

7. In terms of ethic, it is not at all clear whether most people regard work as a necessary prerequisite for making leisure legitimate, or simply as a necessary economic function which interferes with the pursuit of leisure. It *is* quite clear that our heritage has always included those who did not work because they could afford not to. Accordingly, legitimacy of leisure may rest not so much on work as on the idea that the money used to sustain leisure came from a legitimate source; that is, it was either earned by working or inherited. In the Scripps Foundation studies of retirement many middle-income retired people have shown not the slightest reluctance to embrace the leisure role, provided their income was secure.[15] Perhaps if most retired people were not pauperized by retirement, the "portent of embarrassment" mentioned by Miller as an obstacle to increasing acceptance of leisure activity would fade away.

8. Nearly two-thirds of retired men retired as a result of their own

---

[13] Riley and Foner, *op. cit.*

[14] Cottrell, 1970, *op. cit.*

[15] Atchley, 1967; and Cottrell and Atchley, *op. cit.*

decision. Less than *one in five* was retired involuntarily as a result of reaching retirement age.[16]

By leaving out those in poor health and those who voluntarily retired, Miller effectively limited the group he was talking about to less than a third of the retired men and an even smaller percentage of the retired women.

We may seem to have dwelt too long and too deeply on the relationship between leisure and retirement. Nevertheless, if we are to understand the nature of the leisure role among older people, this role must be put in its proper context. Miller's position is a very common one, and it is constantly being used as a basis for decisions that influence older people's lives. Our detailed examination of this approach has shown it to be at least questionable.

To begin with, there is evidence in the Scripps Foundation studies and elsewhere that the adjustment problems sometimes associated with retirement are *not* the result of the loss of work and the identity it provides. In fact, a highly positive orientation toward work had little influence on retirement adjustment. There is no indication that highly work-oriented people are unable to take up the leisure role; in fact, just the opposite is true. We could find no concrete evidence that retirement in and of itself negatively influences the *quality* of one's family life, friendships, or associations.

Accordingly, an alternative to Miller's identity crisis theory of the relationship between retirement and leisure might contain the following points:

Many people are never highly work-oriented and thus may very well provide a model to show others what it would be like to derive self-satisfaction from leisure. The ethic of the system allows this as long as the money used to lead a life of leisure is legitimately earned.

Self-respect *can* be gained from leisure pursuits in retirement if the individual has enough money, and if he has a cohort of retired friends who will accept his full-time leisure as legitimate and help him negate the stigma of implied inability to perform. As retirement becomes more and more an expected part of the life cycle, this orientation should spread beyond the cohort of friends. In any event, the retired individual will continue to *see himself* as a railroader, teacher, and so forth, even though he no longer plays the role. Thus, the crux of this alternative theory is *identity continuity*.

There are many people for whom interpersonal interaction *was* their occupational skill, and it is this *activity* that is useful rather than some abstract goal. In this sense, then, leisure can act as a work-substitute where necessary.

---

[16] Riley and Foner, *op. cit.*, and Cottrell and Atchley, *op. cit.*

Very few people rest their entire identity on a single role. If they did, there would surely be far more suicides than there are now. The only thing that makes failure bearable is that we seldom fail in all of our roles at once.

Each person generally stakes his identity on several roles. Work may be at or near the top, but not necessarily. There simply is not the homogeneous consensus on the value of work that would keep it at the top for everyone. In fact, the many systems of competing values is a complex society *insure* that there will be a wide variety of self-values. Thus, the probability that retirement will lead to a complete identity breakdown is slight, and just as many people may rely on leisure pursuits for self-respect as rely on work, particularly among those with unsatisfying jobs.

Some decline of involvement may be natural as the individual adjusts to declining energy, but most people expand their leisure involvement when they retire. Nevertheless, most retired people do not regard this change negatively. In fact, most people retire voluntarily, and many of these volunteers cite a preference for leisure as their reason for retiring.

There is no doubt that for some people Miller's identity crisis pattern is a grim reality, but it does not appear to be a typical pattern, even among the minority of older people who are forced to retire. Among voluntary retirees, a third retired to devote more time to leisure. The ethical issue may be difficult for some to resolve, but not for the majority, even among the highly work-oriented.

The **identity continuity** theory and the data which give rise to it suggest that leisure can have a great deal of positive value in retirement, and that this value will increase in the future.

Between them, the continuity and identity crisis theories probably account for the majority of cases. Nevertheless, to determine what proportion of retired people fits each model, studies are needed that are broader in scope and wider in range than any thus far brought to bear on the question. One of the intriguing but often infuriating aspects of studying aging in the United States is the sometimes overpowering geographic, social, and psychological diversity of the older population. Perhaps further probing will uncover still other patterns of relationship between retirement and leisure participation.

Yet apart from the question of acceptability, there is also the question of the older person's competence to take advantage of leisure roles. Older people enjoy a wide variety of leisure pursuits, but the data suggest that older people—particularly the less well-educated—are reluctant to engage in autonomous leisure activities such as reading, listening to music, painting, sculpting, or writing. This is at least partly because the older person feels incompetent.

Critics of American education have attacked this apparent deficiency in our orientation toward education. Contemporary education, it is said, devotes anywhere from 80 to 90 percent of the students' time for twelve to nineteen years to teaching him how to fill a job, but makes little effort to prepare him for his life outside the job. As Norman Cousins puts it, "I contend that science tends to lengthen life, and education tends to shorten it; that science has the effect of freeing man for leisure, and that education has the effect of deflecting him from the enjoyment of living."[17] The point is that to open up the full range of leisure possibilities requires some training.

Recent research on exposure to "high culture" in American society has shown that the college educated person is no more likely to enjoy a wide range of leisure pursuits than is the semi-skilled worker.[18] Television, which often requires little competence, is the major leisure pursuit among all people in American society. One can conclude that our education and communication systems do little to develop the potential for the creative use of leisure.

There is some evidence that the learning necessary for a full-blown leisure style of life must begin early. Many gerontologists are pessimistic about the possibility of completely resocializing older people into a life of leisure. This pessimism is mainly based on the slow-down in learning speed that occurs with age, the reluctance most older people show toward attempting anything entirely new, and the extreme stability that activity patterns show. The findings lead to the conclusion that if leisure competence is created early in life it can be maintained into later life, but that if leisure competence is not learned by middle age, it may never be. In these terms the individual should probably begin to develop leisure competence as soon as possible. An active and creative use of leisure in one's youth is the surest way to guarantee a similar pattern in old age, since older people tend to retain patterns and preferences developed in the past.

There is also a physical element in leisure competence, but between age forty and age eighty the physical limits on leisure options often change very little. Only very active sports show drastic declines with age. More sedentary sports such as bowling and golf can be maintained much longer.

Activities differ on several dimensions: at home vs. away from home; spectator vs. participant; solitary vs. group; physical exertion vs. no physical exertion; intellectual vs. manual vs. social; or with family vs. outside family. Zborowski found considerable stability between activities at age forty and activities in later maturity.[19] The stability of activity was slightly

---

[17] Norman Cousins, "Art, Adrenalin, and the Enjoyment of Living," *Saturday Review*, 51:20–24, April 20, 1968.

[18] Harold L. Wilensky, "Social Structure, High Culture, and Mass Culture," *American Sociological Review*, 29:181–194 (1964).

[19] Mark Zborowski, "Aging and Recreation," *Journal of Gerontology*, 17:302–309 (1962).

higher for men than for women. Men showed a significant increase in spectator-home, while women showed significant increases in spectator-home plus solitary-intellectual-outside home. Both groups showed significant declines in activities involving physical exertion, group-manual, and group-intellectual-outside home types of activities.

Leisure roles are extremely diverse, yet seldom will an older individual be able to select from the *entire* range of possibilities. To begin with, physical limitations rule out some alternatives. But perhaps the most important limitation on older people's leisure options is their lack of money. Pursuits such as travel, entertaining, or going to a movie, concert, or play require money, and those without money are shut out. Finally, older people's activities are severely limited by deficiencies in transportation. Obviously, if you cannot get there you cannot participate. Club and church socials or activities, outings, shopping, eating out, and visiting are all examples of leisure pursuits that can be greatly hampered by a lack of transportation.

Faced with the loss of work, there are three general alternatives: finding a work-substitute, engaging in leisure activities, or doing nothing. Idleness is literally deadly for older people, just as it would be for anyone else, and as a result not very many people select this alternative. The other two types of activity are difficult to separate because they may differ only with respect to motivation.

People expand their leisure activities following retirement, but not drastically. Patterns of leisure vary from weekdays to weekends. On weekdays the most frequent activity is watching TV, and this is true of both men and women. On weekends the number one activity is visiting and entertaining, followed by watching TV. The bulk (35 percent) of the older American's leisure is spent at home, and most of it is activity that can be done alone. Following TV, the next most prevalent activities are visiting, reading, gardening, going for walks, and handiwork. Older people do devote a conspicuous amount of time to just sitting, looking out a window, or napping. Idleness does not become an important part of life, however, until the very advanced ages.

There are strikingly few differences between young and old with regard to leisure patterns, but some of these differences are important. Older people read fewer books and magazines but about the same number of newspapers. Older people rate newspapers as more important than television (even though they spend more time with TV). Movie-going falls off rapidly after age fifty. Older people attend the theater, concerts, or sports events less frequently. Older people tend to prefer *serious* content. Their favorite TV programs center around public affairs, news, and information. Also, older people tend to devote more attention to the "local news" section of newspapers. Older people tend to avoid shows designed strictly for entertainment, and they avoid popular music.

Only a small proportion of older people occupy themselves with crafts, hobbies, or intellectual and artistic activities. The only outdoor activities that increase with age are gardening and walking. Vacation and travel are limited to the few who can afford the expense.

Caution: Research data on leisure differences by age come primarily from cross-sectional sources. Therefore the age differences observed may be the result of changes in child-rearing, education, or social fads rather than age changes in leisure preferences.

Summary

In the final analysis, leisure participation in the later years turns out to be an individual thing in the sense that each person is free to choose from a wide variety of possibilities. Yet this variety is limited by physical, financial, and transportation factors. A few older people are hamstrung by an ethic which does not allow play without work. Personality, family, and social class values narrow the field of choice still more. Lack of facilities can also limit the options.

If the older person is to be able to enjoy creative, self-enhancing leisure in his retirement years, then the options must be left as wide open as possible so that he can build on his own personality and his own unique past history.

If one thing is obvious in the studies of leisure among older people who live in their own homes, it is that autonomous and spectator leisure are a big part of the picture, even though many older people prefer participant activities. Perhaps one of the few remaining independent decisions an institutionalized older person can make concerns his leisure activities. In light of this, the ready-made schedules of many retirement homes may be a mistake. A TV set, frequent opportunities to shoot the breeze, and a good light to read by may well be all the person wants.

About the best that can be said of the pursuit of leisure in retirement is that most people seem to be able to cope with it successfully. Those who have good health and money do quite well, but the poorer and sicker people get, the harder it is to accept the constraints of a life of leisure.

Given the nature of the leisure activities older people prefer, few *facilities* are required. In order to maximize opportunities, the key requirements seem to be 1) having enough personal income, 2) being in close proximity to friends and relatives, and 3) having transportation to take advantage of existing community facilities.

Institutional programs in recreation should be constructed with the idea in mind that personal development can be as important as entertainment to older people.

Leisure roles are an integral part of life in American society. Because leisure choices are so often individual decisions, leisure *can be* one of the greatest sources of continuity for the individual across the life span. To make it so, however, one must realize early in life that leisure activities are an important part of life. This realization is particularly important for young adults who expend a great deal of energy on the job and rely mainly on television for their leisure.

Bibliography

Alford, Harold J., *Continuing Education in Action: Residential Centers for Lifelong Learning*. New York: John Wiley, 1968.

Bross, D. R., "Night College Courses for the Older Woman," *Adult Leadership*, 15:233–234, 1967.

Campbell, D. E., "Analysis of Leisure Time Profiles of Four Age Groups of Adult Males," *Research Quarterly*, 40:266–273, 1969.

Christ, Edwin A., "The 'Retired' Stamp Collector: Economic and Other Functions of a Systematized Leisure Activity," in *Older People and Their Social World*, eds. Arnold M. Rose and Warren A. Peterson. Philadelphia: F. A. Davis, 1965, pp. 93–112.

Cowgill, Donald O. and Norma Baulch, "The Use of Leisure Time by Older People," *Gerontologist*, 2:47–50, 1962.

Cunningham, David A., *et al.*, "Active Leisure Time Activities as Related to Age among Males in a Total Population," *Journal of Gerontology*, 23:551–556, 1968.

Curtis, Joseph E. and Dulcy B. Miller, "Community Sponsored Recreation in an Extended Care Facility," *Gerontologist*, 7: (3), 196–199, 1967.

Dumazedier, Joffre and A. Ripert, "Retirement and Leisure," *International Social Science Journal*, 15:438–447, 1963.

Durkee, Stephen, "Artistic Expression in Later Life," in *New Thoughts on Old Age*, ed. Robert Kastenbaum. New York: Springer, 1964, pp. 305–315.

Garfunkel, Florence R. and Gabriele H. Grunebaum, "A New Use of Education in Programming for the Aged," *Journal of Jewish Community Services*, 65:102–110, 1968.

Giordano, Enrico A. and D. F. Seaman, "Continuing Education for the Aging —Evidence for a Positive Outlook," *Gerontologist*, 8: (1, part I), 63–64, 1968.

Groombridge, Brian, *Education and Retirement*. London: National Institute for Adult Education, 1960.

Havighurst, Robert J. and Kenneth Feigenbaum, "Leisure and Life-Style," in *Middle Age and Aging*, ed. Bernice L. Neugarten. Chicago: University of Chicago Press, 1968, pp. 347–353.

Hendrickson, A., "The Role of Colleges and Universities in the Education of the Aging," in *Potentialities for Later Living, ed.* O. B. Thomason. Gainesville, Florida: University of Florida Press, 1968, pp. 111–124.

Hueskinveld, Helen, "Talking Books," *Harvest Years*, 8:29–32, February, 1968.

Hoar, Jere, "Study of Free-Time Activities of 200 Aged Persons," *Sociology and Social Research*, 45:157–163, 1961.

Joelson, J. U. and David Rachlis, "Anticipating the Consequences of Aging;

A Pilot Program in Adult Education," *Journal of Jewish Community Services,* 41:369–377, 1965.

Kent, Donald P., "Current Developments in Educational Programming for Older People," *American School Board Journal,* 149:1–27, 1964.

Kleemeier, Robert W., ed., *Aging and Leisure.* New York: Columbia University Press, 1961.

Kreps, Juanita M., *Lifelong Allocation of Work and Leisure.* Washington, D. C.: Social Security Administration, 1968.

Kuhlen, Raymond G., ed., *Psychological Background of Adult Education.* Chicago: Center for the Study of Liberal Education for Adults, 1963.

Lucas, Carol, *Recreation in Gerontology.* Springfield, Illinois: Charles C Thomas, 1964.

Martin, Alexander R., *Leisure Time—A Creative Force.* New York: National Council on Aging, 1963.

Mary Jeanette, Sister, "Music for the Aging," *Professional Nursing Home,* 8:12–14, July, 1966.

Miller, Stephen J., "The Social Dilemma of the Aging Leisure Participant," in *Older People and Their Social World,* eds. Arnold M. Rose and Warren A. Peterson. Philadelphia: F. A. Davis, 1965, pp. 77–92.

Parker, Edwin B. and William Paisley, *Patterns of Adult Information Seeking.* Stanford, California: Stanford University Institute for Communications Research, 1966.

Pfeiffer, Eric and Glenn C. Davis, "The Use of Leisure Time in Middle Life," *Gerontologist,* 11: (3, part I), 187–195, 1971.

Rosow, Irving, "Retirement, Leisure, and Social Status," in *Duke University Council on Aging and Human Development: Proceedings of Seminars, 1965–1969,* ed. Frances C. Jeffers. Durham, North Carolina: Duke University Center for the Study of Aging and Human Development, 1969, pp. 249–257.

Smigel, Erwin O., ed., *Work and Leisure.* New Haven, Connecticut: College and University Press, 1963.

Spain, Nola, "Recreational Programs for the Elderly," in *Foundations in Practical Gerontology,* eds. Rosamonde R. Boyd and C. G. Oakes. Columbia, South Carolina: University of South Carolina Press, 1969, pp. 180–190.

Steiner, Gary A., *The People Look at Television.* New York: Alfred A. Knopf, 1963.

Whiskin, Frederick E., "On the Meaning and Function of Reading in Later Life," in *New Thoughts on Old Age,* ed. Robert Kastenbaum. New York: Springer, 1964, pp. 300–304.

11　Independence & Dependency

An elderly American woman . . . sits in her hospital bed and talks to her roommate. "Well, now, I've always believed that old folks shouldn't be a burden to young people, because young people need their happiness and independence. I don't know what I'll do when I get out of here—maybe I'll try to get into a nursing home. I want my independence too."

An elderly Japanese woman . . . says to her roommate, "When I leave here, I will live with my eldest son and his wife. My daughter-in-law is not happy about this, but her happiness is not so important just now."[1]

The contrast between these two vignettes illustrates the following points about independence and dependency: (1) our ideas about such things can vary, depending on how we are brought up, (2) independence and dependency are related, but not mutually exclusive, and (3) our ideas about dependency and independence can have a strong influence on the choices we make.[2]

Aging and dependency are linked by the fact that as we grow older, we become increasingly susceptible to a loss of independence. Accordingly, this chapter will examine the origins and development of ideas about independence and dependency, the changes that occur with age in the meaning of independence and dependency, reactions to the dependency and loss of independence that sometimes accompany old age, and some possibilities for preserving independence.

Babies are notoriously self-centered, but at the same time they are the most dependent creatures on earth. The child's inability to do things for

---

[1] Richard A. Kalish, "Of Children and Grandfathers: A Speculative Essay on Dependency," *The Gerontologist*, 7:1:65 (1967).

[2] For a more extensive treatment of dependency see Richard A. Kalish, ed., "The Dependencies of Old People," Occasional Paper No. 6 (Ann Arbor, Michigan: University of Michigan, Wayne State University Institute of Gerontology, 1969).

himself obliges him to depend on others, to lean on them for security, support, sustenance, protection, assistance, sympathy, and love. Early in the individual's life this need to be dependent is encouraged. At the same time, in American society the child is gradually expected to develop his own talents and resources, to make his own decisions, and to solve his own problems.

The child thus learns that there are times to be dependent and times to be independent. He also learns how much independence and dependence is appropriate for people of various ages. He learns that as a small child he can run to his mother when he skins his knee, and he is expected to let his parents decide about his clothes, friends, bedtime, and TV-watching habits. At the same time he is rewarded for learning to go to the toilet by himself, to put away his toys without being asked, to dress himself, and so on.

Gradually, as the child grows older, approval for independent behavior increases and approval for dependent behavior diminishes. Refusing to leave home for school, seeking adult support in arguments with other children, continuous requests for reassurance from parents, and other such dependent acts meet with increasing disapproval from both family and peers. Teasing, humiliation, and ostracism are strong forces which teach the child that as one gets older, dependency is to be avoided.

In the meantime, the child is increasingly rewarded for showing initiative in becoming an independent individual. In fact, a key element involved in creating the achievement motivation that Americans so highly prize appears to be the rewards for doing *new* things independently. As an indicator of independence, mastery of care-taking tasks is much inferior to moving out on one's own, acquiring new skills, and exploring new possibilities. Apparently the dependent child never quite develops the confidence required to compete with others for achievement.[3]

As the child approaches adulthood, he is rewarded by both parents and peers for assuming the adult role and for doing more and more things without supervision. In addition, the independent adolescent is rewarded by the intrinsic satisfaction that comes from being in control of his environment. The expectations concerning independence are so strong that we suspect something wrong when an adolescent does *not* rebel against parental authority. We expect children to gradually assume control over their own decisions, and in fact, it is this very process which separates child from adult.

This pattern of socialization teaches people particular ideas about dependency and independence. Gradually the individual learns to hate the idea of dependency. The terms we use to describe dependents reveal our orientation toward the state of dependency itself. For example, moocher,

[3] Roger Brown, *Social Psycology* (New York: The Free Press, 1965), pp. 445–450.

sponge, leach, lazy good-for-nothing, and bum are all terms we frequently apply to people who cannot take care of themselves financially. We learn very early in life that anyone of adult age who has to rely on others for support is inferior; he is in a subordinate, subservient position in relation to others of his age, and he is expected to give up many of his rights of self-determination in exchange for support. Usually the support required is financial, but our hatred of dependency extends to most other kinds of support as well. To the average, well-reared, adult American, dependency is appropriate only for kids and misfits.

On the other hand, we gradually learn to prize independence very highly. We regard it as a state to be striven for and, once gained, to be jealously guarded. Our heritage of self-reliance and individual autonomy goes back to the dawn of European civilization and even before. It is such an integral part of our culture that most Americans think of it as a basic aspect of human nature, even though it is not.

Our emphasis on self-reliance and autonomy is translated into norms which permeate our lives. We are expected to be self-sufficient in terms of our financial security, to operate an autonomous household, to get around by ourselves, and to manage our own affairs. The very fact that we are free to make our own decisions serves to expand the alternatives we have for solving the problems we face.

But at the same time we also expect these same things of ourselves. When the individual who has been rewarded for acts of independence by his parents, who has been approved of by his peers, who has received the satisfaction of manipulating and controlling his environment, and who has probably experienced the mixed pleasures of having others depend upon him realizes that he is losing his ability to function independently, he must cope not only with society's disapproval of dependence, but also with his own fear and disapproval of the dependent role.[4]

The only respite from this anxiety and fear exists for those segments of the population who are allowed a little dependency. For example, women are allowed to depend on their husbands and their children. Sick people are allowed to be more dependent than are healthy people. These exceptions notwithstanding, anxiety and fear are the usual reactions of older adults who face dependency.

In developmental terms, it appears that becoming independent is a task that cuts across most of childhood, adolescence, and young adulthood. At the same time there is reason to believe that learning to accept dependency is a major developmental task of old age, when old age is defined in symptomatic terms.

The concept of independence has a great many aspects because it refers to *how* we play our various roles as well as to the roles we play. For

---

[4] Kalish, *op. cit.*, p. 67.

this reason, the need for independence is present in almost every aspect of American life that requires individual participation: family, friendships, community, the job, politics, the church, recreation and leisure, and many others. Independence is perhaps *most* important, however, in terms of finances, housing, and mobility.

Financial independence is a necessary condition for maximizing older people's options and opportunities. This has been well documented throughout this book. Lack of financial resources is the most frequent reason that older people cite for having to rely on others—for becoming dependent.

Housing is another important aspect of independence. One of the norms of adult independence requires maintaining one's own household. This norm is reflected in older people's attitudes toward their living arrangements, since only 8 percent of people sixty-five and over say that they would rather live with a child or other relative than in their own homes.[5] It is also reflected in the fact that 87 percent of American older people were living in their own households in 1963.[6] Living arrangements are also related to privacy, another important aspect of independence.

Housing is crucial to independence. In one's own household one has much more privacy and freedom of choice than when one must accommodate oneself to the desires of others. When an older person lives with his child, for example, it is often the child who makes the decisions in the household. For an adult who is accustomed to making decisions not only for himself but for others, this can be a significant reduction in independence.

Mobility is also a vital aspect of independence, particularly in the United States with its spread-out cities. It is quite literally impossible to live an independent life in many American cities without an automobile. The shopping facilities, service facilities such as barber shops, beauty shops, shoe repair shops and the like, and even churches are often located far from the city's residential areas. Our middle-sized cities—those with populations ranging from 50,000 to 200,000—are encountering a steady decline in public transportation.

For the older person who can no longer afford to maintain an automobile, or who is physically unable to operate one, there is seldom an alternative to depending on friends and relatives for transportation. The fact that less than half of the older population owns an automobile suggests how prevalent this kind of limitation on independence is. This area is one in which more research is greatly needed. There are very few data on the extent to which indpendence in the later years is hampered by inadequacies in transportation.

---

[5] Riley, Matilda W. and Ann Foner, *Aging and Society*, Vol. I, *An Inventory of Research Findings*. (New York: Russell Sage Foundation, 1968), p. 549.

[6] *Ibid.*, p. 129.

Often the changes that occur in the individual's physical and social life as he grows older leave him with virtually no alternatives. When this happens, he is almost bound to sense a loss of independence. The significant question is just how much independence older people have, and how much they are forced to give up.

Only about 40 percent of older people in the United States have incomes at or above the modest but adequate level. About four-fifths have housing independence and around half have the use of an automobile. From these data it appears that older people tend to lose their financial independence first, their independence of movement second, and their independence of household last.

A certain level of health is necessary for independence, but it is not very high. As one older person put it, "I'm not looking to be a spring chicken, I just don't want to be an invalid." In fact, twice as many disabled older people live in private homes as in institutions. No doubt this is partly the result of financial problems, but there is a strong possibility that a feared loss of independence may keep away many people who should be in nursing homes.

A definite problem with the concept of sociological independence at this point is the paucity of data. The only research that has dealt extensively with social dependency and its relationship to aging is that done by Clark and Anderson.[7] Their study of aging in San Francisco came upon the idea of dependency almost by accident. They set out to study the cultural aspects of aging with particular emphasis on the relationship between culture and personality. The social institutions they devoted the most attention to were the family, friends and neighbors, organizations, work, retirement, and religion. They attempted to relate the older person's social situation to personal characteristics such as morale, isolation, and loneliness. At the conclusion of their study, Clark and Anderson state:

> The most unequivocal finding to come out of our social analysis of this sample is the singularity of the subjects in it. This singularity is interpreted by these subjects in many ways: it is proud independence; it is autonomy prized as befitting "a good, upstanding American"; or it is shrinking from others for fear of rejection, or an invasion into sacred privacy for purposes of manipulation or the offering of unwanted "charity."[8]

Much of what Clark and Anderson present must be confirmed by additional research, yet something may be gained by considering the implications of their findings, tentative as they may be.

---

[7] Margaret Clark and Barbara Anderson, *Culture and Aging* (Springfield, Illinois: Charles C Thomas, 1967).

[8] *Ibid.*, p. 425.

Apparently the meaning of independence changes with increasing age. To the young adult it means a newly found freedom; to the middle-aged adult it means the normal way of living—as continuing proof of adulthood and self-worth; and to the adult in later maturity or old age it means the same thing as in middle-age with the added feeling that independence is something to be protected. In old age, the need to maintain independence sometimes approaches desperation because of the physical problems involved, but for the majority of older adults the expectation of continued independence, particularly with regard to staying in one's own household, is a realistic one. In the typical situation, when job and income are both long gone, remaining an independent adult is an important source of self-esteem.

Clark and Anderson observed that there were two quite different sets of reasons for wanting to remain independent in one's later years. One set of reasons is basically adaptive for the individual; it includes pride in autonomy and concern for the freedom of others. The pride that comes from making decisions and doing things for oneself is a major source of self-esteem in a society that values independence as highly as ours. The desire to remain independent in order to preserve one's pride is basically an adaptive motive because pride is akin to self-esteem, a personality trait most people seek to attain or maintain.

It is likewise adaptive to respect the independence of others. The aged parent who goes out of his way to avoid imposing on his children has a greater chance of having his children respect his own independence. Many older people in America say they wish to avoid being a burden on their families, and this also provides strong motivation for remaining independent as long as possible. Also behind this notion is the negative evaluation of dependency. Being a burden not only inconveniences the other person, but it also lowers your status in their eyes. In these terms, then, we would expect that the stronger the desire for respect from one's children, the greater the motivation to remain independent.

The maladaptive reasons for wanting to remain independent include fear and mistrust of others and the need for psychological defenses. Older people often seek to remain independent because they are afraid that others will attempt to use them, to manipulate them and thus impose an unacceptable situation on them. There is sometimes an accompanying feeling that once others get into your life, it is not so easy to get them out. There is also a mistrust of the motives for helping older people, the rationale being that the only reason a person would seek out an older person in our society would be for personal gain.

A second maladaptive reason for preserving independence is to use isolation as a defense mechanism. A study of people who refused an in-person interview concluded that a sizeable number of older women held very unrealistic concepts of themselves and sought to restrict their interaction with others in order to avoid a negative reaction to the unrealistic self they presented.[9] Independence in these terms is used as a tool for preserving a vulnerable self-concept. An independent person is more capable of controlling whom he sees and in what situations.

Both of these reasons are maladaptive simply because they lead to isolation. It is very clear from the research findings that isolation is deadly for the older person. Isolation has some important side effects. It increases privacy, but in older people it also increases vulnerability to illness, accidents, malnutrition, and loneliness. In addition, isolation greatly increases the social distance between the generations. If the motives just mentioned became the main reasons for seeking independence, they can gradually lead to complete withdrawal; whereas adaptive motives for retaining independence are positive in the sense that they specify conditions to be sought rather than avoided, and they are also attainable without resorting to isolation.

Given the value placed on independence, it would be very difficult for an adult American to avoid valuing it. There is, therefore, probably a very strong relationship between the value a person puts on independence for himself and his reaction to both the possibility and the fact of dependency.

Older people's attitudes toward dependency tend to be very negative, a fact no doubt related to the generally high degree of motivation among older people to remain independent. The positive value of independence plus the negative value of not encroaching on the independence of others results in strongly negative attitudes toward even the idea of dependency.

Apparently the negative attitudes toward dependency and the strong positive valuation of independence combine to make the dependent older person miserable. In their intensive sample, Clark and Anderson found that the number-one cause of low morale among older people was dependency, either financial or physical.[10]

If the older person is dependent on his children, a great strain is usually put on their relationship—another factor which contributes to a negative attitude toward dependency. If the older person can remain autonomous, or if there is mutual dependence, then the relationship can remain a good one, but apparently there cannot be a happy reversal of roles between parent and child. Many psychologists have remarked about the crisis of authority that most children encounter. This crisis may be a mere shadow in comparison to the authority crisis an older person goes through if he must become dependent on his children. Both the parent and the child resent the change, both feel guilt as a result of their resentment; and both tend to become hostile toward the source of their guilt. This kind of

---

[9] Robert C. Atchley, "Respondents vs. Refusers in an Interview Study of Retired Women," *Journal of Gerontology*, 24:42–47, 1969.

[10] Clark and Anderson, *op. cit.*, p. 222.

relationship is a vicious circle of resentment, guilt, and hostility that tends to grow increasingly worse—often to the point of a breakdown in the relationship between parent and child.

The dread with which most older people regard dependency is thus very realistic. Yet as age increases, so does their need for outside help. Illness, poverty, disability, declining energy, anxiety and loneliness, failing hearing or sight—all of these roads lead to dependency. Often services in the older person's own home might well allow him to retain a measure of autonomy, and in some cases such services are being provided. Visiting nurses, homemaker services, and meals-on-wheels are examples of community services that are available in some areas. Unfortunately, most older people do not have access to these services, and even those who do either do not know about them or find them inadequate.

There is a shortage of medical and service personnel in the United States, especially in rural areas, and providing specialized home service for older people is somewhat erroneously regarded as expensive and inefficient. Instead, efforts are focused on institutions—nursing homes and homes for the aged. Here the needed supports can be provided, but here also even the illusion of self-help or self-determination all too often disappears.

Clark and Anderson found that:

> Some of the aged in our sample feel that, if help can be obtained only at the expense of institutionalization, if the small sphere of respectable autonomy that constitutes the aged person's shrunken life-space can be punctured like a child's balloon—then it may be best to gamble on one's own with survival. Such people will draw their curtains to avoid critical appraisals of their helplessness; they will not get enough to eat; they will stay away from the doctor and forego even vital drugs; they will shiver with cold; they will live in filth and squalor—but pride they will relinquish only as a last resort."[11]

Not all older people react in this extreme fashion, but there is some evidence that older people who do enter institutions are reluctant to do so because they fear loss of independence. More research is needed on the relationship between individual social independence within the institutional setting and adjustment to institutional life. The most reasonable hypothesis would appear to be that the more choices the individual is given in the institutional setting, the better he will like living in the institution and the better his adjustment will be. This hypothesis implies that the decisions left to the individual must be as important as possible.

---

[11] *Ibid.*, p. 391.

Summary

Americans prize their independence highly. From infancy, the American is taught to go it alone, to do things for himself. Adulthood is related to physical and financial independence. Dependency is deplored, and dependents are relegated to inferior positions.

Objectively, social independence means having enough money to get by on, having a household of one's own, and enough health to be able to get around. Independence is a very relative concept. We almost always have some degree of independence, even if it consists of refusing to eat tomato soup. Having money and health are the primary keys to independence in American society, and accordingly there are identifiable phases in the loss of independence. Money generally goes first, often as a result of retirement. Health goes second, partly as a result of the loss in income, and with it often goes a large measure of the individual's ability to get around. Finally, when health declines to the point of incapacity, the individual goes into an institution.

A strong desire for independence has been found to be typical of older people. Sometimes this motivation comes from the pride of being self-sufficient, sometimes from a desire to avoid burdening others, sometimes from a fear and mistrust of others, and sometimes from a desire to defend an unrealistic concept of oneself. The latter two types of motivation are often maladaptive because they tend to increase isolation and vulnerability.

As a result of the high value placed on independence, most older people hold extremely negative attitudes toward dependency. The reaction to dependency is thus highly predictable. It makes older people despise themselves and their situation. Compounding the problem is the fact that older people often must depend on their children—a situation that degrades the older person and puts a strain on his relationships with his children.

It should not be surprising, then, that some older people would literally prefer to die rather than become dependent. This situation is aggravated by the fact that our community supports are inadequate, and many of our medical services are organized in such a way as to deprive the individual of independence.

Accordingly, it appears that one of the key developmental tasks an older person faces is that of accepting dependency. However, this does not mean that older people should be left alone to do or die. It is virtually impossible for a person to change completely; therefore the adjustment required of the older person must be kept as small as possible to give him the greatest chance for success in performing the developmental task. This would require social change in order to support the older person's need for independence while allowing him to gradually accommodate to dependence, and it would also be expensive.

Ideally, the older person with an inadequate income would be able to get a supplementary income from public sources without having to become dependent on his children. Such income would be a right, and the person would not be made to feel like a parasite. Health services, including medicines, would be supported by the public, and community service programs such as homemakers, visiting nurses, and meals-on-wheels would be expanded and made available to all older people.

The object of such provisions would be to help the individual maintain as much independence as possible. The idea here is that an older person is much more likely to accept a certain amount of dependence if he can see that it will enhance his overall independence.

Even in the institutional setting, the individual's negative reaction to dependency may be reduced by respecting his desire for independence by giving him as many choices as possible. Small things such as alternate choices on menus, therapy sequences, or maid service can become important in a world of rapidly diminishing choices. Individual choice in the important things, such as odd jobs in the institution or leisure pursuits, *must* be respected if the individual is to adjust to the degree of dependency found in most institutions.

Experiments on older mental patients using an approach which maximized their opportunities to exercise their independence have shown a high degree of success in rehabilitating such people to a remarkably self-sufficient level. Certainly much more research is needed to establish the role that dependency plays in individual adjustment to aging.

Bibliography

Clark, Margaret and Barbara Anderson, *Culture and Aging.* Springfield, Illinois: Charles C. Thomas, 1967.

Kalish, Richard A., "Of Children and Grandfathers. A Speculative Essay on Dependency," *Gerontologist,* 7:65–69, 1967.

————, ed., *The Dependencies of Old People.* Ann Arbor, Michigan: University of Michigan, Wayne State University Institute of Gerontology, 1969.

Martin, J. David, "Power, Dependence, and the Complaints of the Elderly: A Social Exchange Perspective," *Aging and Human Development,* 2:108–112, 1971.

Solomon, Barbara, "Social Functioning of Economically Dependent Aged," *Gerontologist,* 7:213–217, 1967.

12

Personal Adjustment to Aging

This chapter examines how the aging individual responds to changes in himself and in the social situation that confronts him. This is a difficult topic for several reasons. First, changes associated with aging do not occur all at once for any given individual. Hearing may decline before vision does; personality changes may occur before any of the biological changes. Second, no two individuals are apt to confront *exactly* the same changes at exactly the same stage of their lives. Third, the manner in which different people respond to the same change varies greatly.

Biological decline and increased susceptibility to disease indirectly make certain adjustments inevitable. The relatively inefficient operation of the body reduces the energy available to the individual and restricts the number and the kinds of things he can do and how he can do them. The most frequent response to energy decline is probably to conserve energy. Confronted with too many activities for the amount of energy available, the older person is most likely to drop those activities he considers marginal to his life. Only after a considerable limitation in energy is he apt to drop or restrict activities he considers essential. Retirement and widowhood are major exceptions to this pattern of voluntary choice.

Increased susceptibility to disease also restricts activity. Physical impairment and sickness are in some ways more difficult to adjust to than the decline in energy, because physical impairment often *dictates* the activities that must be dropped.

Inability to recover balance is a change very much like physical impairment, for it too dictates both what things can be done and how.

Deterioration of vision and hearing also restrict older people's activities. Fortunately, most older people can wear corrective glasses or hearing aids and thus maintain adequate social functioning. Only a very small proportion of older people must make a greater adjustment where vision or hearing losses cannot be corrected.

Yet, hearing or vision losses can create problems when the person refuses to recognize them or to use a compensating device. For example, an elderly lady I once interviewed was quite deaf. She had taken a course in lip reading, "so I could teach it to people who need it." She steadfastly refused to admit that she was deaf. Her impaired hearing had resulted in a distorted speech pattern which resembled the slur of a drunkard, and on top of that she literally shouted when she spoke. Her employer was not aware that she was deaf; he thought she was an alcoholic and fired her. If this woman's vanity had allowed her to accept the fact that she was deaf and to do something about it, she might have saved herself a great deal of personal agony.

The findings indicate that most biological and psychological functions in man decline with advanced age. These biological and psychological changes in turn influence the individual's personality and social situation.

The personality of the older person is typically rigid in both attitudes and behavior.[1] Increasing inability to perform new intellectual or psychomotor tasks appears to predispose older people toward sticking to the tried and true, the skills and attitudes developed earlier when their learning abilities were unimpaired. Older people are more restrained, less impulsive, and more cautious than younger people. This fits in with the need to adjust to declining ability by limiting the types of activity one will try. Older people are more passive, more concerned with themselves, and more introverted than younger people. This turning inward could be viewed as a response to an external environment that is viewed as increasingly more hostile and less rewarding.

In addition to the limitations imposed on the older person by illness, declining energy, and declining psychological skills, role changes in later life also present a problem for adjustment. Retirement, widowhood, and dependency are particularly significant role changes which require the older person to adjust.

Some General Reactions to Aging

Neugarten has referred to the increasingly inward orientation of older people.[2] Cumming and Henry have used the term *disengagement* for the process whereby the individual gradually and inevitably withdraws from the various roles he occupied in middle age toward ever-increasing concern with self and isolation.

---

[1] Matilda W. Riley and Ann Foner, *Aging and Society*, Vol. I, *An Inventory of Research Findings*. (New York: Russell Sage Foundation, 1968), pp. 276–279.

[2] Bernice Neugarten, *Personality in Middle and Late Life* (New York: Atherton Press, 1964).

In our theory, aging is an inevitable mutual withdrawal or disengagement, resulting in decreased interaction between the aging person and others in the social system he belongs to. The process may be initiated by the individual or by others in the situation. The older person may withdraw more markedly from some classes of people while remaining relatively close to others. His withdrawal may be accompanied from the outset by an increased preoccupation with himself; certain institutions in society may make this withdrawal easy for him. When the aging process is complete, the equilibrium which existed in middle life between the individual and his society has given way to a new equilibrium characterized by a greater distance and an altered type of relationship.[3]

The reduced frequency of interaction supposedly weakens the hold of norms over the individual. Thus, the disengaged person becomes a free person. Freed from social pressures, the disengaged individual with his declining physical energy is content to live with symbols from the past. To the extent that roles are available to allow him to live in his own self-centered world, his morale will remain high; but if he cannot find roles which allow this, his morale will probably decline with increasing disengagement.

The individual is said to be ready for disengagement when he becomes aware of the short amount of life remaining to him, when he perceives his life space as shrinking, and his ego-energy as lessened.

The disengagement process is molded by the same character traits which influence the individual's behavior at other points in the life cycle. The individual is said to adapt to the world around him in one of two ways: impinging or selecting.[4]

The *impinger* is the other-directed man. He continuously seeks clues as to whether he is behaving properly. He actively seeks interaction with others because only from such interaction can he sustain a self-concept. For such a person disengagement may bring a period of anxiety and intense activity, for the self-concept appropriate to middle age is no longer verified by others, and the impinger must seek frequent interaction in order to modify his behavior and achieve a self-concept which will be supported by those with whom he interacts. The impinger is thus very likely to change his conception of himself as the disengagement process proceeds.

The *selector* is the inner-directed man. He knows what he should be without asking others, and therefore he need not seek interaction to confirm his self-concept. He allows the world to pass him by without interacting with it. And from what interaction he does experience he selectively

---

[3] Elaine Cumming and W. E. Henry, *Growing Old* (New York: Basic Books, 1961), pp. 14–15.

[4] Elaine Cumming, "New Thoughts on the Theory of Disengagement," in *New Thoughts on Old Age,* ed. Robert Kastenbaum (New York: Springer, 1964).

perceives only those clues which support his preconceived ideas about himself. The selector is thus very unlikely to change his image of himself as the disengagement process proceeds. He is likely to further reduce interaction in order to reduce the number of clues which must be ignored.

Engagement is the degree to which the individual is involved with the world around him. He may be *broadly* engaged in a number of roles, *deeply* engaged in a few roles, or *symbolically* engaged as one who stands for something, such as an elder statesman. Obviously, engagement involves not only roles, but a psychological *commitment* on the part of the individual. For example, an older man who is very active in the sense that he interacts frequently with people may simply be a *disengaged impinger* searching for a new identity. Accordingly, in order to measure disengagement the investigator must study changes over time in the individual's commitments to roles, and in the types of roles to which he is committed. The disengaged man is thus one who has a low commitment to various roles normally thought of as important.

Disengagement is thus *one* possible response to shrinking life space and reduced energy. The individual withdraws from the world rather than adjusting to it. More will be said about disengagement later, when we discuss successful aging.

Another general reaction to aging is a rise in over-all anxiety. Constructive attempts are sometimes made to reduce this anxiety through education or therapy, but more often it leads to defensive or handicapping behavior patterns.[5] The conservatism, rigidity, and intolerance of ambiguity sometimes found among older people may be seen as defense mechanisms set up to control this increasing anxiety. The point at which generalized anxiety becomes a problem for the individual is the point at which he discovers that his world is no longer expanding, but has begun to contract. The greater the contraction, the greater the anxiety, and the greater the defenses. In fact, disengagement might be thought of as a particular type of defense mechanism.

Williams and Wirths have advanced the notion that the adjustment an individual makes to aging is very much related to the main focus of his style of life.[6] This idea is more individualistic than those previously discussed, because it contends that the individual's reaction to aging springs from his particular style of life. Williams and Wirths identified six styles of life among the older people they studied.[7]

---

[5] Raymond G. Kuhlen, "Developmental Changes in Motivation During the Adult Years," in *Relations of Development and Aging,* ed. James Birren (Springfield, Illinois: Charles C. Thomas, 1964).

[6] Richard H. Williams, "Styles of Life and Successful Aging," in *Processes of Aging,* eds. Richard H. Williams, Clark Tibbitts, and Wilma Donahue (New York: Atherton, 1963).

[7] Richard H. Williams and Claudine Wirths, *Lives through the Years* (New York: Atherton, 1965).

World of work   People who adhere to this life style focus their attention on work to give meaning to their lives. This is a narrower focus than is characteristic of the other life styles, and accordingly this life style allows little leeway for attempting adjustment. The person with a World of Work style is apt to resist retirement as long as possible, and attempt to replace work as quickly as possible with volunteer jobs or other work substitutes. However, people do develop secondary life styles, and some World of Work people successfully shift to make their secondary style their primary style. When World of Work is the *only* life style the individual has ever attempted, then all alternative styles are closed, and adjustment is usually difficult.

Familism   The focus for people who use this style is their family. Their major decisions are made in relation to the family, their values center around the family, and family is the most important area of their lives. This style is more affective (emotional) than instrumental (as in World of Work) and thus encompasses a much wider range of activities. Individuals with this life style usually have considerable leeway in their reactions to aging.

Living alone   People using this life style are social isolates. Aloneness here does not necessarily refer to living arrangements, but rather to the central focus of the individual's style of coping with the world. When this style is developed in the later years, it is equivalent to total disengagement. It is prevalent among inner-directed people, particularly those who *like* being loners.

Couplehood   The focus of this style is the significant paired relationship. It can be related to Familism, but need not be. For example, two elderly women may live together and focus their lives on the bond between them. Like Familism this style is wide-ranging and is typified by affective rather than instrumental emphasis, but it has an element of precariousness due to the possibility that something could happen to the other person.

Easing through life with minimal involvement   People using this style have only a minimal commitment to most of the roles they play, including work, marriage, and family roles. This is a difficult style to achieve, primarily because there are many informal sanctions against it, and social pressures to become involved are always present. If this style persists throughout life, the person never really becomes engaged in his social world, but if it is adopted later in life, it represents another type of disengagement.

Living fully   People using this style do not focus their energies on any specific part of life; instead they spread themselves rather broadly. Yet their involvement in most aspects of living is more than minimal, and they tend to be the opposite of disengaged. Even when disengagement is forced on them, they deal with it effectively. "Living Fully, as a style, expresses one facet of the Christian ethic, 'I am come that you might have life and that you might have it more abundantly.' It is a socially approved style, and many popular programs of living arrangements and recreation for the aged are based on the assumption that this is a greatly preferred style of life."[8]

Williams and Wirths caution that within each of these life styles can be found varying degrees of commitment to the style, of satisfaction derived from the style, of energy utilization, and particularly of successful aging. Within each of the styles, they found cases of very successful and of very unsuccessful aging.

It should be obvious that no single predictable reaction to the aging process can be expected. Individuals may react by withdrawing, by building walls around themselves, or by increasing their activity. Adjustment to aging is most often shaped by a combination of factors arising from the individual's personality, his physical limitations, and his social situation.

Successful Aging

Implied in the concept of successful aging is a value judgment to the effect that some adjustments are better (successful) than others (unsuccessful). Social gerontology contains many definitions of successful aging.

The *activity theory,* sometimes called life space theory, is perhaps the most prevalent theory of successful aging. It holds that to age successfully one must maintain into old age the activity patterns and values typical of middle age. These values stress maintaining a large number of roles and being very active in them. "To age successfully, in this sense, precaution should be taken against shrinkage of the life space, and substitute activities should be found when necessary."[9]

> The activity theory is favored by most of the practical workers in gerontology. They believe that people should maintain the activities and attitudes of middle age as long as possible and then find substitutes for the activities which they must give up—for work when they are forced to retire, for clubs and associations, for friends and loved ones whom they lose by death.[10]

Evidence indicates that for most older people, the level of activity they have developed over a lifetime tends to persist into their later years.[11]

---

[8] *Ibid.,* p. 155.

[9] *Ibid.,* p. 3.

[10] Robert J. Havighurst, "Successful Aging," in *Processes of Aging, op. cit.,* p. 309.

[11] Riley and Foner, *op. cit.,* p. 418.

Yet activity theory is idealistic, for it sets up the expectation that older people will be carbon copies of middle-aged people with no patterns of behavior peculiar to themselves. This expectation is unrealistic for all but a small minority of older people in view of the limitations imposed by biological changes alone.

The *disengagement* theorists see old age as a potential developmental stage in its own right, with features very different from those of middle age.[12] Disengagement theory looks upon old age as a period during which the individual gradually and voluntarily disinvolves himself from his various positions and roles. Activity reduction in old age is thus welcomed by the individual and should be considered normal. Successful aging in these terms would mean successfully coping with disengagement; and the person who tried to maintain a large array of activities in his old age would be deemed unsuccessful by disengagement theorists. Thus, activity theory and disengagement theory provide opposing definitions of successful aging.

In terms of *personality* theory, a person is said to have aged successfully if he can maintain a mature and integrated personality while going through the aging process. This means essentially that as a person ages, he must be able to make his past experiences and his current experiences live well with each other. This theory is too vague to be usable in this form. But it is important because it formed the basis for the life satisfaction theory.

The *life satisfaction theory* holds that a person has aged successfully if he feels happy and satisfied with his present and past life. This basically subjective theory follows directly from the personality theory and defines success in terms of inner satisfaction rather than external adjustment. Havighurst and Neugarten isolated what they feel to be five components of positive life satisfaction: 1) Zest; showing zest in several areas of life, liking to do things, being enthusiastic, 2) Resolution and fortitude; not giving up, taking good with bad and making the most of it, accepting responsibility for one's own personal life, 3) Agreement between desired and achieved goals; feeling of having accomplished what one wanted to, 4) Positive self-concept; thinking of oneself as a person of worth, 5) Mood tone; showing happiness, optimism, and pleasure with life.[13]

Williams and Wirths have developed a theory of successful aging based on the individual's *personal action system*. The personal action system is defined as follows:

> The social system of an individual actor is a system of action, that is, behavior which is meaningful. Meaningful means oriented toward ends, goals and values which, in turn, can be communicated to and usually shared in by others. Thus, it is composed of all the transactions of an in-

---

[12] Cumming and Henry, *op. cit.,* p. 383.
[13] Havighurst, *op. cit.,* p. 305.

dividual in his social life space. . . . A given actor . . . can be taken as the focal point and questioned about the dimensions and structure of his social life space, modes of interaction in it, attitudinal set toward it, satisfaction or dissatisfaction he derives from it, and degree of its stability over time.[14]

The elements of the personal action system that are said to be pertinent to success in aging are *autonomy* and *persistence*. Autonomy refers to the exchange of energy between the actor and the rest of his action system. If the actor puts about as much energy into his action system as he takes from it, he is said to be *autonomous*. If he takes more from others than he gives to them, he is said to be *dependent*.

Persistence refers to the stability of the personal action system. A persistent action system is one that is apt to remain stable for some time. Opposed to this is the *precarious* system that may collapse or change its characteristics significantly at any time.

Successful aging is defined in terms of autonomy and persistence. "If the overall relation of the individual to his social system is both autonomous and persistent, he is aging successfully. If it is autonomous but precarious, he is aging less successfully. If it is dependent and persistent in dependency, he is aging still less successfully; and if it is dependent and precarious, he is least successful. . . ."[15]

In their Kansas City sample, Williams and Wirths found that 64 percent of those questioned fell into the autonomous-persistent category and were therefore rated as being most successful agers.

Perhaps the most comprehensive and most fruitful theory of successful aging is the developmental theory of Clark and Anderson.[16] Developmental theory in general considers that personality arises out of the response to various developmental tasks. These tasks are things the person must accomplish if he is to achieve the next developmental stage in personality growth. For example, one of the prime developmental tasks might be learning roles appropriate to the various stages of life.

Erikson separates personality development into eight stages: early infancy, later infancy, early childhood, middle childhood, adolescence, early adulthood, middle adulthood, and late adulthood. Late adulthood was typified by the need to accept one's life as having been inevitable, appropriate, and meaningful.[17]

Borrowing elements from various developmental theories, Clark and Anderson have constructed a set of *adaptive* tasks, as they call them, that

---

[14] Williams and Wirths, *op. cit.*, p. 5.

[15] *Ibid.*, p. 10.

[16] Margaret Clark and Barbara G. Anderson, *Culture and Aging* (Springfield, Illinois: Charles C. Thomas, 1967), pp. 392–433.

[17] Neugarten, *op. cit.*

must be accomplished if the person is to age successfully. They differentiate *development*, learning to live with oneself as one changes, from *adaptation*, learning to live in a particular way according to a particular set of values as one changes or as one's culture changes. They depart from what is essentially a personality theory by bringing social pressures into the act. Successful adaptation requires not only internal accommodation to one's own system of needs but also conformity to the demands of society.

Clark and Anderson identify five adaptive tasks which they associate with later adulthood and aging:

1. Recognition of aging and definition of instrumental limitations.
2. Redefinition of physical and social life space.
3. Substitution of alternate sources of need-satisfaction.
4. Reassessment of criteria for evaluation of the self.
5. Reintegration of values and life goals.

Recognition of aging and definition of instrumental limitations "requires an awareness and an acceptance of changes in one's own physical and/or mental capabilities, with acknowledgment that certain activities can no longer be pursued as successfully as they were in one's earlier life."[18] Better adapted older people conserve their health and energies, and they can come to terms with the limitations society puts on the roles they can play. "There must be an awareness of social pressures to relinquish the roles and activities of middle-life and a realistic assessment of what those pressures mean in terms of available supports. . . . The important point in this task is that, although an individual need not *like* his own personal or social circumstances as he grows old, he must not deny the reality of certain limitations, if they exist for him."[19]

Redefinition of physical and social life space involves redefining the boundaries of one's life space. The individual must manipulate his situation to achieve an ideal level of control over his personal action system. As age increases, the individual may no longer be able to control as large a segment of the environment as he did when he was younger. "In social terms, this means that certain roles and activities must be relinquished, and there must follow a reconstitution of one's network of social relationships."[20] Often this reconstruction of social relationships is a *constriction* of them as well.

Here is what can happen when this task is not accomplished:

At sixty-six, Mr. Butler can best be described as a man with a very diffuse life. He is simultaneously headed in several major directions;

---

[18] Clark and Anderson, *op. cit.*, p. 402.
[19] *Ibid.*, pp. 402–403.
[20] *Ibid.*, p. 404.

first, he is trying to finish his term of teaching in order to receive his full pension. His goal in teaching has been to become an administrator: "The reason why I wanted to be an administrator—well, they make much more money. And it gives you the importance and responsibility you seek." Now, with only two years of teaching remaining before his retirement, Mr. Butler is compelled to face the fact that he will never reach this goal. Now he is finding it difficult even to manage his classes. He speaks of difficulties in maintaining discipline in his classroom, in handling "behavior problems," and recently he received a reprimand from his school principal for losing his temper with a student and giving the boy a severe shaking. He admits that, with age, he has become more irritable and less able to cope with the demands of public school teaching. In spite of this fact, however, Mr. Butler is still trying simultaneously to fill his teaching position, study for a state license as a real estate salesman, arrange for the purchase and management of a large apartment building, plan business and stock investments, stabilize a precarious relationship with his wife, support a daughter in Switzerland, and maintain active contacts with a wide circle of friends.

Mr. Butler insists on keeping many irons in the fire. Yet, with the loss of energy due to advancing age, he is finding it increasingly difficult to be successful in this. He admits to making several errors of judgment in business within recent years; we have already pointed to his irritability and impatience with the students; also he admits to some chronic marital difficulties, in part because he is drinking so much more now than he used to (he admits that drinking has become a problem for him); and he is even concerned about maintaining friendships because he fears being "found out a phony."

Interestingly enough, Mr. Butler gave us the following formula for successful aging: "Well, keep your expectations within limits so that you can achieve your goals." Certainly, he himself has not been able to accomplish this, and his control over his environment is being eroded day after day. His horizons, once so far and wide, now seem to be receding beyond his failing grasp. Mr. Butler is a very unhappy man.[21]

Substitution of alternative sources of need-satisfaction requires that aging individuals affect the substitution of feasible interests, activities, and relationships for those they can no longer pursue successfully, thus providing alternative sources of need-satisfaction. Adaptation requires a willingness and an ability to identify and engage in new feasible pursuits; and socially, the individual must have access to possible alternatives within his environment.[22] People who cannot live without work or who cannot cope with widowhood or dependency are failing at this task.

Reassessment of criteria for evaluation of self means that the individual must modify the ideas he uses as the basis for his self-concept. For example, it is not adaptive for the older person to continue to derive his self-concept from his performance in the work role. Likewise, in society there

---

[21] *Ibid.*, pp. 405–406. Reprinted by permission.
[22] *Ibid.*, p. 407.

must be criteria other than work for determining a person's worth. In order to maintain self-esteem, older people must establish their identity on roles other than those of worker, builder, manager, or leader. Without self-approval, the individual is apt to feel utterly useless. As one man put it,

> Now? Now I don't care. You have to be realistic about this. I feel I have lived my life. There is none of me left. . . . What am I good for? I just keep on living. Oh, I'm not a morose man—it isn't a question of that. I have enough money to live decently. My wife is alive and the children come from time to time. I find things to do around the house to keep me busy. But it's not enough. Somehow, it's just not enough. I keep wishing I could do some good—be useful.[23]

Reintegration of values and life goals means revising life goals and values to give coherence, integration, and social meaning to one's new style of life. The older person must not only preserve his self-esteem, but he must also find a new place for himself in the broader scheme of things. This gives his life added meaning and purpose.

A Case of Successful Aging

To complete this discussion, we will describe one additional case, that of Mr. Ed Hart, a man who has skillfully adapted—both personally and socially—to all five tasks. We first saw Mr. Hart when he was ninety years old. He was born in 1870, the only child of middle-aged parents. He started working and contributing significantly to the household budget at a very early age; while still in his teens, he turned over his considerable savings to his parents, enabling them to purchase a home. Still in his youth, he assumed a "parental" role toward his parents, being obliged to do so because much of his father's time was spent in taking care of the then invalid mother. Mr. Hart attended school, learned cabinetmaking from his father, and devoted himself to caring for his parents.

Mr. Hart idolized his father throughout his life. Cabinetwork was always dear to him because it had been taught him by his father. He regarded his father's guidance as invaluable: it was he who kept his son away from the alcohol which he dearly loved, and it was also from his father that he acquired a sincere love for people. The relationship was a very harmonious one, each gladly accommodating himself to the wishes of the other. Although Mr. Hart married at the age of twenty-four, he and his wife continued to live with his parents until their death in 1912. Mr. Hart was closely attached to his wife, but his father had always remained the most important figure in his life.

---

[23] *Ibid.,* pp. 410–411.

He was content with cabinetwork until the age of thirty-five, at which time he bought a ranch, deciding to become a financial success for the sake of his children. He describes himself during this period as over-ambitious and given to excessive chronic worry. His preoccupation with making a fortune from this ranching endeavor led to a nervous break-down and confinement in a sanitarium for two months. This experience, when he was about forty, proved to be the turning point of his life. He emerged with a highly integrated personality and a satisfying personal philosophy. He had formerly been a zealous member of the Methodist Church, but following this hospitalization, he eschewed all organized re-ligions, feeling he needed no one to dictate to him how he should serve God. Nonetheless, Mr. Hart expresses a profound belief in divinity, a love of his fellow man, a full acceptance of everything life has to offer, and an adamant refusal to be unhappy.

Following his hospitalization, Mr. Hart sold his ranch and worked as a vocational teacher for the following six years. Again, he found deep satisfaction in his work and was loved by students and fellow teachers alike. He showed great understanding and evidently displayed remarkable skill in nurturing the talents of his students, adapting his teaching to the individual child's potential. His dislike for the regimentation practiced in the school led him to resign and to return to his former vocation of cabinetmaking, work he pursued up to the age of fifty-five. An injury to his arm, however, finally made him give up this successful occupation (some of his work had been exhibited at the 1939 San Francisco Inter-national Exposition). For the next twenty years, he was employed in the hotel business, work that he found congenial because of his interest in people. Retirement did not find him idle. Up to the age of ninety, he did cabinetwork as a hobby, manufacturing various items to present to his numerous friends.

Mr. Hart looks back on sixty-four years of harmonious and contented married life. His first wife died suddenly after twenty-five years of mar-riage when he was forty-nine years old. After living alone with his chil-dren for two years, he remarried at the age of fifty-one. Thirty years later, he lost his second wife, and it was upon her "last request" that he again remarried. His third wife had been a widowed friend they had both known for almost thirty years. This final marriage lasted for nine years. During the last two years of her life, the third wife was severely ill, and Mr. Hart nursed her through to the end. She died in 1960. Even during his last wife's terminal illness, Mr. Hart showed the same serenity and the same positive acceptance of life he expressed in all of our interviews with him. He does not differentiate among his wives: he describes them all as "dear, loyal women."

Mr. Hart finds it somewhat "humiliating" that he has outlived three wives and both of his sons. He took pains to raise his children as best he could and was anxious to let them develop their own individual ways. Rather than seeing himself as the provider of an estate, a role he had once thought so important, he finally perceived his parental role as that of the provider of good examples and wise guidance. His close relation-ship with his sons changed when they married, and Mr. Hart believes that it is only right that this should be so: "With marriage the offspring form independent units of their own, and parents should release their hold upon them." Mr. Hart was never possessive in his life. The persons closest to him at present are his daughter and step-daughter, who are equally dear. He mentions with pride that both have invited him to come and live with them, but he will not take this step until it is absolutely necessary. He does not wish to inconvenience them, but unlike many other of our subjects, he does not harp on the prospect of "becoming a burden" to somebody else.

From his middle years onward, Mr. Hart suffered a number of major illnesses: in 1926 he was operated on for a bilateral hernia; and in 1949, for a perforated ulcer; finally, a prostatectomy and colostomy in 1953 (he was eighty-three years old at the time) resulted in complete loss of control over his bladder, requiring him to wear a urinal twenty-four hours a day. When he was ninety, his physical condition no longer permitted him to indulge in his hobby of woodworking, and, at ninety-three, his failing eyesight ruled out television and limited his reading to one hour a day. Yet he takes his declining physical functions in stride, not finding it irksome to make necessary adjustments. His mental faculties have remained remarkably intact. He is keenly aware that few men his age are as mentally alert as he is, or have aged as gracefully. He is proud of this fact and attributes it to the philosophical orientation he has worked out for himself and incorporated into his life.

Although Mr. Hart has been obliged to curtail many of his social activities, he still corresponds with numerous friends and receives almost daily visits from solicitous neighbors. He gives much of himself and is warmly appreciated by others; he appears to bring out the best in others, which may be one of the reasons he claims he has never been disappointed by a friend. Mr. Hart has led a full, creative, and serene existence. It is perhaps because his life has been one of fulfillment that he is ready to surrender it at any moment; he still finds life quite enjoyable, but he is as willing to die as he is to continue living.

This man made a profound impression on all our interviewers. They found him alert, intelligent, serene, and wise. His self-acceptance is complete. He found it difficult to answer our self-image questions or to describe himself in terms of the list of various personality traits we submitted to him; he simply stated, more appropriately, "I'm Ed Hart and I don't want to be anyone else—I will be the same ten years from now, if I'm alive."

According to American middle-class standards, Mr. Hart has not been a particularly successful man. Looking at his life in one way, he has no particular reason not to be disappointed with his past and depressed with his present. He failed in his one great effort to become wealthy. After a nervous breakdown, he gave up on this venture altogether. He quit a second time when he dropped out of the teaching profession because he disagreed with established policy. One might expect him to be bitter about this, or terribly lonely, since he has outlived nearly all his friends and relatives—but he is neither. Crippled with disease, forced to wear a urinal at all times, and nearly blind, Mr. Hart gave one of our interviewers his philosophy of life: "I have an original motto which I follow: 'All things respond to the call of rejoicing; all things gather where life is a song.'"

It is clear that Mr. Hart has adapted to aging. He has admitted to and accepted physical limitations, first giving up the demanding manual labor of cabinetmaking, and later retiring without regret from hotel work.

Mr. Hart has no problems in controlling his life space—he does not over-extend himself: "As long as I don't strain myself, I'm okay. I take it easy. The other day I declined an invitation to go on board a ship, since I knew there would be stairs there."

All of his life, Mr. Hart has successfully practiced substitution, so this adaptation has been natural for him. He enjoyed married life and never remained a widower for long. He was capable of substituting one vocation for another, as necessity required, developing a deep interest and satisfaction in each. Even after his retirement from hotel work, his last job, he continued to be interested and active in union affairs. "That's my pork chop, so to speak," he says.

In personal philosophy, Mr. Hart has no problems at all. His standards for self-evaluation are not predicated on mutable factors such as productivity, wealth, or social status. He is first, last, and always himself: "I'm Ed Hart and I don't want to be anyone else." This is a standard not likely to totter with age.

However, his discovery of adaptive values and life goals was hard-won: at forty, he early found himself unable to cope with the instrumental and achievement-oriented values of his society. He suffered a severe emotional upheaval at that time, was hospitalized for a period, and emerged with a warm, humanistic philosophy which has carried him not only through middle age, but through old age as well.[24]

Using their adaptive tasks to define adaptation to aging, Clark and Anderson found that in general older people are adapted. Sixty-one percent of their community sample (San Francisco) was rated as adapted and 39 percent as maladapted. In their hospital sample, however, the percentages were reversed, with only 12 percent adapted and 88 percent maladapted.

In terms of specific tasks, Clark and Anderson found that the maladapted were distributed as follows:

Acceptance of aging	*11%*
Reorganization of life space	*14*
Substitute sources of need-satisfaction	*54*
Revision of criteria for self-evaluation	*14*
Reintegration of values and life goals	*7*

From these data it appears that finding substitutes for the things that satisfy their needs is the skill most lacking among maladapted older people.

Clark and Anderson conclude:

Those in our sample whom we found to be adapted in their old age have suggested the answer to this problem [of maladaptation and alienation in old age]. These are the elderly who have successfully developed personal codes of values which have eased their resolution of the adaptive

---

[24] *Ibid.,* pp. 415–419.

tasks of aging. . . . These codes are not alien to American culture—they are the secondary values—and those who survive best in their later years are simply those who have been able to drop their pursuits of primary values . . . and to go on to pick up, as workable substitutes, the alternative values which have been around all along: conservation instead of acquisition and exploitation; self-acceptance instead of continuous struggles for self-advancement; being rather than doing; congeniality, cooperation, love, and concern for others instead of control of others. These are the values the aged in our society have been forced to embrace.[25]

This model of adaptation is closely akin to the continuity theory presented earlier in connection with retirement and leisure participation. Those who were most able to pick up leisure in retirement were precisely those who had concentrated on "secondary" roles earlier in life.

The Clark and Anderson developmental theory of successful aging makes important additions to the study of aging. First, it assumes that old age is a developmental stage in its own right with its own peculiar set of problems. Second, it recognizes the cultural component in successful aging; and third, it provides a dynamic view of adaptation to aging. In addition, it provides the basis for synthesizing the other theories of successful aging by providing a framework into which to fit their respective concerns. It is more abstract, however, and is thus more difficult to operationalize than most of the other theories. Nevertheless, this developmental theory probably holds the greatest promise for the eventual understanding of success and failure in adjustment to aging.

Summary

Activity limitation in the later years springs simultaneously from biological, physical, psychological, and social phenomena. The individual is often limited in what he can do by the amount of energy he has, his physical health, his mental abilities, and social pressures. All of these forces converge on him to produce tremendous pressure toward restricting activity.

Sometimes age changes can be offset by compensating devices such as hearing aids, eyeglasses, golf carts, electric chairs that help people stand up, and so on; and in the majority of cases even those who must restrict their activities seem to be able to cope with aging. Several different criteria for successful aging all indicated that a majority of older people (around 60 to 65 percent) were successfully adapting in their old age. Evidence

---

[25] *Ibid.,* p. 429.

indicates that a small minority of older people are disproportionately unhappy in old age.

We have found that the style of adaptation an individual adopts is related to his social situation, his personality, his level of anxiety, and his life style (related to his values).

Theories of successful aging involved acceptance of activity limitation and a restriction of life space, satisfaction with life, autonomy and stability of life pattern, and an ability to find substitutes for lost activities that served key needs. The developmental theory of Clark and Anderson, which sees adaptation to aging as a series of problems to be solved, is perhaps the most comprehensive and promising of the theories considered.

Bibliography

Adams, David L., "Correlates of Satisfaction Among the Elderly," *Gerontologist,* 11:(4, part 2),64–68, 1971.

Alleger, Daniel E., "Anomia among the Aged," in *Social Change and Aging in the 20th Century,* ed. Daniel E. Alleger. Gainesville, Florida: University of Florida Press, 1964, pp. 70–77.

Back, Kurt W., and Kenneth J. Gergen, "Personal Orientation and Morale of the Aged," in *Social Aspects of Aging,* eds. Ida H. Simpson and John C. McKinney. Durham, North Carolina: Duke University Press, 1966, pp. 296–305.

Butler, Robert N., "The Life Review," *Psychology Today,* 5:49–51, December, 1971.

Cameron, Paul, "Ego Strength and Happiness of the Aged," *Journal of Gerontology,* 22:199–202, 1967.

Cavan, Ruth S., *et al., Personal Adjustment in Old Age.* Chicago: Science Research Associates, 1949.

Cesa-Bianchi, Marcello, "Mechanisms of Adjustment," *Gerontologist,* 7:86–87, 125–126, 1966.

Goldsamt, Milton R., "Life Satisfaction and the Older Disabled Worker," *Journal of the American Geriatrics Society,* 15:394–399, 1967.

Havens, Betty J., "An Investigation of Activity Patterns and Adjustment in an Aging Population," *Gerontologist,* 8:201–206, 1968.

Havighurst, Robert J., "Successful Aging," in *Processes of Aging,* eds. Richard H. Williams, Clark Tibbitts, and Wilma Donahue. New York: Atherton Press, 1963, I, 299–320.

————, Bernice L. Neugarten, and Sheldon S. Tobin, "Disengagement, Personality, and Life Satisfaction in the Later Years," in *Age with a Future,* ed., P. From Hansen. Copenhagen: Munksgaard, 1964, pp. 419–425.

Kastenbaum, Robert, "Getting There ahead of Time," *Psychology Today,* 5:52–58, December, 1971.

Kerckhoff, Alan C., "Family Patterns and Morale in Retirement," in *Social Aspects of Aging,* eds. Ida H. Simpson and John C. McKinney. Durham, North Carolina: Duke University Press, 1966, pp. 173–192.

Kleemeier, Robert W., "The Effect of a Work Program on the Adjustment

Attitudes in an Aged Population," *Journal of Gerontology*, 6:372–379, 1951.

Lipman, Aaron, "Public Housing and Attitudinal Adjustment in Old Age: A Comparative Study," *Journal of Geriatric Psychiatry*, 2:88–101, 1969.

Loeb, Martin B., Allen Pincus, and B. J. Mueller, "A Framework for Viewing Adjustment in Aging," *Gerontologist*, 6:185–187, 1966.

Lowenthal, Marjorie F. and Deetje Boler, "Voluntary vs. Involuntary Social Withdrawal," *Journal of Gerontology*, 20:363–371, 1965.

———— and Clayton Haven, "Interaction and Adaptation: Intimacy as a Critical Variable," in *Middle Age and Aging*, ed. Bernice L. Neugarten. Chicago: University of Chicago Press, 1968, pp. 390–400.

Maddox, George L., "Activity and Morale: A Longitudinal Study of Selected Elderly Subjects," *Social Forces*, 42:195–204, 1963.

———— and Carl Eisdorfer, "Some Correlates of Activity and Morale among the Elderly," *Social Forces*, 40:254–260, 1962.

Neugarten, Bernice L., "Adaptation and the Life Cycle," *Journal of Geriatric Psychiatry*, 4:71–87, 1970.

————, Robert J. Havighurst, and Sheldon S. Tobin, "The Measurement of Life Satisfaction," *Journal of Gerontology*, 16:134–143, 1961.

Phillips, Bernard S., "A Role Theory Approach to Adjustment in Old Age," *American Sociological Review*, 22:212–217, 1957.

Pihlblad, C. Terence and Robert L. McNamara, "Social Adjustment of Elderly People in Three Small Towns," in *Older People and Their Social World*, eds. Arnold M. Rose and Warren A. Peterson. Philadelphia: F. A. Davis, 1965, pp. 49–73.

Schmidt, John F., "Patterns of Poor Adjustment in Old Age," *American Journal of Sociology*, 57:33–42, 1951.

Schooler, Kermit K., "The Relationship Between Social Interaction and Morale of the Elderly as a Function of Environmental Characteristics," *Gerontologist*, 9:25–29, 1969.

Streib, Gordon F., "Morale of the Retired," *Social Problems*, 3:270–276, 1956.

Thomae, Hans, "Aging and Problems of Adjustment," *International Social Science Journal*, 15:366–376, 1963.

Thompson, Wayne E., Gordon F. Streib, and John Kosa, "The Effect of Retirement on Personal Adjustment: A Panel Analysis," *Journal of Gerontology*, 15:165–169, 1960.

Tobin, Sheldon S. and Bernice L. Neugarten, "Life Satisfaction and Social Interaction in the Aging," *Journal of Gerontology*, 16:344–346, 1961.

Trenton, Jean-Rene, "The Concept of Adjustment in Old Age," in *Processes of Aging*, eds. Richard H. Williams, Clark Tibbitts, and Wilma Donahue. New York: Atherton Press, 1963, I, 292–298.

Williams, Richard H. and Martin B. Loeb, "The Adult's Social Life Space and Successful Aging: Some Suggestions for a Conceptual Framework," in *Middle Age and Aging*, ed. Bernice L. Neugarten. Chicago: University of Chicago Press, 1968, pp. 379–381.

Part Four

Societal Response to the Aging

Thus far aging has been viewed in terms of its importance for the individual. Yet much of the social situation confronting the older person is the product of the way older people are viewed by their society, and of the roles society expects them to play. Accordingly, the remainder of this book is devoted to examining general responses of society to the fact that it has older members; and the roles older people play in the economy, politics and government, the community, religion, voluntary associations, and the family. In addition, the roles of friend and neighbor are also examined in relation to aging.

13 Societal Disengagement

Society's reactions to the fact that many of its members are old is a very important aspect of aging. Thus far we have considered the biological and pyschological aspects of aging, and situational elements such as income, health, retirement, leisure, and independence as they affect aging. But apart from a specific situation, it is important to know *in general* how older people are expected to fit into the family, the peer group, the economic realm, the community, government, politics, voluntary associations, and religion.

Part of the problem arises from the fact that social institutions outlive the people who comprise them, and thus most institutions are constantly phasing young people in and old people out.[1] This is as true of the family as it is of a factory or a state. The process whereby society withdraws from or no longer seeks the individual's efforts is called *societal disengagement*.

As part of an overall theory of disengagement, Newell[2] looked upon societal disengagement as half of the inevitable withdrawal of older people and society from each other.

Societal disengagement is characterized by a "thinning out of the number of members in the social structure surrounding the individual, a diminishing of interactions with these members, and a restructuring of the goals of the system."[3] It was established earlier that individual disengagement reduces the number of interactions for the individual. From the societal point of view, an older person may no longer be sought out for leadership in organizations, his labor may no longer be desired by his employer, his children may no longer want him to become involved in their

---

[1] For a detailed discussion of social institutions see Robert C. Atchley, *Understanding American Society* (Belmont, California: Wadsworth, 1971).

[2] David S. Newell, "Social-Structural Evidence for Disengagement," in *Growing Old,* eds. Elaine Cumming and William E. Henry (New York: Basic Books, 1961), pp. 37–74.

[3] *Ibid.,* p. 37.

decisions, his union may no longer be interested in his financial problems, and his government may no longer be responsive to his needs. These are the realities of societal disengagement. More often than not, societal disengagement is unintended and sometimes even unrecognized, but it is a reality for older people.

To measure societal disengagement, Newell and his associates first took a *role count,* an inventory of the number of separate *active* relationships the individual had. Second, they used an *interaction index* to measure the amount of interaction with others each day. Newell found that role count "is quite stable between the ages of fifty and sixty-four; about 60 percent of this younger group act in six or more roles, but by age sixty-five only 39 percent do, and the proportion decreases steadily until at age seventy-five and over, only 8 percent act in more than five roles."[4] Losses in work and

Table 15. Rates of Interaction, by Age

Age	Percent with High Daily Interaction
50–54	72.2
55–59	58.8
60–64	58.8
65–69	45.2
70–74	34.0
75 and over	15.4

Source: Elaine Cumming, and W. W. Henry, *Growing Old* (New York: Basic Books, 1961), p. 40. Reprinted by permission.

family roles account for most of the role loss for both older men and older women. Thus, the variety of roles an individual plays diminishes with increasing age.

The interaction index was concerned with the density of interaction, and again Newell found a decrease with age. However, here there are marked declines after age sixty-five. Table 15 shows that interaction declines steadily from age fifty onward, the average decline between five-year age groups being just over 11 percent.

The Cumming and Henry theory of disengagement, to which Newell contributed, has been criticized on the ground that some people may be relatively nonengaged throughout their entire lives. For example, one study

---

[4] *Ibid.,* p. 39. (Also see Research Illustration 3.)

showed that 90 percent of *both* engaged and disengaged people over sixty-five were in the same category five years earlier,[5] and another found a high potential for disengagement for professors of all ages.[6] The theory has also been criticized for its assumption that disengagement is both natural and good. Data from one study show that disengagement was associated with low morale and was apparently not as functional as the theory indicates it should be.[7] This criticism relates mainly to the individual aspects.

For those who use society as a point of departure, the major criticism is that the theory of disengagement does not give enough weight to the role of the socially determined situation in the genesis or processes of disengagement.[8] Several studies bear out this last criticism.

The crux of the matter is whether the pattern observed by Newell and others[9] is the result of individual disengagement or societal disengagement or both.

One important aspect of the problem has been dealt with by Frances Carp,[10] who set out to study the effect of moving from "substandard housing and socially isolating or interpersonally stressful situations to a new apartment house" having within it a senior center.

Prior to the move the 204 subjects were assessed in terms of their engagement in three separate roles: paid work, volunteer work, and leisure pastimes. Opportunities for all three were very limited in the premove situations of the study sample. "Special effort was necessary in order to participate in any of the three. Expenditure of this effort was assumed to express a strong need for involvement."[11]

Following the move, opportunities for volunteer work and leisure pastimes were expanded, but opportunities for paid work remained about the same. Carp predicted that those who had expended the effort on leisure or volunteer in the antagonistic premove setting would be happier and better adjusted in an environment that facilitated continued engagement. She also predicted that those who had worked for pay in the premove setting

---

[5] Arnold Rose, *Older People and Their Social World* (Philadelphia: F. A. Davis, 1965), p. 362.

[6] Robert C. Atchley, "Potential for Disengagement among Professors," *Journal of Gerontology*, 26:476–480 (1971).

[7] Aaron Lipman and Kenneth J. Smith, "Functionality of Disengagement in Old Age," *Journal of Gerontology*, 23:517–521 (1968).

[8] Paul Roman and Philip Taietz, "Organizational Structure and Disengagement: The Emeritus Professor," *Gerontologist*, 7:147–52 (1967).

[9] e.g., R. J. Havighurst, B. L. Neugarten, and S. Tobin, "Disengagement and Patterns of Aging," Markyard, Sweden, 1963; Arnold Rose, "A Current Issue in Social Gerontology," *Gerontologist*, 4:45–50 (1964); Richard H. Williams and Claudine Wirths, *Lives through the Years* (New York: Atherton Press, 1965).

[10] Frances M. Carp, "Person-Situation Congruence in Engagement," *The Gerontologist*, 8:184–188 (1968).

[11] *Ibid.*, p. 185.

would be no different in terms of satisfaction or adjustment after the move. Her results fully supported her predictions. People who had been involved in leisure pursuits or volunteer work prior to entering the apartment building tended to become happier, more popular, and better adjusted than the other tenants. On the other hand, those who had worked were not significantly different from the other tenants.

Carp interpreted her findings as supporting the idea that the greater the congruence between the person's desires for continued engagement and the opportunities for such engagement offered by the situation, the higher the degree of adjustment and satisfaction. She concludes:

> The results suggest that involvement is reactive to person-situation congruence, and that engagement-disengagement is not a general trait but one which is specific to various domains of involvement. . . . They suggest also that services for the elderly might profit from prior awareness of prospective clients' engagement in various behavioral domains. . . .[12]

Implicit in these conclusions is the idea that many people want to remain engaged, and that one of the main obstacles preventing them from doing so is societal disengagement, which creates a situation in which continued engagement is difficult.

In order to assess the impact of societal disengagement directly, Roman and Taietz undertook the study of an occupational role in which continued engagement after retirement is allowed, the role of the "emeritus professor."[13] Unlike most organizations, American colleges and universities, instead of removing retired faculty from the organization, make available a formalized, postretirement position with a flexible role, whose definition is a function of the individual's preretirement position, as well as of his own choice of postretirement activity.[14] The important point here is that this system allows the *opportunity* for role-continuity between full-time employment and retirement.

The amount of continuity possible varied. The research professors had the most, since they could generally continue to get research grants through the university. Those involved in teaching, public service, or administration still had opportunities for involvement, but for them the emeritus role was quite different from their preretirement role. They often ended up writing books, consulting, or becoming administrators. In no case, however, was the continuity complete. The emeritus professor always gave up a measure of involvement.

---

[12] *Ibid.*, p. 187.
[13] Roman and Taietz, *op. cit.*, pp. 147–152.
[14] *Ibid.*, p. 147.

This is a perfect situation for studying psychological disengagement, since the societal disengagement is very low. Disengagement theory would lead us to believe that since the individual naturally wants to disengage, he would do so.

Roman and Taietz assumed that disengagement was the product of *particular* social systems, not of systems in general, and that opportunity structures would greatly influence the individual's "readiness to disengage." Cumming and Henry had viewed readiness to disengage as a result of aging, regardless of the social system.

Based on their assumptions about opportunity structures, Roman and Taietz predicted "that a significant proportion of emeritus professors would remain engaged, and that those allowed role continuity would exhibit a higher degree of continued engagement than those required to adopt new roles."[15] They found that 41 percent of the emeritus professors were still engaged within the same university, 13 percent had taken employment in their profession elsewhere, 24 percent were in ill health, and 22 percent were disengaged from both the university and their profession. If these percentages are recomputed leaving out the ill-health group, for whom no determination of voluntary disengagement is possible, and combining both categories of those still engaged, the pattern shows 71 percent still engaged and 29 percent disengaged. In addition, they found that those emeritus professors who had had a research role were still engaged significantly more often than the others. Thus, all of Roman and Taietz's predictions were supported by their findings.

These data suggest that the frequency of disengagement is very much a product of the opportunity for continued engagement. The fact that the organization provided a continuing role after retirement allowed 71 percent of the healthy people to remain engaged, whereas in many occupations the percent allowed to remain engaged would have been near zero. This finding is all the more revealing since almost half of Roman and Taietz's sample was over seventy-five years old.

It is entirely possible that most voluntary individual disengagement has resulted from the fact that people see disengagement as inevitable, *because of the rules of the institutions they participate in.* That is, it is really the result of societal disengagement.

Another study which supports this idea was done by Carp.[16] She found that disengagement from the family role was negatively associated with disengagement from other roles. This finding suggests that when people give up a particular role, their resistance to giving up their other roles increases. Again the implications are that the social situation is an important

---

[15] *Ibid.,* p. 149.

[16] Frances M. Carp, "Some Components of Disengagement," *Journal of Gerontology,* 23:382–386 (1968).

factor influencing disengagement, and that the individual is more reluctant to disengage than the disengagement theory would indicate.

Tallmer and Kutner have attempted to assess the impact of "stress-inducing environmental and circumstantial disturbances" in producing consequences similar to those generally attributed to disengagement.[17] The stress factors they used were such things as illness, widowhood, retirement, receiving welfare, and living alone.

One of the fundamental tenets of the Cumming and Henry disengagement theory is that growing old causes, or is at least associated with, disengagement. *Tallmer and Kutner found that practically all of the relationship between age and engagement was accounted for by the relationship between age and the various stress situations.* They concluded:

> There appears to be substantial evidence for our hypothesis that disengagement among the aged can be predicted to occur as a concommitant of physical or social stresses which profoundly affect the manner in which the life pattern of the person is redirected. Because they have ignored the apparently definitive effect of such factors on disengagement, Cumming and Henry were led to the conclusion that advancing age was a sufficient explanation of the facts obtained in their study. It is not age which produces disengagement in our investigation but the impact of physical and social stress which may be expected to increase with age. It is tempting to hypothesize that as one enters into the later decades, disengagement is bound to grow, and indeed it does. The real difficulty lies in the fact that it is the correlates of old age, i.e., failing health, loss of peers, death of relatives, and the general shrinking of the social world due to factors related to aging, that appear to produce the social withdrawal known as disengagement.[18]

The point is that the external aspects of aging and the socially structured situation can have a far greater influence than personal desires on the social withdrawal of older people. A recurrent theme throughout our examination of how older people fit into a modern industrial society will be that the difficulties many older people face are brought on less by withdrawal on their own part than by decisions, often consciously made, on the part of others to exclude them from the mainstream of society. Illness, loss of peers and relatives through death, and the shrinking pool of alternatives the older person faces are often unnecessarily stressful simply because, in a social system built around production, rationality, and efficiency, it is often more expedient to write off older people than to expend the energy required to create a "citizen emeritus" role.

---

[17] Margot Tallmer and Bernard Kutner, "Disengagement and the Stresses of Aging," *Journal of Gerontology,* 24:70–75 (1969).

[18] *Ibid.,* p. 74.

Disengagement theory is comforting in a way, particularly for the young, because it seems to justify the way older people are treated: after all, being cut off from everything is just what they want. Nevertheless, the research evidence shows that disengagement is *not* what most older people want. It is, however, what older people get.

The confusion concerning the desire to disengage probably results from the failure of most investigators to recognize the possibility that ambivalence can arise from competing values.[19] For example, professors are high in potential for disengagement at all ages, yet most "retired" professors still work. This seeming contradiction is apparently accounted for by the fact that professors are also usually highly committed to a relatively attractive job. This suggests that people in high-status, attractive jobs tend to preserve continuity and remain on the job as long as they can, despite a high potential for disengagement. It is simply a case of competing positive incentives. The corollary is, of course, that people in low-status, unattractive jobs would disengage when given the opportunity, even if they also had the continued opportunity to work. These possibilities need further examination.

Summary

Society disengages from the older individual by isolating him and no longer seeking his efforts. Yet each institution in society accomplishes disengagement in a slightly different way and at a different stage of later life. For example, while retirement is a formalized pattern which occurs for most people between ages sixty-five and seventy, the family often does not withdraw from the individual until he loses his mental faculties.

Societal disengagement is manifested as a decrease in the number of active roles played and in the density of interaction. Research evidence indicates that the relationship between individual desires for disengagement and societal disengagement is very complex. However, it appears certain that much of the "inevitability" of disengagement springs from the roles of society rather than from the motives of the individual. Even in an occupation with high potential for disengagement, continued engagement was the norm when the opportunity existed. Also, people who must disengage from one role tend to resist disengagement from their remaining roles more strongly. Apparently, much of what has been called individual disengagement is a result of various stresses such as retirement and widowhood rather than of aging *per se*.

The separation of older people from society is a fact of modern life.

---

[19] Robert C. Atchley, *op. cit.*

But it is a pattern that has resulted from people's decisions, not from some immutable social force. There can be little doubt at this point that much of the social rejection that older people experience stems from the fact that the societies they live in are more interested in production, rationality, and efficiency than in maintaining a spot for the "citizen emeritus."

Societal disengagement is no more uniform than individual disengagement. Many social institutions allow older people to keep up their ties, while many others cut older people off from participation almost completely. Beginning with the economic institution, the remainder of this book will examine the opportunities for participation that various social institutions afford to older people.

Bibliography

(*See Also the Bibliography for Chapter 2.*)

Atchley, Robert C., "Disengagement among Professors," *Journal of Gerontology,* 26:476–480, 1971.
Carp, Frances M., "Person-Situation Congruence in Engagement," *Gerontologist,* 8:184–188, 1968.
————, "Some Components of Disengagement," *Journal of Gerontology,* 23:382–386, 1968.
Cumming, Elaine and William E. Henry, *Growing Old: The Process of Disengagement.* New York: Basic Books, 1961.
Newell, David S., "Social-Structural Evidence for Disengagement," in *Growing Old: The Process of Disengagement,* eds. Elaine Cumming and William E. Henry. New York: Basic Books, 1961, pp. 37–74.
Roman, Paul and Philip Taietz, "Organizational Structure and Disengagement: The Emeritus Professor," *Gerontologist,* 7:147–152, 1967.
Rose, Arnold M., "A Current Theoretical Issue in Social Gerontology," *Gerontologist,* 4:46–50, 1964.
Tallmer, Margot and Bernard Kutner, "Disengagement and the Stresses of Aging," *Journal of Gerontology,* 24:70–75, 1969.
Williams, Richard H. and Claudine G. Wirths, *Lives through the Years.* New York: Atherton Press, 1965.

14

The Economy

The chapter on retirement indicated that the economy definitely withdraws from older people as producers. But what about other roles in the economic institution, such as consumer, dependent, union member?

Perhaps the best way to begin is by examining the economic roles held by older people in the past. Some care must be exercised here, however, because there is often a tendency to equate older with elderly. As Cottrell has pointed out, in a low-energy society people do not live very long.[1] Nevertheless, the head of the family was most often the oldest surviving member of the group. Those older people who survived without becoming severely decrepit could thus expect to assume control over the family decisions. This is important for understanding the economic roles of older people, because in a rural, agricultural society the family is the basic unit of economic production and distribution. The major economic decisions in such a society are largely a matter of day-to-day operations, and there is often very little conscious effort to coordinate the work of the various producing units. Hence, not only did the patriarch (or matriarch in some cases) make the decisions, but he was relatively free of external social pressures. Naturally there were physical factors which limited the range of alternatives, but there were no fair-trade prices or tariffs and few other governmental controls to take into account.

The older person in such a society enjoyed considerable power over economic production and distribution, almost purely as a result of his position in the family. As industrialization has progressed in modern societies, the family has lost most of its production and distribution functions and is now mainly a consuming unit. With this change, the family patriarch has lost many of his economic roles.

Modern society is compartmentalized. Whereas the family once en-

---

[1] W. Fred Cottrell, "The Technological and Societal Basis of Aging," in *The Handbook of Social Gerontology,* ed. Clark Tibbitts (Chicago: University of Chicago Press, 1960), p. 103.

compassed practically all the institutionalized patterns people needed in order to achieve their goals, we now have a great many relatively autonomous institutions. Position in one institution is no longer *necessarily* related to position in other institutions (although it still *tends* to be). This trend means that being the head of a large family no longer carries with it a large measure of political power in the local community. All of this is to say that the older person has little influence on economic decisions and policy. What powers does he have left?

Older People as Workers

Beyond age forty, the older a person is, the less likely he is to be employed, particularly in industrial societies. The *Manpower Report of the President* gave the following portrait of labor force participation for older Americans from 1948 to 1970[2]:

—Participation of older men dropped from 47 percent to 27 percent.
—Participation of older women remained constant at around 10 percent.
—Participation was slightly lower for older whites of both sexes than for older people of Negro and other races.
—Unemployment rates for older people tended to be lower than for 25 to 34-year-olds.
—Older workers were consistently much more prevalent among the long-term unemployed than among the total unemployed. For example, in 1970 men sixty-five and over constituted 2 percent of the total unemployment, but 6 percent of those unemployed for twenty-seven weeks or more.
—Participation of older people drops sharply after age seventy. (See Table 16.)

By 1985 participation of older people in the labor force will probably decline to somewhere around 21 percent for men and 8 percent for women.[3] In the past, participation rates for women have peaked later and have begun to decline later in the life cycle than have the rates for men. This trend can be expected to continue as more and more women enter the labor force when their children get older.

Older people who do remain in the labor force quite often work only part-time or only part of the year. For example, 98 percent of employed

---

[2] United States Department of Labor, *Manpower Report of the President* (Washington, D. C.: U. S. Government Printing Office, 1971).

[3] *Ibid.,* p. 291.

*Table 16. Labor Force Participation of Older Americans
by Age and Sex: 1960 and 1970*

| | Percent in Labor Force | | | |
| | Males | | Females | |
	1960	1970	1960	1970
Total Age 65 and Over	*32.2*	*26.8*	*10.5*	*9.2*
Age 65–69	*45.8*	*40.7*	*17.3*	*17.0*
Age 70 and Over	*23.5*	*16.9*	*6.5*	*5.4*

Source: *Manpower Report of the President, op. cit.*, p. 291.

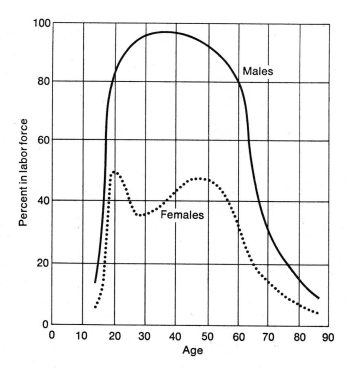

*Figure 10. Labor Force Participation Rates by Age, United
States: 1960.*

Source: U. S. Bureau of the Census, *1960 Census of Population,* Vol. 1, Part 1 (Washington, D. C.: U. S. Government
Printing Office, 1964), p. 501.

men age thirty-five to forty-five work thirty-five or more hours per week, but by age seventy the proportion drops to around 45 percent.[4] In addition, older people constitute less than 5 percent of the American labor force. Similar trends were found in twenty other industrial nations.[5]

Work is thus an economic role which only about a quarter of the older population plays, and over half of those who do work do so only part-time or part of the year. Older workers tend to be relatively powerless. Because of their seniority they are not very likely to become unemployed, but if they do lose their jobs, age discrimination makes it difficult for them to find new ones. The Hilary case cited in Chapter Nine is probably typical of what happens to displaced older workers.

It is illegal in the United States to deny an individual a job because of his age, but such laws have no impact unless businesses voluntarily comply, and they have not. Employment studies show that older workers have superior attendance records, that they are less likely to change jobs, and that their output is equal to that of younger workers. While it is true that some older workers are slow to learn, the range of differences is quite large, and many older people are still quite capable of learning new skills. Age discrimination in employment thus deprives the economy of human resources and creates hardships for older workers. The small number of older workers in job retraining programs probably reflects cynicism about finding a job more than an unwillingness to be retrained.

Older People as Consumers

The largest single economic function remaining for the family is that of consumer. Older people's ability to participate as consumers is determined first, and perhaps mostly, by income. Most older people are living on inadequate incomes, and obviously it is impossible to buy things when you have no money. On the average, older people spend far less for goods and services than younger people do, and are less likely to spend beyond their incomes. A major factor which influences older people's spending is the relatively small size of their families.

Very little attention has been paid to the older person as a consumer.[6] Ad agencies have not yet come to view older people as a significant market. Aside from aspirin, laxative, denture adhesive, and iron-tonic commercials,

---

[4] Matilda W. Riley and Ann Foner, *Aging and Society*, Vol. 1, *An Inventory of Research Findings* (New York: Russell Sage Foundation, 1968), p. 46.

[5] United Nations, "Demographic Aspects of Manpower," *Population Studies*, 33, 1962.

[6] John W. McConnell, "Aging and the Economy," in *Handbook of Social Gerontology, op. cit.,* pp. 489–520.

few appeals are aimed directly at older people. One obvious reason may be that older people buy the same kinds of things most other adults do. Older people tend to retain most of their living habits, and therefore one might expect that their buying patterns would reflect this consistency in ethnic, class, and individual preferences.

Nevertheless, older people have a significant amount of purchasing power. By 1965 older people were spending around 12 percent of the total money spent on goods and services throughout the country. This is almost a perfect proportional share in terms of the percentage of older people in the population (9.6 percent). By 1970, this share reached about sixty billion dollars. One important thing about buying power is that it is passive. It is reactive power. People seldom boycott in an attempt to influence the type of goods produced. The fact that older people buy very few items that are not bought by everyone else makes them a relatively stable and reliable market, although their purchases tend to be more concentrated in the areas of medical care, food, and personal care.

Since much advertising is aimed at encouraging impulse buying of nonessential items, and since most older people cannot afford these items, it is little wonder that business feels no need to court the market older people represent.

Unfortunately, there are some exceptions to this rule. These are mainly the clandestine operators and fringe businesses that deal in fraud, deception, fad, and quackery. While older people are not the sole victims of many of these schemes, they are often the most vulnerable.

To begin with, older people on fixed incomes and with barely enough to live on are very susceptible to any kind of "sure fire" scheme that will yield them more money or a supplementary income. Also, loneliness and isolation often make older people susceptible to deception by a friendly, outgoing person who takes an apparent interest in them. Finally, hopeless illness is more frequent among older people, and many unscrupulous people have exploited the desperation that it can evoke. A few examples should illustrate the point.

Perhaps the most vicious of the "get more money for your money" swindles was the Maryland savings and loan scandal of 1961. From 1958 to 1961, there were many state-chartered savings and loan associations operating in Maryland which were not Federally insured. These companies advertised nation-wide that savings invested with them would yield as high as 8 percent, twice the interest rate of most legitimate, Federally insured institutions. The appeal of increasing yields was particularly attractive to older people who were trying to make the most of a fixed amount of savings which provided them with their living. For people in this situation, it was like saying, "Double your income in one easy step." Hundreds of older people transferred their life's savings into these companies from all over the country.

At best these companies were ill-conceived. They were able to pay such high rates of interest only by investing heavily in second, third, and even fourth mortgages; a very lucrative but also a very risky business.

Following a wide-scale investigation, many of the officers of these companies were indicted on charges of fraud and embezzlement. Most of the companies went bankrupt, and hundreds of people lost their entire life's savings.

Another example is the "investment property" business. Generally, a promoter buys a large tract of cheap land, often swampy land in Florida or desert in Arizona. Then he carves the property up into the smallest parcels allowable. Then he prints beautiful brochures and advertises in newspapers, magazines, and so on. Stress is put on holding the land as an investment for resale later at a profit, or as a place for a retirement home. In the words of a Florida realtor,

> Lots are usually sold on installment contracts, and no deed is recorded until the contract is paid off. Most contracts stipulate that the property reverts to the seller if the buyer misses one or two payments, and the seller is not required to notify the buyer that he is delinquent.
>
> Many, but not all, contracts carry interest on the unpaid balance, usually 5 or 6 percent. Many of these lots are sold over and over again, year after year, as buyers stop their monthly payments for any number of reasons—they die, come upon hard times, come down and see the land, et cetera.
>
> Several years ago I spent almost two days, using a slow plane and a four-wheel-drive, radio-equipped jeep, trying to locate a certain parcel [a Florida development] located approximately ten miles west of Daytona Beach in a dismal swamp.
>
> After two days of some of the roughest riding, we had to give up, as it was impossible to penetrate deep enough into the swamp to the point we had spotted from the air.
>
> Incidentally, this parcel was sold to a woman from Syracuse, N. Y., who had intended to use it as a homesite for a trailer house.[7]

Many other examples could be given of "make money" or "save money" schemes that have bilked older people out of what little they have.

Confidence men have preyed on older people in numerous ways. Perhaps the most ingenious has been the "bank examiner" gambit. A person posing as a bank examiner calls on the intended victim. He explains that one of the employees of the bank is suspected of embezzlement, but unfortunately the bank officials have been unable to catch him in the act. The "examiner" then attempts to elicit the cooperation of the intended

---

[7] United States Senate, Special Committee on Aging, "Frauds and Deceptions Affecting the Elderly" (Washington, D. C.: U. S. Government Printing Office, 1965), p. 34.

victim. He explains that if the victim will go to the bank and withdraw all of his savings, this will force the suspect in the bank to alter his account books, and the bank will then "have the goods on him." If the intended victim takes the bait, and the savings are withdrawn, the "examiner" telephones, says that they have caught the suspect, thanks the victim, and then offers to send a "bank messenger" to pick up the money—"to save you the trouble of having to come all the way down here, since you have been so kind as to cooperate with us." The "messenger" then appears, takes the money, gives the victim an official looking deposit slip, and that is usually the last the victim ever sees of his money. It is surprising the number of unfortunate people who have fallen for this ruse. Older people are particularly susceptible because many of them are flattered to feel needed, and in addition, many of them are too defensive to seek advice in such cases.

Many of the practices found in the "pre-need" funeral business are also fraudulent. People have been sold "complete burial service" for a thousand dollars or more and all the survivors received, if they were lucky, was a hundred-dollar casket. People have been sold crypts in mausoleums that do not exist. One ad read:

> Do you qualify for these U. S. Government death benefits? U. S. Social Security, maximum, $255, United Memorial's answer to the ever-increasing cost of funeral services, the United plan. The preneed plan that costs $10.

For ten dollars, the customer got a "guarantee" from United Memorial that he could have his burial service performed by whatever mortuary he chose. Upon death, however, the relatives found that most of the mortuaries "endorsed" by United Memorial had no contract with them and refused to perform the service for anything like a Social Security benefit price.

It has been estimated that in Colorado alone the annual sales of preneed burial service total eight to ten million dollars.[8] This business thrives on the deep-seated desire of many older people to take care of burial arrangements ahead of time in order to "avoid being a burden" on their relatives. Even for the reputable businessman, it may be unethical to take money from older people for prearranged funerals when they, of all people, fully realize the problems of prearranging funeral services in a society where people travel as much as they do in ours. If the person dies far from the city in which the prearrangements were made, the relatives either lose the money spent for the prearranged funeral or must pay to have the remains shipped back for burial. By encouraging prepayment, the

---

[8] *Ibid.,* p. 72.

funeral director is merely relieving the older person of his savings, often without paying interest on the money held.

The most frequent hazard to older people is medical swindlers and quackery. Arthritis is a good case in point. The Special Committee on Aging found:

> Arthritis offers special opportunities to the unscrupulous. Twelve million Americans have some form of arthritis; and, as one witness testified: "If we fall for the phoney, and sooner or later most of us do, it is because the pains of arthritis are something that you just can't describe because nobody knows why it comes or how or when it goes." . . . Mrs. Bramer also made a comment often expressed by arthritis victims: "There must be an exchange list of arthritic victims because if you get on one list you receive material advertising all manner of devices, items such as vibrators, whirlpool baths, salves, uranium mits, and things of that sort."[9]

—Worthless devices:

> These devices are often used by phoney practitioners to impress victims with "up-to-date" methods or "secret" treatments. One highly mobile pitchman, using and selling a machine that did little more than give colonic enemas to victims of major diseases, made an estimated $2½ million before conviction on a mail fraud charge.[10]

—Misleading claims:

> People will buy almost anything that purports to cure whatever real or imaginary ailments they have. The enforcement of fraud laws is a constant word game between those who are trying to protect the public and those who are trying to swindle it. Thus, "cures" is replaced by "aids in curing" is replaced by "is thought to aid in curing."[11]

—The victims:

> The actual extent of frauds is unknown because many victims either never suspect that they have been taken, or more likely, they are afraid to report it for fear of appearing the fool.[12]

—Complex technology:

> This gives the quack the capability of sowing the seed of doubt about the validity of accepted medical methods because most people are not able to evaluate his claims.[13]

---

[9] *Ibid.*, p. 7.
[10] *Ibid.*, p. 3.
[11] *Ibid.*, p. 8.
[12] *Ibid.*
[13] *Ibid.*

The cost of quackery has been estimated as follows:[14]

Vitamin and Health Food Quackery	$500 million
Arthritis Quackery	$250 million
Ineffective Drugs and Devices for Reducing	$100 million

And this probably only scratches the surface. The true cost of fraud and quackery was summed up well be Sen. Harrison Williams:

> It seems to me that there are losses that go far beyond the original purchase price for the phoney treatment, the useless gadget, the inappropriate drug or pill. How can you measure the cost in terms of suffering, disappointment, and final despair?[15]

One of the heaviest of these costs is surely the attitudes such practices create among older people. They become suspicious and reluctant to get involved with strangers. Unfortunately, it is too often true that only the confidence man feels he has anything to gain from seeking out older people.

It is encouraging, however, that hearings have been held and legislative proposals have been made which would in some ways ease the situation.

The Administration on Aging has instituted a program aimed at collecting consumer data on older people; at preparing information for use by both professional and lay leaders who intend to conduct educational programs for older people and older people themselves; and at supporting demonstration projects concerning

—sound nutrition
—economy food purchasing
—the careful purchase of credit
—avoidance of quackery
—avoidance of fraudulent products and practices
—safe and effective use of drugs
—management of retirement income
—Medicare and supplementary health insurance
—care of clothing and household equipment

AOA has also indicated an interest in exploring the possibilities for consumer cooperatives among older people.

While these attempts are encouraging, little is still known about older people as consumers and about the influence various types of fraud and deception have on their lives. For all we know now, the sad tales just

---

[14] *Ibid.*
[15] *Ibid.*

depicted may be relatively rare. They are, at the least, illustrations of *potential* dangers to be guarded against.

The fact that some theatre owners and transit companies, to name a few, have offered substantial discounts to older people who use their facilities in off hours indicates that the business community can recognize older people as a potential market, and also recognize that price is a prime motivating factor for many older people. Unfortunately, this rationale is not transferable to the essential areas of food, clothing, shelter, or medical care.

Hypothetically, older people may also participate in the economy as dependents or as members of unions. Participation as a dependent is largely passive, although it does sometimes create jobs in state administrations on aging, Social Security offices, welfare department, and the like. Certainly the older person's power is no greater in this role than in the consumer role.

Studies have shown that union contracts do not generally favor or even take into account the needs of retired union members.[16] Sometimes they do, however, as in the case of the rail unions, which have included in their wage contracts a 2 percent increase to be used to pay supplementary benefits to retired railwaymen.[17] In this case, however, it was not the retired railwaymen who applied the pressure, but those who were still working.

There seems to be an ethic in the United States to the effect that if you have no current direct role in producing goods and services, you are not entitled to a voice in how these goods and services are to be divided up. This is an interesting question about which little is known.

Summary

Looking at the economic institution as a whole, one sees a sizeable number of older people still working, but generally on terms that give them little choice. One sees older people consuming their share of the goods and services bought, yet victimized by fraud and quackery on a scale that would be intolerable for the nation as a whole. One sees the older person, once he becomes a public dependent, having his decisions on how he spends his money made for him by an agency bureaucrat, sometimes even being required to turn his home and savings over to the state. One sees the person who is no longer working—whether he is old or not—left completely out of the economic decision-making process.

---

[16] McConnell, *op. cit.,* p. 514.

[17] W. Fred Cottrell, *Technological Change and Labor in the Railroad Industry* (Lexington, Massachusetts: D. C. Heath & Co., 1970).

Bibliography

Agan, D., "The Employment Problems of People over Forty," *Journal of Employment Counseling,* 3:10–15, 1966.

Angel, J. L., *Employment Opportunities for Men and Women after 60.* New York: Regents, 1969.

Bancroft, Gertrude, *The American Labor Force: Its Growth and Changing Composition.* New York: John Wiley, 1958.

Bauder, Ward W. and Jon A. Doerflinger, "Work Roles among the Rural Aged," in *Older Rural Americans,* ed. E. Grant Youmans. Lexington, Kentucky: University of Kentucky Press, 1967, pp. 22–43.

California Department of Employment, *A Survey of the Employment of Older Workers—1964.* Sacramento, California: The Department, 1965.

Clark, Lincoln H., ed., *Consumer Behavior.* New York: New York University Press, 1954.

Clague, Ewan, "Work and Leisure for Older Workers," *Gerontologist,* 11:(1, part II)9–20, 1971.

Crockett, Jean A., "Older People as Consumers," in *Aging and the Economy,* eds. Harold L. Orbach and Clark Tibbitts. Ann Arbor, Michigan: University of Michigan Press, 1963, pp. 127–146.

Crook, Guy Hamilton and Martin Heinstein, *The Older Worker in Industry.* Berkeley, California: University of California Institute of Industrial Relations, 1958.

Ferman, Louis A. and Michael Aiken, "Mobility and Situational Factors in the Adjustment of Older Workers to Job Displacement," *Human Organization,* 26:235–241, 1967.

Fillenbaum, Gerda G., "A Consideration of Some Factors Related to Work after Retirement," *Gerontologist,* 11:(1, part I)18–23, 1971.

————, "The Working Retired," *Journal of Gerontology,* 26:82–89, 1971.

Franke, Walter H., "Labor Market Experience of Unemployed Older Workers," *Monthly Labor Review,* 86:282–284, 1963.

Goldstein, Sidney, *Consumption Patterns of the Aged.* Philadelphia: University of Pennsylvania Press, 1960.

————, "Changing Income and Consumption Patterns of the Aged, 1950–1960," *Journal of Gerontology,* 20:453–461, 1965.

————, "The Effect of Income Level on the Consumer Behavior of the Aged," in *Proceedings of the 7th International Congress of Gerontology.* Vienna: Wiener Medizinischen Akademie, 1966, VII, 1–6.

————, "Urban and Rural Differentials in Consumer Patterns of the Aged," *Rural Sociology,* 31:333–345, 1966.

————, "Home Tenure and Expenditure Patterns of the Aged, 1960–1961," *Gerontologist,* 8:17–24, 1968.

————, "Negro-White Differentials in Consumer Patterns of the Aged, 1960–1961," *Gerontologist,* 11:(3, part I)242–249, 1971.

Kerr, John R., "Income and Expenditures; The Over-65 Age Group," *Journal of Gerontology,* 23:79–81, 1968.

Kreps, Juanita M., "Aggregate Income and Labor Force Participation of the Aged," *Law and Contemporary Problems,* 27:51–66, 1962.

————, "Economic Policy and the Nation's Aged," *Gerontologist,* 8:(2, part II), 37–43, 1968.

National Industrial Conference Board, *Expenditure Patterns of the American Family.* New York: The Board, 1966.

Neef, Arthur F., "International Unemployment Rates, 1960–1964," *Monthly Labor Review,* 38:256–259, 1965.

Orbach, Harold L. and Clark Tibbitts, eds., *Aging and the Economy.* Ann Arbor, Michigan: University of Michigan Press, 1963.

Rusalem, Herbert, "Deterrents to Vocational Disengagement among Older Disabled Workers," *Gerontologist,* 3:64–68, 1963.

Schneider, Betty V. H., *The Older Worker.* Berkeley, California: University of California Institute for Industrial Relations, 1962.

Smith, J. M., "Age and Occupation: A Classification of Occupations by Their Age Structure," *Journal of Gerontology,* 24:412–418, 1969.

U. S. Department of Labor, *The Older American Workers Age Discrimination in Employment.* Washington, D. C.: U. S. Department of Labor, 1965.

Wolfbein, Seymour L., "Work Patterns of Older People," in *Processes of Aging,* eds. Richard H. Williams, Clark Tibbitts, and Wilma Donahue. New York: Atherton Press, 1963, II, 303–312.

Youmans, E. Grant, "Objective and Subjective Economic Disengagement Among Older Rural and Urban Men," *Journal of Gerontology,* 21:439–441, 1966.

15

Politics and Government

Politics refers to the process of carrying on or settling the power struggles that center around various conflicts of interest between groups. Power, the ability to realize one's own goals even against opposition, is the central core of politics, and people engage in politics as a way of securing power. Practially all large-scale institutions have their power and political aspects, but we generally reserve the label of politics for the relationships that surround the struggle for power over the machinery of the state.

In examining the relationship between aging and politics, we will concentrate on three fundamental issues: the political *participation* of older people, the political *power* of older people, and finally older people as the *object* of governmental programs and policies.

Political Participation

Political participation takes many forms in American society. It involves expressing political opinions, voting, participation in voluntary associations centered around politics, or holding political offices.

Forming political opinions requires the least involvement on the part of the individual. Several researchers have found that the proportion of people who answer "no opinion" to political pool questions increase with age,[1] and this has been taken as an indication of the relatively disengaged status of older people in American society. However, Glenn has found

---

[1] Herman Turk, Joel Smith, and Howard P. Meyers, "Understanding Local Political Behavior: The Role of the Older Citizen," in *Social Aspects of Aging,* eds. Ida H. Simpson and John C. McKinney (Durham, North Carolina: Duke University Press, 1966); K. G. Gergen and K. W. Back, "Communication in the Interview and the Disengaged Respondent," *Public Opinion Quarterly,* 30:385–398 (1966).

that if the effect of *education* is controlled, there is no evidence that older people become less interested in political affairs or less likely to form political opinions.[2] In fact, he found that when education was precisely controlled, older people were slightly *more* likely to hold opinions than were younger people. Also, Turk, Smith, and Meyers found that among people who were committed to the community, anchored to the community through social ties, and generally community-oriented, there was a tendency for opinionation to increase with age.[3] While the tendency to form political opinions may possibly decline with age, education and involvement in the community are strong forces which more than counteract this trend for many people.

Opinion formation is no doubt related to information-seeking, and research results indicate that older people try hard to remain informed about political affairs. In comparison with the young, older people give greater attention to political campaigns and are more likely to follow public affairs in the newspapers and on television.[4] In addition, older people are more apt to seek practical knowledge, such as the name of their own Congressman, than academic knowledge such as the makeup and purpose of the House Ways and Means Committee. This leads one to suspect, without necessarily being able to prove, that older people recognize that they have an interest in politics, and that they are at least predisposed toward political action. Glenn found, for example, that those showing the highest interest in politics were consistently those aged sixty or over.[5]

Voting behavior ranks just above opinion formation in terms of participation. It is still a relatively mild form of involvement in politics compared to other roles. Voting behavior shows a pattern of change with age as complex as it is interesting. In general, it appears that voting participation is lowest at age twenty-one; it builds to a plateau in the fifties, and then begins a gradual decline after age sixty-five. Voters in their eighties still vote more than voters in their early twenties. Men and women show approximately the same curve of voter participation, although the overall participation of women is lower for all ages. Hence, a substantial part of the apparent decline in voter participation among older people results from sex differences in voter participation and the higher mortality rates among older men.

Table 17 leads us to conclude that education has a significant impact

---

[2] Norval Glenn, "Aging, Disengagement, and Opinionation," *Public Opinion Quarterly,* 33:17–33 (1969).

[3] Turk, Smith, and Meyers, *op. cit.*

[4] Matilda W. Riley and Ann Foner, *Aging and Society,* Vol. I, *An Inventory of Research Findings* (New York: Russell Sage Foundation, 1968), p. 368.

[5] Norval D. Glenn, "Aging, Voting, and Political Interest," *American Sociological Review,* 33:563–575 (1968).

Table 17. Voter Participation, by Age and Education, United States, November, 1964

Age	Elementary		High school		College		Total	"Effect" of education (high—low education)
	0–7 years	8 years	1–3 years	4 years	1–3 years	4 years or more		
Males								
21–24	14	30	34	56	70	80	53	+66
25–44	43	58	65	76	82	87	71	+44
45–64	63	79	81	88	88	93	79	+30
65+	66	79	80	88	91	88	74	+22
Total 21+	58	73	69	80	82	88	73	+30
"Effect" of age (old—young)	+52	+49	+46	+32	+21	+ 8	+21	
Females								
21–24	22	21	33	55	69	78	52	+56
25–44	34	52	53	76	85	87	68	+53
45–64	52	69	75	84	87	92	74	+40
65+	46	63	72	76	82	93	61	+47
Total 21+	45	63	63	76	83	89	68	+44
"Effect" of age (old—young)	+24	+42	+39	+21	+13	+15	+ 9	

Source: U. S. Bureau of the Census, *Current Population Reports*, Series P-20, No. 143, pp. 16–19. (1965)

on the age pattern of voting. Among men, there is very little difference between the voting patterns of those aged sixty-five or over and those aged forty-five to sixty-four, if comparisons are restricted to those with similar education (read down the columns in the table). Among women, age makes more difference, but there is still more similarity of voter participation within education categories than within age categories. Among those with some college, the difference between older men and older women in terms of voter participation is quite small, whereas it is greatest among those who did not complete elementary school. Increased education thus decreases the influence of both age and sex on voter participation in the United States.

In an interesting analysis of aging, voting, and political interest, Glenn found that there was scarcely any change in voting turnout when the same age cohort was examined over the course of six presidential elections (twenty years).[6] This analysis suggests that people develop a style of participation as a result of their own unique political socialization and then stick to it. The importance of this finding is its implication that as the general level of education in our population increases, we should expect the age curve of voter participation to rise faster, peak higher, remain at the high plateau longer, and decline even more slowly than the cross-sectional data given in Figure 11 indicate. It also implies a genera-

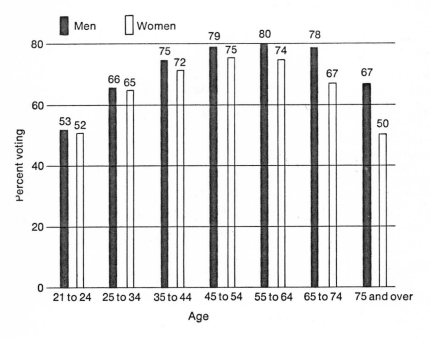

Figure 11. Voter Participation, by Age and Sex,
United States, November, 1964
Source: U. S. Bureau of the Census, *Current Population*
Reports, Series P-20, No. 143, p. 9.

tional change in the direction of greater voter participation on the part of older people.

In fact, Glenn carries his analysis even further to hypothesize that "only widespread disability and lack of transportation keep the voter turn-out of the elderly down near that of the middle-aged persons with the same amount of education."[7] Otherwise, older people would vote in *higher* proportions than middle-aged persons with the same education and sex.

---

[6] *Ibid.*
[7] *Ibid.,* pp. 570–571.

In support of this idea, Turk and his associates found an increase with age in the proportion voting among people who were involved in the community.[8]

Party affiliation is another significant role in the political institution. The proportion who identify strongly with a political party increases gradually with age, but unlike voting behavior, party identification does not decline in the later years.[9] The strength of a person's party attachment appears to be a function less of age than of the duration of that particular bond. Age provides the opportunity for the long-term identification that appears to be necessary for a strong bond, but among those with the same duration of affiliation age is *negatively* associated with the strength of the bond. The end result, however, is that a person in his twenties is only half as likely as a person over sixty-five to identify himself with a major party.

Consistent with this high level of party identification is the fact that among people who are involved in their communities there is an increase with age in political activities (working for the party in a local vote, signing petitions, belonging to political groups).[10]

Among older people, there are about equal proportions of Republicans and Democrats. This implies a substantial change with age, since at the younger ages there are many more Democrats than Republicans. Again, however, we run into the difficulty of trying to infer changes through time from data collected at one point in time. A closer examination of the longitudinal data suggests that when those who entered politics during and after the New Deal become a majority among older people, a preponderance of Democrats may emerge. Nevertheless, there will probably continue to be a small but consistent drift of Democrats to the Republican party as age increases.[11]

Older people seem to be amply represented in party organizations. What evidence there is indicates that older people represent about the same percentage of the party organization that they represent of the total population. In addition, one study has shown that older people have a disproportionately great influence in the nominating conventions.[12] Thus it appears that older members of the party organizations have a great deal of influence over the selection of party candidates for political office.

Indeed, close examination reveals that older people are also over-represented in various political offices. Leadership in all areas related to public affairs seems to be amply accessible to older political leaders.

---

[8] Turk, Smith, and Meyers, *op. cit.*, p. 273.

[9] Riley and Foner, *op. cit.*

[10] Turk, Smith, and Meyers, *op. cit.*

[11] Riley and Foner, *op. cit.*, p. 472.

[12] R. L. Kapnick, J. S. Goodman, and E. E. Cornwell, "Political Behavior in the Aged: Some New Data," *Journal of Gerontology,* 23:305–310 (1968).

Presidents, cabinet ministers and ambassadors usually acquire their positions in their late fifties, and often retain them well beyond age sixty. Supreme Court Justices are also most likely to be appointed in their late fifties, and most continue to serve well beyond age sixty-five, since retirement usually depends on their own personal desire. In the 91st Congress (1969) there were forty-two Senators and ninety-six Representatives aged sixty or over. In both houses combined there were twenty-nine members over age seventy. Proportions of older people in state and local offices (whether elected or appointed) are substantially higher than among the rank and file of other occupations.[13]

One reason why older members of political organizations are influential is the weight that sheer tenure carries in politics. In politics perhaps more than in any other institution the older person is still able to play the role of sage. This is probably partly because political processes have felt the impact of industrialization and rationalization to a lesser degree than has the economic institution or even the family. The professionalization of politics is much less complete than that of education or the economy. As a result political prowess is still felt to be largely something one learns from experience rather than out of a book or in a professional school.

Thus, older people do not seem to be at any great disadvantage in terms of access to political roles. Yet what does this accessibility mean to the older person?

Glenn feels that people turn increasingly *toward* political activity as they age simply because they have no other absorbing interests or activities. He further suggests that as one grows older, politics tends to be viewed more as a means of personal fulfillment and less as a means to some instrumental end.[14] This rationale gains support from studies showing that as they grow older people maintain and perhaps even increase an interest in politics, while simultaneously feeling that individual action neither does nor can have an impact on the political process.[15] In short, older people appear to enjoy political participation but at the same time to be cynical about its concrete effects.

Political Power

There are many approaches to the study of older people's political power. Some say that older people serve primarily as a pressure group

---

[13] Riley and Foner, *op. cit.*, p. 477.

[14] Glenn, 1968, *op. cit.*

[15] John Schmidhauser, "The Political Influence of the Aged," *The Gerontologist*, 8:1(II):44–49, 1968.

that attempts to coerce politicians into either enacting legislation beneficial to them or opposing legislation harmful to them. Others see the problems of aging as the central focus for the formation of a social movement that involves not only older people but people of all ages in an attempt to solve these problems. Still others view older people as a category that, because of the discriminatory and categorical treatment it receives at the hands of society at large, is rapidly developing a subculture of its own in much the same way that Oscar Lewis depicts the development of a "culture of poverty."[16] Still others view politics as being run by a gerontocratic power elite who make many policy decisions without having to account to anyone for their actions.

Political success for political groups formed around older people's interests has been more often a hope than a reality. As Carlie concludes:[17]

> We have indicated [previously] that the old age political organization left a great deal to be desired as pertains to such matters [as] organization (a failure to develop strong secondary leadership), pressure (if there were not too few members then they were regionally segregated), votes (the aspiring representatives of old age political programs failed to secure enough votes to place them in pivotal political positions), and money (recall the 30¢ a month dues of the Ham and Eggers).

And further:

> It seems as though one of the necessary conditions for the formulation and maintenance of interest groups is a homogeneity of characteristics among the membership. An effective interest group, then, should have more in common than just age. Other important shared characteristics may be ethnicity, nativity, educational background, occupational status, race, and rural-urban residency. Lacking similarity beyond age (and perhaps the state of retirement), the old age political movements were handicapped from their very inception.

Effective political pressure groups have to be able to deliver votes in a bloc. The leadership must be able to guarantee the vote in return for favorable political action. There has never been an instance in the history of the United States in which the leadership of an old age interest group could deliver what would even approach "the old folks' vote." Thus, the view that older people comprise a unified interest group that can mobilize political pressure by bloc voting is an illusion, and it is quite likely to remain one.

---

[16] Oscar Lewis, *Five Families* (New York: Basic Books, 1961). See also his *La Vida* and *Children of Sanchez.*

[17] Michael K. Carlie, "The Politics of Age: Interest Group or Social Movement?" *The Gerontologist,* 9:4(I):259–263 (1969).

Arnold Rose was perhaps the strongest proponent of the idea that patterns of aging in American society are producing a subculture of the aging.[18] According to Rose, a subculture will develop whenever people in a given category interact with each other more than they interact with people in other categories. The subculture grows as a result of the positive affinity that draws like people together and the discrimination that excludes these same people from interacting with other groups. Rose cites the growing numbers of older people with common problems—usually related to health—living out their retirement in self-segregated retirement communities where a relatively high standard of living makes possible the development of a unique life style. And he contends that older people are rapidly shifting from the status of a category to that of a group. He further states that in addition to pure self-interest there is also an interactional basis for the development of an age-conscious group. This results from our society's policy of phasing older people out of almost every other kind of group, forcing them to seek each other out. Rose sees this trend as cutting across the subcultures based on occupation, sex, religion, and ethnic identification that typify the middle-aged population. It is this type of old age group identification rather than any specific *organization* of older people that leads Rose to conclude that "the elderly seem to be on their way to becoming a voting bloc with a leadership that acts as a political pressure group."[19]

This type of analysis is intuitively attractive to many because it postulates the existence of the old age pressure group without necessarily requiring that this group manifest itself in an overt form of organization. The "leaders" speak for a kind of silent group—a group that recognizes itself and is capable of the bloc voting required to achieve political influence. Again, however, history deserts us when we attempt to find evidence for the trends that Rose leads us to search for.

To begin with, most older people interact more *across* generational lines than within them, simply because their most frequent source of interaction is their children.[20] Neighbors and friends come far behind in terms of both frequency and duration of interaction. Second, the stereotype that older people are flocking *en masse* to retirement communities is largely a myth. The data on migration show that over a five-year period less than 10 percent of older people moved across county lines.[21] In fact, most older people have lived in the same residence for a long time. As a result, older people tend to be interspersed among the general population, even

---

[18] Arnold M. Rose, *Older People and Their Social World* (Philadelphia: F. A. Davis Co., 1965), pp. 3–16.

[19] *Ibid.*, p. 14.

[20] Riley and Foner, *op. cit.*, p. 545.

[21] *Ibid.*, p. 145.

though they may be seen rarely in newer apartment complexes because of the high rents. Third, while there may be a rising number of older people who can afford a unique leisure life style, our examination of the economics of aging must lead us to conclude that life styles vary widely among older people. Thus, several of the key conditions that led Rose to make a case for the subculture approach turn out to be nonexistent. There are still no adequate grounds for assuming that older people have the kind of political power that comes from bloc voting.

The view that political action favoring older people stems from a social movement involving not only the aged but others as well is the view most often expressed by the political scientists.[22] According to this approach, older people have a great deal of *potential* power by virtue of the fact that in the more rural areas they constitute a larger proportion of the population, and that these rural areas are overrepresented in both the state legislatures and the U. S. Senate. The reason that this potential has never been realized, however, is that the older population is divided among a great many interest groups, most of which do not make the welfare of the aged their primary goal. If this is true, how did legislation in behalf of older people manage to get passed?

To begin with, old age political organizations, while they were not effective as pressure groups, *were* effective in making the older person's plight politically visible. As a result, the "cause" of the elderly was picked up by non-age-based groups such as unions and political parties. The readiness of various groups interested in the general welfare to commit themselves to programs for the aged was due largely to the existence, at almost every level of organization, of large numbers of adult children who were anxious to shift the growing burden of financial support for older people off themselves and onto the government. It is for this reason, as well as the votes the elderly themselves command, that no major political party, trade union, or other large-scale organization dares oppose the income provisions of Social Security.

This view of older people's power fits the facts better than any other so far. It describes relatively accurately the political processes whereby the two most sweeping legislative proposals affecting older people, Social Security and Medicare, were passed.

The view that older people form a large part of the power elite which can act in favor of older people is questionable on the same grounds as the view that "old folks' power" is the power of an interest group or sub-culture. Age simply does not appear to be a variable that unites people regardless of their differences. This can be seen among people of all age

---

[22] W. Fred Cottrell, "Governmental Functions and the Politics of Age," in *Handbook of Social Gerontology,* ed. Clark Tibbitts (Chicago: University of Chicago Press, 1960).

groups, and older people are certainly no exception. Even if there is such a thing as a power elite—and it is by no means clear that there is—political, financial, and business interests would take a much higher priority than the mere age of the decision-maker as a factor influencing the directions decisions might take. Decision-makers tend to be older than the rank-and-file, but they retain their positions only so long as their decisions adequately represent the rank-and-file. Therefore, older decision-makers may support programs for older people only to the extent that the organizations they represent favor such programs.

The view we emerge with is that older people themselves have relatively little power *as older people*. Some powerful people are old, but they are not powerful *because* they are old. Most of political power behind programs for older people is generated by others on behalf of older people rather than by older people themselves. There are good reasons to expect that this situation will continue to exist.

To begin with, the sense of group identity that has created large ethnic voting blocs such as the Negroes, Catholics, or Italians is not now present among older people, and it is unlikely that such an identity will develop, for the reasons stated earlier. Second, older people are dispersed throughout the population both socially and geographically. This creates even less possibility of concentrating their votes, because this dispersal brings with it a dispersion of interests. Third, older people are among the least likely to desert a long-term party affiliation to vote on a specific issue. Thus, the organizational leader cannot guarantee the votes of older people because these votes are largely already committed, and furthermore, most politicians know that they can usually count on the votes of the older members of their party without giving in to pressure group demands. This is particularly true at the state and national levels. Finally, it should be recalled that older people represent an almost evenly divided vote. As a result, what power they might have is cut in half.

The role the older person is left to play in politics is generally confined to the local area, unless he has been involved in politics steadily throughout his life. At the local level, older people may indeed be influential, particularly in close elections on nonpartisan issues, but nationwide politics offers older people as such very little in terms of either power or participation. This means that while politics is relatively unique in not *demanding* disengagement from its older participants, it does not very often offer older people the opportunity to *increase* their active participation, even though they might like to. Older people can increase their efforts to form strong opinions in political affairs, and they can increase their involvement in voting; but unless they have "paid their dues" in the form of earlier participation in politics, they are not apt to gain access to positions within party organization or government itself.

Government and Older People

It is well known that the United States government operates Social Security and Medicare primarily for the benefit of older people. The goals of these programs are to shift the financial burden of income and health maintenance for older people onto the federal government. Older people have other needs, however, which many people feel could best be served by government. Consider the following list:

vocational rehabilitation
housing
transportation
taxes
recreation
mental health
consumer protection
suicide prevention
referral services
independence
poverty
activity
design factors (in buildings, furniture, clothing, etc.)
long-term care
nursing home financing
inflation
homemaker services
retirement
protective services
alcoholism
blindness and deafness
education
mass media coverage
isolation
dental care

How likely is the government to respond to these needs? To satisfy them first requires a commitment to spend government money on the aged and then some consensus concerning priorities. The first requirement brings us to perhaps the most fundamental problem that politicians face— the problem of choosing the things that are possible from among the many things that people want, given the fact that government can almost never command enough resources to satisfy everybody. And as Cottrell has pointed out.

They [the politicians] know that to gain anything people must sacrifice something else they might have had. They try to judge the worth of an objective in terms of what the voter is willing to sacrifice to achieve it. If they judge correctly, they can continue to make policy; but if they err too greatly, policy will be made by others who have organized a more effective coalition in support of [other] policies.[23]

To build the power necessary to design, develop, and implement governmental programs for older people, the politician must find out in which areas older people's interests coincide enough with those of other groups to form an effective voting coalition—since we have already seen that older people do not by themselves have the necessary power. He must also stay out of areas, however strong the need may be, that most people consider none of the government's business. As we shall see, there are some sizeable obstacles which block governmental programs for the aged *per se*.

The first of these obstacles is conflicts of interest. Meeting the needs of older people often conflicts with meeting the needs of the young, and often the choice that must be made resembles the choice between aid to schools and aid to nursing homes. Most of the time the needs of youth are placed first. The same can be said of other categories and programs such as Aid to Dependent Children, the Economic Opportunity Act, the 1965 Voting Rights Act, and so on.

Vested interests also play their part. The most recent example is the American Medical Association's opposition to Medicare. The physicians did not oppose the idea of better medical care for older people. They opposed the idea of government involvement in programs that have traditionally been dominated by doctors. It was to protect this vested interest that the AMA opposed Medicare. This is quite evident from the fact that within six weeks after Medicare was put into operation, over 80 percent of doctors expressed approval. By this time it had become obvious to most of them that the government had no intention of becoming involved in their everyday decisions. The fact that the AMA's fears for their vested interest were unfounded is unimportant. The fact that they *felt* that the threat was real was enough to block the passage of Medicare for quite some time.

Another factor that inhibits programs for older people is the inertia of bureaucratic organizations. One of the factors which worked against the Social Security legislation was the fact that at the time it was being considered there was no recognized bureaucratic structure in the government around which those interested in supporting income programs for the aged could rally. At that time the Townsend Movement and Eliminate

---

[23] W. Fred Cottrell, "Aging and the Political System," in *Aging and Social Policy,* eds. John C. McKinney and Frant T. deVyver (New York: Appleton-Century-Crofts, 1966), p. 96.

Poverty in California under Upton Sinclair were both going strong, but there was no office in Washington through which their support could be funneled. At the time Medicare was being considered there was an Office of Aging under the Department of Health, Education and Welfare (HEW) and the Special Committee on Aging in the U. S. Senate. These mechanisms made gaining support for programs for older people easier in the sense that there was an office staff paid by the government to keep tabs on the interests of the aged. Part of the Older Americans Act which set up Medicare also set up the Administration on Aging (AOA). This agency now serves as a locus for information and research on aging going both to and from the Federal Government. It also serves as a primary advisory agency to the President where legislative programs for older people are concerned.

The fact that AOA is within HEW is no accident. Because the old Office of Aging was under HEW, the secretary assumed prior claim on programs in aging. As we shall see later, this may not be entirely unfortunate, but it is a case where bureaucratic inertia denied the Administration on Aging a certain amount of autonomy. In this respect AOA may be contrasted to the Office of Economic Opportunity. While AOA was buried in the bureaucratic maze in HEW, OEO was free to establish its own program, including quite a few genuine innovations. Each setup has its advantages and disadvantages. But the point is that the poverty coalition had the power to force its way out of the existing bureaucracy at least for a time, while the aging coalition did not.

Going back to the list of needs presented earlier, probably not a single one would receive enough general support in competition with other programs to make possible a self-contained legislative proposal. This leads to a fundamental question: Is it better to have low priority in a system having great power (i.e., a large coalition), or to have high priority in a system competing for and receiving much less (i.e., the National Council on Aging)? Everything we have discovered thus far indicates that if success is the measure of good, then low priority in a large coalition is the only hope older people have. Their needs must be incorporated into general programs to enjoy any real possibility of success. For example, combining the transportation needs of older people with those of the poor could result in gains for both, and this is the essence of political coalitions. Many political scientists are convinced that since Social Security and Medicare have both been enacted, there will never again be an issue relating primarily to older people that will mobilize the support of the young. Accordingly, the only hope that older people seeking government action on their problems have is to attach their requirements to broader ranging proposals.

This brings us to the political role of the "expert." It is the trained or experienced gerontologist who has the greatest potential impact in terms of formulating policies related to older people. He has access to more information about older people than perhaps anyone else, and as a society we are accustomed to letting the experts handle our problems. With AOA as a base of operations, the government experts in gerontology can influence programs that are being developed in other agencies. It is for this reason that we said that the location of AOA in HEW had certain advantages, for HEW programs are precisely those in which the interests of older people need to be represented.

The only difficulty with this system is the fact that in gerontology the "experts" are in fact much less expert than the experts in, let us say, the Agriculture Department. There is simply not enough evidence yet for the gerontologist to make policy recommendation with full confidence that he knows what is best or what most older people want. This is largely because we do not know enough yet about the changes with age that occur in people's values.

Fortunately the Senate Special Committee on Aging serves a very useful function here by allowing input from interested citizens concerning older people's problems. By holding hearings throughout the country, the committee attempts to give as many older people as want it a chance to be heard. Of course, a great many older people are never heard from, but the access is there should they need it.

With regard to governmental programs, then, we can expect to see the needs of the aged being combined with broader ranging programs. We should not expect to see old age programs emerge as a separate issue. We should expect to see the influence of gerontological "experts" on old age programs increase, although their knowledge of older people's needs is far from perfect.

Aside from the issue of how programs for older people can win political support, there is the equally important issue of how these programs should be organized and coordinated. The Federal Government can do a reasonable job of providing direct support to older people through programs such as Social Security. However, solutions to a great many of the problems older people face must be based on personal considerations and the *local* situation. In cases where personalized want-to-action-to-satisfaction service is necessary, the local community is the only governmental agency capable of doing the job.

Cottrell has outlined several important questions concerning the nature of governmental programs:[24]

—What should be the functions of a central agency on aging and what are the relationships between it and other departments and agencies within the Federal Government?

---

[24] W. Fred Cottrell, "Government and Non-Government Organization," Technical Paper for the 1971 White House Conference on the Aging, pp. 1–2.

—What should be the functions of official State agencies on aging? Where should they be located, and what should be their relationships with other units of State government?

—What type of agency is needed at the community level to serve as a focal point for broad action in aging? What should its functions be? From whence should it derive its authority and financial support?

—What is the most desirable method of integrating or interrelating the activities of overall agencies in aging at Federal, State, and community levels?

—How can government at each level best maintain working relationships with voluntary organizations and with the private sector of the economy?

—What should be the division of responsibility among public and private agencies and organizations?

—Should government take initiative in stimulating roles in aging on the part of organizations? If so, what types of organizations?

At present, most of these questions remain unanswered. The existing intergovernmental division of labor with respect to programs for older people has resulted from variations in the ability of various agencies to muster the political clout necessary to enact legislation. The track record at the national level is familiar. Social Security, Medicare, and agencies on aging in various Federal departments attest to a small but sometimes effective political power base at the Federal level.

At the state level the picture is clear. In most states, programs for older people are very limited, and the average state agency for aging consists of three people. Only very recently have Governor's Conferences on Aging, forums, and so on brought home to state politicians the fact that there is an interest group to be served. However, state involvement in programs for older people is hindered primarily by the fact that the four major programs —Social Security, Medicare, Aid for the Aged, and Federal Housing— all bypass state government on their way to the people.

At the local level the only governmental agency serving older people is usually the welfare department. Given the connotations attached to welfare programs by the public and by older people themselves, this is a very unsatisfactory situation. Only in very large cities has the concentration of older people at the local level been great enough to produce a separate office to respond to their needs. Recently, however, the multipurpose senior center has emerged as an effective community agency for translating public programs for older people into action.

Perhaps the ideal system would consist of a strong Federal agency capable of mustering political support for national fund-raising legislation, and strong state agencies to administer Federally funded programs, through local governmental agencies in the large metropolitan areas, and through multipurpose senior centers or other agencies in the small towns and rural areas.

Summary

Politics is the route to political power, and political power means control over the machinery of government. Older people are concerned with politics and government because they participate in politics through voting, working in political organizations, and holding office; and they are the object of governmental programs.

Older people seek to remain informed about and interested in politics, particularly if they are well educated or involved in local affairs. Older people vote in about the same proportions as they did when they were middle-aged. Each age cohort apparently develops its own level of participation which stays relatively stable throughout life. But differential mortality and the tendency for women to vote less reduce the actual proportion voting.

Older people have stronger party identification than the young only if they have been associated with the party over many years. It is years of affiliation, not age *per se,* which produces a strong party identification. Older people are evenly split between the Republican and Democratic parties. Since they are overrepresented among people who have served long apprenticeships in politics, older people are also overrepresented at nominating conventions and public offices. However, there is no evidence that this is the result of deference to age. In politics, youth apparently still bows to experience, and experience rather than age is the crucial variable. Older people have equal opportunity in politics, *but only if they have been lifelong participants.* There is little room for the retired grocer who suddenly decides he would like to get into politics.

In terms of political power, pressure groups of older people have seldom counted for much. Lack of leadership, regional segregation, heterogeneity of interests among older people, and lack of funds have all proved too much for those who would create an "old folks' power" bloc. These same factors have prevented older people from developing into a subculture or a genuine minority group.

Action in behalf of older people has almost always depended on the political support of non-age-based organizations such as unions or political parties. The role of old age interest groups is to make the need for action highly visible. If, once the need is visible, the cause is not picked up by a broad-based organization, little action is likely to result. This leads to the conclusion that older people have little genuine political power of their own.

Governmental programs for older people seek to shift the responsibility for meeting some of their needs from the family to the various levels of government. The Federal Government operates programs in income and health maintenance. But many other needs require involvement on the part of state and local governments.

The biggest problems in creating governmental programs for older people are to convince the public at large that older people deserve a higher priority than other needy groups, setting priorities among older people themselves, and deciding how these programs should be organized and coordinated, particularly in terms of intergovernmental relations.

In terms of realistic prospects, the best bet for older people is probably to settle for being one of many claimants on broad-ranging programs. They have found it extremely difficult to get action based on their needs alone. Older people tend to agree that income, housing, and transportation deserve top priority. In terms of organization, the best system for governmental programs would seem to be a strong Federal agency capable of gathering support for national fund-raising legislation, and strong state commissioners on aging to administer federally funded programs through local governments and multipurpose senior centers. More will be said on community organization for meeting the needs of older people in the next chapter.

Bibliography

Atchley, Robert C., W. Fred Cottrell, Linda K. George, and Ruth W. Smith, *Ohio's Older People*. Oxford, Ohio: Scripps Foundation, 1972.

Campbell, Angus, "Politics through the Life Cycle," *Gerontologist*, 11:(2, part I)112–117, 1971.

Carlie, Michael K., "The Politics of Age; Interest Group or Social Movement?" *Gerontologist*, 9:259–263, 1969.

Carp, Frances M., "Differences Among Older Workers, Volunteers, and Persons Who Are Neither," *Journal of Gerontology*, 23:497–501, 1968.

Cottrell, Fred, "Governmental Functions and the Politics of Age," in *Handbook of Social Gerontology*, ed. Clark Tibbitts. Chicago: University of Chicago Press, 1960, pp. 624–665.

———, "Aging and the Political System," in *Aging and Social Policy*, eds. John C. McKinney and Frank T. de Vyver. New York: Appleton-Century-Crofts, 1966, pp. 77–113.

———, "Political Deprivation and the Aged," in *Perspectives on Human Deprivation*. Washington, D. C.: National Institute of Mental Health, 1968.

———, *Government and Nongovernment Organization*. Washington, D. C.: White House Conference on Aging, 1971.

Crittenden, John, "Aging and Party Affiliation," *Public Opinion Quarterly*, 26:648–657, 1962.

———, "Aging and Political Participation," *Western Political Quarterly*, 16:323–331, 1963.

Donahue, Wilma and Clark Tibbitts, eds., *Politics of Age*. Ann Arbor, Michigan: University of Michigan Press, 1962.

Feingold, Eugene, *Medicare; Policy and Politics*. San Francisco: Chandler, 1966.

Fries, Victoria and Robert N. Butler, "The Congressional Seniority System: The Myth of Gerontocracy in Congress," *Aging and Human Development,* 2:341–348, 1971.

Glenn, Norval D. and Michael Grimes, "Aging, Voting, and Political Interest," *American Sociological Review,* 33:563–575, 1968.

Holtzman, Abraham, "Analysis of Old Age Politics in the United States," *Journal of Gerontology,* 9:56–66, 1954.

——, *The Townsend Movement: A Political Study*. New York: Bookman Associates, 1963.

Kapnick, Philip L., Jay S. Goodman, and Elmer E. Cornwell, Jr., "Political Behavior in the Aged; Some New Data," *Journal of Gerontology,* 23:305–310, 1968.

Kent, Donald P., "Government and the Aging," *Journal of Social Issues,* 21:79–86, 1965.

McKinney, John C. and Frank T. deVyver, eds. *Aging and Social Policy*. New York: Appleton-Century-Crofts, 1966.

National Council of Senior Citizens, *Legislative Approaches to the Problems of the Elderly: A Handbook of Model State Statutes*. Washington, D. C.: The Council, 1971.

Philibert, Michel, "La Politique Nationale de la Vieillesse en France," *Gerontologie,* November, 1970, pp. 10–13.

——, "L'Aspect Politique de la Gerontologie de Secteur," *Gerontologie,* March, 1971, pp. 13–19.

Pinner, Frank A., Paul Jacobs, and Philip Selznick, *Old Age and Political Behavior; A Case Study*. Berkeley, California: University of California Press, 1959.

Polner, Walter, "The Aged in Politics: A Successful Example, the NPA and the Passage of the Railroad Retirement Act of 1934," *Gerontologist,* 2:207–215, 1962.

Ruck, S. K., "Policy for Old Age," *The Economist,* 195:619, 1960.

Schmidhauser, John, "The Political Influence of the Aged," *Gerontologist,* 8:(2, part II),44–49, 1968.

Smith, Joel *et al.*, "Understanding Local Political Behavior: the Role of the Older Citizen," *Law and Contemporary Problems,* 27:280–298, 1962.

Taber, Merlin, "Application of Research Findings to the Issues of Social Policy," in *Older People and Their Social World,* eds. Arnold M. Rose and Warren A. Peterson. Philadelphia: F. A. Davis, 1965, pp. 367–379.

Tibbitts, Clark, "Politics of Aging: Pressure for Change," in *Politics of Age,* eds. Wilma Donahue and Clark Tibbitts. Ann Arbor, Michigan: University of Michigan Press, 1962, pp. 16–25.

Townsend, Peter and Dorothy Wedderburn, *The Aged in the Welfare State*. London: G. Bell and Sons, 1965.

Trela, James E., "Some Political Consequences of Senior Center and Other Old Age Group Membership," *Gerontologist,* 11:(2, part I)118–123, 1971.

Wedderburn, Dorothy, "Financial Resources Available to Older People; Lessons for Social Policy," in *Age with a Future,* ed. P. From Hansen. Copenhagen: Munksgaard, 1964, pp. 513–525.

16 Community

Community has been variously defined as a source of identity, as a location in geographic space, as a way of life, and as a social system. We will be concerned primarily with community as a social system, but it might be useful first to consider briefly how aging influences community as defined in these other ways.

While the identity a person draws from the community varies from person to person and from community to community, it is possible to say that in general, as people get older, they tend increasingly to identify themselves as members of a particular community, especially if they have remained in the same community for many years.

As locations in space, communities have certain ecological and physical characteristics that make a difference to the individual as he grows older. Climate is perhaps the most obvious of several factors that can either drive older people away from or attract them to an area. This is largely because of the impact that climate has on health. As people grow older they become less able to endure harsh climates. Another factor is air pollution, because older people are more susceptible to respiratory problems than the young. Older people are also more sensitive to noise. There are many other physical and ecological factors that serve to make some communities more attractive than others. Nevertheless, in the final analysis, these considerations have little influence on older people's choice of residence. Family, friends, a house, and historical identity are all more important factors for most older people.

Communities differ from each other in that each community has a somewhat individual culture. This means that local politics, groups, opinions about government spending, criteria for establishing social class membership, family attitudes and values, and many other features will differ slightly from one community to another. Thus moving from one community to another can be a difficult experience if the cultures in the two communities are quite different. Older people are particularly susceptible to difficulties of this kind because they tend to be more committed than younger people to the cultures of communities they have lived in for many years. This accounts in part for the reluctance many older people show toward moving. They realize that a new community will mean many new ways of doing things. Of course, this cultural commitment also helps explain the attractiveness of communities housing like-minded older people.

Communities are social systems that are tied to a relatively small geogrpahic area. The system begins with people who have needs they would like to satisfy. They join groups for this purpose, but access to various goal-oriented groups often depends on what categories the individual is assigned to. Age in itself is used as a criterion for categorizing just as race, religion, and ethnicity are.

When a set of groups forms an interrelated cluster around a long-range goal, we attach the label *social institution* to the entire cluster. When the various social institutions are interrelated with a small geographic area we call the resulting social system a *community*. Communities are in turn organized into states and states into nations.

The important point to remember about communities as social systems is that they are the smallest form of human organization that involves a full array of social institutions. Accordingly, the community is where most people come into their most intimate contact with social institutions. The ideal community is one in which the interrelated social institutions function so smoothly that everyone who attempts to solve his personal problems within the community context is given at least one realistic and effective alternative.

The prime question in assessing the impact of aging on community thus becomes: In what ways does aging influence the ability of the community to function for the individual? Function in the sense used here means both giving older people access to institutional means and achieving results for older people through the operation of the institution.

Consider the following list of social institutions:

Family	Health
Education	Welfare
Religion	Recreation
Economy	Leisure
Politics	Government

Although they are all interrelated, these institutions are not organized in the same ways in relation to the community. They differ particularly in the areas of responsibility and control. Some institutions are defined as primarily the responsibility of an individual or group; others are defined as a community responsibility; while still others are defined as both a public and a private responsibility. In terms of control, some institutions are informally controlled, some are formally controlled, and some are both. The institutions in our list could be roughly categorized as shown in Figure 12.

From the diagram it seems obvious that public responsibility produces a tendency toward formal control, while private responsibility produces a tendency toward informal control. Thus, in our discussion of the impact of aging on community will concentrate on formally controlled institutions in which public responsibility is a significant element. We will consider health only briefly, since it is considered in more detail elsewhere. In the

	Control		
	Formal	Combination	Informal
Public	Education Government Welfare		
Combination	Economy Health	Politics Recreation	
Private		Religion	Family Leisure

(Responsibility)

Figure 12. Institutions by Type of
Control and Responsibility

area of interaction at the community level among the economy, education, government, and welfare we will consider social services, housing, transportation, protective services, and educational programs.

Health

Health care in American Society is primarily a private matter to be arranged between the individual and the organizations providing care. The major exceptions to this pattern are VA hospital facilities and community health facilities for the poor. Many communities maintain well-baby clinics for the poor and sometimes long-term care facilities for the aged and disabled. Communities thus take responsibility for the health care of some older people—not necessarily because they are old, but because they are *both* old *and* poor. As we saw earlier, this type of relationship forces the older individual into a dependent status and makes adjustment to aging more difficult.

Another alternative is to provide public payment for the private health care of welfare clients, but the difficulty with this approach is that it excludes those who are poor, but who do not qualify for welfare.

Two conclusions come out of prolonged study of health care in America: we have yet to find a method of payment that will open up adequate health care to the poor—aged poor, included; and health care is so poorly organized that genuinely adequate care is both scarce and expensive. This is largely because health is still considered to be an institution that communities are responsible for setting up and supporting; while control is considered to be largely a matter for private enterprise or private nonprofit organizations. The result thus far appears to be a situation in which the planning and coordination needed to get the most out of the health care resources in the community are very difficult to achieve. This situation hits older people as a category harder than almost any other, because so many of them are poor and because older people have a greater need for health care than any other age group with the possible exception of small children.

Social Services

Social services consist of a broad range of often unrelated programs which revolve around a general goal of helping people when they need help to get the things they want. It includes such things as income assistance and counseling, senior centers, the foster grandparent program, talking books, meals-on-wheels, employment services, clearinghouse services, and protective services. Communities vary widely with regard to the number and range of such programs; therefore, instead of trying to describe the typical community, it is probably more useful to examine the various programs in the abstract.

Income assistance not tied to Social Security or private pension plans usually comes from local welfare departments, but now and then it comes from various philanthropic or religious organizations. In most major cities, for example, the Jewish community provides income assistance for indigent older people of their faith. While public welfare programs are usually administered at the local level, they are formulated at the state and national level. It is for this reason that local communities are often forced into a fairly inflexible posture which allows very little leeway for adjustment to fit local problems. Private programs theoretically have more flexibility, but they usually get bogged down in their own unique rigidities, usually over rules of "eligibility." That we have such difficulty in deciding who is "needy" probably reflects our preoccupation with preventing people from "getting something for nothing" rather than with more humanitarian motives.

Most communities do not have the power in the tax or distribution systems to be able to do their own planning or operations in the area of income assistance. They are thus left in the often thankless position of carrying out and being held responsible for policies which are not under their control.

Income counseling, on the other hand, is generally carried on apart from government agencies. In general such programs aim at helping people to get maximum use of their income resources by making sure they are aware of all possible sources of income and by helping them with the transition from a pre- to a post-retirement budget. Income counseling often includes such things as how to buy consumer goods at the lowest prices, how to take advantage of seasonal sales, the cost of credit buying, how to form consumer co-operatives, how to save on rent or get into low-rent public housing, ways to save on auto insurance, ways to save on building repairs, and so on. While this type of assistance is highly valued by older people, very few communities offer it.

Senior centers are usually operated as private nonprofit corporations, often underwritten with United Fund money. There are several hundred senior centers in the United States, and these organizations usually constitute the sole community attempt to offer recreational and educational programs for older people. In assessing the impact of senior centers and measuring their effectiveness as an institution, the small percentage of older people who utilize them (one to five percent) would seem to indicate that they do not constitute a viable alternative for recreation and education among the overwhelming majority of older people.

Of course, many older people who might otherwise use a senior center's facilities are prevented by difficulties of access—poor transportation service, disability, health, and so on. Yet even in communities where all-out efforts have been made to give older people access to senior centers, only a small minority took advantage of them.

For some older people the senior center is a beacon in the night, a place for self-renewal. For others it is a continued reminder that older people are treated like isolated outcasts. Perhaps the difficulty is that in any community older people's needs are too complex to be effectively satisfied by any single organization, particularly one that gets a very low-priority share of community funds.

The average multi-purpose senior center tends to adopt a flexible program—one that involves informal companionship, community services, self-government within the center, and a wide variety of other possible features. Membership in senior centers tends to be drawn from a wide area rather than from a single neighborhood. Initial membership is often related to a major life change such as retirement or widowhood, and joiners tend to be healthy and able to get around. Members of senior centers do not seem to be very different from other older people.

At this point we still do not know how widely accepted senior centers are as an institution in the American community. Part of the reason is that many senior citizens' organizations are semi-formal groups operating under the auspices of churches, unions, fraternal organizations, and the like. One "directory" of senior centers in the United States listed only about 350 for the entire country as of 1966. Certainly there are more than this, but much more research is needed before we will know very much about regional trends in the acceptance of senior centers, community attitudes toward senior centers, and the variety of services provided. The growing tendency for Federal support of programs in local areas to be channeled through senior centers should provide considerable impetus for such research.

The Foster Grandparent Program has been very successful in many areas. This program seeks to utilize the services of impoverished older people as a way of providing personal, individual care to children who live in institutions. Right now about 8,000 children are being cared for by 4,000 older people who work four hours a day, five days a week at giving them the kind of individual attention many of them have never had before. The program began as a Federal project, funded by the Office of Economic Opportunity and administered by the Administration on Aging. There were sixty-eight projects in various hospitals, schools, and other institutions throughout forty states in January, 1970. There was a great deal of enthusiasm for the program in many areas, and the states themselves have shown interest in continuing and expanding it.

In a series of studies, the impact of the Foster Grandparent Program has been shown to be of great benefit to both the older people involved and the children they served. After exposure to the program, children in one project were observed to be more outgoing and to have improved relationships with both their peers and institutional authorities. There was evidence of increased self-confidence, decreased insecurity and fear, and improved language skills.[1]

Older people get many gratifications from the program. To begin with, the older person is able to augment his income by $30 to $35 per week, and for most older people this is quite a help. Many reported feelings of increased vigor and youthfulness, of an increased sense of personal worth, of a renewed sense of purpose and direction to life, and of pleasure in renewed personal growth and development.[2]

Administrators were pleased with the way older people seemed to adapt to the various tasks—many of them involving new skills which the older people had to learn. Special assignments in day-care, physical therapy,

---

[1] "Foster Grandparents Get High Ratings in Five Studies," *Aging,* December, 1968, p. 14.

[2] *Ibid.,* p. 15.

speech therapy, and as teacher's aides were made possible by the willingness and ability some of the older people showed. As one study put it: "There need not be any great concern about the comfort and staying power of the aged. . . ."[3] From the experience of the Foster Grandparent Program several inferences can be drawn. For one thing, low income older people will work for modest but reasonable pay if the job proves satisfying to them, and thus they offer a vast pool of relatively inexpensive labor that can be utilized to do needed work within the community. The role that older people might play in day care alone is enough to stagger one's imagination. It has also shown that older people are interested in continued participation in community affairs, particularly a useful and dignified participation.

Table 18 shows a compilation of the various types of community service programs intended primarily for older people. About half of these programs attempt to do something *for* older people, and half attempt *to utilize older people* as a means of doing something for the community. Also, a great many of them owe their initial financial push to Federal programs under the Administration on Aging (AOA).

It becomes obvious as one surveys various programs in various communities that there is very little coordination of programs within communities. It is rare to find a community that attempts to offer a coordinated range of services to its older people.

One such community is Bucks County, Pennsylvania. With the help of several grants from AOA, Bucks County has developed a complex of services around Neshaminy Manor, a modern public nursing home. The services are available not only to indigent older people, but to all who want them. Payment is scaled according to means.

The nursing home and the Bucks County Adult Welfare Department *work closely together*. The Welfare Department refers patients to the nursing home for admission, and the nursing home refers patients to the Welfare Department for foster home care. In addition, the nursing home provides services such as meals, physical therapy, and occupational therapy to the day-care patients of the Department.

The Welfare Department runs a counseling and referral service, a foster home care program, and volunteer service which provides volunteer workers for the nursing home. Activity centers are maintained in locations around the community by the Bucks County Association for Retired and Senior Citizens.

A day-care center for the chronically ill is used to care for eighteen people and give them physical and recreational therapy. The Welfare Department intends to purchase a bus to solve some of the transportation problems.

---

[3] *Ibid.*

Table 18. A Survey of Community Programs for Older People

Program Title	Description	Reference
Meals-on-Wheels, also called Operation: Loaves and Fishes	*Provides home delivered meals to older people. Provides improved nutrition and increases independence among those who participate.*	*National Council on the Aging, 49 W. 45th St., N. Y. See also* Aging, *April, 1968, p. 15.*
Friendly Visitor	*Provides regular, but limited visits by volunteers to shut-ins. Primarily an extension of welfare casework services.*	*Patterns for Progress in Aging, Case Study No. 13, Office of Aging, HEW. See also* Aging, *Oct., 1967, p. 11.*
Senior Citizens as Teacher Aides	*Provides supplemental income and a source of satisfaction to the older people involved.*	*Operation: Seasoned Service, Dade County Board of Public Instruction. Report available from AOA. See also* Aging, *July, 1968, p. 8.*
Project TLC	*Older people are utilized in a variety of positions that involve giving tender, loving care to very young children.*	*National Council on the Aging*
Project FIND	*Community action program to find older people who are friendless, isolated, needy, and disabled and help them utilize community services.*	*National Council on the Aging*
Green Thumb	*Older farmers are employed in beautification projects.*	*National Farmers Union,* Aging, *Oct.–Nov., 1969, p. 18. See also Nov., 1967, p. 4.*
Green Light	*Older low-income women are used in community service work. Used to fill gaps in service to rural areas.*	*National Farmers Union,* Aging, *Oct.–Nov., 1969, p. 18.*
Senior Orchestra	*Retired union musicians in New York City. Provides free concerts for the public.*	Aging, *June–July, 1969, p. 18.*

Table 18 (cont'd)

Referral and Counseling Services	*Information, counseling, and referral services are provided to older people in South Bend, Ind. by means of a clearinghouse.*	Aging, *May, 1969, p. 10. See also* Aging, *Oct., 1967, p. 12 for another referral program.*
Library Aides	*Older people are paid to work in libraries. Training investment was small, and there was little absenteeism. Libraries continued employment after Federal aid stopped.*	Aging, *March–April, 1969, p. 9.*
TOCER	*Tuscon on Call Employment Service. No charge to job seekers or employers. Placed over 4,000 people over 40 in jobs in the Tuscon area in 10 years.*	Aging, *March–April, 1969, p. 15.*
Senior Guides	*Older people were used as paid tourist guides in two Michigan counties.*	Aging, *March–April, 1969, p. 15.*
Senior College Tuition Waiver	*Six colleges reported a waiver of tuition for older people.*	Aging, *February, 1969, p. 12.*
Roadrunners	*An Austin, Texas group that serves as a source of transportation, companionship, letter-writing, nurses aides, shopping, etc.*	Aging, *Oct.–Nov., 1968, p. 11.*
Reachout	*Uses student interns from Albany to find and assist older people in getting the services available to them.*	Aging, *Oct.–Nov., 1968, p. 27.*
Employ Ability	*Connecticut State Labor Dept. program which has successfully placed a number of old (70-plus) applicants.*	Aging, *Oct.–Nov., 1968, p. 31.*
Craftmobile	*Provides instruction and materials for use in ceramics, needlepoint, knitting, etc.*	Aging, *July, 1968, p. 14.*
Service Corps of Retired Executives	*3,300 retired executives have rendered assistance to over 37,000 small businesses.*	Aging, *May, 1968, p. 17.*
Talking Books	*Provides recorded books to blind and disabled people.*	Aging, *Sept., 1967, p. 16.*

Table 18 (cont'd)

Program Title	Description	Reference
Home Care	*Rehabilitative care by home-care nurses. Proved as effective as institutional programs.*	Aging, *July, 1967,* p. 3.
Home Health Aides	*Older people are trained and employed as health aides.*	Aging, *March, 1967,* p. 6.

Here is how the services work:

A call to the Counseling and Referral Service at the Department will bring an immediate response. If the problem is a complicated one, a caseworker will visit the person who needs help. Last year there were more than 700 inquiries and the two caseworkers attached to the Service traveled 8,824 miles to provide help for 485 county residents—133 men and 352 women with an average age of seventy-six.

With their knowledge of the resources of the county, the caseworkers can help with many types of problems. If an older person is incapable or incompetent, and has no family or friends to assume responsibility, the Department mobilizes medical, psychiatric, and legal services for his protection. Sometimes this may mean that he will be placed in a foster home for responsible care.

During 1967, seventy-six aged persons were cared for in foster homes as an Adult Welfare service under the foster home supervisor. Of these, thirty-eight were receiving public assistance, while the others had enough income to pay their own expenses. In addition, a retired occupational therapist, who is also employed part-time in the day care center, provides service to some of the people in the homes, and others are now being transported to Day Care at the Neshaminy Manor Center for additional physical and recreational therapy.

Neshaminy Manor usually has a waiting list of at least 100, but often one of the Homemaker Service's forty-eight trained homemaker-home health aides may be needed. In 1967, the agency provided 32,875 hours of service, 72 percent to elderly clients. The Homemakers are carefully selected and trained women, ranging in age from twenty-four to eighty-one. It is the eighty-one-year-old who has volunteered to do twenty-four-hours-a-day service. Twice a year the Service conducts a training class and employs the new graduates, and in July of this year it is certified to begin providing services for reimbursement under Medicare.

If an elderly resident of the county has suffered a stroke or needs physical-occupational therapy to help him use his hands or legs, he may be accepted in the Day Care Program. In that case, he will be given a multiphasic medical screening and his physical rehabilitation and corrective therapy planned by trained professionals.

In addition, as a special service to the older people of Bucks County, caseworkers of the Department of Adult Welfare are available to visit each of the five senior activity centers—in Bristol, Doylestown, Perkasie,

Quakertown, and Feasterville—one day each week to provide counseling and referral.[4]

From this description it is not too difficult to see that most communities are far behind Bucks County in their ability to provide efficient, co-ordinated services to older people.

Another problem area which often requires public services goes by the name of *protective services*. Generally speaking, this type of service means taking over the affairs of older people who are no longer capable of taking care of themselves. Everyone has heard of the aging, confused hermit who has outlived his family and who is starving because he had hidden his Social Security check and can't recall where he put it. A case illustration may help:

For several years Mr. M. has been complaining to a variety of agencies about Mrs. S., an eighty-eight-year-old woman whose house is adjacent to his—and he finally reached Senior Information Center. Mrs. S. is a recluse who has harassed the M's by making loud noises in their bedroom window, banging her porch door, calling over vile and obscene things to their children playing in the yard. Her house is run down, weeds and bushes are overgrown, and neighbors photographed her feeding rats in her back yard. They described her as resembling the witch of fairy tales—with flowing grey hair and long dirty skirts, living in seclusion in a silent house. The only relative is a niece, who for the last several years has refused to be involved. Her income in only $72.00 a month from Social Security.

A home call confirmed the grim picture. Mrs. S., suspicious at first, refused to let the caseworker into the house, but came out on the porch to talk. She tried to hide a dirty, stained slip; and there was a strong odor of urine about her. She denied having any problems other than those caused by the "gangsters" next door, and there was a paranoid trend in her thinking. As she talked she became almost friendly, joked about getting a mini-skirt, and assured the caseworker that there was nothing to worry about in her situation.

Later, a city sanitation inspector went through the house, saw one rat and evidence of their presence throughout the house. He believes that she does actually feed rats. The odor of urine and feces was strong, for Mrs. S. apparently does not bother to use the upstairs toilet or is incontinent. The inspector also found about fifty wine bottles, which adds to the frightening picture. Suppose she became intoxicated and a rat attacked her?

Another aspect was recently uncovered. Mr. M. in his anger over the continued harassment, nailed shut the back door to her house. Fortunately, another neighbor, realizing the danger in case of fire, removed the nails.[5]

---

[4] "Bucks County, Pa., Initiates Program to Provide Coordinated Services for Older People," *Aging*, July 1968, pp. 10–12.

[5] Hugh A. Ross, "Protective Services for the Aged," *Gerontologist*, 8:(1, part II)50 (1968).

Protective services are brought to bear when it becomes clear that "the individual's behavior indicates that he is mentally incapable of caring for himself and his interests."[6] It is thought that something on the order of one in every twenty older people needs some form of protective service. In addition, this proportion can be expected to increase as the proportion of older people over age seventy-five increases.

The typical response to someone like Mrs. S. is to put her away in a mental hospital, but this solution is coming under increased scrutiny. Many older people in mental hospitals could easily be left at home with a minimum of help in securing the support services that are already available to them. Often commitment to mental hospitals is done against the will of the older person "for his own good," but a U. S. District Court of Appeals has ruled that a person cannot be involuntarily committed until it has been shown that all other alternatives for caring for him have been exhausted.[7] In addition, mental hospitals are already too crowded to be able to care for incompetent older people.

The most difficult problem is often to find someone to initiate action. In many states the law assumes the proceedings will be initiated by a relative, and in the absence of a relative no one is willing to take the responsibility. Laws need to be changed in such a way that responsibility is pinpointed.

Ultimately, protective services are casework, outreach services rather than deskbound ones. Legal intervention is usually a last resort, used only when all other alternatives have been exhausted, and agencies must often seek out people who may not want the service at all. It is obvious that protective services must be a part of any community service program for older people, but assigning responsibility for such services is a difficult task.

Transportation

In this country we have been experiencing a long-term trend away from public transportation. Its use is declining in all but our largest cities. No longer a paying proposition, and usually requiring tax subsidy, public transportation is most used for travel to and from work. The needs of the elderly are not considered in most decisions about public transportation.

Older people fall into two categories with regard to transportation: those who can utilize present facilities and those who cannot. Those with

---

[6] *Ibid.*

[7] Gertrude H. Hall, *The Law and the Impaired Older Person: Protection or Punishment?* (New York: National Council on the Aging, 1966).

no transportation problem tend to be the ones who can afford to own and operate their own cars, represented by about 46 percent of those sixty-five and older. For these people, public transportation is something to be used when it snows or when going on a long trip.

The elderly with a transportation problem fall into three groups: (1) those who could use existing public transportation but cannot afford it, (2) those who for one reason or another need to be picked up and returned directly to their homes, and (3) those who live in areas where there is no public transportation.

Cost is an important factor. In this country we have roughly ten million older people who are hampered by the cost of transportation. Some of the limiting factors are: they cannot afford a car; bus fares of $.50 or higher are beyond their means; and they cannot pay cab fares of $1.25 or more. For these people, lack of adequate, inexpensive transportation is one of the most important limitations on their independence and activities.

Studies have shown that among the older people with transportation problems, most are still able to get to the doctor, dentist, and grocery store. But many do not get out to see their friends and relatives or go to church or recreation facilities. Although they still manage to keep alive, they are unable to do the things that give meaning to life. They can maintain the body, but not the spirit. Pride and a sense of dignity often prevent older people from relying on friends and relatives to transport them. What is needed is a dependable transportation system at prices they can afford.

Solutions that have been tried in various communities include: (1) reduced fares for older people at specific hours; (2) public subsidy to improve bus schedules and routing; (3) use of volunteers in private automobiles; (4) nonprofit transportation services operated by senior centers; and (5) use of church buses.

The ideal transportation plan for older people would consist of: (1) fare reductions or discounts on all public transportation, including interstate transport; (2) public subsidies for adequate scheduling and routing of existing public transportation; (3) reduced taxi fares for the disabled or infirm; and (4) funds to be used by senior centers to purchase and equip vehicles to use in transporting older people, particularly in rural areas and in places with no public transportation.

Perhaps the most pressing need is for reduced fares and door-to-door transportation programs, even in some of our larger cities.

Older people's transportation problems are specifically two: poor public transportation service and a low-income older population. Yet even if the income problem were largely solved, a great many of the problems would remain, because even if they could afford it, older people do not represent a sufficiently large market to support a profit-making transportation system on their own.

Housing

Housing is a key feature in the relationship between the older person and his community for several reasons. First of all, where a person lives largely determines his opportunities for contact with other people. It also has a bearing on access to various community services. The relationship between the housing preferences of older people and the availability of the preferred types of housing in a community are also important factors in an older person's overall evaluation of the desirability of a particular community. Finally, one's home is where a large part of one's life is led, and it can either help or hinder the individual in his attempts to enjoy life.

Riley and Foner report that "Neighborhood ties tend to increase as size of place decreases. This does not necessarily mean, however, that all residents of large cities are isolated, for there are important variations among neighborhoods within the city and among individuals according to their length of residence in the neighborhood."[8]

In the larger cities the neighborhood tends to be a less important source of friendships for older people than in the case in medium-sized or smaller towns, a trend that is at least partly due to the greater instability of low income residential areas in the metropolis. Older people in big cities often find themselves deserted by their former neighbors and surrounded by strangers, and the newcomers are often not only of a different age but a different subculture as well. Thus, what could be a source of life-style continuity is often a source of alienation for older people in the big cities.

Apparently the two crucial determinants of neighborhood interaction among older people are the length of residence in the area and the concentration of older people from a similar background in the area. These two factors can overcome the influence of city size.

From an ideal point of view, then, one would expect the maximum integration of older people into their neighborhoods to occur in medium-sized or smaller cities with stable neighborhoods having large proportions of older people in them. One of the tragedies of urban renewal has thus been the destruction of the social web of interaction, and while this is a problem for anyone, it is doubly so for older people. Another implication of the findings on neighborhood interaction is that older people actually fare better in neighborhoods with a disproportionately high number of older people in them.

In terms of use of community facilities, older people in larger cities seem to be better off. The larger the city, the more likely it is that older people will use various facilities in the community (e.g., shops, post office,

---

[8] Matilda W. Riley and Ann Foner, *Aging and Society*, Vol. I, *An Inventory of Research Findings* (New York: Russell Sage Foundation, 1968), p. 125.

doctor's office, and senior center). The facilities most often used tend to be grocery stores, public transportation, and churches.[9]

Older people generally prefer to remain in independent housing as long as possible. Table 19 shows some stages on the continuum from independent to dependent housing.

As we saw earlier, nearly 75 percent of older people live in their own independent households, and this percentage is on the increase. They tend to own their own homes, and continue to live in them as long as possible. As age increases, however, more and more of them are forced to give up their homes. Death of one spouse is also very likely to produce a move

Table 19. Levels of Housing by Degree of Independence

Housing Type		Significant Criteria
Independent	Fully independent	Self-contained, self-sufficient household; residents do 90% or more of the cooking and household chores.
	Semi-independent	Self-contained but not entirely self-sufficient; may require some assistance with cooking and household chores. Example would be independent household augmented by meals-on-wheels and/or homemaker services.
Group Housing	Congregate Housing	Can still be self-contained, but is less self-sufficient; cooking and household tasks are often incorporated into the housing unit. Most common type is the retirement hotel.
	Personal Care Home	Neither self-contained nor self-sufficient; help given in getting about, personal care, grooming, etc., in addition to cooking and household tasks. Most common type is the retirement home.
	Nursing Home	Neither self-contained nor self-sufficient; total care, including health, personal, and household functions.

from an owned home. More than a third of older people living in their own homes have lived there twenty years or longer, compared with 13 percent for all households.[10]

Older people tend to live in dwellings that are slightly older than average, that have lower values, and that are more often dilapidated. Three-fourths of these are detached houses, as distinct from duplexes or apartments, a figure which is about average for the country as a whole.

[9] Riley and Foner, op. cit., p. 128.
[10] Ibid., p. 131.

Older people tend to have more room in their households than the young do, but many of them wish they had less.[11]

Negro-white differences in value of housing are notable. As Figure 13 shows, Negro older households are concentrated at the bottom of the housing value scale as compared to white older households. The same trends appear in terms of monthly rent.

It is not clear just what percentage of these independent households are semi-independent. Certainly some of them are. Research on this subject is greatly needed. It would probably be a safe guess, however, that a great many so-called independent households desperately need the support services involved in semiindependence. The truth is that very few communities have the facilities to provide such services, and as we saw earlier, many older people would prefer to suffer and perhaps even die rather than give up their independence. The chances are that the semiindependent type of housing would be popular not only with many older people now living in marginally independent households but also with some now living in less self-contained housing.

Only about 5 percent of the older people in the United States live in some type of group housing. Of these, about 1 percent live in congregate housing, and the remainder is split almost evenly between personal care and nursing homes.[12] A small percentage of older people live with their children. This pattern will be discussed later, when we examine the family.

To a large extent, older people use their homes as the center for their social contacts. They entertain there, they have overnight guests there, they have people in for meals. Home ownership also appears to encourage involvement in community affairs. It is therefore extremely significant for most communities that the overwhelming majority of older people have living arrangements that do not limit their community participation.

It is harder for older people living in group housing to maintain community identification and participation. It is for this reason that some nursing homes seek to develop a sense of community within the home.

Finally, in planning housing especially for older people, there are many design features that can help the individual stay independent. Ramps to go up and steps to come down, wide doorways, large rooms with few hallways or corners, and sturdy hand-support fixtures in the bath are some of these.[13] However, in the long run it is the social rather than the physical conditions that appear to be most important.

---

[11] *Ibid.*, p. 134.

[12] *Ibid.*, pp. 141–142.

[13] See also U. S. Department of Housing and Urban Development, *Housing for the Physically Impaired: A Guide for Planning and Design* (Washington, D. C.: U. S. Government Printing Office, 1968).

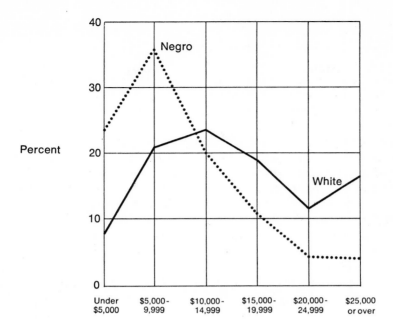

Value of owner-occupied housing units.

Figure 13. Percent of Husband-Wife Families with Head Sixty-five Years and Over, by Race of Head, by Value of Owner-Occupied Housing Units, United States: 1970
Source: U. S. Department of Housing and Urban Development, *Population, Housing and Income, and Federal Housing Programs* (Washington, D. C.: Government Printing Office, 1971), p. 22.

Education

Here we see perhaps the ultimate in the withdrawal of support from older people. Education systems in the United States are youth-oriented and job-oriented. The purpose of school in America is primarily to prepare the student for a job. Even adult education tends to be oriented around the types of skills needed to secure a better job or a promotion. Only a very tiny portion of the young person's education is devoted to the skills involved in the enjoyment of living, and few of the adult education programs throughout the country are so oriented. It should not be too surprising, then, to find that education programs are the last thing most older people would consider in terms of community participation. There is some question how relevant education is for the young, but there can be no question that most formal educational programs are almost totally irrelevant for older people.

One bright light on the horizon is a growing trend for universities to offer courses to older people truition free. At present there are very few such programs, but the prospects for more in the future seem good. The prime difficulty, however, is that the very people who need educational programs the most are often also the least able to take advantage of free college programs because their public school education has not prepared them to enjoy college-level courses of study. Another difficulty is that gradually the colleges have become more and more specialized, and the liberal arts—which include most of the courses that interest older people—are fast becoming the weakest part of public higher education.

Other educational programs of note include the Institute for Lifetime Learning in Washington, D. C., where members of the American Association of Retired Persons and National Retired Teachers Associations can go to learn such subjects as typing, sewing, painting, stamp collecting, or public speaking. Community colleges have also shown an interest in programs for older people.

Another significant educational program is the community education concept now in operation in Flint, Michigan. Through grants from the Mott Foundation, Flint has been engaged for twenty years in creating a genuine cradle-to-grave educational system—a system that would meet the needs of community citizens not just as children, but throughout their lives. Senior centers are operated as part of the public school program in Flint, and it is perhaps a commentary on the rigidity of our notions about education that this seems unusual.

Summary

For older people the community is important, particularly if they have lived there a long time. Nevertheless, older people are, in general, either expected to withdraw from participation or prevented from participating by the structure of the various public-responsibility institutions in the community. Educational participation is largely nonexistent. Economic participation is curtailed by retirement and low incomes. In the areas of health and welfare a great deal is being done *for* older people, but precious little of it *by* older people. In social services, there is a mixture of uncoordinated programs; and older people are only just beginning to be relied on as a community resource. Protective services often tend to serve the public rather than the older person himself.

Transportation systems largely ignore the needs of older people, as do housing plans, particularly in the area of semiindependent housing.

The ideal community is one in which the interrelated social institutions function so smoothly that everyone who attempts to solve his personal problems within the community context is given at least one realistic and effective alternative. We might refer back to Clark and Anderson, who cite the following as the adaptive tasks of aging: acceptance of aging, reorganization of life space, substitute sources of need satisfaction, reexamination of criteria for self-evaluation, and reintegration of values and life goals.[14] By far the most frequent cause of maladjustment in old age is the failure to find substitute sources of need satisfaction.

There can be little doubt that this failure is brought about partly by the ineffective organization of most communities. They simply are not prepared to help older people in this regard. The pressures of formal control mechanisms make it impossible to deal flexibly with what often turn out to be highly individualized problems.

Bibliography

A. General

Belcher, J. C. and S. Deutschberger, *Needs of Older Persons in Non-Metropolitan Communities*. Athens, Georgia: Georgia Gerontological Society, 1966.

Britton, Joseph H., "Living in a Rural Pennsylvania Community in Old Age," in *Patterns of Living and Housing of Middle-Aged and Older People*, eds. Frances M. Carp and W. M. Burnett. Washington, D. C.: Public Health Service, 1964, pp. 99–105.

————, William G. Mather, and Alice K. Lansing, "Expectations for Older Persons in a Rural Community: Community Participation," *Rural Sociology*, 27:387–395, 1962.

Cantilli, Edmund J. and June L. Shmelzer, eds., *Transportation and Aging: Selected Issues*. Washington, D. C.: U. S. Government Printing Office, 1970.

Edwards, Mabel I., comp., *Selected References on Homemaker-Health Aide Services; An Annotated Bibliography*. Iowa City, Iowa: State University of Iowa Institute of Gerontology, 1966.

————, *Selected References on "Meals-on-Wheels" Service; An Annotated Bibliography*. Iowa City, Iowa: State University of Iowa Institute of Gerontology, 1966.

---

[14] Margaret Clark and Barbara Anderson, *Culture and Aging* (Springfield, Illinois: Charles C. Thomas, 1967), p. 420.

Hutchinson, Bertram, *Old People in a Modern Australian Community*. Victoria: Melbourne University Press, 1954.

Kent, Donald P., *Meeting the Needs of Older People at the Community Level*. Washington, D. C.: U. S. Government Printing Office, 1965.

Kutner, Bernard, *et al., Five Hundred over Sixty, A Community Survey on Aging*. New York: Russell Sage Foundation, 1956.

McKain, Walter C., Jr., "Community Roles and Activities of Older Rural Persons," in *Older Rural Americans,* ed. E. Grant Youmans. Lexington, Kentucky: University of Kentucky Press, 1967, pp. 75–96.

Rosenblatt, Aaron, "Interest of Older Persons in Volunteer Activities," *Social Work,* 11:(3),87–94, 1966.

Taietz, Philip, "Community Structure and Aging," in *Proceedings of the 7th International Congress of Gerontology*. Vienna: Wiener Medizinischen Akadamie, 1966, VI, 375–378.

Thune, Jeanne, Sebastian Tine, and F. E. Booth, "Retraining Older Adults for Employment in Community Services," *Gerontologist,* 4:5–9, 1964.

B. Community Programs

Eckstein, Rebecca, ed., *Senior Centers Today: New Opportunities, New Challenges*. New York: National Council on the Aging, 1968.

Fendell, N., "Foster Grandparents Join the Rehabilitation Team," *Journal of Rehabilitation,* 33:(3),22–23, 1967.

Frankel, Godfrey, "The Multi-Purpose Senior Citizens' Center: A New Comprehensive Agency," *Gerontologist,* 6:23–27, 1966.

Gaitz, Charles M., M. Powell Lawton, and Raymond Harris, *Goals of Comprehensive Health Care in Advanced Old Age*. Ann Arbor, Michigan: University of Michigan, Wayne State University Institute of Gerontology, 1968.

Greenleigh Associates, *An Evaluation of the Foster Grandparent Program*. New York: The Associates, 1966.

Kaplan, Jerome, Caroline S. Ford, and Harry Wain, "An Analysis of Multiple Community Services through the Institution for the Aged," *Geriatrics,* 19:773–782, 1964.

Morris, Robert and Ollie A. Randall, "Planning and Organization of Community Services for the Elderly," *Social Work,* 10:96–102, 1965.

Nash, B. E., "Foster Grandparents in Child-Care Settings," *Public Welfare,* 26:272–280, 1968.

Spear, Mel, "Paramedical Services for Older Americans," *Journal of the American Geriatrics Society,* 16:1088–1094, 1968.

Tissue, Thomas, "Social Class and the Senior Citizen Center," *Gerontologist,* 11:196–200, 1971.

United States Department of Health, Education, and Welfare, Office of Aging, *Foster Family Care for the Aged*. Washington, D. C.: U. S. Government Printing Office, 1965.

————, *A Rural County Cares for Its Aging*. Washington, D. C.: U. S. Government Printing Office, 1967.

Vassey, Wayne, "Organization of Community Social Services for the Aging," *Gerontologist,* 8:(2, part II), 54–56, 1968.

Vickery, Florence E., "A Multi-Service Senior Center—Its Unique Role and Function," *Gerontologist,* 5:246–249, 1965.

C. Housing

Andrews, R. B., "Housing for the Elderly; Aspects of Its Central Problem," *Gerontologist,* 3:110–116, 1963.

————, "Housing for the Elderly; State and City-County Based Market Analysis, An Outline of Method and Administration," *Gerontologist,* 3:148–151, 1963.

Beckman, R. O., "Acceptance of Congregate Life in a Retirement Village," *Gerontologist,* 9:281–285, 1969.

Beyer, Glenn H., "Living Arrangements, Attitudes, and Preferences of Older Persons," in *Social and Psychological Aspects of Aging,* eds. Clark Tibbitts and Wilma Donahue. New York: Columbia University Press, 1962, pp. 348–369.

————, *Economic Aspects of Housing for the Aged.* Ithaca, New York: Cornell University Center for Housing and Environmental Studies, 1963.

————, *Housing and Society.* New York: MacMillan, 1965.

———— and F. H. J. Nierstrasz, *Housing the Aged in Western Countries; Programs, Dwellings, Homes, and Geriatric Facilities.* New York: Elsevier, 1967.

————, and S. G. Wahl, *The Elderly and Their Housing.* Ithaca, New York: Cornell University Center for Housing and Environmental Studies, 1963.

Blenkner, Margaret, "Environmental Change and the Aging Individual," *Gerontologist,* 7:101–105, 1967.

Bultena, Gordon L. and Vivian Wood, "The American Retirement Community; Bane or Blessing?" *Journal of Gerontology,* 24:209–217, 1969.

Burgess, Ernest W. ed., *Aging in Western Societies.* Chicago: University of Chicago Press, 1961.

Carp, Frances M., "Effects of Improved Housing on the Lives of Older People," in *Patterns of Living and Housing of Middle-Aged and Older People,* eds. Frances M. Carp and W. M. Burnett. Washington, D. C.: U. S. Public Health Service, 1966, pp. 147–167.

————, *A Future for the Aged: Victoria Plaza and Its Residents.* Austin, Texas: University of Texas Press, 1966.

————, "Housing and Minority-Group Elderly," *Gerontologist,* 9:20–24, 1969.

Chase, John A., "Better Housing for Senior Citizens," in *Foundations of Practical Gerontology,* eds. Rosamond R. Boyd and Charles G. Oakes. Columbia, South Carolina: University of South Carolina Press, 1969, pp. 207–210.

Dick, Harry R., *et al.,* "Residential Patterns of Aged Persons Prior to Institutionalization," *Journal of Marriage and the Family,* 26:96–98, 1964.

Donahue, Wilma, "Rent Supplement Experiment; Tests Mingling Low-Income, Moderate-Income Elderly," *Journal of Housing,* 22:447–481, 1965.

————, "Impact of Living Arrangements on Ego Development in the Elderly," in *Patterns of Living and Housing of Middle-Aged and Older People,* eds. Frances M. Carp and W. M. Burnett. Washington, D. C.: U. S. Public Health Service, 1966, pp. 1–9.

Fried, Marc, "Grieving for a Lost Home," in *The Urban Condition,* ed. Leonard Duhl. New York: Basic Books, 1963, pp. 151–171.

Gairey, T., "Housing of the Elderly," *Gerontologia Clinica,* 10:187–191, 1968.

Goldscheider, Calvin, "Differential Residential Mobility of the Older Population," *Journal of Gerontology,* 21:103–108, 1966.

Hamovitch, Maurice B. and J. E. Peterson, "Housing Needs and Satisfactions of the Elderly," *Gerontologist,* 9:30–32, 1969.

Hoyt, George C., "The Life of the Retired in a Trailer Park," *American Journal of Sociology*, 59:361–370, 1954.

Kasteler, Josephine M., R. M. Gray, and M. L. Carruth, "Involuntary Relocation of the Elderly," *Gerontologist*, 8:276–279, 1968.

Lake, Wilfred, S., "Housing Preferences and Social Patterns," in *Social and Psychological Aspects of Aging*, eds. Clark Tibbitts and Wilma Donahue. New York: Columbia University Press, 1962, pp. 341–347.

Langford, Marilyn, *Community Aspects of Housing for the Aged*. Ithaca, New York: Cornell University Center for Housing and Environmental Studies, 1962.

Lawton, Alfred H. and Gordon J. Azar, "Consequences of Physical and Physiological Change with Age in the Patterns of Living and Housing for the Middle-Aged and Aged," in *Patterns of Living and Housing of Middle-Aged and Older People*, eds. Frances M. Carp and W. M. Burnett. Washington, D. C.: U. S. Public Health Service, 1966, pp. 19–26.

Lawton, M. Powell, "Supportive Services in the Context of the Housing Environment," *Gerontologist*, 9:15–19, 1969.

———, "Planning Environments for Older People," *AIP Journal*, 36:124–129, March, 1970.

Lenzer, Anthony, "Mobility Patterns among the Aged," *Gerontologist*, 5:(1, part I),12–15, 1965.

McGuire, Marie C., "The Status of Housing for the Elderly," *Gerontologist*, 9:10–14, 1969.

Montgomery, James E., "Housing for the Rural Aged," in *Older Rural Americans*, ed. E. Grant Youmans. Lexington, Kentucky: University of Kentucky Press, 1967, pp. 169–194.

Musson, Novere and Helen Heusinkveld, *Buildings for the Elderly*. New York: Reinhold, 1963.

Rutherford, Robert B. and Arnold J. Holst, *Architectural Designs: Homes for the Aged: the European Approach*. Peoria, Illinois: Howard, 1963.

Sauer, Herbert I., "Migration and the Risk of Dying," in *Proceedings of the Social Statistics Section, 1967*. Washington, D. C.: American Statistical Association, 1968, pp. 399–407.

Sherman, Susan R., *et al.*, "Psychological Effects of Retirement Housing," *Gerontologist*, 8:170–175, 1968.

United States Department of Housing and Urban Development, *Housing for the Physically Impaired; A Guide for Planning and Design*. Washington, D. C.: U. S. Government Printing Office, 1968.

———, *Minimum Property Standards; Housing for the Elderly, with Special Consideration for the Handicapped*. Washington, D. C.: U. S. Government Printing Office, 1967.

Vance, Mary, comp., *Housing for the Elderly*. Eugene, Oregon: Council of Planning Librarians, 1963.

Weiss, Joseph D., *Better Buildings for the Aged*. New York: Hopkinson and Blake, 1969.

Wilner, Daniel M. and Rosabelle P. Walkley, "Some Special Problems and Alternatives in Housing for Older Persons," in *Aging and Social Policy*, eds. John C. McKinney and F. T. deVyver. New York: Appleton-Century-Crofts, 1966, pp. 221–259.

———, *et al.*, "Demographic Characteristics of Residents of Planned Retirement Housing Sites," *Gerontologist*, 8:164–169, 1968.

D. Protective Services

Blenkner, Margaret, Edna Wasser, and Martin Bloom, *Protective Services for Older People; Progress Report for 1966–67*. Cleveland, Ohio: The Benjamin Rose Institute, 1967.

Cumming, Roger J., "Growing Problems in Protective Services for the Aged," *Geriatrics*, 21:(9),163–173, 1966.

Hall, Gertrude H., ed., *The Law and the Impaired Older Person: Protection or Punishment?* New York: National Council on the Aging, 1966.

———— and Geneva Mathiasen, eds., *Overcoming Barriers to Protective Services for the Aged*. New York: National Council for the Aging, 1968.

Larson, N., "Protective Services for Older Adults," *Public Welfare*, 22:247–252, 1964.

Lehman, Virginia and Geneva Mathiasen, *Guardianship and Protective Services for Older People*. New York: National Council on the Aging, 1963.

E. Social Welfare

American Public Welfare Association, *Program Planning for Strengthening Services to the Aging Through Welfare Agencies*. Chicago: The Association, 1965.

Banay, Isabel, "Social Services for the Aged; A Reconsideration," in *New Thoughts on Old Age*, ed. Robert Kastenbaum. New York: Springer, 1964, pp. 205–212.

Beattie, Walter M., Jr., "The Aging Negro: Some Implications for Social Welfare Services," *Phylon*, 21:131–135, 1960.

Binstock, Robert H., "Some Deficiencies of Gerontological Research in Social Welfare," *Journal of Gerontology*, 21:157–160, 1966.

Bucke, M., "The Contributions of Voluntary Bodies to the Welfare of the Aged," *Gerontologia Clinica*, 9:217–226, 1967.

Carp, Frances M., *Factors in the Utilization of Services by the Mexican-American Elderly*. Palo Alto, California: American Institute for Research, 1968.

————, "Use of Community Services and Social Integration of the Aged," in *Duke University Council on Aging and Human Development. Proceedings of Seminars 1965–69*, ed. Frances C. Jeffers. Durham, North Carolina: Duke University Center for the Study of Aging and Human Development, 1969, pp. 169–176.

Herz, Kurt G., "New Patterns of Social Services for the Aging and Aged," *Journal of Jewish Community Services*, 44:236–245, 1968.

Kaplan, Jerome and Gordon J. Aldridge, eds., *Social Welfare of the Aging*. New York: Columbia University Press, 1962.

Morris, Robert and Robert H. Binstock, *Feasible Planning for Social Change*. New York: Columbia University Press, 1966.

Randall, Ollie A., "Some Historical Developments of Social Welfare Aspects of Aging," *Gerontologist*, 5:40–49, 1965.

United States Department of Health, Education, and Welfare, Welfare Administration, *Planning Welfare Services for Older People*. Washington, D. C.: U. S. Government Printing Office, 1966.

17

Moorings in the Community: Religion and Voluntary Associations

Religion

Consider the following list of topics:

religious identification
church attendance
religious associations
personal religious observances
participation in religious ritual
religious faith
religious "experience"
religious beliefs
personal importance of religion
religious morality

All of these topics can change as the individual grows older.

One of the things that makes religion an interesting and also infuriating area for study is the diversity of meanings that attach to the term. What does it mean to say that a person is "religious"? What do we mean when we talk about a religious faith? There are a great many possibilities.

Attempting to answer these questions is so frustrating partly because there are many variables that prevent religion from being a unified institution. For one thing, the range and variety of religious groups is considerable, all the way from the one-of-a-kind store-front church to the most stately denomination. There is also considerable variety even among congregations of the same denomination or sect. Within denominations there are also factions which differ in the emphasis they put on various aspects of church doctrine. Religions also differ in terms of the amount of participation and interest demanded of their adherents, the degree of organization they possess, and the opportunities they offer for the individual to achieve his goals through the church. Consequently, we can make only limited, general statements about religion and aging. Caution should be used in drawing inferences from these generalizations.

Most people apparently identify with some religion. In a sample of 35,000 households, the Census Bureau found that only 2 to 3 percent of those responding reported no religion. The older people in this sample were neither more nor less likely to report no religion. Proportionally, there are slightly more Protestants and slightly fewer Catholics among older people than among the general population, but the differences are very small and can be largely explained by changes in differential rates of immigration, fertility, and mortality.[1]

While most people identify with some religion, they do not nesessarily attend church. About half of the general population attends church regularly (twice a month or more). Catholics are much more likely to attend regularly than Protestants or Jews, and a higher proportion of women than men attend frequently. Also, church attendance is related to income, education, and length of residence in the community. Age is thus only one among many factors that influence church attendance. The age pattern of church attendance in general shows a steady increase from the late teens until it peaks in the late fifties to early sixties. After that, the curve shows a consistent but very slight decline. The only significant trend appears to be the increase in percent never attending among older people. Only the Jews do not show a discernible age pattern in church attendance. One study that attempted to determine the influence of age on church attendance while holding other variables constant found no consistent age trends.[2]

Some people increase their church attendance as they grow older; therefore, probably a larger proportion of people reduce their attendance than would appear from the composite data alone. At this point we simply do not have enough longitudinal data to be able to tell what impact this factor has on overall attendance figures.

In their study of older people in San Francisco, Clark and Anderson found that only a minority of their subjects attended church services even as often as once a month.[3] Interestingly, they found that "frequent church attendance is more characteristic of the mentally ill than of the mentally healthy subjects, in spite of the fact that more of the latter attend on special occasions from time to time."[4]

Their analysis is particularly enlightening in terms of the factors they discovered that tended to discourage church attendance. Most of the non-churchgoers were people who had never developed an association with a church or had had some sort of antagonistic experience with church organi-

---

[1] Matilda W. Riley and Ann Foner, *Aging and Society,* Vol. I, *An Inventory of Research Findings* (New York: Russell Sage Foundation, 1968), pp. 484–5.

[2] *Ibid.*

[3] Margaret Clark and Barbara Anderson, *Culture and Aging* (Springfield, Illinois: Charles C. Thomas, 1967), p. 329.

[4] *Ibid.,* p. 329.

zations early in life, usually in adolescence. For some, the demands of religious doctrine were too difficult to reconcile with the events of their lives. Still others based their antagonism on hostility toward a particular minister.

Clark and Anderson found two basic reasons why mentally ill older people were more preoccupied with religion. First, mentally ill people are anxious and fearful. They seek strength wherever they can—and sometimes they find it in religion. Second, mentally ill people can become obsessed with just about anything, including religion. The mentally ill people sought emotional support from religion; the normal controls gave it more social value. Another factor is feelings about immortality and death. Compared with the controls, the mentally ill older people had less tolerance for ambiguity concerning death. They needed to *know* what was going to happen. The controls seemed more able to accept death as an inevitable fact of life. As one said: "Death? Well, darling, I know from nothing about death. But one thing I'm sure of—I'll look back on it as an experience."[5]

The declines in church attendance, where they occur, are probably at least partially offset by increases in regular listening to church services and other religious broadcasts on radio and TV and in Bible reading.

Religious voluntary associations are second only to lodges and fraternal associations as membership groups for older people. Membership in these associations tends to increase with age until seventy-five. Leadership positions in these associations also tend to be concentrated among older people. Studies indicate that participation in religious organizations declines among older people at a much slower rate than participation in other types of organizations.

In terms of personal observances, older people are more likely to read the Bible at home, to react favorably to the idea of religious meditation, to pray in private, and to describe Sunday as a day for religious observance rather than for relaxation. In one study, the aspects of religious involvement were identified as (1) *knowledge* of the Bible; (2) *activism,* including church attendance, financial support, organizational participation, and leadership; (3) *creed* or adherence to doctrine, and (4) *devotional observance,* including personal prayer and private ritual. The percent of people who were religiously oriented on each of these dimensions was then measured and classified by age of the respondent. All dimensions except the devotional showed a decline in the seventy-or-over age group, but on this dimension there was a sizable increase over the group in their sixties. Devotional observance apparently does not become very important until the fifties, whereas the other dimensions of religious orientation reach peak levels much sooner.[6] Either that, or else there are some fairly sizable

---

[5] *Ibid.,* p. 342.

[6] Riley and Foner, *op. cit.,* p. 491.

changes in the devotional practices of later generations. As with so many other questions, reliance on cross-sectional data leaves us at a loss.

Although they are not very likely to participate in adult education generally, older people are more likely to study religion than most other subjects when they do decide to become students. It is for this reason that Maves emphasizes the importance of religious instruction in the formulation of church programs for older people.[7] This indicates an interest on the part of older people in religious knowledge. On the other hand, the few studies that have been done are unclear as to the effect of age on religious knowledge. This is an area greatly in need of research.

Regarding religious beliefs, there is some evidence that "belief in life after death may increase with age; at least a higher proportion of old people than of younger generations believe that there is a life after death. Older people also are more certain that there is a God and apparently are more inclined to hold to traditional and conservative beliefs of their religion."[8] But again we cannot tell whether the apparent differences are due to age or to the fact that the early childhood experiences with religion took place in different historical eras for the different cohorts.

Older people are more likely to feel that religion is important to them than are their younger counterparts. This is indicated by the larger proportions of older people who say that religion is very important in their lives, that religion is important to them aside from church attendance, that they are religious, and that they have a strong interest in religion.[9] In terms of life-cycle changes, there is a wide variety of individual patterns. Some feel that the usefulness of religion declines, but more think that it increases. The saliency of religion to the individual's self-image seems to increase with age, as does the stability of self-image. As age increases, the tendency to identify oneself as a religious person increases, and so does indecision about this aspect of the self.[10]

Religion also tends to be related to life satisfaction. Compared with older people in general, those who are church members, who read the Bible or attend church frequently, who are church leaders rather than followers, or who frequently listen to religious broadcasts are more likely to be well adjusted in their old age.[11] At this point, however, we cannot tell whether religious involvement aids adjustment or whether it is adjustment that leads to religious involvement. It would be possible to find out, but as yet this has not been done.

---

[7] Paul B. Maves, "Aging, Religion, and the Church," in *Handbook of Social Gerontology,* ed. Clark Tibbitts (Chicago: University of Chicago Press, 1960), pp. 698–749.

[8] David O. Moberg, "Religiosity in Old Age," *The Gerontologist,* 5(2):80, 1965.

[9] Riley and Foner, *op. cit.,* p. 495.

[10] Moberg, *op. cit.,* pp. 83–84.

[11] Riley and Foner, *op. cit.,* p. 496.

Contrary to popular belief, interest and participation in religious activities does not appear to protect people from loneliness or fear of death. Only among the most conservative of religious people does serenity and a decreasing fear of death seem to appear.[12] On other personal dimensions, such as self-esteem, identity, attitudes, values, beliefs, and norms, religion appears to increase in importance with age. Again, however, we do not know if this is a change with age or simply an intergenerational difference.

From what we have seen so far, it should be clear that a great many gaps still exist in our knowledge about the place of religion in the lives of older people. One reason is that research in this area has a very low priority. Therefore, we cannot expect to see many of these gaps filled for some time.

What about older people's place in the church? Because aging is often linked closely with death in people's minds, and because death is central to the question of the meaning of life, most religions take cognizance of the meaning of aging. Based on belief in a supernatural, Christian doctrine tends to consider aging a sometimes uncomfortable way station between life here and life hereafter. Implicit in this attitude is the idea that older people should be preparing to meet their Maker. This is perhaps one of the basic notions underlying the treatment of older people in Western culture. In many Eastern religions and in Judaism, on the other hand, there is no belief in a hereafter; thus a person has only one life to live. Behavior in this life is not a mere prelude to something better (or worse, depending on the religion), and respect is due to every phase of life. It is quite possible that these two conflicting views of the meaning of old age in the total sphere of human life have significantly affected patterns of aging in the two groups.

Jews have probably the highest respect for older people among the major faiths in the United States. Consequently, Jewish programs for older people have been more responsible, imaginative, and creative than either Protestant or Catholic programs.[13]

Protestants tend to view the misfortunes that often befall older people as somehow related to moral terpitude or a lack of responsibility. This individualistic approach has been somewhat mitigated by the tendency for Protestant groups to found church-related old-age homes. However, these homes tend to be only distantly related to the church and open to persons of all faiths; therefore, the church membership usually considers them philanthropy rather than a support service for "their own."

Catholics have been forced to develop their own institutions by a strong sense of responsibility for members of the faith, and by the difficulty of providing the required religious care within public quasi-Protestant in-

---

[12] Moberg, *op. cit.,* p. 84.
[13] Maves, *op. cit.,* p. 712.

stitutions. They have also developed a considerable array of health services open to older people of all faiths.

Jewish and Catholic doctrines both encourage their followers to support public social services for older people. The Protestants, on the other hand, are ambivalent, for theirs is a conflicting doctrine. On one side there is the individualism of the Protestant ethic and on the other the pietistic trend toward being a Good Samaritan. Thus far, the Protestant ethic has won out oftener than not, and this has been a major factor shaping social welfare support—or the lack of it—for older people in the United States.

However, the Protestants do appear to be changing. For one thing, the denominations are beginning to create positions on their national boards whose primary responsibility it is to promote programs for older people. Accordingly, national denominational magazines have run articles to acquaint the membership with problems of aging; manuals and booklets have been developed for use by local congregations in setting up programs; and workshops have been held to prepare ministers and lay workers for work with older people.[14]

On the local level, most ministers assume that worship services are as available to older people as they are to others. It is usually through contacts with shut-ins, hospitalized older people, and older people in nursing homes that local congregation pastors first confront the problems of older members of the congregation. Only gradually do they come to recognize that many of their ambulatory older members also have problems.

Some churches set up Golden Age clubs; others allow their facilities to be used by such groups. The churches are also getting interested in housing programs, particularly retirement homes for middle-income older people. They are beginning to see this as a legitimate service, and not merely as an act of charity. Since the proportion of older people in the average congregation is about the same as the proportion in the total population, it is not too surprising that the churches have begun to feel some pressure from their older members concerning housing problems.

At this point, however, church programs for older people are few and far between. While 80 percent of the Presbyterian churches, for example, report special social groups for older people (including age-segregated Sunday school classes), only two-thirds report any type of educational program specifically for older people, and very few have employment, homemaker, or health services, or room registries. Only about 13 percent have special budget items involving ministries to older people.[15] There is some indication, however, that Negro older people participate in and receive more from their churches than do older whites.[16]

---

[14] *Ibid.,* pp. 718–719.

[15] Riley and Foner, *op. cit.*

[16] Donald P. Kent, "The Negro Aged," *Gerontologist,* 11:(1, part II),49, 1971.

Thus, while it appears that most churches are quite willing to *passively accept* the participation of older people in church affairs, few are willing or able to *actively solicit* the participation of ill, handicapped, or isolated older people.

Voluntary Associations

A voluntary association is a group that develops around a collective desire to achieve some purpose or pursue some interest. It differs from other groups in that it is voluntary—voluntary in the sense that the individual is not compelled by social pressure or necessity to join, but instead is free to weigh the advantages and disadvantages of group membership and decide for himself whether or not to do so.

Many sociologists believe that voluntary associations have taken over American society because they serve the large-scale functions that were performed by the extended family in agrarian eras. No matter how we got that way, however, we are said to be the "joiningest" nation in the world.

Voluntary association membership appears to decline with age, but the decline is much less pronounced among women and among members of the higher socioeconomic classes.[17]

Only about 4 percent of older people show a significant amount of participation, but for this group, voluntary associations take up more time than any other leisure activity.[18] Trends over the life cycle show that most people persist in their established patterns; they remain either joiners or nonjoiners. Extraneous factors such as retirement or moving sometimes produce declines in participation, but if the individual's situation remains stable, his participation tends to do the same.

Older people who are still working, still married, and still entertaining friends occasionally are more likely to continue to participate in voluntary associations. For many, however, there is a perceived decline in the satisfaction they get from participation as they see the groups "letting in a different sort of people" or "having changed so much." Others are self-conscious about their age and would "rather leave it for the youngsters."

Health certainly influences participation, for it determines both the energy available and the individual's ability to get around. But there are other factors that reduce participation, the most important being fear of going out at night and transportation problems.

To a certain extent, participation in urban-industrial society requires

---

[17] Riley and Foner, *op. cit.*, p. 504.
[18] *Ibid.*, p. 515.

participation in voluntary associations. If nothing else, the 4 percent participation in voluntary associations shows the extent to which older people are alienated from what many feel is an essential area of life.

Earlier we considered senior centers and special clubs for older people and found that they suffer from the dual handicap of serving a group with no money, and of often forcing the older person to disrupt the continuity of his leisure style if he is to participate. Under these conditions we should not be surprised that Golden Age clubs do not abound in our land. Such organizations are infinitely more viable in cases where 1) the members have good retirement incomes, and 2) they carry over former work associations. The latter can provide the necessary continuity.

When we see in what types of organizations older people continue to participate, the continuity theory takes on added credence. In the civic or service area, where participation is often linked to the occupational role, older people show a substantial decline in participation. In lodges, fraternal and patriotic organizations, and church organizations there are no declines in participation with increasing age. This indicates a great deal of continuity in group participation in *leisure*-oriented voluntary associations.

In addition to church groups and fraternal organizations, there are union organizations. The United Auto Workers, for example, has set up centers open to all older people in order to provide a meeting place for retired members. Other unions have similar facilities, and many have a local union hall that is also a meeting place for retired union members and other older people.

Voluntary associations could perform many necessary functions for most older people. To begin with, the association often enables its members to obtain certain services, such as credit, with a minimum of red tape. Voluntary associations also serve as a source of social contacts and of personal identification. They also serve as a means of keeping a routine in the individual's lifestyle, and for some people this is important. Perhaps most important, associations give the individual a means of staying in the flow of things, of feeling worthwhile. For all of these reasons it is very unfortunate that so few older people are participating members of voluntary associations.[19]

Conclusion

As was true of several of the institutions we have already studied, older people can continue to participate in religious organizations or voluntary

---

[19] Some of these benefits of voluntary association membership go to mere members, but most are reserved for participating members.

associations, provided the involvement begins in middle age. Once begun, a position can be carried into old age. Beginning from scratch as an older person is difficult, if not impossible, depending on the particular situation.

The "portent of embarrassment," used earlier to describe some older people's failure to take up new leisure pursuits in retirement, can also be used to explain why few people take up roles in religious or voluntary associations late in life.

Once again, we are confronted with institutions that have much to offer older people, but which are not particularly well-oriented toward doing so. Religion and voluntary associations may occupy a big spot in the hearts of many older people, but unfortunately these institutions seldom reciprocate.

Bibliography

Ailor, James W., "The Church Provides for the Elderly," in *Foundations of Practical Gerontology*, eds. Rosamonde R. Boyd and C. G. Oakes. Columbia, South Carolina: University of South Carolina Press, 1969, pp. 191–206.

Downing, Joseph, "Factors Affecting the Selective Use of a Social Club for the Aged," *Journal of Gerontology*, 12:81–84, 1957.

Gray, Robert M. and David O. Moberg, *The Church and the Older Person*. Grand Rapids, Michigan: W. B. Eerdmans, 1962.

Havighurst, Robert J., "Life Beyond the Family and Work," in *Aging in Western Societies*, ed. E. W. Burgess. Chicago: University of Chicago Press, 1960, pp. 299–353.

Jacobs, Ruth H., "The Friendship Club; A Case Study of the Segregated Aged," *Gerontologist*, 9:276–280, 1969.

Maves, Paul B., "Aging, Religion and the Church," in *Handbook of Social Gerontology*, ed. Clark Tibbitts. Chicago: University of Chicago Press, 1960, pp. 698–749.

————, "Research on Religion in Relation to Aging," in *Duke University Council on Gerontology, Proceedings of Seminars 1961–65*, ed. Frances C. Jeffers. Durham, North Carolina: Duke University Regional Center for the Study of Aging, 1965, pp. 69–79.

Moberg, David O., "The Integration of Older Members in the Church Congregation," in *Older People and Their Social World*, eds. Arnold M. Rose and Warren A. Peterson. Philadelphia: F. A. Davis, 1965, pp. 125–140.

————, "Religion in Old Age," *Geriatrics*, 20:977–982, 1965.

————, "Religiosity in Old Age," *Gerontologist*, 5:78–87, 1965.

———— and Marvin J. Taves, "Church Participation and Adjustment in Old Age," in *Older People and Their Social World*, eds. Arnold M. Rose and Warren A. Peterson. Philadelphia: F. A. Davis, 1965, pp. 113–124.

Orbach, Harold L., "Aging and Religion: A Study of Church Attendance in the Detroit Metropolitan Area," *Geriatrics*, 16:530–540, 1961.

O'Reilly, Charles T., "Religious Practice and Personal Adjustment," *Sociology and Social Research*, 42:119–121, 1958.

Rose, Arnold M., "The Impact of Aging on Voluntary Associations" in *Hand-*

book of Social Gerontology, ed. Clark Tibbits. Chicago: University of Chicago Press, 1960, pp. 666–697.

Rubenstein, Daniel, "An Examination of Social Participation Found among a National Sample of Black and White Elderly," *Aging and Human Development,* 2:172–188, 1971.

Storey, Ruth T., "Who Needs A Senior Activity Center?" *Gerontologist,* 2:216–222, 1962.

Taietz, Philip and Olaf F. Larson, "Social Participation and Old Age," *Rural Sociology,* 21:229–238, 1965.

Wilensky, Harold, "Life Cycle, Work Situation, and Participation in Formal Associations," in *Aging and Leisure,* ed. Robert W. Kleemeier. New York: Oxford University Press, 1961. pp. 213–242.

Wingrove, C. Ray and Jon P. Alston, "Age, Aging and Church Attendance," *Gerontologist,* 11:(4, part I)356–358, 1971.

18 Primary Relationships: Family, Friends, and Neighbors

Interpersonal relationships vary considerably in terms of the degree of intimacy involved. Highly intimate relationships are called *primary,* and relationships involving little intimacy are called *secondary.*

Most of the social relationships considered up until now have been secondary. As MacIver and Page put it:

> The relations within which people confront one another in such specialized group roles as buyers and sellers, voters and candidates, officials and citizens, teachers and students, practitioners and clients, are *secondary,* involving categoric or "rational" attitudes.[1]

Secondary group contacts are rational in the sense that they do not involve emotional intimacy or sentiment, and as such they are relatively impersonal. A great many of older people's relationships in politics, government, the community, the church, and the economy are of this type.

At the other end of the continuum is the primary relationship, one that is intimate, durable, and personal. Primary relationships are usually limited to certain types of social situations, and a group is apt to develop primary relationships if the members are in frequent and enduring interaction, if they are close to each other in space, if the group membership remains small, if there is basic equality among the members, and if the membership remains relatively stable. Each and every one of these preconditions limits the extent to which any given group could develop primary relationships, and cases in which such relationships develop without these preconditions are rare.

Primary relations are not unheard of in institutions such as politics, government, or the economy. In fact, they are quite common. The essential

---

[1] Robert M. MacIver and Charles H. Page, *Society: An Introductory Analysis* (New York: Rinehart, 1949), p. 221.

point is that although the close working relationship between coworkers may produce a primary relationship, the nature of the *essential* relationships in the economy does not *require* a primary bond, only a secondary one.

Only a few institutions in American society are oriented primarily toward the development and nurturance of primary relations. The most obvious is the family. It meets all of the preconditions for primary group formation.

The family is perhaps the most basic of social institutions. Almost everyone is born into a family. Most people spend most of their lives residing in a family group. Most people play several family roles—son, husband, father, grandfather, uncle—in the course of a lifetime. For many people, the family group is the center of their world, the highest priority in their system of values.

There are a great many different types of family organizations throughout the world, but we will concentrate on the American pattern. The family has a life cycle just as people do. It usually begins with marriage, the formation of a couple from two previously unrelated people. The typical phases of the family life cycle could be listed as follows:

marriage
birth of first child
birth of last child
last child starts to school
first child marries or leaves home
last child marries or leaves home
birth of first grandchild
birth of first great-grandchild
death of first spouse
death of second spouse

Of course, since the children and grandchildren usually begin their own family cycles, the chain seldom stops. As we shall see, increasingly it is only the last three phases of the family cycle that occur in later maturity or old age.

The family that produces these relationships (spouse, parent, grandparent, great grandparent, widow) is called the *family of procreation* because it is the family within which a person's own procreative behavior occurs.

People also belong to a *family of orientation,* usually the family they are born into. Older people very often carry into their later years the roles from this family (son, daughter, brother, sister) as well as from the family of procreation.

There are also family roles such as cousin, uncle, nephew, brother-in-law, and so on, that derive from an *extended family,* the complex network of kin that parallels both the family of procreation and the family of orientation, usually through the sibling relationship or the marital bond uniting two separate families of orientation.

Kinship is an extremely complex subject. We will not emphasize extended kinship, but will concentrate on roles in the family of procreation and in the family of orientation as they relate to the effects of aging. We will start with marital status, since it is the most obvious criterion for distinguishing older people who are in families from those who are not.

The Older Couple

Most older people are married and live with their spouses in separate households. It is becoming unusual for people to live through the entire life cycle without marrying, and in 1960 fewer than one in ten older people had never married. Among older people, however, there are some important age differences in marital status.

Table 20. Marital Status by Age: United States, 1960

Marital Status	Age 65–69	Age 70–74	Age 75–79	Age 80–84	Age 85+	Total Age 65+
Males						
Married	79.4	73.1	64.7	53.7	38.7	70.8
Widowed	10.2	16.8	25.3	37.2	52.8	19.1
Divorced	2.7	2.4	2.1	1.7	1.4	2.3
Single	7.7	7.8	7.9	7.4	7.1	7.7
Females						
Married	51.6	39.1	27.4	16.2	8.2	37.4
Widowed	37.9	50.4	62.2	73.1	81.4	52.1
Divorced	2.7	2.1	1.5	1.1	.8	2.0
Single	7.9	8.4	8.8	9.5	9.6	8.5

Source: U. S. Bureau of the Census, *1960 Census of Population*, Vol. 1, Part 1 (Washington, D. C.: U. S. Government Printing Office, 1964.), pp. 424–425.

The proportion of single older people stays about the same as age increases. The proportion divorced shows a small but steady decline with age. This trend may be related to changes in the feelings of various generations about the acceptability of divorce, and it may also reflect the higher death rate for divorced people. The major changes occur in the married and widowed categories. The proportion married declines each year, but the decline starts sooner and is steeper for older women. At age eighty most men are still married, while only 16 percent of women are. This trend reflects the fact that men tend to marry women younger than themselves, and also the fact that women currently live an average of six years longer than men.

All of this means that couples are very prevalent among older people. Marriage tends to be the focal point in the lives of most older people who have a living spouse, especially when the departure of the children and retirement have limited other sources of primary relationships.

As the average life span has increased and the age of childbearing decreases, the average number of years a couple lives together after the children leave home has increased greatly. One consequence has been to create a greater sharing of activities between spouses. One study found that if the children were *all* gone, the older couple was much more likely to do things together than if one or more children were still living at home.[2]

Older couples appear to be no less happy than young couples. In fact, older people are less likely than the young to say that their marriages are characterized by feelings of inadequacy or by recurrent problems.[3]

For the happily married older couple, marriage is a godsend. It is a source of great comfort and support as well as the focal point of everyday life, and happily married couples often experience an increasing closeness as the years go by. In addition, there is often a high degree of inter-dependence in these couples, particularly in terms of caring for each other in times of illness. The older husbands in this happily married category are particularly likely to view their wives as indispensable pillars of strength. For people in these happy marriages widowhood is a dismal prospect indeed.

One key finding about these happy marriages is that they tend to be characterized by a much greater equality between the partners than is true of unhappy older couples. This is brought about especially by a gradual loss of boundaries between the sex roles and a decreasing sexual definition of the household division of labor.[4]

While most older couples fit more or less into the happy category, a few are filled with hostility. Some older people feel that their spouses are the cause of all their troubles, and they often wish that they could somehow terminate their marriages. Religious orthodoxy, such as the strong Catholic policy against divorce, has no doubt keep couples together who otherwise would have separated. The same could be said of social pressure in the

---

[2] Matilda W. Riley and Ann Foner, *Aging in Society,* Vol. I, *An Inventory of Research Findings* (New York: Russell Sage Foundation, 1968), p. 538.

[3] *Ibid.,* p. 539.

[4] Margaret Clark and Barbara Anderson, *Culture and Aging* (Springfield, Illinois: Charles C. Thomas, 1967), pp. 237–241.

community: the stigma of divorce has kept people together for years under a more or less armed truce. Many of these unhappy older people simply cannot cope with the increased demands that illness generates for the old.[5]

One of the key elements in the married couple's adjustment to aging is the issue of retirement. Apparently there are wide differences in the response to retirement shown by older couples in the various social classes. Table 21 summarizes these differences.

Men retired more than five years seemed to be slightly *less* favorable toward the retirement experience than those retired less than five years, and wives were apparently less involved and less affected by the retirement process than their husbands.[6]

*Table 21. Pre- and Postretirement Experience
of Married Couples*

Occupational Status	Preretirement attitude	Postretirement experience
Upper	negative	positive
Middle	positive	less positive
Lower	passive	negative

Source: Adapted from Alan C. Kerckhoff, "Husband-Wife Expectations and Reactions to Retirement," *Journal of Gerontology*, 19:510–516 (1964), p. 516.

Retirement contributes to the equalitarian nature of the happy older couple by promoting the sharing of household tasks and by emphasizing the expressive aspects of marriage, such as giving love, affection, and companionship. These trends also tend to reduce the differences between male and female roles, another characteristic of happy older marriages. The trend in successful older marriages thus appears to be moving away from social bonds based on the instrumental functions of marriage, such as providing money and status, to bonds based on a common identity that comes from sharing and cooperating in many of the same roles.[7]

No doubt all marriages have both instrumental and expressive aspects. Nevertheless, most marriages concentrate on one aspect or the other at any given point in time. Older couples who approach retirement life from a

---

[5] *Ibid.*, pp. 241–243.

[6] Alan C. Kerckhoff, "Husband-Wife Expectations and Reactions to Retirement," *Journal of Gerontology*, 19:510–516 (1964), p. 516.

[7] Aaron Lipman, "Role Conceptions and Morale of Couples in Retirement," *Journal of Gerontology*, 16:267–271 (1961).

predominantly expressive perspective apparently have a better chance for a successful adjustment to retirement than those with an instrumental orientation. One study indicates that women who stress instrumental aspects such as housework rather than the expressive functions such as love or understanding have much lower morale than their counterparts.[8]

Note that throughout this discussion we have emphasized the need not only of the individual but of the couple to adjust to retirement.

Not all older couples have to make the transition into retirement, however, since some of them are not formed until the partners are already retired. The factors involved in marrying in later life are numerous, but two of the most important are income and the sex ratio. Before older people will marry there generally has to be enough money between them to support the marriage. This is a limiting factor, particularly for the lower income males, who find it difficult to find a marriage partner unless they can bring their share of financial support to the union. The other factor is the overabundance of older women. Because older men are vastly outnumbered by women of their own age, and because men tend to marry women younger than themselves, older men always have a much larger field of eligibles than older women. There are about seventy-five males per hundred females in the age category sixty-five and over. In addition, only 29 percent of these males are unmarried as compared with 62 percent of the females. Thus, if everyone were matched evenly by age, more than half of the unmarried older women would still be left over. These data help to explain the fact that no matter how much a happy marriage may ease the pain of adjustment to aging, this option simply will not be available to many older women.

In a study of 100 older couples who married in later maturity, McKain found that the desire for companionship was by far the most frequently given reason.[9] Previous experience with marriage also predisposed older people to remarry. Few of the couples believed in romantic love, but they were interested in companionship, lasting affection, and regard. As McKain states, "The role of sex in the lives of these older people extended far beyond love-making and coitus; a woman's gentle touch, the perfume on her hair, a word of endearment—all these and many more reminders that he is married help to satisfy a man's urge for the opposite sex. The same is true for the older wife."[10] A few older people remarried to allay their anxiety about poor health, and some remarried to avoid having to depend on their children.

Many older people tended to select mates who reminded them of a previous spouse. Also, older couples followed the same pattern of

---

[8] Riley and Foner, *op. cit.*, p. 540.

[9] Walter C. McKain, *Retirement Marriage* (Storrs, Connecticut: Storrs Agricultural Experiment Station Monograph 3, 1969).

[10] *Ibid.*, p. 36.

homogamy, the tendency for people of similar backgrounds to marry, that is found among younger couples.

Using such unobtrusive measures as displays of affection, respect and consideration, obvious enjoyment of each other's company, lack of complaints about each other, and pride in their marriage as indicators of successful marriage, McKain found that successful "retirement marriage" was related to several factors. Couples who had known each other well over a period of years before their marriage were likely to be successfully married. A surprisingly large number of the couples McKain studied were related to each other through previous marriages. Probably the prime reason that long friendship was so strongly related to successful marriage in later life is that intimate knowledge of the other allowed better matching of interests and favorite activities. Marriages in which interests were not alike were less successful.

Approval of the marriage by children and friends is also important for the success of marriage in later life. Apparently there is often considerable social pressure against marriage in later life, probably growing out of a misguided notion that older people do not *need* to be married. Older people are very sensitive to this pressure, and encouragement from children and from friends is important in overcoming it. Also, a marriage which alienates older people from their families or friends is not likely to be successful.

People who experienced difficulty in adjusting to the reduced life space of the older person also had a difficult time adjusting to marriage in later life. There is apparently an element of adaptability involved in adjustment to life changes in general which influences the ability to adjust to retirement marriage in particular. And unless both the bride and the groom were reasonably well-adjusted individuals, marriage in later life was not likely to be successful.

Financial factors were also related to successful marriage in later life. If both partners owned homes, success was more likely than if one or neither did. The importance of dual home ownership was probably symbolic, indicating that each partner brought something equally concrete to the marriage. If both partners had a sufficient income prior to marriage, they usually had a successful marriage. The arrangements for pooling property or giving it to children were important for predicting success of the marriage because they indicated the priority one partner held in the eyes of the other. It was important for the marriage partner to have first priority on resources, if the marriage was to be successful.

Widows and Widowers

By age seventy a majority of older women are widows, but a majority of men are not widowers until after age eighty-five. As we said earlier, this trend results from lower female mortality rates and the tendency for men to marry women younger than themselves. Most women have to adjust to widowhood sooner or later, but the trend is for widowhood to come increasingly later.

One objective consequence of widowhood appears to be a higher mortality rate. Suicide rates are also higher for widowed older people than for those who are still married. Divorced older people have the highest mortality and suicide rates, however.

Although most people are able to cope with widowhood, studies show that older widows and widowers are preoccupied with grief, show a greater tendency toward worry and unhappiness, and fear death more than those whose spouses are still with them. Morale appears to be particularly low among those widowed within the last ten years.[11]

Most older couples are not entirely unprepared for widowhood, because most of them have thought about the possibility of losing their spouses. These thoughts usually take the form of anxiety, and are often ambivalent. Many people genuinely do not care to survive their partners, but on the other hand, someone must go first and someone must be left a widow or widower.

The most common response to widowhood is to try to keep occupied, but often circumstances make this response difficult. For one thing, widowhood often comes at the end of a spouse's long, financially and physically taxing illness. This tends to minimize the physical and financial resources available to keep "in the swing of things."

Many widows seek a male companion in widowhood in order to feel needed by someone and to have someone to escort them to the places they want to go. More common, however, is the pattern referred to earlier as "the merry widows" in which a group of widows gets together to provide each other with companionship and someone to go places with.

Widows and widowers face slightly different situations. The older widower can replace his lost wife more easily than the older widow can replace her husband. On the other hand, the widow is often better prepared to live a self-sufficient life alone than is the widower. About all that can be said is that the two sexes face different adaptive tasks and situations when death destroys the couple.[12]

Older Bachelors and Spinsters

In 1960, 7 to 9 percent of the older people in the United States had never married. On the surface, one would expect that as these people

---

[11] *Ibid.*

[12] Clark and Anderson, *op. cit.,* pp. 249–256.

reach old age, they would have trouble getting along as isolated individuals. Clark and Anderson found, however, that apparently because they learn very early in life to cope with loneliness and the need to look after themselves, older bachelors and spinsters are well practiced in the autonomy and self-reliance so often required of older people.[13] In addition, because they have never been close to others, the *isolated* single person is spared the grief that comes from watching one's friends and relatives die. Thus, while it is possible to argue that the person who never marries and perhaps lives an isolated existence is missing a lot of the "good" parts of life, he also apparently misses some of the "bad" too.

Most men stay bachelors because they want personal freedom from involvement. The bachelor appears to be motivated by an intense desire to escape the kind of involvement present in his family of orientation. The spinster, on the other hand, often appears to be motivated by her desire to stay close to her family of orientation and by her choice of career (this latter factor is becoming less important because today there are very few careers that require one to remain a spinster).

Sexuality in Older People

Earlier we found that older people who have some degree of continuity in their sex lives continue to enjoy sexual relationships throughout the entire life span. Sexual ability does appear to deteriorate in old age (late seventies to early eighties), particularly among the men. But evidence indicates that part of this problem is psychological rather than physical.

Sex is an integral part of the couple's relationship. In American society the married couple is the only legitimate place where a sexual outlet is possible. In counseling older couples and older people in general, it is essential that the sexual component of human interaction be taken into account.

Masters and Johnson have done the most complete research on the sexual response of older people.[14] For older females, they found that there were several major factors which served to limit sexual response: 1) steroid starvation, which makes coitus painful; 2) lack of opportunity for a regular sexual outlet; 3) the lingering Victorian concept that women should have no innate interest in sexual activity; 4) physical infirmities of the desired partner; and 5) the fact that many women never learn to respond to sexual desire, and use menopause as an excuse for total abstinence. They also found, however, that with hormone therapy to eliminate the pain associated with coitus and with the uterine contractions that often

---

[13] *Ibid.,* pp. 256–261.

[14] William H. Masters and Virginia E. Johnson, *Human Sexual Response* (New York: Little, Brown and Co., 1966), pp. 223–270.

accompany orgasm, there was "no time limit drawn by the advancing years to female sexuality."[15]

Among older men, there is little doubt that sexual performance wanes with age. Levels of sexual tension, ability to establish coital connection, ability to ejaculate, and masturbation or nocturnal emission all show declines as age increases. Yet for those older men who have established a high sexual output, by whatever means, in their middle years, there appears to be a much less significant decline.

Masters and Johnson tie the upturn in sexual inadequacy to a number of factors, the least of which is physical. The Victorian myth that older men have no sexuality is identified by Masters and Johnson as being a major force leading to self doubts and secondary impotence among older men. Research evidence indicates that a large proportion of the older men who suffer secondary impotence can be trained out of it by adequate counseling.

Masters and Johnson state that once a high sexual output is established in the middle years, it is usually possible to maintain it physically into the eighties provided health is maintained. They go on to say that several factors reduce this possibility: (1) boredom with one's partner, (2) preoccupation with career or economic pursuits (this would affect only a tiny proportion of older men), (3) mental or physical fatigue, (4) overindulgence in food or drink, (5) physical and mental infirmities, and (6) fear of poor performance.[16] They further state: "There is no way to overemphasize the importance that the factor 'fear of failure' plays in the aging male's withdrawal from sexual performance."[17]

The available data indicate that wives very often lack insight into the "fear of failure" problem and as a result are very likely to feel personally rejected by their husbands' alienation from marital sexual activity. Thus, the older couple faces some serious sexual problems that do not usually confront younger couples. Very often the older couple is not aware of the exact nature of these problems.

To solve them in a genuinely satisfactory fashion, the couple must understand what conditions are necessary to the maintenance of sexual functioning and what can be done to create these conditions.

Trends in Marital Status

More people get married today than got married fifty years ago. If this trend continues, the percentage of older people who are married should

---

[15] *Ibid.*, p. 247.

[16] *Ibid.*, p. 264.

[17] *Ibid.*, p. 269.

continue to increase throughout this century. The increase in average length of life for the general population should result in a larger proportion of couples surviving into later maturity. This would also result in an increase in the proportion married. The widening differential in average length of life between men and women will tend to increase the proportion of widows among those over seventy.

The overall impact of these trends should be to substantially increase the percent married between ages sixty-five to seventy-five during the next twenty years. But at the same time the percent widowed at age seventy-five or over should also increase during this same period.

The Older Parent Role

The role of parent is without doubt one of the pivotal roles that Americans play in their middle years, and this is particularly true for the housewife. Three out of four older people in the United States have at least one living child; and of those who have living children, four out of five have seen one of their children within the past week.[18] Over 60 percent reported seeing their child either that day or the day before. Most older people with children, then, play the older parent role quite frequently.

Even parents with adult children very far away manage to see their children on holidays and special occasions, and contacts with children seem to be maximized if the children live nearby, and if there are only one or two children. Retirement seems, if anything, to increase contact with children.[19]

As was true of the older married couple, there are significant differences in older parent-adult child relationships. Clark and Anderson found:

A good relationship with children in old age depends, to large extent, on the graces and autonomy of the aged parent—in short, on his ability to manage gracefully by himself. It would appear that, in our culture, there simply cannot be any happy role reversals between the generations, neither an increasing dependency of parent upon child nor a continuing reliance of child upon parent. The mores do not sanction it and children and parents resent it. The parent must remain strong and independent. If his personal resources fail, the conflicts arise. The child, on the other hand, must not threaten the security of the parent with requests for monetary aid or other care when parental income has shrunk through retirement. The ideal situation is when both parent and child are functioning well. The parent does not depend on the child for nurturance or social interaction; these needs the parent can manage to fulfill by himself else-

---

[18] Riley and Foner, *op. cit.*, pp. 160 and 541.
[19] *Ibid.*, pp. 542–544.

where. He does not limit the freedom of his child nor arouse the child's feelings of guilt. The child establishes an independent dwelling, sustains his own family, and achieves a measure of the hope the parent had entertained for him. Such an ideal situation, of course, is more likely to occur when the parent is still provided with a spouse and where a high socio-economic status buttresses the parent and child.[20]

Most older parents, particularly the men, apparently dread the day when they may become dependent on their children. Part of this reluctance is based on the perceived differences in values between the generations. Differences in drinking practices, childbearing attitudes, manners and etiquette, and religious beliefs are all major obstacles to good communication between the generations. Another obstacle is the adult child's reluctance at times to accept advice from an older parent, often accompanied by a strong need on the part of the older parent to give advice. Finally, the strong paternalistic bent among foreign-born older parents sometimes produces difficulties in inter-generational relations.

Given all of these difficulties, one might expect to find a great deal of alienation among older parents, and this notion is indeed prevalent among those working with older people. Nevertheless, study after study has failed to support this view.[21] As Blenkner says,

> the older person prefers to maintain his independence as long as he can, but . . . when he can no longer manage for himself, he expects his children to assume that responsibility; his children in turn expect to, and do, undertake it, particularly in terms of personal and protective services.[22]

Perhaps the reasons for the myth are to be found in the attitudes of professional workers and childless older people. The childless older person is the one most likely to believe that children neglect their older parents, and while they may be very vocal about it, these childless people are in perhaps the worst position to judge the validity of this particular idea. The same criticism applies to the perceptions of professionals who work with older people. Their view of the situation is biased by the fact that, by definition, the older people they see are disproportionately alienated and neglected; otherwise there would be no occasion for them to seek professional help.[23]

---

[20] Clark and Anderson, *op. cit.*, pp. 275–276. Reprinted by permission.

[21] Margaret Blenkner, "Social Work and Family Relationships in Later Life with Some Thoughts on Filial Maturity," in *Social Structure and the Family,* eds. Ethel Shanas and Gordon F. Streib (New York: Prentice-Hall, 1965), pp. 46–59.

[22] *Ibid.,* p. 48.

[23] *Ibid.,* p. 49.

The evidence indicates that most parents understand and comply with the norms for older parent-adult child relationships (note that we do not refer here to simple parent-child relationships). The demands on the older parent are to recognize that the adult children have a right to lead their own lives, to not be too demanding and thus alienate oneself from one's adult children, and above all, not to interfere with their normal pursuits.[24] At the same time, the adult child is expected to leave behind the rebellion and emancipation of adolescence and young adulthood, and to turn again to the parent, "no longer as a child, but as a mature adult with a new role and a different love, seeing him for the first time as an individual with his own rights, needs, limitations, and a life history that, to a large extent, made him the person he is long before his child existed."[25]

This type of relationship requires that both the older parent and the adult child be mature, secure persons, and it is for this reason that mental, physical, and financial resources on both sides improve the chances of developing a satisfactory relationship.

Before we leave this particular family role, it might be worthwhile to mention that a growing number of the children of older people are themselves older people. About one out of ten older people has a child who is over sixty-five. In these cases an even greater strain is usually put on both parties by the financial squeeze they find themselves in and the greater incidence of disabling illness among the very old.

The Grandparent Role

Seventy percent of older people have living grandchildren, and about 5 percent of households headed by older people contain grandchildren. Yet from the research evidence it appears that the grandparent role is not one that brings continuing interaction into the lives of the grandparents. If older people are separated from their children by the need for autonomy and independence, they are separated even farther from their grandchildren. Ideological differences between generations can become a chasm across three generations, and the strong peer orientation of adolescents in American society leaves little room in their lives for older people.

The satisfying period of grandparenthood is usually when the grandchildren are small, but with the trend toward early marriage and early parenthood, most people become grandparents in their mid- or late forties. Few have very young grandchildren after age sixty-five. Since teenage grandchildren usually shy away from their grandparents, the

---

[24] Clark and Anderson, *op. cit.,* p. 284.
[25] Blenkner, *op. cit.,* p. 58.

grandparent role is basically an inactive one for most older people. As times goes on, the decline in marriage age since World War II should make this trend even more prevalent.

Grandmothers appear to have a somewhat better chance of developing a relationship with their granddaughters than grandfathers have in developing one with their grandsons. The key to this trend is the relative stability of the housewife role in comparison with the occupational roles of men. It is simply a matter of the grandmothers' having more to offer their granddaughters that is pertinent to the lives they will lead. Sewing, cooking, and childbearing are but a few of the subjects that granddaughters often want to learn about. In contrast, the grandfathers very often find their skills to be unwanted, not only by industry but by their grandsons as well. As women's roles in society change, however, there is a good chance that the grandmothers' knowledge will be less pertinent to the aspirations of their granddaughters.

Research Illustration 7
The Changing American Grandparent*
Bernice L. Neugarten and Karol K. Weinstein

Noting that sociologists have tended to neglect grandparenthood as an aspect of the family life of older people, Neugarten and Weinstein sought to examine three dimensions of grandparenthood: the degree of comfort with the role (as expressed by the grandparent), the significance of the role as seen by the role player, and the style with which the role was enacted.

Through open-ended interviews with seventy sets of middle-class grandparents in the metropolitan Chicago area, Neugarten and Weinstein were able to secure data on how often and on what occasions the grandparents saw their grandchildren, and on the significance of grandparenthood in their lives and how it had affected them. Table A shows their results.

While a clear majority of the grandparents expressed comfort and pleasure in the role, nearly a third were uncomfortable enough to mention this discomfort to the interviewer. The sources of discomfort or disappointment included the strain associated with thinking of oneself as a

---

* Bernice L. Neugarten and Karol K. Weinstein, "The Changing American Grandparent," *Journal of Marriage and the Family,* 26:199–204 (1964).

Table A. Ease of Role Performance, Significance
of Role, and Style of Grandparenting
in Seventy Pairs of Grandparents

	Grandmothers N = 70	Grandfathers N = 70
	%	%
Ease of Role Performance		
Comfortable/Pleasant	59	61
Difficulty/Discomfort	36	29
(Insufficient Data)	5	10
Significance of the Grandparent Role		
Biological Renewal and/or Continuity	42*	23*
Emotional Self-fulfillment	19	27
Resource Person to Child	4	11
Vicarious Achievement through Child	4	4
Remote; Little Effect on the Self	27	29
(Insufficient Data)	4	6
Style of Grandparenting		
Formal	31	33
Fun-Seeking	29	24
Parent Surrogate	14*	0*
Reservoir of Family Wisdom	1	6
Distant Figure	19	29
(Insufficient Data)	6	8

   * Differences between proportions for grandmothers and grandfathers are significant at the .05 level for this category.
   Source: Adapted from Bernice L. Neugarten and Karol K. Weinstein, "The Changing American Grandparent," *Journal of Marriage and the Family*, 26:201 (1964).

grandparent, conflict with parents over the rearing of a grandchild, and self-chastisement about indifference toward taking care of or assuming responsibility for a grandchild.

While it was recognized that grandparenthood usually had multiple significance for grandparents, Neugarten and Weinstein nevertheless categorized all of the grandparents into one of five somewhat overlapping categories on the basis of their rating of the *primary* significance of grandparenthood to the individual as expressed throughout the interview. As Table A shows, the prime significance of grandparenthood was in terms of biological renewal and/or continuity and of emotional self-fulfillment. Through biological renewal or continuity the grandparent sees himself extended into the future. The authors caution that the difference between grandfathers and grandmothers in the significance of this factor may be because only one-third of the grandparents studied were the parents of the young husband. They consider it likely that grandfathers are more inclined to trace their biological continuity through their sons than through their daughters. Neugarten and Weinstein could have explored this notion further by examining the percentages while holding sex of immediate offspring constant, but apparently they did not do so. For some, grandparenthood offers the opportunity to succeed in a new emotional role—to be a better grandparent than he was a parent.

The other large group comprised those who felt relatively romote from their grandchildren, and who acknowledged that grandparenthood had relatively little effect in their own lives. Most people in this category felt that this was an unusual sentiment, and while a few expected that as their grandchildren grew older the relationship might develop more fully, most of them—men and women alike—perceived the role as basically empty of meaningful relationships.

Table B. Age Differences in Styles of Grandparenting*

	Under 65 *N = 81* %	*Over 65* *N = 34* %
Formal	*31*	*59*
Fun-Seeking	*37*	*21*
Distant Figure	*32*	*21*

* These age differences are significant at the .02 level.
Source: Adapted from Bernice L. Neugarten and Karol K. Weinstein, "The Changing American Grandparent," *Journal of Marriage and the Family*, 26:203 (1964).

As for *style of* grandparenting, Neugarten and Weinstein found that few of their respondents served primarily as reservoirs of family wisdom, and considering the rapidly changing nature of knowledge, this should not be surprising. And being a parent surrogate was apparently a style reserved for grandmothers, although few grandmothers served primarily as parent surrogates to their grandchildren.

The majority of grandparents exhibit a style that is either formal or distant. The formal style emphasizes the "proper" role of the grandparent. It leaves parental functions up to the parents, but there is constant interest in the grandchild. The "distant figure" style is similar except that contact is fleeting and infrequent—often reserved for holidays and special occasions such as Christmas or birthdays.

The fun-seeking style emphasizes informality and playfulness. Authority lines are considered irrelevant, and the emphasis is on making the relationship between grandparent and grandchild a mutually satisfying one. A quarter of the grandparents showed this style.

Neugarten and Weinstein were also interested in the impact of age on the style of grandparenting. Table B shows that grandparents were more likely to be under sixty-five, and that those who were under sixty-five were much more likely to adopt a fun-seeking or distant figure style; whereas better than half of those over sixty-five had adopted a formal style. They conclude that this may be the result of the socialization processes in different eras (secular trends) or simply the influence of age on the role itself. Neugarten and Weinstein conclude that grandparenthood as a role is perhaps more salient in middle age than in later maturity or old age, particularly in terms of the assumption of new roles or adult socialization.

Perhaps more important, Neugarten and Weinstein conclude that the younger grandparents are much less concerned with a style that revolves around an authority relation than are their older counterparts.

The Great-Grandparent Role

About 40 percent of the older people in the United States are great-grandparents, and this role, unlike the grandparent role, does involve older people with very young children. This can create problems, because young children, particularly American children, are very active and are apt to irritate very old people with their impatience.

While there are many four-generation families, little attention has been paid to this phenomenon by gerontologists. We know something about mutual aid patterns in multigenerational families, but we know very little about the psychological and sociological consequences of having a four-generation family, particularly in terms of intergenerational relationships.

The Sibling Role

About 80 percent of older people have living brothers and/or sisters. Clark and Anderson found that the most common kinship role among their sample of older people was that of sibling.[26]

With the advent of old age, many older people seek to pick up old family loyalties and renew old relationships. More effort is made to visit siblings, even at great distance, in old age than in middle age, and the narrower the older person's social world, the more likely he is to sponta-

---

[26] Clark and Anderson, op. cit., p. 294.

neously mention a sibling as a source of aid in time of trouble or need. Next to adult children, siblings are the best prospects for providing older people with a permanent home. Except in those cases which involve long-term family feuds, siblings offer a logical source of primary relationships, particularly for older people whose primary bonds have been reduced by the death of a spouse or the marriages of children. The death of a sibling, particularly when the relationship was a close one, may shock an older person more than the death of any other kin. Such a loss apparently brings home one's own mortality with greater immediacy.[27]

Summary of Kinship Roles

Having a spouse is one of the greatest possible assets in terms of a successful adjustment to aging. Unfortunately, it is very vulnerable to attrition, and widowhood often serves as an obstacle to adjustment in old age.

Rather than replacing lost spouses with new ones, most widowed older people substitute platonic relationships with men and women friends. Relationships between the generations are restricted by the norms which call for individual autonomy, and this may be related to the strong trend toward seeking primary contacts among siblings.

Thus, for older people the deepest primary relationships come from kin, and sometimes from kin of the same generation. There is a great deal of interchange between generations, but some older people are reluctant to lean too heavily on their children for personal contacts for fear of disrupting their lives.

Family Structure

Thus far we have considered relationships within the family of procreation and the family of orientation separately. In order to get a good overall view of family structure, however, it is necessary to view the family as a collection of relationships, many of which might involve a single person. Thus, the family involves these roles: mother, daughter, grandmother, wife, and aunt (or father, son, grandfather, husband, uncle)—all of which might be held by a single person, although not usually at the same time and in the same situation.

A number of contemporary changes have influenced the constellation

---

[27] *Ibid.,* pp. 294–301.

of roles within the family. To begin with, the decline in mortality rates since 1900 has had the result of adding a fourth generation to many families; thus the positions of great-grandparent, great-aunt, and so on have become a more evident part of the American family in the latter part of this century. Another important trend which also affects family structure is the family cycle. As the parent's age at birth of the last child declines, the result is a shorter period between generations. Hence, in fifty years the length of time between generations has declined from about thirty to about twenty years. This factor also promotes a greater number of generations in the family.

Finally, family size has a strong influence on the structure of the family. In 1910 the average completed family had produced 4.5 children, but by 1960 this number had declined to 2.5. This means that not only were there fewer children per completed family, but that there were fewer family roles *within* each generation. The result of this trend is that increasingly an older person will have fewer live siblings to relate to, even should he want to. It also means that there will be fewer extended kin (uncles, aunts, and so on) in each family.

If American family structure is anything, it is diverse. Around 5 percent of older people have no spouse, children, or brothers and sisters. On the other hand, most older people have at least two children, and they have grandchildren and great-grandchildren. In addition, most older people have surviving brothers and sisters. The older person may thus either have no kin at all or be incorporated into a very complex kinship network involving several generations.

Many studies have documented the fact that at least 40 percent of the older population have great-grandchildren and are thus members of a four-generation family. The question remains, however, how much older people are *involved* in these extended structures. Some researchers claim that the conjugal pair is the central focus of family life in American society, and that it makes little sense to examine relationships that are very far removed from the isolation of the family of procreation.[28] Many others, however, contend that extended family systems are the most typical and functional. These systems are seen as complicated networks of aid and service activities in which nuclear units are linked together both within and across generations.[29] At this point the evidence seems to weigh more heavily on the side of those who see the extended family system as typical.

---

[28] Gordon F. Streib and Wayne E. Thompson, "The Older Person in a Family Context," in *Handbook of Social Gerontology,* ed. Clark Tibbitts (Chicago: University of Chicago Press, 1960).

[29] Bernice L. Neugarten, *Middle Age and Aging* (Chicago: University of Chicago Press, 1968). Articles by Sussman and Burchinal, Townsend, Hill and Shanas all suggest that older people are frequently involved with extended kin.

Family Values

Obviously the trends presented thus far do not represent a unity. The different patterns in the family lives of older people result largely from differences in values. Kerckhoff has done perhaps the most thorough study of this matter.[30] He found three relatively clear norm-value clusters, based mainly on the older person's conception of the norms in the parent-child relationship. In what he called the *extended family* cluster, both husband and wife expected to live near their children, to enjoy considerable mutual aid and affection with their children, and to divide the family tasks between husband and wife according to a definition of woman's work and man's work. These people did not attach much value to change, and they saw considerable conflict between self-improvement for the children and family values.[31] At the other end of the continuum was the *nucleated family* cluster in which the older couple expected neither to live near their children nor to aid or be aided by them. They expected to share equally in the same tasks, they accepted change as a benefit, and they saw little conflict between family values and the children's attempts to improve on the social position given to them by their parents. A third cluster, called a *modified extended family,* accepted mutual aid and affection, rejected nearness as a requirement, and took an intermediate position on the other values. These were genuine middle-of-the-roaders.[32]

Kerckhoff found that these norm value clusters were strongly related to social position. Families allied with the extended family cluster were very likely to have heads with blue-collar occupations and low levels of education, to have lived on a farm, to have not moved around much in their lives, and to have large families. In other words, the extended family cluster was associated with a complex of characteristics we normally link with the rural working class. Those allied with the nucleated family cluster tended to be just the opposite—to have a head with a white-collar occupation, to have high levels of education, to be city-bred, to have been geographically mobile, and to have relatively small families. Those allied with the modified extended family cluster were again in between on all measures, but tended more toward the extended family pole.[33] About 20 percent of the families fell into the extended family cluster and 20 percent

---

[30] Alan C. Kerckhoff, "Norm-Value Clusters and the Strain Toward Consistency Among Older Married Couples," in *Social Aspects of Aging,* eds. Ida H. Simpson and John C. McKinney (Durham, North Carolina: Duke University Press, 1966), pp. 138–159.

[31] *Ibid.,* pp. 156–157.

[32] *Ibid.,* p. 157.

[33] *Ibid.*

into the nucleated family cluster, with the remaining 60 percent in the modified extended family cluster. It appears that most older people are getting about what they think they ought to have from the parent-child relationship.

In comparing the differences between the value norm clusters and actual family experiences, Kerckhoff brings up an interesting point. Since most of the experience falls into the modified extended family pattern, those who hold extended family values are very likely to be disappointed in their expectations, while those who hold the nucleated family view are apt to be pleasantly surprised by more mutual aid and affection than they expect.[34] All of the data we have on changes in occupation, education, and urban-rural residence lead us to expect that the group identifying with the extended family cluster will decline in proportion in the future.

Family Functions

As outlined by Streib and Thompson, the functions normally performed by the family include procreation, socialization, maintenance, placement, and affection.[35]

Procreation refers, of course, to the reproduction of new human beings to take the place of older generations that die. Normally we might think that older people would have little or nothing to do with this function in the family. However, there is some reason to think that an important part of the pressure on young married couples to have children comes from their parents, who want grandchildren to brag about, to have fun with, or to carry on the family name.

There is also the possibility of reproduction for older males married to younger females. Technically, males are capable of reproduction well into their seventies. It does not often happen, simply because marriages of partners thirty years apart do not happen very often.

When we speak of socialization, we normally think of teaching the young, but as Brim and Wheeler have pointed out, socialization is a lifelong process.[36] Our earlier discussion should lead us to expect a minimal role for older people in the socialization of their young grandchildren or great grandchildren, but what about a continued role in the socialization of their adult children? One of the primary ways we learn is by example, and one of the things older people offer their adult children, and the

---

[34] *Ibid.,* p. 159.

[35] Gordon F. Streib and Wayne E. Thompson, *op. cit.*

[36] Orville Brim and Stanton Wheeler, *Socialization After Childhood* (New York: John Wiley, 1966).

younger generations as well, is an illustration of how or how not to grow old gracefully. Whether the learning be positive or negative, the lives of older people serve as a resource that younger people can use in patterning their own lives when they reach their later years. Ways of handling retirement, grief, poverty, and illness are some of the lessons to be learned from watching older people.

A great deal of socialization also takes place within the older couple. When older husbands successfully make a transition from an instrumental orientation on the job to an expressive orientation in retirement, the wives usually deserve a great deal of credit for helping the husbands learn to reorient themselves. On the other hand, older wives must often be helped through the crisis of the empty nest that occurs when children marry and move away.

The maintenance function refers to the providing of food, clothing, and shelter. Again common sense tells us that older people are more likely to be receivers than givers in this regard, and by and large this is true. Nevertheless, among the high-income aged there are substantial proportions who still give financial support to their middle-aged children. We always tend to assume that the children end up in a better position than their parents. But what happens if they end up in a worse position? In these cases, the older parents are very likely to continue to support their children as best they can.

Of course, for many older couples the maintenance function is tied to the husband's retirement income, and often his death leaves the widow not only grief-stricken but poorer financially. Many cases exist where both members of a couple contributed to Social Security, and the widow loses all benefits from her own labor if she is to accept the widow's pension from her spouse's Social Security.

In any case, maintenance places one of the greatest strains on the older couple. Many older husbands who provided well for a family during their working years suddenly find themselves not only emasculated in terms of labor, but also in terms of being able to provide for themselves and their wives.

The placement function refers to the social position a child has at birth by virtue of the social position of his parents. The primary problem here has been assumed in the past to be the strain and tension that arises if the children improve on the position given them by their parents. As we saw earlier, this fear represents a small obstacle, if any at all, to older parent-adult child relationships. The only parents that would be strongly affected are those with extended family values and norms. Also, it sometimes happens that children who have a higher social position than their aged parents are ashamed of them and seek to avoid involving themselves too deeply with their parents' lives. No matter how we might decry this as the result of insecurities, the fact remains that it happens, and some older people are forced to go through the pain of adjusting to it. They often need help.

The affectional function of the family refers to providing emotional support and security within the framework of family roles. As we saw earlier, this is the main type of interchange between generations, and it is also a major function of the family for the older couple. Most of the affection and support they receive comes from each other.

Family Dynamics

Some very practical considerations that have a significant impact on the family relationships of older people include living arrangements, proximity to children, frequency of contacts, and exchange of family services.

Table 22 shows the living arrangements of older people in the United States, by marital category.

Table 22. Family Living Arrangement of Older People: United States, 1962

Living Arrangements	People with Living Children	
	Married	*Divorced, Widowed, Single*
Total	*100.0*	*100.0*
Living Alone	*–0–*	*46.5*
Living with:		
Spouse only	*77.9*	*–0–*
Married daughter	*1.0*	*14.5*
Married son	*1.1*	*4.1*
Unmarried child	*14.6*	*24.1*
Sibling	*1.3*	*2.5*
Grandchild	*2.3*	*2.2*
Other relative	*.8*	*1.4*
Nonrelative only	*1.0*	*4.6*

Source: Riley and Foner, *op. cit.*, p. 171

It shows basically what one would expect. Married older people tend to live by themselves, and unattached older people tend to live alone. Unmarried older people are much more likely to live with an unmarried child, but both groups are more likely to live with an unmarried child than with anyone else, relative or nonrelative. Perhaps the most interesting statistic is the percentage living with married children. Less than 10 percent of the unattached older people live with married children. Perhaps there is no better indicator of the reluctance on both sides to enter into such an arrangement, and given our earlier discussion about the norms of autonomy between generations we should not be surprised.

Living in a different household from children does not mean isolation from them. About 90 percent of the older people in the United States with living children live less than an hour's trip from at least one of their children. This proportion is even higher for unmarried older women.[37] (See Table 23.)

Table 23. Proximity of Older People to Their Nearest Child: People with Living Children, United States, 1962

Proximity	Percent
Same household	*27.6*
10 minutes journey or less	*33.1*
11–30 minutes	*15.7*
31 minutes to 1 hour	*7.2*
Over 1 hour but less than 1 day	*11.2*
1 day or more	*5.2*

Source: Riley and Foner, *op. cit.*, p. 169.

Concerning contacts with family, Riley and Foner found that, "Altogether, most older people, with or without children, maintain contacts with relatives, though the frequency varies with the geographical (as well as the geneological) closeness of the older person's relatives, his ties to home and community and other factors."[38] (See Table 24.)

In terms of exchange of family services, Reuben Hill has made perhaps the most comprehensive study.[39] Table 25 represents a summary of his data.

These data reveal some interesting patterns. We are usually quite willing to assume that the differential between help given and help received would be greatest for older people in the economic sphere, particularly since so many older people are poor. Yet the differential in the economic sphere turns out, in fact, to be the smallest. In terms of emotional gratification,

---

[37] Riley and Foner, *op. cit.*, pp. 170–171.

[38] *Ibid.*, p. 544.

[39] Reuben Hill, "Decision Making and the Family Life Cycle," in *Social Structure and the Family: Generational Considerations,* eds. Ethel Shanas and Gordon F. Streib (Englewood Cliffs, New Jersey: Prentice-Hall, 1965), pp. 113–139.

Table 24. Frequency of Stopping by to See
Older People (percentage distribution)

| | Person who stopped | | | | |
Frequency	Someone	Relative	Neighbor	Friend	Other
Daily	35	22	10	4	3
Once or twice a week	29	19	8	7	1
Less than once a week	6	3	1	3	—
No one in this group stopped	—	26	51	56	66
No one stopped	30	30	30	30	30
Total	100	100	100	100	100
Number reporting	(4,926)	(4,926)	(4,926)	(4,926)	(4,926)

Source: Riley and Foner, *op. cit.*, p. 545.

household management, and illness, grandparents received much more than they gave, but in the economic area, grandparents gave almost as much as they received. The middle generation is the one that apparently gives the most in terms of economic aid.

Table 25. Comparison of Help Received and Help Given by
Generation for Chief Problem Areas*

| | Type of Crisis | | | | | | | | | |
| | Economic | | Emotional Gratification | | Household Management | | Child Care | | Illness | |
	Gave Percent	Received Percent	Gave Percent	Received Percent	Gave Percent	Received Percent	Gave Percent	Received Percent	Gave Percent	Received Percent
Total	100	100	100	100	100	100	100	100	100	100
Grandparents	26	34	23	42	21	52	16	0	32	61
Parents	41	17	47	37	47	23	50	23	21	21
Married children	34	49	31	21	33	25	34	78	47	18

* Percents may not total 100 due to rounding.
Source: Reuben Hill, "Decision Making and the Family Life Cycle," in *Social Structure and the Family: Generational Considerations*, eds. Ethel Shanas and Gordon F. Streib, (Englewood Cliffs, New Jersey: Prentice-Hall, 1965), p. 125. Reprinted by permission.

Another important point is the extent to which aid is exchanged. The picture is very balanced in terms of exchange of economic aid across generations. It is uneven with regard to child care, for obvious reasons, and it varies for the other kinds of aid. No one generation comes off clearly a giver or receiver when all types of aid are considered.

Friends and Neighbors

Friends and neighbors are important sources of primary relationships in later life. They also provide help and contact with the outside world, although they are less important in this regard than children or other relatives.

Friendships tend to be retained into later life from middle age, and the higher the socioeconomic status of the individual, the more likely this is. Older people tend to pick their friends from among people with similar characteristics (including age). As a result, the longer the person lives in a given neighborhood, the more extensive his ties are apt to be.[40]

Most people report a decline in friendships over the years, but a small minority of older people report that they have *more* friends than ever before.[41] Numerous friendships among older people are related to high socioeconomic status, good health, high density of older people in the neighborhood, long-term neighborhood residence, and residence in a small town rather than a large city. They are unrelated to marital status, parental roles, or retirement.[42]

Regardless of how many friends they have, there is evidence that older people are fairly restrictive in terms of *who* they will accept. To begin with, age peers seem to have priority as potential friends. Also, friends tend to be selected from among those of the same sex, marital status, and socioeconomic class.[43]

On the surface it would seem that friend is one of the roles that older people can hang onto indefinitely. Long after the roles of worker, organization member, or even spouse have been lost, the role of friend remains. The demands of the friend role are flexible and can be adjusted to fit the individual's capability in terms of health and energy. It is the greatest source of companionship next to that of spouse.

How do older people define friendship? Quite a range of relationships are lumped together under this label. They go from close, intense, and continuous interaction marked by mutual understanding and concern all

---

[40] Riley and Foner, *op. cit.,* p. 561.
[41] *Ibid.,* p. 563.
[42] *Ibid.,* pp. 562–571.
[43] *Ibid.,* pp. 571–573.

the way to cursory contacts over the years with people whose names one happens to know.[44] Probably the best way to divide them is to call the former *friends* and the latter *associates.*

Clark and Anderson observed that older women seemed to have an abundance of friends, while older men had an abundance of associates.[45] In comparison to men, women appeared to speak more about their friendships and to place more value on them. They also tended to depend more on them. Men were much more passive about their friendships, and Clark and Anderson attribute this to the fact that many more of the men were married and thus had less need for friends as a source of primary bonds. Yet men seemed to feel the implied stigma that being old and friendless brings. In addition, men were apparently less willing to continue friendships via correspondence or telephone, and this may have shut them off from potential contacts.

Most older people recognize that the loss of friends is an inevitable accompaniment to growing older, and most also believe that replacing lost friends is a very difficult task. Older people cite difficulties in transportation, geographic moves, lowered economic status, and a life style limited by illness or disability as significant obstacles to the replacement of lost friends.

Research Illustration 8
Social Integration of the Aged*
Irving Rosow

Rosow studied the relationship between the residential density of older people and the integration of older people into friend and neighbor roles. The study was conducted in several hundred apartment buildings in Cleveland. These buildings were divided, in terms of the density of aged households, into *normal,* with 1–15 percent aged households; *concentrated,* with 33–49 percent aged households; and *dense,* with 50 percent or more aged households.

The study included 1,200 people. The men had to be at least sixty-five and the women sixty-two to be included. A range of social classes was purposely included in the sample by screening apartment buildings for occupation of head of household and by using public housing units.

---

[44] Clark and Anderson, *op. cit.,* pp. 303–310.

[45] *Ibid.,* p. 305.

* Based on Irving Rosow, *Social Integration of the Aged* (New York: Free Press, 1967).

Interviews were conducted on three successive occasions with a 25 percent dropout rate, about average for panel studies.

Rosow predicted that dense neighborhoods would produce more friendships among older people, and that the friends of older people would come disproportionately from among their old, as opposed to their younger, neighbors.

It was found that middle-class older people had significantly more friends than the working class, and that working-class older people depended more on the neighborhood for friendships than did those of the middle class.

Middle-class older people formed slightly more new friendships than those in the working class. Also, those in the working class were "far more sensitive and vulnerable to variations in residential age composition in making and maintaining friendships."[46]

The basic hypotheses of the study were borne out. Older people did have more friends when there were more older neighbors in the neighborhood, and these friends were drawn from among their age peers. The implication of this finding is that in terms of fighting social isolation among older people it is apparently better to have a *dense* concentration of older people than a cross-section of the general population in the neighborhood.

In cases of high role loss, such as might occur through retirement or bereavement, a high residential density of older people afforded greater opportunities for replacing friends. Even though the middle-class older person did not usually base his friendships on locality, he could and would do so if the density was high. This was particularly true for women. For working-class older people, of course, the pattern of finding one's friends locally is well established. Rosow noted that before the residential density would produce an increase in social ties, the proportion of aged households had to exceed half.

Nevertheless, Rosow cautioned that we should avoid looking upon high residential density of older households as a panacea. In his study there were many who simply did not care to associate with neighbors. Table A shows an array of categories that could be used to type people in terms of their contacts with neighbors and their desire for contacts with neighbors.

Rosow was interested in the effect of density on the relationship between neighboring and morale. He found that as density increased, the morale of the isolates *declined*. They felt depressed, apparently, by their continued inability to make friends even in the face of improved opportunity. The morale of the sociables remained the same because they retained a relatively constant level of interaction, as they wished to. The morale of the insatiables *increased* because they increased their

---

[46] *Ibid.,* p. 294.

*Table A. Functions of Neighboring in
Older People's Lives*

Type	Contact with Neighbors	Desired Contacts with Neighbors
Cosmopolitan	*low*	*none*
Phlegmatic	*low*	*none*
Isolated	*low*	*more*
Sociable	*high*	*no more*
Insatiable	*high*	*more*

opportunities for new contacts. The cosmopolitan and phlegmatic did not figure in the analysis because neither type was socially motivated as far as the neighborhood was concerned; therefore, density had no bearing on morale.

Rosow's data indicate that at least half of the isolated group could not take advantage of a dense neighborhood without assistance. The cosmopolitans found their friends outside the neighborhood, and the phlegmatics were just that.

Rosow also examined the extent to which neighbors served as a reference group. He found that neighbors were almost never asked for financial help. In terms of identity, loyalty, and closeness, he found that older people attached a greater salience to current friends and neighbors than to those of the past, if the two did not coincide. Finally, in terms of help in times of illness, he found two patterns. For those older people who lived with someone, less than 10 percent got help from outside the family. For those who lived alone, however, there was quite a different pattern, particularly if they had no local family.

Dense areas were apparently the only way older people with no relatives and no money could cope with illness. "These neighbors take care of more solitary people in longer illness than do friends, as many as relatives, and almost as many as children. This attention is not confined to brief sickness, but is sustained longer if necessary. For all their stoicism and self-reliance, solitary residents do use neighbors' help for longer illness when they can get it, but dense apartments are the only ones that can provide this to any significant element" (p. 308). The result is that tenants in dense housing learned to rely on their neighbors in a crisis, and this reduced their apprehensions about living alone. The interesting point here is that older neighbors in dense apartments can be an effective reference group even for people who have never personally made use of them in this capacity.

Summary

Unlike most other institutions, the family allows the older person to remain a full participant. In later life the family is still the individual's main source of primary relationships, just as it is in middle age.

Most older people are married and living with their spouses, but as age increases, progressively more of them, particularly women, are widowed. Older couples are generally happy, particularly where there is equality in the relationship, and retirement can enhance the success of older couples by providing more opportunities for equality. Older people who concentrate on the expressive aspects of marriage instead of the instrumental aspects tend to adjust better to retirement.

Those who marry in later life tend to seek companionship above all, and the success of such marriages depends on many of the same factors which influence the success of marriage among younger people. Knowing each other well, having approval of friends and family, being well adjusted individuals, and having financial security were all important for the success of "retirement marriages."

Widowhood is difficult to cope with, but most older people succeed in doing so. Most respond to widowhood by increasing their involvement in various activities. Variations in urbanization and cultural norms can apparently produce a wide variety of responses to widowhood.

Sexual problems in later life stem very often from the influence of various myths about the effects of age on sexual capacity, cultural norms which lead people to avoid sex when they get older, and fear of failure among older men. Older people apparently need to understand more about their own sexuality than they do now.

The proportion of older people under seventy-five who are married can be expected to increase in the future, while the proportion seventy-five or over who are widowed can also be expected to increase.

Older parents with adult children tend to see their children often and to regard these as their most important relationships. The more autonomous the parent, the better the relationship, but when the time comes, most children take up the responsibility for their aged parents. There is little evidence that reluctance to accept such responsibility is widespread. The norms of the relationship tend to emphasize the independence and dignity of both older parent and adult child.

The grandparent role is one that most older people enjoy, but for most of them it is not a meaningful primary relationship. It tends to be pursued, if at all, out of interest in their grandchildren or out of a desire to have fun with them. There is some indication that grandparent roles are being viewed as more informal and that the salience of the role is higher in middle age than in later maturity or old age.

About a third of older people are great-grandparents, but this role probably has little interactive meaning for most of them.

The sibling role seems to be more important in later life than it is in middle age, particularly as a substitute for lost friends and spouses. Next to children, siblings are the most important source of primary relationships the older person has.

Changes in family structure over the past fifty years have reduced the chances that kin can provide a substantial reservoir of potential relationships. Smaller families mean fewer aunts, uncles, cousins, siblings, children, and grandchildren. Nevertheless, extended kinship relations typify the family lives of most older people.

Older people who expect many extended family relationships are mainly concentrated in the working class, and they are very likely to be disappointed by the amount of mutual aid and affection they actually receive from their extended families. Those who expected little in the way of extended kin support were concentrated in the urban upper-middle class and were generally pleasantly surprised at the amount of mutual aid and affection they actually received from their families. Those in between expected a medium amount from the extended family and got about what they expected.

In terms of family dynamics, most older people live in their own household, but near at least one of their children. They are in contact with their children often. In terms of exchange of family services no one generation comes off clearly as giver or receiver when all types of aid are considered.

In our examination of primary roles we encounter a familiar pattern. If primary relationships are carried over from middle age, they tend to be maintained, but beginning new ones as an older person is a difficult task. Thus, the role of spouse can easily be carried over into old age, but to find a new spouse in old age is another matter, particularly for older women. Most other family roles, such as father, grandfather, uncle, and brother, once lost can never be replaced.

The role of friend or neighbor is also easy to carry over but difficult to replace, except in the relatively unusual case where 50 percent or more of the neighboring households are made up of older people.

Family values, family functions, and family dynamics all reflect some distance expected between the generations. On the other hand, as a practical matter it is obvious that there is a great deal of contact and mutual aid among the generations. Certainly if there is disengagement by the family or by friends it occurs on a much smaller scale than in the other areas of social life we have discussed

Bibliography

A. Family

Adams, Bert N., "The Middle-Class Adult and His Widowed or Still-Married Mother," *Social Problems,* 16:51–59, 1968.

Albrecht, Ruth, "The Family and Aging Seen Cross-Culturally," in *Foundations of Practical Gerontology,* eds. Rosamonde R. Boyd and Charles G. Oakes. Columbia, South Carolina: University of South Carolina Press, 1969, pp. 27–34.

Apple, Dorrian, "The Social Structure of Grandparenthood," *American Anthropologist,* 58:656–663, 1956.

Axelson, Leland L., "Personal Adjustments in the Postparental Period," *Marriage and Family Living,* 22:66–70, 1960.

Baumert, Gerhard, "Changes in the Family and the Position of Older Persons in Germany," in *Social and Psychological Aspects of Aging,* eds. Clark Tibbitts and Wilma Donahue. New York: Columbia University Press, 1962, pp. 415–425.

Belcher, John C., "The One-Person Household: A Consequence of the Isolated Nuclear Family," *Journal of Marriage and the Family,* 29:534–540, 1967.

Bellin, Seymour S. and Robert H. Hardt, "Marital Status and Mental Disorders of the Aged," *American Sociological Review,* 23:155–162, 1958.

Bengtson, Vern L. and Joseph A. Kuypers, "Generational Difference and the Developmental Stake," *Aging and Human Development,* 2:249–260, 1971.

Bettelheim, Bruno, "The Problem of Generations," *Daedalus,* 91:(1),68–96, Winter, 1962.

Blenkner, Margaret, "Social Work and Family Relationships in Later Life with Some Thoughts on Filial Maturity," in *Social Structure and the Family: Generational Relations,* eds. Ethel Shanas and Gordon F. Streib. Englewood Cliffs, New Jersey: Prentice-Hall, 1965, pp. 46–59.

Boyd, Rosamonde R., "Emerging Roles of the Four-Generation Family," in *Foundations of Practical Gerontology,* eds. Rosamonde R. Boyd and Charles G. Oakes. Columbia, South Carolina: University of South Carolina Press, 1969, pp. 35–50.

Britton, Joseph H. and Jean O. Britton, "The Middle-Aged and Older Rural Person and His Family," in *Older Rural Americans,* ed. E. Grant Youmans. Lexington, Kentucky: University of Kentucky Press, 1967, pp. 44–74.

Brody, Elaine M., "Aging as a Family Crisis: Implications for Research and Planning," in *Proceedings of the 7th International Congress of Gerontology.* Vienna: Wiener Medizinischen Akadamie, 1966, VII, 49–52.

———, "The Aging Family," *Gerontologist,* 6:201–206, 1966. Burgess, Ernest W., "Family Structure and Relationships," in *Aging in Western Societies,* ed. Ernest W. Burgess. Chicago: University of Chicago Press, 1960, pp. 271–298.

———, "The Transition from Extended Families to Nuclear Families," in *Processes of Aging,* eds. Richard H. Williams, Clark Tibbitts and Wilma Donahue. New York: Atherton Press, 1963, II, 77–82.

Cavan, Ruth S., "Family Tensions Between the Old and the Middle-Aged," *Marriage and Family Living,* 18:323–327, 1956.

Christenson, Cornelia V. and John H. Gagon, "Sexual Behavior in a Group of Older Women," *Journal of Gerontology,* 20:351–356, 1965.

Deutscher, Irwin, "The Quality of Postparental Life," in *Middle Age and Aging,* ed. Bernice L. Neugarten. Chicago: University of Chicago Press, 1968, pp. 263–268.

Glick, Paul C. and Robert Parke, Jr., "New Approaches in Studying the Life Cycle of the Family," *Demography,* 2:187–202, 1965.

Goldfarb, Alvin I., "Psychodynamics and the Three-Generation Family," in *Social Structure and the Family: Generational Relations,* eds. Ethel Shanas and Gordon F. Streib. Englewood Cliffs, New Jersey: Prentice-Hall, 1965, pp. 10–45.

Hill, Reuben, "Decision Making and the Family Life Cycle," in *Social Structure and the Family: Generational Relations,* eds. Ethel Shanas and Gordon F. Streib. Englewood Cliffs, New Jersey: Prentice-Hall, 1965, pp. 111–139.

Jackson, Jacquelyne J., "Sex and Social Class Variations in Black Aged Parent-Adult Child Relationships," *Aging and Human Development,* 2:96–107, 1971.

Kahana, Eva and Boaz Kahana, "Theoretical and Research Perspectives on Grandparenthood," *Aging and Human Development,* 2:261–268, 1971.

Kerckhoff, Alan C., "Nuclear and Extended Family Relationships: A Normative and Behavioral Analysis," in *Social Structure and the Family: Generational Relations,* eds. Ethel Shanas and Gordon F. Streib. Englewood Cliffs, New Jersey: Prentice-Hall, 1965, pp. 93–112.

———, "Norm-Value Clusters and the Strain Toward Consistency among Older Married Couples," in *Social Aspects of Aging,* eds. Ida H. Simpson and John C. McKinney. Durham, North Carolina: Duke University Press, 1966, pp. 138–159.

Kreps, Juanita M., "The Economics of Intergenerational Relationships," in *Social Structure and the Family: Generational Relations,* eds. Ethel Shanas and Gordon F. Streib. Englewood Cliffs, New Jersey: Prentice-Hall, 1965, pp. 267–288.

LeVine, Robert A., "Intergenerational Tensions and Extended Family Structures in Africa," in *Social Structure and the Family: Generational Relations,* eds. Ethel Shanas and Gordon F. Streib. Englewood Cliffs, New Jersey: Prentice-Hall, 1965, pp. 188–204.

Lipman, Aaron, "Role Conceptions of Couples in Retirement," in *Social and Psychological Aspects of Aging,* eds. Clark Tibbitts and Wilma Donahue. New York: Columbia University Press, 1962, pp. 475–485.

Lopata, Helena Z., "Widows as a Minority Group," *Gerontologist,* 11:(1, part 2)67–77, 1971.

———, *Occupation: Housewife.* New York: Oxford University Press, 1971.

McKain, Walter C., *Retirement Marriage.* Storrs, Connecticut: University of Connecticut Press, 1969.

Neugarten, Bernice L. and Karol K. Weinstein, "The Changing American Grandparent," *Journal of Marriage and the Family,* 26:199–204, 1964.

Pineo, Peter C., "Disenchantment in the Later Years of Marriage," in *Middle Age and Aging,* ed. Bernice L. Neugarten. Chicago: University of Chicago Press, 1968, pp. 258–262.

Rheinstein, Max, "Duty of Children to Support Parents," in *Aging in Western Societies,* ed. E. W. Burgess. Chicago: University of Chicago Press, 1960, p. 442.

———, "Motivation of Intergenerational Behavior by Norms of Law," in

Social Structure and the Family: Generational Relations, eds. Ethel Shanas and Gordon F. Streib. Englewood Cliffs, New Jersey: Prentice-Hall, 1965, pp. 241–266.

Rosenheim, Margaret K., "Social Welfare and Its Implications for Family Living," in *Social Structure and the Family: Generational Relations,* eds. Ethel Shanas and Gordon F. Streib. Englewood Cliffs, New Jersey: Prentice-Hall, 1965, pp. 206–240.

Rubin, I., "The 'Sexless Older Years'—A Socially Harmful Stereotype," *Annals of the American Academy of Political and Social Sciences,* 376:86–95, 1968.

————, *Sexual Life after Sixty.* New York: Basic Books, 1965.

Schorr, Alvin L., "Filial Responsibility and the Aging, or Beyond Pluck and Luck," *Social Security Bulletin,* 25:4–9, May, 1962.

Shanas, Ethel, "Family and Household Characteristics of Older People in the United States," in *Age with a Future,* ed. P. From Hansen. Copenhagen: Munksgaard, 1964, pp. 449–454.

————, "Family Help Patterns and Social Class in Three Countries," *Journal of Marriage and the Family,* 29:257–266, 1967.

———— and Gordon F. Streib, eds., *Social Structure and the Family: Generational Relations.* Englewood Cliffs, New Jersey: Prentice-Hall, 1965.

———— et al., *Old People in Three Industrial Societies.* New York: Atherton Press, 1968.

Smith, Harold E., "Family Interaction Patterns of the Aged. A Review," in *Older People and Their Social World,* eds. Arnold M. Rose and Warren A. Peterson. Philadelphia: F. A. Davis, 1965, pp. 143–161.

Stehouwer, Jan, "Relations Between Generations and the Three-Generation Household in Denmark," in *Social Structure and the Family: Generational Relations,* eds. Ethel Shanas and Gordon F. Streib. Englewood Cliffs, New Jersey: Prentice-Hall, 1965, pp. 142–162.

Streib, Gordon F., "Family Patterns in Retirement," *Journal of Social Issues,* 24:46–60, 1958.

Schorr, Alvin L. "Filial Responsibility and the Aging, or Beyond Pluck and Luck," *Social Security Bulletin,* 25:4–9, May, 1962.

Shanas, Ethel. "Family and Household Characteristics of Older People in the United States," in *Age with a Future,* ed. P. From Hansen. Copenhagen: Munksgaard, 1964, pp. 449–454.

————. "Family Help Patterns and Social Class in Three Countries," *Journal of Marriage and the Family,* 29:257–266, 1967.

————, and Gordon F. Streib, eds. *Social Structure and the Family: Generational Relations.* Englewood Cliffs, New Jersey: Prentice-Hall, 1965.

————, et al. *Old People in Three Industrial Societies.* New York: Atherton Press, 1968.

Smith, Harold E. "Family Interaction Patterns of the Aged: A Review," in *Older People and Their Social World,* eds. Arnold M. Rose and Warren A. Peterson. Philadelphia: F. A. Davis, 1965, pp. 143–161.

Stehouwer, Jan. "Relations between Generations and the Three-Generation Household in Denmark," in *Social Structure and the Family: Generational Relations,* eds. Ethel Shanas and Gordon F. Streib. Englewood Cliffs, New Jersey: Prentice-Hall, 1965, pp. 142–162.

Streib, Gordon F. "Family Patterns in Retirement," *Journal of Social Issues,* 24:46–60, 1958.

————, "Intergenerational Relations: Perspectives of the Two Generations on the Older Parent," *Journal of Marriage and the Family,* 27:469–476, 1965.

Sussman, Marvin B., "Relationships of Adult Children with Their Parents in the United States," in *Social Structure and the Family: Generational Relations*, eds. Ethel Shanas and Gordon F. Streib. Englewood Cliffs, New Jersey: Prentice-Hall, 1965, pp. 62–92.

Townsend, Peter, "The Effects of Family Structure on the Likelihood of Admission to an Institution in Old Age: The Application of a General Theory," in *Social Structure and the Family: Generational Relations*, eds. Ethel Shanas and Gordon F. Streib. Englewood Cliffs, New Jersey: Prentice-Hall, 1965, pp. 163–187.

————, "The Emergence of the Four Generation Family in Industrial Society," in *Proceedings of the 7th International Congress of Gerontology*. Vienna: Wiener Medizinischen Akademie, 1966, VIII, 555–558.

————, *The Family Life of Old People; An Inquiry in East London*. Glencoe, Illinois: Free Press, 1957.

————, "Problems in the Cross-National Study of Old People in the Family; Segregation Versus Integration," in *Methodology Problems in Cross-National Studies in Aging*, eds. Ethel Shanas and John Madge. New York: S. Karger, 1968, pp. 41–60.

Troll, Lillian E. "Issues in the Study of Generations," *Aging and Human Development*, 1:199–218, 1970.

————, "The Family of Later Life: A Decade Review," *Journal of Marriage and the Family*, 33:263–290, 1971.

Verwoerdt, Adriaan, Eric Pfeiffer, and Hsioh-Shan Wang, "Sexual Behavior in Senescence: Changes in Sexual Activity and Interest in Aging Men and Women," *Journal of Geriatric Psychiatry*, 2:168–180, 1969.

von Hentig, Hans, "The Social Function of the Grandmother," *Social Forces*, 24:389–392, 1946.

Willmott, Peter and Michael Young, *Family and Class in a London Suburb*. London: Routledge and Kegan Paul, 1960.

Young, Michael and Peter Willmott, *Family and Kinship in East London*. London: Routledge and Kegan Paul, 1957.

B. Friends and Neighbors

Blau, Zena S., "Structural Constraints on Friendships in Old Age," *American Sociological Review*, 26:429–439, 1961.

Bultena, Gordon L., "The Relationship of Occupational Status to Friendship Ties in Three Planned Retirement Communities," *Journal of Gerontology*, 24:461–464, 1969.

Lawton, M. Powell and B. Simon, "The Ecology of Social Relationships in Housing for the Elderly," *Gerontologist*, 8:108–115, 1968.

Long, Barbara H., Robert C. Ziller, and Elaine E. Thompson, "A Comparison of Prejudices: The Effects upon Friendship Ratings of Chronic Illness, Old Age, Education, and Race," *Journal of Social Psychology*, 70:101–109, 1966.

Rosenberg, George S., "Age, Poverty, and Isolation from Friends in the Urban Working Class," *Journal of Gerontology*, 23:533–538, 1968.

Rosow, Irving, "Local Concentrations of Aged and Intergenerational Friendships," in *Age with a Future*, ed. P. From Hansen. Copenhagen: Munksgaard, 1964, pp. 478–483.

————, "The Aged, Family and Friends," *Social Security Bulletin*, 28:18–20, November, 1965.

Rosow, Irving, "Housing and Local Ties of the Aged," in *Patterns of Living and Housing of Middle-Aged and Older People,* eds. Frances M. Carp and W. M. Burnett. Washington, D. C.: U. S. Public Health Service, 1966, pp. 47–64.
————, *Social Integration of the Aged.* New York: Free Press, 1967.
Smith, Joel, "The Narrowing Social World of the Aged," in *Social Aspects of Aging,* eds. Ida H. Simpson and John C. McKinney. Durham, North Carolina: Duke University Press, 1966, pp. 226–242.

19

Epilogue: What Does It All Mean?

Obviously, lots of work is needed in social gerontology. But where do we go from here? What are the implications of the facts, figures, and perspectives given in this book? It would require another book to answer these questions fully. Yet as one observer put it, a book shouldn't "just end." Therefore this chapter attempts to outline some of the implications of this book for the field in general. Be forewarned that a generous helping of my own educated opinions is included.

Research

There is not a single area of social gerontology that does not need more answers to crucial questions. In fact, the past decade of work in social gerontology has only just enabled us to begin to ask the right questions. Yet there are some areas where the research needs are particularly pressing. For example, we know very little about America's minority-group older people. We still do not fully understand the retirement process. Very little is known about transportation as it relates to older people. We still do not understand why some people are devastated by old age and others are not. We do not fully understand the dynamics of the age differentiation process. The vast amount of aging research in the United States needs to be complemented by research in other areas of the world.

In addition to the many stones as yet unturned, there is a crying need for *replication*. Scientific knowledge is built piece by piece, and it takes many repeated studies to establish a scientific proposition. Social gerontology is loaded with conflicting research evidence, and only more research can give us the tools to sort it out.

Because their focus is narrower than all of social reality, social gerontologists have many opportunities to do genuinely interdisciplinary research. The Kansas City Study of Adult Life and the Langley Porter Institute Studies in Aging were noteworthy in that their study designs brought together psychologists, social psychologists, sociologists, psychiatrists, and social anthropologists to do simultaneous longitudinal studies on the same samples of older people. In fact, the interplay of various traditions that goes on in social gerontology could be viewed as a step in the direction of needed theoretical integration in the social sciences. The literature of social gerontology is full of cases where supposedly general social theories failed the test when applied to older man, and of cases where insights gained from theories of personality or developmental psychology have helped to refine sociological theories that have been found wanting. And there are also many cases where the reverse is true.

In my opinion, detailed research on community systems holds great promise for understanding how the various social institutions and aging interact. Often institutions and organizations pick up each other's slack, and needs not being met by one will be met by another. This kind of give and take is most observable at the local level. Also, it is at the local level that the individual most often comes into direct contact with the economy, politics, religion, health and welfare institutions, and his family, friends, and neighbors. The impact of any given institution or organization thus occurs in the content of a locally based *system* of institutions and organizations.

To date there have been all too few attempts to study the *interdependent situational context* in which the individual experiences later life. To my mind, more interdisciplinary, community-based research like the Kansas City Study of Adult Life and the Langley Porter Institute Studies in Aging is needed. Much was learned from those studies which could be used to do new and better community studies. The work of Clark and Anderson[1] in particular shows that both the individual's personal system and his interaction with the social system can be studied successfully in a community context. More studies of this kind are especially needed to partially offset the tunnel vision one tends to get in large-scale survey research studies of specific topics such as retirement, widowhood, or voting behavior done by scholars in a single discipline.

Large-scale studies are also necessary in order to get a view of a particular phenomenon, such as retirement or income, that is *representative* of an entire nation or set of nations and not just of a particular community. To date, the large-scale studies that have been done have tended to suffer greatly from sampling problems. I hope that future survey research in aging can utilize better techniques, and thus give better, more representative answers.

---

[1] Margaret Clark and Barbara G. Anderson, *Culture and Aging* (Springfield, Illinois: Charles C. Thomas, 1967).

An important key to the quality of research in social gerontology is the amount of research money available in the United States. When the Older Americans Act was passed in 1965, it established the U. S. Administration on Aging and included funds for research in social gerontology. For a while there was a flurry of research activity, but slowly the funds for aging research were diverted to other purposes, and by the time of the 1971 White House Conference on Aging there was only a trickle of research money available. There are signs that the level of research funding may increase somewhat in the 1970's, but the important question is whether or not this support will be *sustained*. Gerontology research centers cannot be established and maintained with only sporadic sources of funds. A persistent commitment is needed. The funding of research has always been a complicated matter, but with the rising cost of social research and the growing inability of state and local governments to raise public revenue, the Federal Government is the prime realistic source of research funds. And until there is greater Federal support of research in social gerontology, closing the research gaps listed in this book will be a slow process.

Training

Obviously, if there is to be an increased research effort in social gerontology, people must be trained to do it. There has been an encouraging increase during the 1960's in the number of institutions offering research training in social gerontology at both the graduate and undergraduate levels. A large part of this increase was financed through Federal programs. Thus, not only the actual research but also the existence of trained people to do it depends on a continuing Federal commitment to research in social gerontology.

In addition to the need for research training, more training in social gerontology is needed for professionals working in fields that serve older people, and in turn there must be organizations to provide this training. All too often the practitioner finds himself hampered by the same faulty stereotypes about older people that pervade industrial societies.

Policy and Planning

The theme of the 1971 White House Conference on Aging was "Toward a National Policy on Aging." Just how far toward that goal the conference got is debatable, but the issues raised there show considerable consensus concerning needed changes in planning and policy that derive from the present status of older people in American society. It is impossible to present all of the issues or recommendations which came out of the conference, but here are a few that are particularly pertinent to this book:[2]

Education

—Adult education should be expanded to include more of the specific concerns of the elderly.
—Federal funds should be earmarked specifically for library services to older people.
—Knowledge relative to aging should be part of educational curricula from preschool through higher education.
—Preretirement education should be available to *everyone* and well in advance of retirement.

Employment and Retirement

—Employment and retirement policy should create a climate of *free choice* between continuing in employment as long as one wishes and is able, or retiring on adequate income with opportunities for meaningful activities.
—More vigorous efforts are needed to eliminate age discrimination in employment.
—Retirement ages should be more flexible.
—More effort should be made to utilize the talents of older people in public service jobs.

Physical and Mental Health

—Present health care delivery systems should be expanded to include preventive medicine, long-term health care, special needs such as eyeglasses and dental services, and rehabilitation services.
—Adequate, appropriate alternatives to institutional care should be developed.

Housing

—Housing programs should give special attention to the housing needs of older people who are poor, who live in rural areas, who are members of minority groups, who are disabled, or who are isolated.
—The range of housing choice for older people should include long-term care facilities; facilities with limited medical, food, and homemaker services; congregate housing with food and personal services; and housing for independent living with recreational and activity programs.
—Housing for older people should adopt architectural guidelines based on the needs of the elderly and the disabled.

---

[2] The material in this section was drawn from "A Report to the Delegates from the Conference Sections and Special Concerns Sessions, 1971," White House Conference on Aging. November 28–December 2, 1971.

Income

—Older people (individuals as well as couples) should have a total cash income in accordance with the "American standard of living."
—More earnings should be allowed without penalty under Social Security.
—Private pension plans should be solvent and should provide for early vesting, portability, survivor benefits, and complete disclosure of provisions to those covered.
—Tax relief should be given to older people.

Nutrition

—Research should be conducted on the nutritional status of older Americans.
—Nutrition should be emphasized in health care programs and in education for older people.
—·The equivalent of the National school lunch program should be developed for all older people, not just those with low incomes.

Spiritual Well-Being

—Institutions for the aged should include chaplaincy services.
—More religious programs should be available to older people in their own homes.
—Religious bodies and the government should affirm the right to, and reverence for, life and recognize the individual's right to die with dignity.

Transportation

—Increased transportation services should be provided to both rural and urban older people. Both system subsidies and payments to elderly individuals should be available, depending on the availability and usability of public and private transportation.
—Individualized, flexible transportation should be part of social service programs.
—Insurance companies should be prevented from raising premiums on, or canceling, auto insurance on the basis of age alone.
—Special attention should be given to the transportation needs of the rural elderly.

Facilities, Programs, and Services

—All older persons should have real choices as to how they shall spend their later years.
—Older people should be enabled to maintain their independence and their usefulness at the highest possible levels.
—Older people should have the opportunity for continued growth, development, and self-fulfillment and for expanded contributions to a variety of community activities.
—An effective network of facilities, programs, and services should be readily available and accessible to permit older people to exercise a

wide range of options, regardless of their individual circumstances or where they live.

—Specific agencies at the local, state, and Federal levels should be assigned the responsibility for planning and coordinating services to older people.

—Consumer protection of the elderly should be emphasized.

—Protective services should be developed for those older persons in the community who are unable to manage their affairs because their mental and/or physical functioning is seriously impaired.

Government and Nongovernment Organizations

—Planning and programing for the aged should coordinate the efforts of both private and public agencies at the local, state, and Federal levels.

—Government action on issues pertaining to older people must include a local-state-Federal partnership.

—Agencies responsible for programs in aging should be strong advocates for older people's interests.

—Responsibility for planning and coordinating programs for older people should be consolidated under a single, high-level office of government, and this should apply at all levels of government.

Planning

—Comprehensive planning in aging should be done on both a state-wide basis and a local basis.

Research and Demonstration

—Research aimed at understanding the basic processes of aging and alleviating the suffering of those who encounter difficulty in adapting to this phase of life should be accelerated.

—Research on racial and ethnic minority groups should assume a proportional share of the total research effort.

—A major increase in research and research training funds in aging should be appropriated and allocated.

Training

—Additional Federal funds should be provided for training professionals both in colleges and universities and on an in-service basis.

—All service programs for older people should contain funds earmarked for the training of personnel.

This incomplete list of the concerns of the 1971 White House Conference on Aging shows that many of the problems highlighted in this book are receiving the attention of politicians and planners. However, implementing these policy recommendations is a political problem, and in order for the efforts of the Conference to bear fruit, older people and their advocates must exert enough political pressure to make it costly for politicians to ignore their needs. While these observations are based primarily on American society, they probably apply to most industrial societies.

The Future of Social Gerontology

The U. S. Bureau of the Census estimates that by the year 2037 the population of *older people* in the United States could reach nearly 60 million (over twice the number of older people in 1970). Twenty million of those would be over seventy-five (three times as many as in 1970). Older people would then represent about a *fifth* of the total population.[3]

With the older population growing this fast, there is little chance that interest in aging will lessen. In fact, during the coming decades, services to older people may well represent one of the fastest-growing areas of employment in the Western world. And the demand for knowledge in the field of social gerontology can be expected to grow accordingly. All of this implies a rosy future for social gerontology—and it's about time.

There are plentiful career opportunities in social gerontology. We are just beginning to grapple with the problems in many areas of research and practice. There is a relatively small "establishment" in the field, and interest in research results and innovative programs is high. Funding levels for gerontology research and demonstration projects are increasing, and institutes of gerontology are just getting started in several universities. This situation offers people ready to embark on a new career an opportunty to "get in on the ground floor." I hope that this book will motivate some of its readers to join me in this fascinating field.

Bibliography

Atchley, Robert C., W. Fred Cottrell, Linda K. George, and Ruth W. Smith, *Ohio's Older People.* Oxford, Ohio: Scripps Foundation, 1972.

Baltes, Paul B., "Longitudinal and Cross-Sectional Sequences in the Study of Age and Generation Effects," *Human Development,* 11:145–171, 1968.

Bennett, Ruth, "Social Context—A Neglected Variable in Research on Aging," *Aging and Human Development,* 1:97–116, 1970.

Binstock, Robert H., "The Gerontological Society and Public Policy; A Report," *Gerontologist,* 9:69, 1969.

---

[3] United States Bureau of the Census, "Protections of the Population of the United States (Interim Revisions): 1970 to 2020," *Current Population Reports,* Series P-25, Number 448, 1970.

Birren, James E., "Research on Aging: A Frontier of Science and Social Gain," *Gerontologist,* 8:7–13, 1968.

Breen, Leonard Z., "The Discipline of Gerontology," in *The Daily Needs and Interests of Older People,* ed. Adeline M. Hoffman. Springfield, Illinois: Charles C. Thomas, 1970, pp. 5–24.

Carp, Frances M., "Compound Criteria in Gerontological Research," *Journal of Gerontology,* 24:341–347, 1969.

———, "Research Goals and Priorities in Gerontology," *Gerontologist,* 11:(1, part I)67, 1971.

Cohen, Elias S., "The White House Conference on Aging: Will It Fail?" *Aging and Human Development,* 1:51–60, 1970.

Eisdorfer, Carl, "Patterns of Federal Funding for Research in Aging," *Gerontologist,* 8:3–6, 1968.

———, "The Implications of Research for Medical Practice," *Gerontologist,* 10:(1, part 2),62–67, 1970.

——— and F. Wilkie, "Research in Aging—Biological, Social, and Psychological," in *Daily Needs and Interests of Older People,* ed. A. M. Hoffman. Springfield, Illinois: Charles C. Thomas, 1970, pp. 401–426.

Gerontological Society, "Research Designs and Proposals in Applied Social Gerontology: Third Report, 1971," *Gerontologist,* 11:(4, part II), 1971.

———, "Research Proposals in Applied Social Gerontology," *Gerontologist,* 11:(1, part II),2–4, 1971.

Gottesman, Leonard E., "Long-Range Priorities for the Aged," *Aging and Human Development,* 1:393–400, 1970.

Hayflick, Leonard, "Quantity, Quality, and Responsibility in Aging Research," *Gerontologist,* 11:68–73, 1971.

Jackson, Hobart C., "National Goals and Priorities in the Social Welfare of the Aging," *Gerontologist,* 11:88–94, 1971.

Kreps, Juanita M., "Career Options After Fifty: Suggested Research," *Gerontologist,* 11:(1, part II),4–8, 1971.

Maddox, George L., "Selected Methodological Issues," in *Normal Aging,* ed. Erdman Palmore. Durham, North Carolina: Duke University Press, 1970, pp. 18–27.

Martin, John B., "Gerontological Challenges of the Seventies," *Aging and Human Development,* 1:3–4, 1970.

National Council on Aging, *The Golden Years—A Tarnished Myth.* New York: The Council, 1970.

National Retired Teachers Association and American Association of Retired Persons, *Proposals for a National Policy on Aging.* Washington, D. C.: The Association, 1971.

Paillat, Paul, "Gerontological Research: Present Situation and Prospects," *International Social Science Journal,* 20:263–272, 1968.

Rockstein, Morris, "The Challenges of Gerontology," *Gerontologist,* 6:177–178, 1966.

Sax, Sidney, "The Goals of Gerontology," *Gerontologist,* 7:153–160, 1967.

Sontag, Lester W., "The Longitudinal Method of Research: What It Can and Can't Do," in *Duke University Council on Aging and Human Development. Proceedings of Seminars 1965–69,* ed. Frances C. Jeffers. Durham, North Carolina: Duke University Press, 1969, pp. 15–25.

Tibbitts, Clark, "Title V Training Grants Program," *Aging,* No. 154:14–15, 1967.

———, "Manpower Needs in the Field of Aging," *Aging,* Nos. 173–174:3–5, 1969.

United States Senate, Special Committee on Aging, *Long-Range Program and Research Needs in Aging and Related Fields. Part I.* Washington, D. C.: U. S. Government Printing Office, 1968.

————, *Developments in Aging, 1970.* Washington, D. C.: U. S. Government Printing Office, 1971.

White House Conference on Aging, *Report of the Delegates from the Conference Sections and Special Concerns Sessions.* Washington, D. C.: The Conference, 1971.

General Bibliography

Allenger, Daniel E., ed., *Social Change and Aging in the Twentieth Century.* Gainsville, Florida: University of Florida Press, 1964.

American Association for the Advancement of Science, *Aging—Some Social and Biological Aspects.* Washington, D. C.: The Association, 1960.

Arth, Malcolm, "An Interdisciplinary View of the Aged in Ibo Culture," *Journal of Geriatric Psychiatry,* 2:33–39, 1968.

Barron, Milton L., *The Aging American: An Introduction to Social Gerontology and Geriatrics.* New York: Thomas Y. Crowell Co., 1961.

Belbin, R. Meredith, "Industrial Gerontology: Origins, Issues, and Applications in Europe," *Industrial Gerontology,* 1:12–25, 1969.

Berwick, Keith, "The 'Senior Citizen' in America: A Study in Unplanned Obsolescence," *Gerontologist,* 7:257–260, 1967.

Birren, James E., ed., *Handbook of Aging and the Individual.* Chicago: University of Chicago Press, 1959.

———, *The Psychology of Aging.* Englewood Cliffs, New Jersey: Prentice-Hall, 1964.

———, ed., *Relations of Development and Aging.* Springfield, Illinois: Charles C. Thomas, 1964.

Blau, David and M. A. Berezin, "Some Ethnic and Cultural Considerations in Aging," *Journal of Geriatric Psychiatry,* 2:3–5, 1968.

Boyd, Rosamonde R. and Charles G. Oakes, eds., *Foundations of Practical Gerontology.* Columbia, South Carolina: University of South Carolina Press, 1969.

Burgess, Ernest W., ed., *Aging in Western Societies.* Chicago: University of Chicago Press, 1960.

Busse, Ewald W. and Eric Pfeiffer, eds., *Behavior and Adaptation in Late Life.* Boston: Little, Brown and Co., 1969.

Cain, Leonard D., Jr., "Life Course and Social Structure," in *Handbook of Modern Sociology,* ed. Robert E. L. Faris. Chicago: Rand McNally & Co., 1964, pp. 272–309.

———, "Age Status and Generational Phenomena: The New Old People in Contemporary America," *Gerontologist,* 7:83–92, 1967.

———, "Aging and the Character of Our Times," *Gerontologist,* 8:250–258, 1968.

Clark, Margaret and Barbara G. Anderson, *Culture and Aging.* Springfield, Illinois: Charles C. Thomas, 1967.

Cumming, Elaine and William E. Henry, *Growing Old: The Process of Disengagement.* New York: Basic Books, 1961.

Donahue, Wilma and Clark Tibbitts, eds., *The New Frontiers of Aging.* Ann Arbor, Michigan: University of Michigan Press, 1957.

Hansen, P. From, ed., *Age with a Future.* Copenhagen: Munksgaard, 1964.

Havighurst, Robert J. and Ruth Albrecht, *Older People.* New York: Longmans Green, 1953.

Kastenbaum, Robert, ed., *New Thoughts on Old Age.* New York: Springer, 1964.

Kent, Donald P., "Aging Within the American Social Structure," *Journal of Geriatric Psychiatry,* 2:19–32, 1968.

Kreps, Juanita M., *Lifetime Allocation of Work and Income.* Durham, North Carolina: Duke University Press, 1971.

Loether, Herman J., *Problems of Aging: Sociological and Social Psychological Perspectives*. Belmont, California: Dickenson, 1967.

Lowenthal, Marjorie F., *Lives in Distress*. New York: Basic Books, 1964.

Morris, Robert and Robert H. Binstock, *Feasible Planning for Social Change*. New York: Columbia University Press, 1966.

National Council on the Aging, *Directory; National Organizations with Programs in the Field of Aging, 1971*. Washington, D. C.: The Council, 1971.

Neugarten, Bernice L., ed., *Middle Age and Aging*. Chicago: University of Chicago Press, 1968.

————, "Grow Old Along with Me! The Best Is Yet to Be," *Psychology Today*, 5:45–48, December, 1971.

————, Joan W. Moore, and John C. Lowe, "Age Norms, Age Constraints, and Adult Socialization," *American Journal of Sociology*. 70:710–717, 1965.

Palmore, Erdman, ed., *Normal Aging: Reports from the Duke Longitudinal Study, 1955–1969*. Durham, North Carolina: Duke University Press, 1970.

Richardson, Ian M., *Age and Need: A Study of Older People in North-East Scotland*. Edinburgh: Livingstone, 1964.

Riley, Matilda White and Anne Foner, *Aging and Society*, Vol. I, *An Inventory of Research Findings*. New York: Russell Sage Foundation, 1968.

————, John W. Riley, Jr., and Marilyn E. Johnson, *Aging and Society*. Vol. II. *Aging and the Professions*. New York: Russell Sage Foundation, 1969.

————, Marilyn Johnson, and Anne Foner, *Aging and Society*. Vol. III. *A Sociology of Age Stratification*. New York: Russell Sage Foundation, 1971.

Rose, Arnold M. and Warren A. Peterson, eds., *Older People and Their Social World*. Philadelphia: F. A. Davis, 1965.

Rosenberg, George S., *The Worker Grows Old*. San Francisco: Jossey-Bass, 1970.

Rosow, Irving, *Social Integration of the Aged*. New York: Free Press, 1967.

Shanas, Ethel, *et al.*, *Old People in Three Industrial Societies*. New York: Atherton Press, 1968.

————, issue ed., "Aging in Contemporary Society," *American Behavioral Scientist*, 14:5–128, 1970.

Shock, Nathan W., *A Classified Bibliography of Gerontology and Geriatrics*. Stanford, California: Stanford University Press, 1951. (Updated bi-monthly in the *Journal of Gerontology*.)

Simon, Anne W., *The New Years: A New Middle Age*. New York: Alfred A. Knopf, 1968.

Simpson, Ida H. and John C. McKinney, eds., *Social Aspects of Aging*. Durham, North Carolina: Duke University Press, 1966.

Talland, George A., ed., *Human Aging and Behavior*. New York: Academic Press, 1968.

Tibbitts, Clark, ed., *Handbook of Social Gerontology*. Chicago: University of Chicago Press, 1960.

———— and Wilma Donahue, eds., *Social and Psychological Aspects of Aging*. New York: Columbia University Press, 1962.

Townsend, Peter and Dorothy Wedderburn, *The Aged in the Welfare State*. London: Bell and Sons, 1965.

Tunstall, Jeremy, *Old and Alone: A Sociological Study of Old People*. London: Routledge and Kegan Paul, 1966.

United States Department of Health, Education, and Welfare, *Aging in the Modern World, An Annotated Bibliography*. Washington, D. C.: U. S. Government Printing Office, 1964.

Vedder, Clyde B., ed., *Gerontology: A Book of Readings.* Springfield, Illinois: Charles C. Thomas, 1963.

———— and Annette S. Lefkowitz, *Problems of the Aged.* Springfield, Illinois: Charles C. Thomas, 1965.

Williams, Richard H., Clark Tibbitts, and Wilma Donahue, eds., *Processes of Aging.* 2 vols. New York: Atherton Press, 1963.

———— and Claudine G. Wirths, *Lives Through the Years.* New York: Atherton Press, 1965.

Youmans, E. Grant, ed., *Older Rural Americans: A Sociological Perspective.* Lexington, Kentucky: University of Kentucky Press, 1967.

Glossary

Included in this glossary are only those words which are unique to gerontology. Common terms from the various social sciences are not included, nor are terms which are adequately defined in the various collegiate dictionaries.

Age changes   Changes in an individual as a result of the aging processes. (See also *aging; age differences.*)

Age, chronological   Age measured by number of years lived.

Age differences   Differences among categories of people of different chronological age at a particular point in time. Such differences are only *partly* the result of the aging process. (See also *age changes.*)

Age grading   A social process whereby eligibility and responsibility for various positions in the group are primarily determined by chronological age.

Age identification   The individual's stage of life as he perceives it; how old the individual *thinks* he is.

Age strata   Categories used to classify persons into a given age interval. Used to compare age *differences* within a given population at a particular point in time.

Age, symptomatic   Age measured by symptoms of biological, psychological, and social aging. Wrinkled skin, difficulty in remembering things, and involuntary retirement are examples of usable symptomatic indicators of age.

Aging   A general term used for various biological, psychological, and social processes whereby an individual acquires the socially defined characteristics of old age. (See also *senescence; old age.*)

Cohort   All individuals of approximately the same age; for example, all persons born in the year 1900.

Dependency   A social state in which the individual must rely on others for financial or physical support.

Disengagement, psychological   The process whereby the individual withdraws commitments to various social roles. May be manifested either by dropping various roles or by "going through the motions."

Disengagement, societal   The process whereby society withdraws support from the individual and ceases to seek a commitment from him. May be active, such as in compulsory retirement, or passive, as in no encouragement of the older individual to stay on.

Engagement   A commitment on the part of the individual to a particular social role. Commitment can be to one role or to several, it may be deep or superficial, and it may be real or symbolic.

Gerontology   Literally, the logic of aging. A field of investigation comprised of the results from various traditional disciplines and professions directed toward understanding the processes of aging and their consequences.

Golden Age Club   A voluntary organization for older people which does not have its own facility and which offers a limited program (usually recreational) to its members. (See also *Senior Center.*)

Institution   A housing facility organized primarily to perform services such as personal care, housekeeping, mental health care, and/or medical care for its residents.

Later maturity   A life-cycle stage socially defined or typified by marked energy decline; awareness of sensory loss; onset of chronic health problems; difficulty in remaining future-oriented; recognition that one's time is growing short; loss of social contacts through retirement, widowhood, and movement of children; and freedom from responsibilities such as work or child rearing.

Life cycle   The life of an individual seen as a series of stages, such as infancy, childhood, adulthood, middle age, later maturity, and old age. The life history of an organism.

Life expectancy   The *average* length of time a group of individuals of the same age will live, given current mortality rates. Life expectancy can be computed from any age, but is most often computed from birth.

Life review   The process whereby an individual reviews the past events of his life in an effort to identify, evaluate, and give meaning to the forces that have shaped his life.

Life space   The field or network of social interactions unique to a particular individual.

Life span   The *theoretical* maximum length of life, estimated to be about 120 years for human beings. (See also *life expectancy; longevity.*)

Longevity   The actual length of life of a particular organism. (See also *life expectancy; life span.*)

Middle age   A stage of the life cycle socially defined or typified by obvious energy decline; shifting from physical to mental activities; feelings of having reached a goal or plateau in one's career; awareness that life is finite; shrinking of family as children leave home; entry of women into the labor force; employment troubles; and feelings of restlessness, of not getting anywhere. (See also *later maturity; old age.*)

Nursing home   A group housing facility which offers skilled health care plus personal care. (See also *personal care home.*)

Old age   A stage of the life cycle socially defined or typified by increasing frailty and disability; much introspection and concern over the meaning of life; distinct awareness of approaching death; financial and physical dependency; isolation, boredom, and loneliness. (See also *middle age; later maturity.*)

Older person   Conceptually, an individual in the later maturity or old age stages of the life cycle. Socially, people are usually classified as older if they are chronologically sixty-five or older. Legally, there are several chronological ages which are used to define people as old, beginning as early as forty-five. (See also *later maturity; old age.*)

Pension   A periodic payment to a person or his family, given as a result of previous on-the-job service.

Personal care home   A group housing facility which offers personal care, help in getting about, cooking, and household services, but which does not offer nursing services. Sometimes called domiciliary home. (See also *nursing home.*)

Retirement   The period following a career of job-holding, in which job responsibilities and often opportunities are minimized and in which economic wherewithal comes by virtue of having held a job for a minimum length of time in the past.

Retirement cohort   A group of coworkers who retire at the same time from the same place of employment or in the same neighborhood or community.

Retirement processes   The processes whereby the individual prepares for, accomplishes, adjusts to, and lives out his retirement. (See also *retirement.*)

Senescence   The group of biological processes whereby the organism becomes less viable and more vulnerable as chronological age increases. Manifests itself as an increased probability of disease, injury, and death.

Senior Center   A voluntary organization for older people which offers its members a range of services (recreation, nutrition, education, transportation, referral, etc.) and which has a specific facility for this purpose.

Social gerontology   A subfield of gerontology dealing with the developmental and group behavior of adults and with the causes and consequences of having older people in the population.

Index

activity, drive toward, 76, 91
activity theory of adjustment to aging, 34–35, 36, 38, 179, 204–205
adaptation, 84
  to aging, 206–13, 214
adaptive tasks, 206–207, 208–209, 212, 275
adjustment, 284
  to aging, 198, 199–215, 259
  to dependency, 197
  influence of retirement on, 169–72
Administration on Aging (AOA), U. S., 8, 235, 251, 252, 262, 263, 329
adolescence, 6, 191, 206, 282–83
adolescent, 102, 190
adulthood, 6, 15, 88, 190, 194, 197, 206
age graph, 51
aging, 16, 49
  adaptation to, 206–13, 214
  adjustment to, 198, 199–215, 259
  behavioral aspect of, 5
  biological aspect of, 5, 41, 43–50
  Christian doctrine on, 285
  psychological aspect of, 5, 41, 51–72, 73–95
  sociological aspect of, 5, 49
Aid for the Aged, 141–42, 253
Aid to Dependent Children, 250
aloneness, as a life style, 203
AMA. See American Medical Association
American Association of Retired Persons, 274
American Medical Association (AMA), 250
Anderson, Barbára G., 193, 194, 195, 196, 206, 207, 212, 213, 214, 275, 282, 283, 299, 301, 307, 317, 328
Anderson, Nancy N., 89
anger, 79–81
anxiety, 196, 201, 202
AOA. See Administration on Aging
Atchley, Robert C., 179
attitudes, 73, 81–82, 91, 200
  defined, 81–82, 91
  family, 257
  relationship of religion to, 285
  toward death, 7, 82, 283, 285, 298
authority crisis, 195
autoimmune reaction, 45, 46
"autoimmunity" theory of senescence, 45

bachelor. See single older person
Back, Kurt W., 168, 180
Backman, Carl, 90
balance, 55–56, 199
behavior, 100, 101, 200, 201, 205, 285
  psychological foundations of, 73–95
beliefs, 285
Bible reading, 283, 284
biological aspect of aging, 5, 41, 43–50, 199, 200, 205
Birren, James E., 83
birth rates, 155
black older persons, 17. See also minority group older persons; Negroes; nonwhite population
Blenkner, Margaret, 302
blindness, 54, 121. See also vision
boredom, 7, 79–81
Botwinick, Jack, 76
Bucks County (Pennsylvania) Adult Welfare Program, 263, 266–67
Burgess, E. W., 156

calendar. See chronological age
cardiovascular system, 47–78
Carlie, Michael K., 245
Carp, Frances M., 221, 222
Catholics, 282, 285–86, 294
central nervous system, 56
central processes, 58, 59, 60, 61, 70
  defined, 58
child, 102, 144, 189–90, 194, 228, 260, 262, 272, 297, 301–3, 320
childhood, 6, 15, 191, 206
child-rearing, 186
Christian:
  doctrine, 285
  ethic, 204
chronological age, 6, 7–8, 14–15, 18, 26–27, 35, 83, 84
church, 192, 262, 269, 271
  attendance, 282–83, 284
  programs for older persons, 286
Clark, Margaret, 193, 194, 195, 196, 206, 207, 212, 213, 214, 275, 282, 283, 299, 301, 307, 317, 328
clearinghouse services, 260
climate, 257
closure, 57, 88
clubs for older persons, 111, 185, 204, 286, 288
"collagen" theory of senescence, 45
color vision, 53–54

community, 192, 217, 219, 240, 252, 255, 257–79
defined, 257
services for older persons, 196, 197, 198
concept formation, 68, 69
condition, 113–23, 131, 132, 133 (*See also* health)
categories of, 114
defined, 113–14
consumer, older person as, 230–36, 261
continuity theory, 35–36, 38–39, 182, 183, 213, 288
Cottrell, W. Fred, 179, 181, 227, 249, 252
couple, older, 293–94, 313, 320
adjustment to aging, 295
response to retirement, 295–96
couplehood, as a life style, 203
Cousins, Norman, 184
covert response, 83
creativity, 68, 70, 71, 77
Cumming, Elaine, 104, 200, 220, 223, 224
Curtis, Howard J., 45

Davis, Robert, 89–90
Dean, Lois R., 79, 80, 81
death, 125, 128–29 (*See also* mortality rates)
attitudes toward, 7, 82, 283, 285, 298
defense mechanisms, 77, 92, 194, 202
Democrats, 243, 254
Dennis, Wayne, 86
dependency, 4, 107–108, 110, 112, 126, 189–98, 200, 208, 236, 259
developmental stages, 206, 213
developmental theory of aging, 206–7, 213, 214
disability, 88, 108–10, 112, 121–23, 131, 133, 193, 196, 261, 269
discrimination, on the basis of age, 37, 161–62, 163, 230
disease, susceptibility to, 48, 199
disengagement, 31–34, 36, 200–202, 203, 204, 205, 239, 321
a defense mechanism, 202
defined, 31
individual, 32–34, 219–20
influences on, 224
psychological, 223
societal, 32, 33–34, 219–26
theory, 31–34, 35, 36, 38, 179, 205, 219, 220–21, 223, 224
digestive system, 48
divorce, 294–95
divorced older people, 293, 298
DNA, 45, 46

Donahue, Wilma, 162
Dorfman, Robert, 140
drives, 73–76, 91

Economic Opportunity Act, 250
economy, 217, 219, 226, 227–38, 244, 328 (*See also* finances; income; retirement income)
economic power of older people, 12–13
economics of aging
education, 158, 160, 186, 202, 240–42, 244, 273–74, 310, 311, 330
for leisure, 183–84
of older people, 259, 261, 273–74
relationship between I.Q. and, 64
effector, 58
Eliminate Poverty in California, 250–51
emotions, 73, 79–81, 91
defined, 79, 91
employment, 158–59, 330
services for older persons, 260
See also job occupation, position, work
energy, 196, 199, 200, 201, 202, 207
engagement, 202, 221–22, 224 (*See also* disengagement)
defined, 202
Erikson, Erik, 206
errors, in research, causes of, 22
"error" theory of senescence, 46
ethnicity, 246, 248, 258
expectancies, 73, 79, 91

facilities for the aged. *See* institutions for the aged; mental institutions
Familism, 203
family, 182, 186, 192, 193, 203, 217, 219, 227, 228, 230, 257, 272, 291–326
extended, 292–93, 309, 310, 311
functions of, 311–13
life cycle of, 292, 309
nuclear, 309, 310, 311
of orientation, 292, 299, 308
of procreation, 292, 308, 309
role, 203, 220, 223
structure of, 12–13, 308–9
values, 310–11
Filer, Richard N., 77, 78
finances, 139–51, 192, 193 (*See also* economy; income; retirement income)
financial help, 314–16
financial independence, 192, 193, 197
financial quackery, 231–34
Foner, Ann, 270, 314

food, 146, 149, 236
foster grandparent program, 260, 262–63
friend, 178, 182, 186, 192, 193, 204, 217, 257, 269, 291–326

generations, social distance between, 195
genetic mutation, 45–46
geographic distribution of older people, 11
gerontology, definition of, 4–5, 18
Glenn, Norval, 239, 240, 241, 242, 244
government, 217, 219, 220, 239–56
governmental programs for older people, 239, 249–53, 254–55, 332
Governor's Conferences of Aging, 253
grandparent role, 303–307, 320–21
Gray, Robert M., 131
great-grandparent role, 307, 321
guilds, medieval, 154
Guptill, Carleton S., 168

habits, 74
Hall, Calvin, 85–86
Havighurst, Robert J., 205
health, 64, 113–37, 147, 160, 170, 171, 193, 197, 207, 219, 249, 257, 261, 287, 328, 330 (See also mental health)
  care, 132, 133, 147, 149, 197, 198, 236, 259–60, 274
  cause for retirement, 160, 162, 164–65
  defined, 113
hearing, 6–7, 51, 54–55, 121, 196, 199–200
heart. See cardiovascular system
Henry, Jules, 127
Henry, William E., 104, 200, 220, 223, 224
heredity, 46–47
HEW. See U.S. Department of Health, Education and Welfare
Hill, Reuben, 314
hormone:
  imbalance, 74, 75
  therapy, 75
housing, 160, 192, 236, 259, 270–72, 275, 286, 330
  costs of, 145, 146–47
  Negro-white differences in, 272

identity, 177, 178, 179, 183, 285
identity continuity theory. See continuity theory
identity crisis theory, 37, 39, 179, 182, 183

illness, 6, 88, 108–10, 112, 122–23, 126, 191, 196, 199, 200, 224, 231, 287, 294, 295, 303, 312, 315, 317, 319
impairment, 121–23, 199
income, 139, 141–44, 145, 147–48, 158, 193, 194, 198, 219, 230, 231, 249, 331 (See also economy; finances; retirement income)
  assistance, 260–61
  counseling, 260, 261
  programs, 250–51
independence, 189–98, 219
industrialization, 9, 13, 15, 18, 227, 244
industrial revolution, 155
I.Q. See intelligence quotient
Institute for Lifetime Learning, 274
intelligence, 62–65, 70, 73
intelligence quotient (I.Q.), 62–65, 69
institutions for the aged, 110, 112, 114, 123–28, 133, 186, 193, 196, 197, 263, 272, 286, 331 (See also mental institutions)
  aid to, 250
  mortality in, 125
  percent of older persons in, 110, 123, 133
institutions, social. See social institutions
interaction index, 220
interpersonal relationships:
  primary, 291–326
  secondary, 219, 292
irritation, 79–81
isolation, 193, 195, 200, 203, 231, 261, 287, 299, 318–19

Jewish community, 260, 282, 285, 286
job, 177, 179, 180, 181, 187, 192, 193, 198, 225, 230 (See also employment; occupation; position; work)
  retraining programs, 230
Johnson, Virginia, 74, 75, 76, 299, 300
Judaism, 285

Kansas City Study of Adult Life, 3, 80, 104, 328
Kerckhoff, Alan C., 310, 311
kinship, 293, 308, 309
Kosa, John, 169, 170
Kuhlen, Raymond G., 76, 77
Kutner, Bernard, 224

labor force, 13, 15, 141, 147, 161, 172, 228–30
Langley Porter Institute Studies in Aging, 328
later maturity, 6, 7, 101, 194, 307
learning, 65, 69, 70
legal aspects of retirement, 161

leisure, 111, 160, 167, 168, 173, 177–88, 192, 198, 213, 219, 221–22, 287, 288, 289
  defined, 177
  relationship between retirement and, 177–83, 185
life expectancy, 10
life cycle, 15–16, 27, 36, 102, 201, 293
  stages of, 6
life satisfaction theory of aging, 205
life space theory. *See* activity theory
life styles among older people, 202–204, 214, 246–47, 288
limitations on activity, 199–200, 207, 211, 213, 214
living fully, as a life style, 203–204
loneliness, 7, 79–81, 126, 193, 195, 196, 231, 285, 299
Lopata, Helena Z., 107
Lowenthal, Marjorie Fiske, 118, 120

MacIver, Robert M., 291
McKinney, John C., 180
maladaptation, 212. *See also* adaptation
malnutrition, 48, 146, 195
marital status of older people, 293–94, 300–301
marriage, 203, 292, 293–94, 320
Masters, William H., 74, 75, 76, 299, 300
Maves, Paul B., 284
meals-on-wheels, 132, 260, 264
medical care. *See* health care
Medicare, 131, 140, 148, 247, 249, 251, 253, 266
  opposition of AMA to, 250
menopause, 7, 74
memory, 65, 66–67, 70
mental functioning, 51, 61–70
mental illness, 116–20, 121, 123, 132, 160, 282–83, 330
  rates of, 132
mental institutions, 123, 132, 268
  See also institutions for the aged
mental sets, 79, 91
methodological problems in study of older people, 26–30, 38
Mexican-Americans, 142. *See also* minority group older persons; nonwhite population
Meyers, Howard P., 240
middle age, 6–7, 34–35, 65, 100, 101, 102, 132, 184, 194, 200–201, 204–5, 212, 246, 300, 301, 307, 316, 321
Miller, Stephen J., 103, 106, 177–79, 181, 182, 183
Mills, C. W., 154

minimal involvement, as a life style, 203
minority group older persons, 16, 17–18, 327
  theory that older people are a minority group, 37, 39
mobility, 192, 193
  geographical, 155, 181
morale, 193, 195, 201, 221
mortality, 169
  rates, 130–33
motives, 73, 76–79, 91
"mutation" theory of senescence, 45–46

National Council on Aging, 251
National Retired Teachers Associations, 274
Negroes, 142, 228, 248, 272, 286
  See also black older persons; minority group older persons; nonwhite population
neighborhoods, 11–12, 270
neighbor, 193, 217, 291–326
nervous system, 47, 48
Neugarten, Bernice L., 83, 84, 86, 87, 91, 200, 205, 304, 305, 306, 307
neurosis, 117
Newell, David S., 219, 220, 221
nonwhite population, 130–31
  See also black older persons; Mexican-Americans; minority group older persons; Negroes
norms, 14–15, 16, 32–33, 171, 178, 201, 285
nursing homes. *See* institutions for the aged; mental institutions
nutrition, 48, 132, 331

occupation, 158, 246. *See also* employment; job; position; work
occupational:
  identity, 103, 177, 178
  role, 222, 288
O'Connell, Desmond O., 77, 78
OEO. *See* Office of Economic Opportunity
Office of Aging, 251
Office of Economic Opportunity (OEO), 251, 262
Old Age Assistance, 148
Old Age, Survivors, Disability and Health Insurance (OASDHI). *See* Social Security
old age, 6, 7, 194, 205
Older Americans Act, 251, 329
older person, defined, 6, 9, 18, 26–27
Orbach, Harold, 162
organizations, social, 193

Page, Charles H., 291
parent-child relationship, 13, 108, 195–96, 210, 301–303, 310, 311, 320
    older parent-adult child relationship, 312, 320
peer group, 219
pension plans, private, 142–44, 148, 260
perception, 51, 61, 70, 73
personal action system, 205–6, 207
personality, 73, 82–86, 91, 92, 99, 186, 194, 200, 204, 210, 214, 328
    changes in, 77, 99, 199
    defined, 82, 91
personality theory of aging, 205, 207
political participation, 239–44, 254
politics, 32, 110–11, 192, 217, 239–56, 257, 328
    defined, 239
Pollak, Otto, 162
Pollman, A. William, 164
population:
    growth, 9–10, 18
    of older people, 333
    proportion of older people in, 9–10
    ratio of older men to older women, 296
positions, 99, 100, 101, 102, 110, 111, 112, 205 (See also employment; job; occupation; work)
    defined, 99
    old age causes loss of eligibility for, 101, 110, 112
poverty, 139, 140–41, 196, 251, 312
power of older persons, 101
    economic, 12–13, 231
    political, 239, 244–48, 254
problem-solving, 67–68, 69–70
protective services, 259, 260, 267–68, 275
Protestant ethic, 286
Protestants, 282, 285, 286
psychological aspects of aging, 5, 41, 51–72, 73–95, 200
psychomotor performance, 51, 58, 61, 70, 200
psychosis, 116–17
Public Assistance. See Aid for the Aged

"rate of living" theory of senescence, 44
recreation, 147, 177–88, 192, 204, 261, 269
    defined, 177
rehabilitation, 132, 133, 198
religion, 110, 193, 210, 217, 219, 246, 258, 281–90, 294, 328, 331
reproductive system, 48
Republicans, 243, 254
respiratory system, 48

responses, covert and overt, 83
retirement, 7, 15, 88, 102–106, 107, 112, 131, 133, 147, 148, 153–76, 193, 199, 200, 203, 204, 210, 213, 219, 222, 223, 224, 225, 227, 232, 246, 261, 287, 301, 312, 320, 327, 328, 330
    attitudes toward, 157–59, 161, 170
    communities, 246
    consequences of, 168–72, 173
    defined, 102, 153
    first program, 155
    homes, 286
    income, 147, 158, 159–60, 162, 166, 167, 169, 170, 172–73, 181, 288, 312
    influence on adjustment, 169–72
    policies, 13, 15, 32, 144, 156, 162–63, 172
    preparation for, 157, 159–61, 173
    reasons for, 161–66, 173
    relationship between leisure and, 177–83, 185, 186
    response to by older couples, 295–96
    role, 166, 167–68, 173, 222–23
    rewards, 77, 78, 103, 190
Riley, Matilda W., 270, 314
RNA (ribonucleic acid), 46, 67
Rogers, Carl, 86
roles, 85, 87, 88, 89, 91–92, 99–112, 113, 157, 167, 172, 173, 178, 183, 191, 200, 201, 202, 203, 204, 205, 207, 217, 220, 223, 225
    defined, 87, 91–92, 99
    learning of, 206
Roman, Paul, 222, 223
Rose, Arnold M., 246
Rosow, Irving, 317, 318, 319

Schultz, James H., 143, 144
Scripps Foundation, 179, 181, 182
Secord, Paul F., 90
self, 85, 86–87, 90, 91, 92, 200, 207
    effect of retirement on, 168, 169
self-concept, 86–87, 87–88, 89, 91, 92, 179, 201, 205, 208
    defined, 86–87, 91
    effect of retirement on, 168
self-esteem, 87, 89–90, 91, 92, 177, 194, 209
    defined, 87, 89, 91
    effect of retirement on, 169
    relationship of religion to, 285
self-evaluation, 208, 212, 275
self-image, 133, 284
self-ideal, 89
self-respect, 177, 178, 182, 183

senescence, 43–50
  defined, 43, 48
  results of, 47–48
  theories of, 44–46
senior centers, 260, 261–62, 269, 271, 288
sensation, 56–57, 61
sensory:
  experience, 51
  mechanism, 58
  organs, 51
  process, 51–57
  threshold, 51–52, 59
sex, 246
  drive, 74–76, 91
  roles, 294, 295
sexuality in older people, 299–300, 320
Shanas, Ethel, 17, 139 n, 166
shelter. See housing
sibling role of older people, 307–308, 321
sickness. See illness
Simpson, Ida H., 180
Sinclair, Upton, 251
single older persons, 293, 298–99
Smith, Joel, 240
Smith, Madorah E., 85, 86
social:
  change, 14–16, 18
  class, 37, 186, 257, 310, 317–18
  criticism, 24–25
  gerontology, 1, 5–6, 8, 18, 21–40, 90, 327–38
  institutions, 193, 201, 219, 226, 228, 258, 292, 328
  interaction, 85, 86, 88, 89
  roles. See roles
  services, 259, 260–68, 274, 331–32
  situation of older people, 97, 99, 193, 199, 200, 204, 214, 217, 223–24
  status, 100 n, 100–101, 180, 316
socialization, 159, 190, 307, 311–12
  defined, 159
Social Security, 27, 28, 141–42, 143, 144, 147–48, 149, 156, 160, 162, 172, 233, 236, 247, 249, 250, 251, 252, 253, 260, 267
spending patterns of older persons, 146–47
spinster. See single older person
sports, 177, 184
Steiner, Peter O., 140
stigma:
  of old age, 14
  of retirement, 178, 182
stimulus generalization, 68
Streib, Gordon F., 169, 170, 311
stress, 77, 126, 131, 224

subculture:
  older people as, 245–47, 254
  theory of older people as, 37, 39
suicide, 129, 183, 298

Taietz, Philip, 222, 223
Tallmer, Margot, 224
television, 111, 184, 185, 187, 283
temperature control system, 48
Thaler, Margaret, 86
theory, 22, 30
thinking, 67–69, 70
Thompson, Wayne E., 169, 170, 311
Tibbitts, Clark, 5
Townsend Movement, 250
trade union. See unions
transportation, 259, 261, 268–69, 275, 331
Turk, Herman, 240

unions, 236, 247, 254, 262, 288
United Fund, 261
urbanization, 9, 10–13, 15, 18, 155
urban renewal, 270
U. S. Administration on Aging, 8, 235, 251, 252, 262, 263, 329
U. S. Bureau of the Census, 27, 28
U. S. Department of Health, Education and Welfare (HEW), 251, 252
U. S. Senate Special Committee on Aging, 251, 252

values, 186, 207, 212, 214, 225, 275
  family, 257, 310–11, 321
  middle age, 204
  reintegration of, 209
  relationship to religion, 285
vision, 6–7, 52–54, 55, 196, 199–200
voluntary associations, 281, 287–88
volunteer work, 203, 221–22
voting behavior of older people, 240–43, 254, 328
Voting Rights Act (1965), 250

WAIS. See Wechsler Adult Intelligence Scale
"waste product" theory of senescence, 44
"wear and tear" theory of senescence, 44
Wechsler Adult Intelligence Scale (WAIS), 62–63, 68
Weinstein, Karol K., 304, 305, 306, 307
welfare, 224, 236, 253, 260, 263, 266–67, 274, 286, 328
White House Conference on Aging (1971), 329, 332

widowhood, 88, 106–7, 110, 112, 126, 133, 199, 200, 208, 224, 261, 293, 294, 297–98, 308, 320, 328
Williams, Richard H., 202, 204, 205, 206
Wirths, Claudine, 202, 204, 205, 206
work, 7, 193, 208, 221, 225, 230 (*See also* employment; job; occupation; position)
a source of self-respect, 178
a temporary part of life, 181
force. *See* labor force
orientation of retired people, 179–80, 182, 183

work (continued)
relationship between life style and, 153–54
relationship between man and, 154–55
role, 167, 172, 178, 183, 203, 208, 220
substitute, 178, 182, 185, 203
World of Work life style, 203

young adulthood, 6, 16, 102, 191, 194
youth, 184, 187, 250

Zborowski, Mark, 184